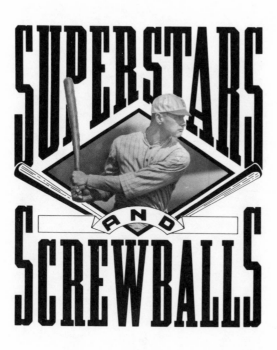

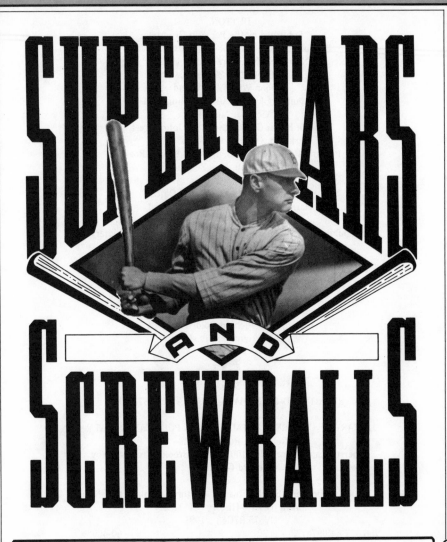

SUPERSTARS AND SCREWBALLS

100 YEARS OF BROOKLYN BASEBALL

Richard Goldstein

A DUTTON BOOK

DUTTON
Published by the Penguin Group
Penguin Books USA Inc., 375 Hudson Street,
New York, New York 10014, U.S.A.
Penguin Books Ltd, 27 Wrights Lane,
London W8 5TZ, England
Penguin Books Australia Ltd, Ringwood,
Victoria, Australia
Penguin Books Canada Ltd, 2801 John Street,
Markham, Ontario, Canada L3R 1B4
Penguin Books (N.Z.) Ltd, 182–190 Wairau Road,
Auckland 10, New Zealand

Penguin Books Ltd, Registered Offices:
Harmondsworth, Middlesex, England

First published by Dutton, an imprint of New American Library,
a division of Penguin Books USA Inc.
Distributed in Canada by McClelland & Stewart Inc.

First Printing, March, 1991
10 9 8 7 6 5 4 3 2 1

LIBRARY OF CONGRESS CATALOGING IN PUBLICATION DATA:
Goldstein, Richard, 1942–
Superstars and screwballs : 100 years of Brooklyn baseball / by
Richard Goldstein.
p.   cm.
1. Brooklyn Dodgers (Baseball team)—History.   2. Baseball—New
York (N.Y.)—History.   I. Title.
GV875.B7G63   1991
796.357′64′0974723—dc20   90-46089
                                                     CIP

Printed in the United States of America
Set in Clarendon and ITC Clearface
Designed by: Kathleen Herlihy-Paoli

For Nancy

Contents

Acknowledgments

A word of thanks to the men who shared their memories with me, from George Daubert, who was watching Brooklyn baseball before there was an Ebbets Field, to Carl Erskine, who was there the wintry day they tore the old ballpark down.

My photo research was smoothed by Patricia Kelly and Dan Bennett of the National Baseball Library at the Hall of Fame, Brent Shyer and Mindi Cabe of the Los Angeles Dodgers' staff, and Elizabeth White of the Brooklyn Public Library.

I'm grateful to Kevin Mulroy and Mitch Horowitz of NAL/Dutton for believing in the idea for this book and to Basil Kane for enthusiastically representing me.

I will always be indebted to my wife, Nancy, for her loving encouragement and to Dad and Uncle Joe, Brooklynites who showed me the way.

Preface

One day during the spring of 1934, a curious piece of fan mail arrived for the Brooklyn Dodger infielder Tony Cuccinello.

The writer wanted to know whether the ballplayers at Ebbets Field paid much attention to their uniforms, and if so, did any of them know how to spell?

Cuccinello had been wearing his jersey for nearly two months with no hint of anything amiss. Now he took another look. In block letters, it proclaimed BROOKYLN.

The stitching job had indeed been botched, but Cuccinello and his mates deserved no ridicule. The players could hardly be expected to notice the spelling on their uniforms when their fans were famous for fracturing the language whenever they opened their mouths.

Brooklyn had long been dismissed as an outpost for the unsophisticated, a backwater of culture in comparison with the city of glitter and power across the East River.

In an essay in January 1892 titled "The Brooklyn Man," the *New York Tribune* sneered: "Brooklyn men, as we see them about in town in the daytime, seem peaceable and quiet. When they get off this end of the Bridge in the morning there may be a slightly confused air about them, but it is apt to be seen in anyone when he arrives in a great city like New York."

A year later, *Harper's Magazine* asked Julian Ralph, known for his articles about the American West, to travel among Brooklyn's exotic natives.

Ralph found Brooklyn to be a place where bowling, choral singing and churchgoing were the major amusements, a sorry contrast with New York's theatrical attractions and political intrigue.

"Many a countryman who comes to New York and prospers never masters the metropolis or feels safe in it," wrote Ralph. "Sooner or later such ones move to Brooklyn."

The image would be undimmed in the years to come.

Long after graduating from Brooklyn College, the novelist Irwin Shaw would recall how his alma mater was "a wonderful school. It was free and it taught me all I needed to know to get out of Brooklyn."

In *A Walker in the City*, a remembrance of his youth in Brooklyn's Brownsville section, Alfred Kazin observed: "We were the end of the line. We were the children of the immigrants who had camped at the city's back door, in New York's rawest, remotest, cheapest ghetto, enclosed on one side by the Canarsie flats and on the other by the hallowed middle-class districts that showed the way to New York. 'New York' was what we put last in our address, but first in thinking of the others around us. THEY were New York, the Gentiles, America. . . ."

Once, Brooklynites were looked down on as a bunch of farmers. The isolation would fade in the late nineteenth century with the opening of the Brooklyn Bridge. But the unworldly image would remain, for Brooklyn would be swamped by European immigrants who mangled English and congregated in insulated neighborhoods.

"Dere's no guy livin' dat knows Brooklyn t'roo an' t'roo, because it'd take a guy a lifetime just to find his way aroun'. . . ." wrote Thomas Wolfe in *Only the Dead Know Brooklyn*.

It was easy to get lost in such strange-sounding domains as "Canarse an' East Noo Yawk an' Flatbush, Bensonhoist, Sout' Brooklyn, duh Heights, Bay Ridge, Greenpernt . . ."

All this was, of course, an exaggeration. Brooklyn did—and still does— have the Academy of Music, the Brooklyn Museum, a fine public library at Grand Army Plaza, trendy shops on the Heights, and Irwin Shaw's well-regarded Brooklyn College.

And once it had baseball.

Here, Brooklynites could rally together and strike back at their tormentors.

With the possible exception of small boys and upstate New York politicians, no one believes anymore that baseball was born in a cow pasture at Cooperstown. What may not be so well known is that the game's roots are urban.

At baseball's dawn in the 1850's, dozens of teams were playing in the City of Brooklyn.

A quarter-century before the Dodgers and Giants were born, Brooklyn had a baseball rivalry going with Manhattan. In the summer of 1858, all-star teams from Brooklyn and New York faced each other in a ballyhooed three-game series at a Long Island race track.

Brooklyn lost the encounter, 2 games to 1. But the following year, its teams swept their games from New York clubs, and for one major voice in town, prowess on the diamond had cast aside a collective inferiority complex.

"If we are ahead of the big city in nothing else, we can beat her in baseball," crowed the *Brooklyn Eagle.*

Brooklyn dominated baseball in the 1860's with its Eckford and Atlantic teams claiming unofficial national championships.

In 1883, the year the great bridge opened, a less heralded event occurred: The team that would become the Dodgers first took the field. For one summer, the new ballclub in South Brooklyn toiled in obscurity as a minor-league entry. But in the spring of 1884, Brooklyn went big time when the franchise joined the American Association, a major league circuit. In 1890, there was another step upward when Brooklyn made its debut in the National League.

On New Year's Day 1898, Brooklyn was a city no more. It was swallowed up in a consolidation, leaving it simply one of five boroughs of the City of New York.

But Brooklynites hadn't lost their Dodgers, and the ballclub brought home pennants in 1899 and 1900.

Then came some lean years as the Giants dominated the National League.

Not only did the hated gang at the Polo Grounds leave the Dodgers behind virtually every season, but the long-time rival managers presented a contrast perfectly in tune with those who would mock the natives of Brooklyn.

The Giants' John McGraw was on the fringe of the Broadway world, hob-nobbing with actors at the Lambs Club when he wasn't haranguing his men to ever greater feats. The Giants drew the Wall Street crowd, the smart set. They were Manhattan and all the sleekness it represented.

From 1914 to 1931, the Dodger dugout was occupied by Wilbert Robinson. He was fat, he was profane, and while he won a pair of pennants and knew a thing or two about pitching, he would just as soon argue strategy with the fans than wake the players from their slumbers.

The year before Uncle Robbie arrived, Charlie Ebbets opened the ballpark he modestly called Ebbets Field.

Mrs. Ed McKeever, the wife of one of Charlie's partners, was given the honor of raising the stars and stripes on the very first afternoon. She marched to the outfield, but then came an embarrassing pause. The flag had been left behind in a storage room. Eventually it was found, but the tone was set for many a goofy day in Flatbush.

By the 1920's, the Dodgers had become known as the Daffiness Boys, thanks in good measure to a gawky young man named Babe Herman. One afternoon, the Babe rapped a drive off the right-field wall, then wound up on third base holding hands with two of his fellow baserunners. Herman was a terrific hitter and hardly a loon, but he became a symbol of Dodger misdeeds.

In the Depression years, the franchise was as much sad as funny. The team was in permanent embrace of sixth place, the ballpark had become shabby, the fans were nowhere in sight. Willard Mullin's cartoon character "Bum," the Dodgers' unofficial mascot, was inspired by the down-and-out ballclubs of the 1930's.

Then the stormy and imaginative Larry MacPhail arrived in 1938 and brought new life.

Red Barber, hired by MacPhail to launch broadcasting of the Dodger games, recalled long afterward how a rejuvenated team renewed a sense of pride for Brooklynites.

"When I came to Brooklyn in 1939—and I know this for a fact—there were people living in Brooklyn who had never been to Manhattan," Barber would write. "If these people had to go downtown they might go to Flatbush Avenue or one of the other big streets in Brooklyn. Manhattan was another country. But these people who thought in terms of their own group and then their own neighborhood began to think in terms of Brooklyn. This was their town—not New York."

As America moved toward war, the Dodgers brought a pennant to Brooklyn in 1941 after twenty-one years as also-rans. And then the mystique of Brooklyn grew with an assist from Hollywood.

Every war movie seemed to have a brash Brooklynite in the infantry platoon teaming up with the Texan, the Italian-American and the Midwestern farm boy.

The sportswriter Tom Meany toured Italy in the winter of 1944–45 with a troupe of baseball personalities including Dodger manager Leo Durocher.

On his return, Meany wrote in the New York newspaper *PM*: "You didn't have to be overseas any length of time to realize that Brooklyn isn't a geographical entity as much as a state of mind.

"There were more Dodger fans in Italy than there ever had been at Ebbets Field. Roughly we saw 70,000 G.I.'s and every one of them had an opinion one way or another about Brooklyn. There were Yankee fans and Giant fans, too, and just plain baseball fans, but it was the Brooklyn club which received the laughs, cheers and hoots any time it was mentioned."

Just before World War II, a Brooklynite named Sid Ascher and some friends formed the Society for the Prevention of Disparaging Remarks Against Brooklyn. By 1946, the group claimed to have 40,000 members and it reported uncovering 3,000 uncomplimentary references.

And then parochial Brooklyn taught the rest of America a lesson in democracy. Long before the term "America's Team" was coined by TV sports promoters, the Dodgers were indeed America's team for the nation's blacks. Branch Rickey brought Jackie Robinson to Ebbets Field in 1947, and Roy Campanella and Don Newcombe would soon follow. The Dodgers became baseball's first integrated team.

Along with the great black players would come names like Hodges and Snider and Furillo as Rickey built a powerhouse.

And yet, season after season, the Dodgers fell short. Four times they won the pennant in the post-war years and four times they lost to the Yankees in the World Series. Then came 1955—a championship team at last after sixty-six seasons in the National League.

Two years later, it was all over. Turned down by city officials in his quest for a new ballpark in downtown Brooklyn, enticed by a huge land offer in downtown Los Angeles, Walter O'Malley took the Dodgers west.

Back in 1857, a group of ballclubs from Brooklyn had gathered in Lower Manhattan for baseball's first convention. On a cool September evening 100 years later, the final pitch was thrown at Ebbets Field.

One of the Dodger players making the move to California was Carl Erskine, a particular favorite of the Brooklyn fans. Erskine was a Hoosier—like so many other Dodger players his roots were elsewhere—but to Brooklynites he would be "Oisk."

More than thirty years after the Dodgers' departure—by then president of the First National Bank of Anderson, Indiana—Erskine would reflect on how he got caught up in the Brooklyn vernacular.

"I was called up from Fort Worth, Texas, in July of 1948," he remembered. "The Brooklyn fans, from reading the papers, were aware that this kid pitcher was coming up. I took the subway from the St. George Hotel out to the Ebbets Field stop. I had my duffel bag with me, 'Fort Worth Cats' on the side. As I got near the rotunda of Ebbets Field, people were waiting in line, milling around, and spotted me. Not that they knew me, but they saw this 'Fort Worth Cats.' And I could hear these Brooklyn people. My first introduction to Ebbets Field was 'Hey, there's Oiskine. From Fort Woith.' "

On a wintry day in 1960—the Dodgers had been in Los Angeles for two seasons by then—Oisk came back to Flatbush. It was Tuesday, February 23. The Ebbets Field gates had been locked since the fall of '57, but now they were thrown open for anyone who cared to come in.

Some 200 people had shown up, a few sitting in the box seats, others wandering around. The turf was scarred, the outfield signs faded. But still there were reminders. On the right-field scoreboard, "AT BATS," "UMPIRES," and "BATTING ORDER" stood out.

A brass band was on hand, and a few old Dodgers had accepted invitations: Otto Miller, 70 years old, the Brooklyn catcher in the first game ever played at Ebbets Field. Roy Campanella, the catcher in the final game, now in a wheelchair. Ralph Branca, destined to be remembered always for an afternoon up at the Polo Grounds. And Carl Erskine.

The old ballpark was about to be torn down.

Erskine recalled the scene:

"We were jovial enough and kidded each other and took pictures. Then came the moment, and they wheeled this crane over and held this big iron ball—I don't know how much that thing weighed, a ton or a half a ton. It was painted like a baseball.

"They held it over the visitors' dugout. As many times as I sat in Ebbets Field and looked across into that dugout with professional hate at the Giants and Leo, and some of these teams that came in—and all the taunts that we heard come out of that dugout at Jackie—when they dropped the ball, and it hit the end of the dugout just about where that old drinking fountain had been, and caved that top in, I got sick.

"I told the guys, 'I'll see ya.' I didn't say goodbye to anybody. I just left."

As the ballpark began to crumble around him, a glance by Erskine at the outfield roof would have provided a sense of the good old times. An American flag was still flying, as if there would be a ballgame there that afternoon.

When the place opened back in 1913, the ceremonies had been thrown out of whack because the flag was missing. Now, a zany parting note. In the finale to Brooklyn baseball, they still couldn't get it right. The flag was flying upside down.

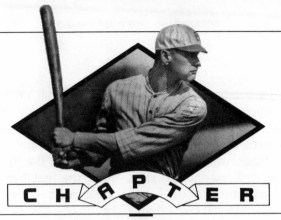

1

Of Eckfords
and Excelsiors

O ne hundred years later, Pee Wee Reese, the captain of the Brooklyn
Dodgers, would lead his ballclub against the New York Yankees
in a succession of dramatic October encounters. The teams would
confront each other before huge crowds and a national television audience
in the millions. Their meetings would be American spectacles.

But all that could hardly be imagined by a young Brooklynite who
was absolutely thrilled over a new game he and his mates had just learned
to play.

If at the end there was Pee Wee Reese, in the beginning there was
Frank Pigeon.

In the mid-1850's, baseball was beginning to stir on the fields of
Brooklyn and New York City. What had been largely an informal recreational
activity was now blossoming into a sport that attracted scores of youths
organizing into ballclubs and testing their primitive skills against each
other.

And, as in the autumns to come a century later, it was Brooklyn
against the Bronx.

Among baseball's first teams were the Eckfords of Brooklyn, a group
of workingmen who squeezed in time away from their trades to go out
with bat and ball. One of their founders was Frank Pigeon. On an afternoon
in late September 1856, they traveled to the Old Red House grounds in
Harlem for their first match. The opponents were the Unions, representing
Morrisania, now a part of the Bronx.

It proved a wonderful day for the new Brooklyn team. When the very first run was scored, it was almost too exciting to bear.

"We pulled off our coats, and rolled up our sleeves, we stood up to the rack, but were very nervous—first appearance on any stage!" Pigeon, the Eckford pitcher, would remember in describing the game for a local sports publication a few months later. "After the first two batters made out, the third man up gave the ball a regular crusher and reached third base as one desperate yell burst from eight throats. The next hitter drove him home. Glory! One run. Ah, how proud the Eckford Club were of that run. Some ran to the Umpire's book, to see how it looked on paper."

The Eckfords thrashed the Unions, 22–8, and, recalled Pigeon, "About seven o'clock that evening, nine peacocks might have been seen on their way home with tail feathers spread. Our friends were astonished, as well as ourselves."

Brooklyn was a hotbed of baseball in the decade before the Civil War, boasting more than 100 regular and junior teams. As the sports newspaper *Porter's Spirit* put it in 1857:

Verily Brooklyn is fast earning the title of the "City of Baseball Clubs," as well as the "City of Churches." As numerous as are its church spires, pointing the way to heaven, the present prospect indicates that they may be soon outnumbered by the rapidly increasing ball clubs.

But Manhattan lays claim to baseball's pioneer team, the Knickerbockers. A gentlemen's organization of professional men, merchants and white collar workers, they played ball as far back as 1842 on a vacant lot at Fourth Avenue and Twenty-seventh Street in what is now the Murray Hill section.

After the Knickerbockers spent a few years playing informally, one of their members, Alexander J. Cartwright, Jr., a black-whiskered, 25-year-old volunteer fireman, prevailed on his teammates to draw up a club constitution and a set of rules.

They devised a four-base diamond with ninety feet between the bases and decreed three outs to an inning along with regular rotation for the batting order and nine-man teams. It was a system built to last.

Their pitching rules did not, however, envision a Walter Johnson or a Nolan Ryan. The pitcher stood on a plate forty-five feet from home and had to throw the ball gently in an underhand motion. And the Knickerbocker uniforms—long blue woolen trousers, white flannel shirts, webbed belts and straw hats—were modeled on what a well-dressed cricket team would wear.

When open space became scarce in their neighborhood, the Knickerbockers went to the wilds of New Jersey for their games, finding a permanent site at the Elysian Fields, a tract of perhaps five acres fronting on the Hudson River.

On June 19, 1846, they began match play by taking on the New York Club in a four-inning game. It was a rough debut. They were beaten by 23–1.

Brooklyn's first important team was the Excelsiors, one of seven clubs formed there in 1854 and 1855. The squad was founded by a fan named John H. Suydam and some friends who decided to start a club of their own after watching a game between the Knickerbockers and Eagles in November 1854. A few days after that game they met for practice, calling themselves the Jolly Young Bachelors' Base Ball Club.

At first they played in South Brooklyn at Smith and DeGraw streets, then eventually found open space at the foot of Court Street, not far from what is now the Brooklyn Borough Hall.

In August 1855, the Eckfords began playing ball in the Greenpoint section near the waterfront. Composed mainly of mechanics and shipworkers, they were named for Henry Eckford, a Scotch-Irish immigrant who was New York's most successful shipbuilder in the pre–Civil War period. But Eckford evidently was not so benevolent as to give his men much free time to learn the game. A full year went by before the Eckfords got up the courage to face another squad. When they played that first game against the Unions—the encounter Frank Pigeon recalled so breathlessly— many of their supporters stayed away, fearing the team would be crushed.

Two other Brooklyn clubs that would thrive—the Putnams and the Atlantics—were also formed about this time.

Baseball was a gentlemen's game at its dawn, with good fellowship much prized. Wining and dining after the game was as important as winning.

One autumn evening in 1856, the Putnams, after defeating the Excelsiors, played host to them at Trenor's Dancing Academy in the Williamsburgh section. There was some serious eating along with a few light speeches, and toasts were offered to the Knickerbockers, as baseball's pioneers, and to the press, which presumably had yet to misquote a ballplayer. To conclude the happy evening, the Putnams escorted the Excelsiors to the horse cars taking them back to their homes in South Brooklyn.

Proper etiquette in the locker room was as important as proper form on the ballfield. The Excelsior rules required that a member have "written permission" before "wearing or using the apparel of a fellow-member." Anyone flouting the regulation would be fined one dollar.

The young gentlemen—most of them sporting mustaches, some add-ing long sideburns, others full-flowing beards—played most of their games on Saturday afternoons, journeying to the ballfields in horse-drawn coaches, steamer trains or ferries. Sunday was decidedly a day of rest.

As baseball began to gain popularity, so Brooklyn was growing rapidly, expanding through immigration and the gobbling up of neighboring towns.

On January 1, 1855, just a few weeks after the Excelsiors were or-ganized, Brooklyn became America's third largest city—after New York City and Philadelphia—when it annexed the Williamsburgh and Bushwick areas. The expansion brought an additional 55,000 residents, making Brooklyn a city of some 200,000.

First settled by the Dutch in 1636, then coming under British control in 1664, Brooklyn had developed from the gradual joining of country vil-lages. A township in its early days, it became a city in 1834. By the time baseball arrived, most Brooklynites lived along the East River waterfront, including the area around the great Navy Yard and the downtown business district near the major ferry slips. The lands to the east, toward Long Island, containing communities such as Flatbush and New Utrecht, were mostly farmland.

According to a popular joke of the day, General William Howe had captured Brooklyn for the British before moving across the East River so he would have a place to sleep while taking New York. But Brooklyn was not so sleepy anymore. It was more than farms and a place to live for commuters who would cross to work in New York on the thirteen ferries that ran each day. Among Brooklyn's twenty-five square miles were more than eight miles of waterfront lined with shipyards, warehouses, sugar refineries, chemical works, grain elevators and breweries. And some thirty miles of railroad track had been laid for horse-drawn omnibuses.

The depiction of Brooklyn as the borough of churches was no idle imagery. At mid-nineteenth century, Brooklyn had more than 100 churches, the most famous being the Plymouth Church on Orange Street in the Heights where the Reverend Henry Ward Beecher had become a national figure with his passionate sermons denouncing slavery.

With ballclubs sprouting throughout the New York City area, it wasn't long before moves were made to organize things. In January 1857, at the invitation of the Knickerbockers, delegates from more than a dozen clubs—among them the Excelsiors, Eckfords, Putnams and Atlantics—assembled at Smith's Hotel on Broome Street in Lower Manhattan. It was the first convention in baseball history.

The teams drew up a formal set of rules and then, in a March 1858 meeting in Manhattan's Bowery area, the first league was created—the National Association of Base Ball Players.

Things were getting serious now. Before long, the game's genteel aura would fade away and baseball would become a tough business marked by bully boys on the field and gambling, drinking and whoring off it.

Junior clubs and their fans were especially rough and tumble.

In the summer of 1858, the secretary of Brooklyn's Niagara junior team announced that his club would no longer play the North Stars because "they would come down on the ballgrounds in South Brooklyn and swagger up to some of our members and say, with oaths: 'If we cannot whip you with bats and ball, we can with fists.' "

That was only a warmup. In a June 1871 game between the Fly Aways and Silver Stars for the national junior championship, the 400 spectators at Brooklyn's Union Grounds spent their afternoon fighting, cursing and spitting tobacco juice in each other's faces. Before the game was half over, the players grabbed their bats and joined in the melee. The match somehow was completed (the Fly Aways won, 14–13) and the umpire got away alive, escorted by two policemen.

Few clubs were scared off by the kind of tough talk and threats the Niagaras had faced, and the game's popularity soared. In 1855, there had been only a dozen truly organized teams in Brooklyn and New York City. By 1858, there were seventy-one clubs in Brooklyn and twenty-five in New York.

Before long, people would even pay to watch others play ball. In the summer of 1858, Brooklyn challenged New York to see who had the best team. After lengthy haggling, a three-game series was set up at the Fashion Course racetrack on Long Island, a neutral site that could accommodate a big crowd. It was announced that each fan entering the stone grandstand would be charged fifty cents to cover the expense of getting the grounds in shape, the first admission fee at a baseball game.

The excitement was great when all-star squads from Brooklyn and New York played their first game on July 20, a cool, cloudy afternoon.

Brooklynites crowded the little steamers running from the Fulton Ferry dock to Hunt's Point on Long Island's North Shore, where they switched to special trains put on by the Flushing Railroad. Hundreds of private carriages crowded the roads running to the course through farm-land. The players from the Excelsiors arrived in style on an omnibus of the Fulton Avenue line drawn by fourteen gray horses with feathers in their head gear.

Outside the gates, the sounds and sights of a carnival greeted the fans. Card sharks snared the more naive. At one shaky table, a group of men set up three-card monte games to relieve the "greenie" victims of a lot more than the fifty-cent admission charge.

Others looking for more honest odds could win twenty-five cents by hurling a ring around a spike driven into a plank or could match wits with a weight-guesser.

When the players took the field at two-thirty, the stands were jammed (the crowd numbered somewhere between 1,500 and 8,000, depending on what account is to be believed). Those without seats watched from carriages parked alongside the field. Even the ladies joined in the glorious social event, packing the special section reserved for wives, daughters and girl-friends of the players. To spare the women any scenes of rowdiness, hard liquor was banned from the site. The men made do with beer or water.

The only problem on an otherwise wonderful day was the condition of the field. In baseball's infancy, balls caught on one bounce were out. This particular afternoon, the field was a bit too soft for many one-bouncers to be snared.

The Brooklyn ballplayers went home losers in this first great spectacle involving a New York rival, dropping the opener by 22–10.

In August, the Brooklyn all-stars took the second game, 29–8. There was plenty of action in the stands as well, the *Times* apologizing in its account of the game that "space does not admit of descriptions of gambling, and cadging, and other delectable modes of making the dimes and dollars."

The betting provided extra incentive for a New York ballplayer named John Holden. Two fans made a $100 bet on whether Holden could hit a home run. The spectator betting on Holden's prowess offered him $25 if he could deliver, and wallop one he did, sending a pitch by Brooklyn's Matty O'Brien to the far reaches of right-center field.

The final game of the series was played in September, and, as in many an autumn to come, Brooklyn emerged on the losing end. The New Yorkers took the deciding game by 29–18.

But Brooklyn recovered a measure of pride in 1859 when its teams swept the early games against New York clubs. And in short order, a rivalry was in full swing.

Porter's Spirit newspaper implored the New York teams to bounce back from the springtime defeats, asking, "Is New York to rank second to the village over the other side of the river?"

Some village.

As the *Brooklyn Eagle* exulted: "Nowhere has the National game of Baseball taken firmer hold than in Brooklyn and nowhere are there better players. If we are ahead of the big city in nothing else, we can beat her in baseball."

And beat her Brooklyn did. Its teams dominated baseball in the years to come, the Eckfords winning the unofficial national championship in 1862 and 1863 and the Atlantics taking the title in 1864 and 1865.

Off the field, an English-born Brooklynite named Henry Chadwick was making a huge contribution to the growth of baseball. Chadwick had come to America with his family in 1837 as a boy of thirteen. Having played cricket as a youngster, he tried baseball and found a niche as shortstop for

◆ *Henry Chadwick, the Brooklyn sportswriter dubbed the Father of Baseball for his chronicling of the game's early years. (National Baseball Library, Cooperstown, N.Y.)*

an amateur team in Hoboken. But soon he turned his energies to reporting on the game rather than playing it, becoming baseball's first sportswriter.

In the late 1850's, Chadwick began covering games for several newspapers, including the *Brooklyn Eagle* and *New York Clipper*. He soon invented the box score and a shorthand system of scoring. In 1860, Chadwick published the first baseball guide—*Beadle's Dime Baseball Player*— a collection of his newspaper articles along with statistics and a compilation of rules. It sold 50,000 copies.

Chadwick served on rules committees and, as a gentleman of the old order, fought an uphill battle against gambling, drunkenness and rowdy play. In 1881, he began editing the Spalding guides and put them out every year until his death in 1908. In 1938, the "Father of Baseball," as he had been known, was elected to the Hall of Fame.

Chadwick was buried at Greenwood Cemetery in Brooklyn beneath a monument of ornamental crossed bats and a baseball. Not far away was a towering granite monument similarly adorned in tribute to baseball's first superstar, James Creighton of Brooklyn's Excelsiors.

In 1860, as Chadwick was putting out his inaugural baseball guide, Creighton's pitching prowess was bringing the Excelsiors to the top of the baseball world. Pitchers were still required to use a stiff-armed motion and were accustomed to laying the ball in easily. It would not be until 1884 that overhand deliveries were allowed. But Creighton skirted the rules and managed to get away with it. He used a barely noticeable wrist snap and arm bend that enabled him to overpower batters with speed and spin. And he starred at the plate, becoming one of the game's most powerful hitters. A man like this would be rewarded. Violating baseball's amateurism code, the Excelsiors secretly paid Creighton, making him the only known professional in the pre–Civil

♦ *The Excelsiors' James Creighton, baseball's first superstar. (National Baseball Library, Cooperstown, N.Y.)*

◆ *Dickey Pearce* (third from right), *who pioneered shortstop techniques and bunting, with his teammates on the Atlantics of Brooklyn, one of baseball's top teams during the 1860's. The lone bearded Atlantic is the manager, Peter O'Brien. (Brooklyn Public Library–Brooklyn Collection)*

War days.

The Excelsiors decided to show their stuff beyond Brooklyn, and in 1860 they became the first baseball team to go on an extended road trip. Playing less experienced teams on a two-week tour of upstate New York, they swept six games.

Upon returning to Brooklyn, the Excelsiors accepted a challenge from the Atlantics, the only club in the nation considered likely to hold its own against Creighton and company. It was no contest: the Excelsiors romped, 23–4.

The Excelsiors then skipped out of town again, touring Pennsylvania, Delaware and Maryland and scoring more one-sided victories.

When they returned undefeated from their second trip, they took on the Atlantics again, this time at the Atlantics' field. With hundreds of players representing clubs from as far away as Buffalo and Boston in the crowd— presumably hoping to decipher the game's finer points—the Excelsiors were finally beaten, losing by 15–14.

Having split their first two games, the teams agreed on a third match,

◆*Arthur (Candy) Cummings, a Hall of Famer as the supposed discoverer of the curveball. (National Baseball Library, Cooperstown, N.Y.)*

to be held on neutral territory, for the unofficial national championship. On August 23, some 20,000 fans converged on the Putnams' field at Gates and Lafayette avenues for the most important game in Brooklyn's brief baseball history.

It would end in violence and an enduring enmity between the teams.

The potential for trouble was there before a pitch was thrown. Gambling, having become common at games, could always inflame things. Beyond that, there was social-class antagonism: The Atlantics' fans were mostly Irish immigrant workingmen while the Excelsiors' backers were mainly from the old Anglo-Saxon stock, in white-collar positions and the professions.

When the Atlantics began bickering with the umpire in the early going, their supporters were quick to anger. After each close play, the Atlantic fans showered abuse on the umpire and the Excelsior players. Things got even uglier when the Atlantics' McMahon was called out for overrunning third base in the fifth inning. Despite pleas for calm by the Atlantic players, the 100 policemen at the game were hard-pressed to keep the crowd under control.

With the Excelsiors leading, 8–6, in the sixth inning, their captain, Joseph Leggett, finally pulled them off the field.

Leggett supposedly handed the baseball to Matty O'Brien, the Atlantics' captain, and declared, "Here, O'Brien, the ball, you can keep it."

O'Brien, reciprocating the sporting gesture, is said to have replied: "Will you call it a draw?"

"As you please," Leggett icily responded.

The Excelsiors then departed in their horse-drawn omnibus, pursued by Atlantic fans hurling stones at them.

The uproar was not forgotten. Never again would the Excelsiors and the Atlantics face each other.

Two years later, baseball lost its greatest pitcher. On October 14, 1862, batting for the Excelsiors against the Unions in the final game of the season, James Creighton hit a tremendous drive. As Creighton rounded first base, he collapsed in pain. He managed to make it around the bases for a home run, then was taken to his father's house. Four days later, at the age of twenty-one years seven months, he died. According to the *Eagle*, he had ruptured his bladder taking his powerful swing and had died of internal bleeding.

Another early Brooklyn pitcher who could do unusual things with the baseball was a 120-pounder named Arthur (Candy) Cummings, who was elected to the Hall of Fame in 1939 as the reputed inventor of the curveball.

Cummings would maintain he fathomed the principle of a curve back in 1863 when he was fourteen years old. As he told it, "A number of boys and myself were amusing ourselves by throwing clamshells and watching them sail along through the air, turning now to the right and now to the left."

He supposedly began using the curve around 1866 while playing amateur ball in Brooklyn with the Fulton Hercules team and then the Excelsior Juniors.

Cummings explained years later that he held the ball toward the end of his fingers in a "death grip" and gave a quick wrist turn, which was then illegal. He recalled having to wear a kid glove to keep his fingertips from blistering and making his hand "a ragged wreck after a few innings." Being a pioneer did have its price. In snapping the ball, Cummings once dislocated a wrist bone and had to wear a support device.

The batters may have noticed something peculiar going on, but Cummings recalled that he waited until the end of the 1867 season before publicly claiming he could curve a ball. He announced he would provide proof in a game against Harvard. Physics experts scoffed, but Cummings remembered, "I curveballed them to death."

Cummings pitched for the Stars of Brooklyn in the late 1860's and early 1870's. In 1872, he joined the Mutuals, a big league club nominally representing New York City but actually playing its home games in Brooklyn, and curved his way to a 33–20 record that season.

Despite his slender build, Cummings managed to win 124 games with various pro clubs from 1872 to 1875. He then joined the Hartford Blues of the newly formed National League, winning sixteen games in 1876. In nineteenth century slang, "candy" meant being the best. Cummings's manager, Bob Ferguson, is said to have remarked: "God never gave him any size, but he's the candy."

Ferguson, who had been a third baseman for many years with the Atlantics, possessed an even more colorful nickname. His knack for spearing line drives in an era when fielders had yet to don gloves brought him the sobriquet "Death to Flying Things."

Cummings pitched until 1877, finishing his career with Cincinnati. By then, thanks to the relentless pioneering work of Henry Chadwick, there should have been no doubt that a baseball could indeed be made to curve.

Chadwick had put together a little experiment at Brooklyn's Capitoline ballfield in August 1870. Challenging Fred Goldsmith, another early curveballer, to prove he could make his delivery bend, Chadwick placed two stakes set twenty feet apart in a line from the center of the pitcher's box to the center of home plate. To the cheers of onlookers, Goldsmith threw a half-dozen pitches that sailed to the right of the nearer stake and then to the left of the farther one.

Another Brooklynite who pioneered baseball techniques was Dickey Pearce. Pudgy and only five foot three, Pearce didn't seem to have much range, so when he joined the Atlantics in 1856, he was put at shortstop. In those days, the fielder at that position simply stationed himself between second and third base and seldom moved very far. But Pearce revolutionized shortstop play, shifting his spot depending on where the batter was likely to hit the ball and moving back to grab shallow outfield flies.

He also developed the "fair-foul hit." Pearce would bunt the baseball so that it bounced fair and then bounded away from the fielder, toward the crowd, before reaching the first-base or third-base bags. A ball taking that route was considered in play until a rules change in 1877.

But as baseball developed some sophistication and grew in popularity, the nation became preoccupied with events far removed from the playing field.

At four-thirty on the morning of April 12, 1861, secessionists opened fire on Fort Sumter, South Carolina. Soon, hundreds of thousands of men would be off to the battlefields. The number of teams in New York City and Brooklyn would decrease by more than 60 percent during the first three years of the Civil War.

Still, there were enough young men left behind to keep baseball going, and important games attracted big crowds. On October 21, 1861, three months to the day after the first Battle of Bull Run, 15,000 fans flocked to Hoboken's Elysian Fields to see the "Silver Ball" all-star game between squads from Brooklyn and New York. The game, arranged by the tireless baseball impresario Henry Chadwick, was played for a silver ball prize presented by the *New York Clipper* newspaper. The Brooklyn squad, with players from the Atlantics, Excelsiors and Eckfords, won by 18–6, atoning for Brooklyn's loss to New York in that Fashion Course all-star series three years before.

A few months later, Brooklyn baseball took some bizarre turns. The opening of the Central Park skating rink in the winter of 1858–59 had brought an ice-skating craze to New York. Not to be outdone, the Atlantic and Charter Oak squads of Brooklyn inaugurated baseball on ice in the winter of 1861. A few modifications were made. Powdered charcoal circles were sprinkled on the ice to simulate bases, and a runner was permitted to skate beyond the circles for a distance of five feet before being vulnerable to a tag. The baseball was soft so as not to injure the players in the cold air. Some 10,000 bundled-up spectators saw the Atlantics glide their way to a 20–9 victory over the Charter Oaks amid "mishaps" that were, as the *Clipper* put it, "a source of infinite merriment." Baseball on ice would continue in Brooklyn throughout the 1870's, with the Washington Skating Pond and the Capitoline Skating Lake among the more popular "fields."

In the spring of 1862, William Cammeyer, the owner of the Union ice-skating rink in Brooklyn's Williamsburgh section, opened baseball's first enclosed ballpark on the site.

Now there would be fences to shoot for as Cammeyer put up six-foot-high outfield walls. But inside-the-park homers would hardly be a relic of the past as the fences were more than 500 feet from home plate. A clubhouse was built and wooden benches seating about 1,500 were placed around the field. The overflow would stand, as usual. A dash of color was provided by the American flag and the club banners snapping in the breeze from newly erected flagpoles. To complete the amenities, a saloon opened up outside the park. Total cost: about $12,000.

Games had been free to the fans with the exception of that Fashion Course series of 1858, but somebody would have to pay for progress so Cammeyer charged a ten-cent admission fee. He did, however, have a problem with freeloaders. An embankment enabled fans on foot or in carriages to peer over the fences.

On May 15, 1862, with a band playing the "Star-Spangled Banner"—apparently the first time a musical touch was provided at a ballgame—the Union Grounds opened for baseball.

The grounds, bounded by Marcy, Lee and Rutledge avenues, eventually

◆ *Baseball on ice—a fad of the 1860's and 1870's—at Brooklyn's Washington Skating Pond. (National Baseball Library, Cooperstown, N.Y.)*

became a big league ballpark. The field would be used by the Mutuals, Eckfords and Atlantics in the early 1870's when the first professional league was formed. The Mutuals continued to play there upon joining the fledgling National League in 1876. The Hartford Blues, unable to arouse much interest back home, played their "home" games at the Union Grounds in 1877 before giving up altogether.

Cammeyer would have competition in the Brooklyn ballpark business. Soon after he built his Union Grounds, a man named Reuben S. Decker constructed an enclosed ballfield in what is now the Bedford-Stuyvesant section. Called the Capitoline Grounds, the park was a relatively convenient three-mile horsecar trip from the downtown ferry docks.

A row of stables—the equivalent of today's parking lot—was erected along Putnam Avenue, behind a restaurant, bandstand, sitting rooms for the female fans and clubhouses. Two sets of bleachers seating a total of 5,000 fans were put up along Nostrand Avenue and Halsey Street.

Each November, the grounds were flooded from a nearby water main and converted into a rink for skating and baseball on ice. Then the following spring, the water would be drained off, Phineas T. Barnum would bring in his circus for a few appearances, and finally it would be time to play ball again.

Soon the players would begin getting a share of the wealth, modest though it still was. Although James Creighton is viewed as baseball's first professional, he evidently did not get a regular salary. Another Brooklynite would have the distinction of being the first salaried pro. In 1863, Al Reach, baseball's top player following Creighton's death, received money offers from several teams to jump from Brooklyn's Eckfords. He would abandon

his team but not the New York area. Reach eventually went to the Philadelphia Athletics, picking them because he could commute to his home in
Flushing, Long Island. Later the founder of a major sporting goods firm,
he is the only man known to have received a flat fee for playing baseball
before 1865.

Baseball had, meanwhile, won the battle with cricket for the fans'
devotion. When the Atlantics played the Mutuals in September 1863 at the
St. George cricket grounds in Hoboken (admission fee ten cents), the *Times,*
while failing to give a crowd figure, reported that the game had attracted
more fans than had all the cricket matches in the area for the whole season.

In the springtime of 1865, the guns of the Civil War were finally
stilled. Baseball would begin a sensational period of growth to become
America's premier sport.

2

The Atlantics' Marvelous Afternoon

Only three weeks before, in the tiny village of Appomattox Court House, Virginia, Robert E. Lee—garbed in a new full-dress uniform with sash and jewel-studded sword—had surrendered the armies of the Confederacy to Ulysses S. Grant.

Now, after four years of carnage, the soldiers were coming home and the nation would begin to rebuild. In Brooklyn, as the springtime of 1865 arrived, the air was alive with the start of what promised to be the best baseball season ever.

"Both the base ball and cricket fraternity of New-York and Brooklyn have made ample preparation for a brilliant campaign this season, and the prospects are that both games will flourish to a greater extent this Summer than they have done since the inauguration of the great rebellion," declared the *New York Times* on May 1 as it described the baseball stirrings around town.

The Excelsiors had left behind their old grounds—the meadow at the foot of Court Street—and had moved into the Capitoline Grounds where a new clubhouse had been erected. In a special effort to lure female fans, a dance was to be held in the clubhouse at the conclusion of the home opener. The Atlantic and Enterprise baseball teams along with the Long Island cricket club would also be playing at Capitoline.

The Eckford and Resolute baseball clubs and the Satellite cricket squad were preparing to open their seasons at the Union Grounds, and more than forty junior baseball teams had been organized in Brooklyn.

Just how much the game was flourishing became evident on a brutally hot August 3 afternoon when the Atlantics took on the Mutuals of New York at Hoboken's Elysian Fields for the unofficial national championship.

The fans overloaded Hudson River ferries for the crossing to Jersey, and carriages crowded the dusty roads to the ballfield. Two hours before the game's start, all the seats had been filled. The overflow wandered around the meadow, causing the game to be delayed forty-five minutes.

When play began, a crowd estimated at 15,000 to 20,000 was on hand under what the *Times* described as "a burning August sun." It was clear, said the paper, that "Gotham had baseball on the brain."

For their trouble, the fans eventually were drenched as a thunderstorm ended the game in the sixth inning. The Atlantics escaped with a 13–12 victory.

Baseball was thriving as well beyond the New York area. The National Association, whose membership consisted of a few New York metropolitan area ballclubs in pre-Civil War days, boasted 202 teams from seventeen states and the District of Columbia by 1866.

While the game flourished, the widespread gambling that had gone with it for years remained, in the eyes of critics, as a blemish on the sport.

With ballplayers still forbidden to play for pay, but with gamblers all over the place, the temptation was there for an athlete to make some quick money by doing less than his full duty on the field.

And so, long before the days of the Black Sox, a "fix" was uncovered. A Brooklyn team had the distinction of being the beneficiary.

In reporting on the game between Brooklyn's Eckfords and the New York Mutuals at Hoboken on September 28, 1865, the *New York Times* wondered about a sudden reversal of form by the Mutuals in the fifth inning when the Eckfords scored eleven runs.

"Over-pitched balls, wild throws, passed balls and failures to stop them in the field marked the play of the Mutuals to an unusual extent," the newspaper noted.

When it was all over, the Eckfords had emerged with a 23–11 victory.

The Mutuals had always had a taint to them resulting from the club's close ties to the notoriously corrupt Tammany Hall political organization and its head, Boss Tweed, who was president of the team from 1860 to 1871. Rumors of fixed games continually enveloped them. This time, the suspicions proved out. A few months after the 1865 season ended, three Mutual players—Thomas Devyr, the shortstop; Ed Duffy, the third baseman, and William Wansley, the catcher—were found to have conspired with gamblers to fix the Eckford game.

Devyr testified before a special investigating committee of the ballclub that Wansley had approached him and said, "Now, you ain't got a cent, nor neither has Duffy; you can make this money without anyone being a bit the wiser of it."

In a letter of confession, Devyr claimed that Wansley offered him $300—of which he received only 30 bucks—as a bribe to dump the game, although he was not told to do anything specific to earn the money.

The Mutuals expelled all three fixers, but they weren't gone for long. Devyr was reinstated in 1867, Duffy in 1868 and Wansley in 1870. The incident had little impact on either the lust for betting or the enthusiasm for the game.

As crowds grew larger, men with imagination got to work making money off the rage for baseball. There was the matter of feeding the fans. Enter Brooklyn's Charles Feltman, who owned a shop at East New York and Howard avenues in what is now the Brownsville section. One day in 1867, Feltman hit upon the idea of selling boiled sausages on rolls. He may, therefore, be the father of the hot dog that goes so inexorably with small boys and baseball. Feltman was a man of high ambition. Four years after hitting upon the hot dog-to-be, he opened a small stand on the beach at Coney Island, and by the late 1870's, he was running a Coney restaurant and beer garden serving 80,000 customers annually. Success spawned imitators. A local historian noted that by 1887, there were more hot dog stands at Coney Island than houses of prostitution.

By the spring of 1869, at least ten ballclubs around the country— among them the Atlantics, Eckfords and Mutuals—were ignoring the ban on professionalism by giving their players a share of the gate receipts or providing outright salaries.

In Cincinnati, Aaron B. Champion, an attorney and transplanted New Yorker, was launching the first team to pay all its players under yearly contracts.

Champion had gone to Cincinnati in 1865, intent on organizing a cricket club. He discovered that baseball was of more interest in the city, and a few years later took over management of the Red Stockings, who had been vying for fans with the Buckeye squad.

With a group of talented players brought in from the East, the Red Stockings eventually drove the Buckeyes out of business. The big money men were Harry Wright, the center fielder, and his brother George, both of whom earned $1,800 for the 1869 season. Harry had a particularly eventful career before heading to Ohio. Born in England, he had played cricket professionally for the St. George Club in Hoboken and then baseball for the Knickerbockers.

In 1869, the Red Stockings were the rage of baseball, going undefeated on an 11,000-mile road trip. Journeying by railroad and steamboat from New York to California, they played before some 200,000 fans, winning perhaps fifty-seven games—the exact number is in dispute—and not losing once. Only a disputed tie in Troy, New York, marred a perfect record.

The Red Stockings began the 1870 season with another twenty-seven victories. Then, on Tuesday, June 14, a sweltering day for late spring—the thermometer at Hudnut's pharmacy in Lower Manhattan registered 86 degrees—the mighty Cincinnati club came to the Capitoline Grounds for a match with the Atlantics. It would be the most memorable game of the nineteenth century.

Game time was 3 P.M., but fans started streaming into the park shortly after noon. The grounds could seat only 5,000, but perhaps three times as many New Yorkers and Brooklynites got some sort of view. For those who wouldn't come up with the fifty-cent admission fee or who got there too late, a peek from a crack in the fence, a perch atop the outfield wall or a spot on a tree limb would do.

The Red Stockings, showing no signs of slowing down, had trounced the Mutuals the previous afternoon. The Atlantics had already lost three games and were rumored to be torn by dissension. Their captain, Bob (Death to Flying Things) Ferguson, had been accused by a *New York Herald* sportswriter of alienating his best players by his foul temper. Ferguson proved the point by threatening to knock out the writer's teeth, frightening him so that he didn't show up to cover the game.

So it was no wonder the betting line was 5 to 1 on the Red Stockings.

◆ *The Atlantics in the process of snapping the Cincinnati Red Stockings' two-year winning streak at Brooklyn's Capitoline Grounds in June 1870. (National Baseball Library, Cooperstown, N.Y.)*

The mystery was why so many fans bothered to make the horsecar journey out to the park.

The Atlantics, dressed in long dark blue trousers, white shirts with an "A" embroidered on the chest, and light buff linen caps, took the field with George Zettlein on the mound and the fearsome Ferguson catching. Zettlein, the greatest fastballer of the era, would indeed be bearing down with his underhand deliveries—he soon stripped off his jersey and pitched in a silk undershirt.

The Cincinnati players, wearing the knickers they had introduced to baseball back in 1868 amid considerable sneering, and donning bright red woolen stockings and shirts with an Old English *C,* were deluged with jeers from the fans. But they seemed ready to romp, taking a 3–0 lead by the third inning behind the pitching of mutton-chopped Asa Brainard.

The Atlantics were hardly done for. They fought back, and at the end of nine innings, they had held the Red Stockings to a 5–5 tie. Under the rules, the game could have ended as a draw if both captains agreed to go home. The Atlantics were willing to settle for the deadlock but Aaron Champion, the Cincinnati owner, ordered his captain, Harry Wright, to demand that play continue. While the two sides argued, most of the Atlantic players went to their lockers and changed clothes, and the fans swarmed

onto the field. Finally, Champion jumped up on a bench and announced that the Reds would claim a forfeit victory if the Atlantics didn't resume play. The players put on their uniforms again and the teams went to extra innings.

The Red Stockings seemed rewarded for their obstinacy when they scored two runs in the top of the eleventh. But the Atlantics staged a rally. Charley Smith, the Atlantics' third baseman, led off with a sharp single to left, then went to third on a wild pitch. Joe (Old Reliable) Start, the Atlantics' first baseman, followed with a drive over the head of the Red Stocking right fielder, Cal McVey. The ball wound up among fans standing on the field, Start made it to third base, and now it was a 7–6 game.

As the *Cincinnati Commercial* told it: "In pushing the crowd aside to get at the ball, McVey was kicked at by a scoundrel." A policeman supposedly clubbed the exuberant fan and dragged him away. (Years later, McVey claimed in an interview that contrary to all the press accounts of the famous play, he was not, in fact, interfered with.)

The next batter, John Chapman, the Atlantics' left fielder, grounded out to third, with Start staying put. Now Ferguson came to the plate. He drove the ball into right field, Start came home, and the game was tied. The fans went wild, running onto the field and shrieking for their Atlantics. Eventually, the grass was cleared and Zettlein strode to the plate.

The Atlantic pitcher hit a hot grounder to the right of Charley Gould, the first baseman. Gould had trouble handling it, finally picked the ball up, then threw to second. The ball was in the dirt, it skipped past Charley Sweasy, the second baseman, and rolled into the outfield. Ferguson dashed home and the Atlantics had scored an astonishing 8–7 victory.

For Aaron Champion, the father of the Red Stockings, it was a bitter hour. He returned to his hotel room after the game and, it was said, "wept like a child."

3

The National Association: Disorganized Baseball

On St. Patrick's Day 1871, delegates of ten ballclubs from around the East and Midwest—among them the Brooklyn-based Eckfords and Mutuals—gathered in Manhattan at the Collier's Rooms hotel on Broadway. They weren't there for the wearin' of the green, but to find a coherent way of making it.

The Red Stockings of Cincinnati had become a drain on their stockholders and had returned to amateur status following the 1870 season. But their spectacular success had inspired other clubs to pay players in violation of the ban on professionalism. Widespread gambling, meanwhile, was continuing to overshadow the game. It was becoming clear that the amateur element had lost the fight.

The baseball-is-a-business contingent founded the first professional baseball organization at the St. Patrick's Day meeting, creating the National Association of Professional Base Ball Players.

The old playing rules were kept in force, but the new organization would attempt to run the game on a more businesslike basis. Any club seeking to join it would have to come up with a membership contribution. What seemed fair? The Association decided on a ten dollar fee, reasoning that if an official banner were to be bought for the pennant-winners to fly, the money would have to come from somewhere. The Eckfords could not, however, bear to part with ten bucks and refused to join up.

The Association lasted from 1871 to 1875, but chaos was never far off. Few teams played their quota of games, a reliance on volunteer umpires led to numerous disputes over the calls and the clubs argued about division of gate receipts. Since the Association was really controlled by the players, little was done to combat drunkenness, contract-jumping and fixes.

Although the Eckfords—hanging on to their ten dollar bill—stayed away when play began in the spring of 1871, Brooklyn did have the Mutuals, and one of the first big series in professional baseball was played at their Union Grounds field. The Chicago White Stockings arrived in town leading the league, one-half game in front of the Mutuals. On June 5, a crowd of 6,000 packed the ballpark, and another 3,000 fans surrounded the field, looking on from the porch of the clubhouse, from carriages on a grassy embankment and from rooftops. The Mutuals rewarded their fans with an 8–5 victory and went into first place.

The White Stockings continued along doing just fine, but eventually found themselves without a ballpark. The great Chicago fire of October 8 destroyed their lakefront field, forcing them to play out the season on the road. The close pennant race among Chicago, Philadelphia and Boston was decided in, of all places, Brooklyn. The Union Grounds was selected as a neutral site for the season's finale on October 30 between Chicago and Philadelphia.

The Chicago players came dressed as if all their possessions had been lost in the fire. Brooklyn-born Ed Pinkham, the second baseman, displayed a touch of his old hometown, wearing a Mutual uniform shirt and pants. To add a final perverse touch, the White Stocking infielder had on a pair of red socks. Tom Foley, the center fielder, was attired in an Eckford uniform: white flannel pants, a white shirt with an orange *E,* and an orange belt and matching socks. The White Stockings' pitcher, George Zettlein, having hurled the Atlantics to their famous victory over the Red Stockings a year earlier, showed up with his old Atlantic jersey. Some of the Chicago players wore baseball caps, others black hats and a few went bare-headed.

Zettlein's old jersey brought him no luck. The White Stockings were dressed for defeat as the Athletics scored a 4–1 victory and came away with the Association's first pennant.

The Mutuals faded to sixth place, finishing with a 17–18 record. The Eckfords must have had second thoughts about raiding their treasury, for they had joined the Association in July, taking the place of the Kekionga club of Fort Wayne, Indiana, which disbanded. Since the Eckfords were latecomers, their games did not count in the standings.

When the 1872 season opened, Brooklyn baseball was going strong. There were now three Brooklyn teams in the Association—the Mutuals,

Eckfords and the newly arrived Atlantics—and a Brooklynite had been named the league's president.

J. W. Kerns, the president of the Troy (New York) Haymakers, had headed the Association in its first year. But then it was decided to give someone from the players' ranks a chance to run things. The Association turned to Death to Flying Things Ferguson, who would spend the '72 season fielding administrative matters when he wasn't wrestling with grounders as the Atlantics' third baseman.

If Ferguson made any executive decisions favoring his ballclub, it wasn't evident in the standings. The Atlantics finished in seventh place with a record of 8–27.

The terrible-tempered Ferguson, having threatened to punch out that *New York Herald* reporter a few years back, was hardly mellowed by the responsibilities of high office. In July 1873, while umpiring a game between the Mutuals and the Baltimore Canaries, Ferguson was loudly abused by the Mutual catcher, Nat Hicks, a notorious umpire-baiter. Hicks had received a bloody mouth three weeks before when he was hit by a foul tip (catching masks were yet to come), but the mishap had not quieted him. By the ninth inning, Ferguson had heard enough. He grabbed a bat and walloped away at Hicks's arm. When the game ended, a policeman tried to arrest Ferguson for assault, but the gallant Hicks refused to press charges, claiming he was not badly hurt. He was wrong. The arm turned out to be broken in two places and Hicks was sidelined for almost two months.

Brooklynites of the 1870's had grand fun cheering on ballfield mayhem while drinking and gambling in the stands. But there were entertaining moments far removed from the ballpark. The times were spiced with a sensational criminal case: the adultery trial of the Reverend Henry Ward Beecher.

The 3,000 seats at Plymouth Church on the Heights—the biggest hall in Brooklyn—were regularly packed for the powerful sermons that made Beecher a celebrity far beyond Brooklyn.

He had taken over the church in 1847 upon arriving from Indianapolis, and as passions over the slavery issue rose, Beecher had become one of the loudest voices for abolitionism. One day, in a burst of moral fervor designed to outrage his fellow Brooklynites, he auctioned off a slave named Sarah from the church pulpit.

As Beecher's fame spread, Lincoln came to hear him speak and so did Charles Dickens. His orations intrigued Mark Twain, who described him in action: "He went marching up and down the stage, sawing his arms in the air, howling sarcasms this way and that, discharging rockets of poetry, and exploding mines of eloquence, halting now and then to stamp his foot three times in succession to emphasize a point."

In 1874, a sensational story broke. Theodore Tilton, an associate of

Beecher, accused him of having seduced Tilton's wife. The paper that first ran the accusation sold 100,000 copies, and the adultery trial that followed, lasting almost six months, was the biggest national story since the Civil War days. Beecher was finally found not guilty, the church raised $100,000 to pay his legal fees, and he continued to bask in his fame.

On a more serene note for Brooklyn, 1874 also marked completion of Prospect Park, a magnificent 526 acres of rolling meadows, wooded hills and a fine lake created during the previous eight years by the renowned park architects Frederick Law Olmsted and Calvert Vaux, who designed Central Park as well.

When Brooklynites turned their attention from the sensations of an adultery trial and the beauty of their new park, they encountered a dismal 1875 baseball season. The year was the worst one for the National Association—only seven of the thirteen clubs that began the season were still there at its end. The Atlantics finished out their schedule, but could brag of little else. They had a record of 2–42.

When the Mutuals and Atlantics played at home, the excitement seemed mostly confined to the stands: Fans of the ballclubs may have led the league in gambling. Betting on baseball—common in the 1860's—was booming in the decade that followed.

Back in 1870, *Porter's Spirit* newspaper estimated that only 1,000 people had bothered to attend a game between the Chicago White Stockings and the Atlantics because the Brooklyn club was "getting into such bad repute, from the constantly flying rumors of 'sells' and 'thrown' games, that few people cared to expend their time and money in going to witness what may turn out to be merely a 'hippodroming' exhibition."

Read "hippodroming" as the nineteenth century term for "fix."

The formation of the new National Association in 1871 had done little to clean up the game. There was so much open betting in one section of the Atlantics' park that it became known as the Gold Board because its activity seemed to rival that of the stock exchange.

Amid the mess, there emerged in Chicago a man named William Hulbert. Brooklyn baseball would go into eclipse, but Hulbert would help save the game.

4

"A Disgraceful Scene on the Union Grounds"

O n the morning of February 2, 1876, executives from eight baseball teams trudged through a fresh snowfall to a meeting near Manhattan's Washington Square.

Gathering at the Grand Central Hotel on Broadway, just ten blocks south of the spot where the National Association had been formed five years earlier, they would bring baseball into a new era.

Behind it all was the White Stockings' William Hulbert, who had pulled a coup the year before with a quite illegal maneuver. Hulbert had obtained secret agreements from several top players, among them Boston's pitching ace Al Spalding and Philadelphia's batting star Cap Anson, to join his Chicago club for the 1876 season. A commitment by a ballplayer in the midst of one season to join another team the following year was against the rules, loose as they were. So when Chicago sportswriters exposed Hulbert's deal, a furor erupted.

Fearful that the National Association would expel the players he had grabbed, Hulbert outsmarted his foes by organizing a new league. He enticed clubs from a few Midwestern cities and some teams from the Association—among them the Mutuals—to overthrow the old order.

The National League was born.

The rebels proclaimed a crackdown on crookedness, announcing that all dishonest players would be banned for life and that betting by fans on club grounds would be forbidden. Amid the professed devotion to clean play, an eye for profit seemed, however, to take precedence over principle.

The Mutuals had a reputation as the most notorious fixers of the old Association. But without them, the new league would have no presence in America's largest city. So the Mutuals—still playing at Brooklyn's Union Grounds although formally a New York franchise—were welcomed into the family.

The Mutuals made a superficial attempt to shed their image. In the Association days, their players usually wore green or brown leggings, and the club had alternately been known as the Green Stockings or Chocolate Stockings. Now they switched to red leggings to go with the white uniforms. And the team dropped New York from its name, calling itself the Brooklyn Mutuals.

But as the 1876 season got under way, the franchise found it could not live down its unsavory reputation. The *Chicago Tribune* reported that some of the Mutual players had agreed to fix a game but that William Cammeyer, the manager as well as owner, had learned of the plot so they played it on the level and actually won. The *New York Herald* told of an unsuccessful attempt by a gambler to bribe Bobby Mathews, the Mutuals' one and only pitcher.

Outside the National League, crooked games seemed to be continuing with no let-up. A bizarre game on September 21 between Brooklyn and New York teams composed of players from various clubs in each city inspired the *New York Times* headline, "A Disgraceful Scene on the Union Grounds."

Early in the afternoon, the New York team had been 25–10 favorites, but just before game time the smart money shifted to the Brooklyn squad. The word was that at least two New York players had agreed to throw the game.

In the first inning, Hovey, the New York center fielder, let a ball go through his hands, turning a single into a triple. In the fourth, Hovey dropped an easy fly ball, prompting Fallon, his pitcher, to stop the game and accuse him of dumping.

In the eighth inning, the Brooklyn pitcher, a fellow named Rule, became disgusted with Hovey, even though the Brooklyn team was benefiting by his generosity. Rule angrily accused Hovey of trying to persuade one of his own men to wander off third base so he could be tagged out.

"The crowd hissed and hooted, and demanded that Hovey be put off the field, but after some little delay the game went on," the *Times* reported.

In the final inning, Frank Hankinson, the New York third baseman, who had earlier made "several suspicious throws to first base," hit a drive to right-center field that could easily have been a home run, tying the game.

But, the *Times* reported, Hankinson "did little more than walk around the bases" and got no farther than third base. He was, however, forced to score when the next batter made a base hit.

With that, the two teams called it quits.

"Rule and Fallon, the two pitchers, now shook hands, and refusing longer to engage in such a disgraceful affair, walked off the field," the *Times* continued. "At the solicitation of the two captains the umpires called the affair a draw. While the players were changing their uniforms in the club-house some one accused Hovey of selling the game. A disgraceful fight ensued, to suppress which the Police had to be called in, a fitting finale to the most disreputable proceeding that has been witnessed on a ball field in this vicinity for years."

Hankinson may have been disgraced but he was hardly undone by the poor press notices. Seven years later, he would be the starting third baseman for the New York Giants in their first National League game.

The League would not have to worry for long about whether the Mutuals were still fixing games. When the Mutuals and the Philadelphia Athletics both refused to go through with their final western trip of the 1876 season, explaining they had lost money and couldn't afford any additional expenses, both were expelled.

Brooklyn would not, however, be without National League baseball in 1877. The Hartford Dark Blues had lost money in 1876 despite finishing second to the Chicago White Stockings. So their owner, Morgan Bulkeley, decided on a change of scenery for the club's home games, shifting them from Connecticut to the Union Grounds. Why he thought Brooklynites would support a team that couldn't draw fans in its own hometown is a mystery. The club was, in fact, essentially ignored by Brooklyn fans and after the '77 season it went out of business.

If the Mutuals were dumping games in 1876, they were hardly the only crooked team in the National League's early days. The Mutuals may have been gone from the league in '77, but thanks to two of their alumni, the team's moral values were not forgotten.

When the Louisville Grays came east late in the 1877 season for games with Boston and with the Hartford club at its Brooklyn field, they collapsed amid a flood of errors.

The team's play was so poor that the *Louisville Courier-Journal* ran bewildered headlines reading "!!!-???-!!!" and "What's the Matter?" Soon there was an explanation: The games had been fixed.

After the season, an investigation found that four Louisville players— Jim Devlin, a pitcher; William Craver, the captain and second baseman; Al Nichols, another infielder, and George Hall, an outfielder—had taken bribes to throw games. Perhaps $300 had been paid to them by New York gamblers, half of the money going to Devlin. They were banned from baseball for life.

Three of the four had a Brooklyn baseball pedigree. Nichols had played for the Atlantics in 1875 and both he and Craver were members of the Mutuals in '76. Hall had been on the 1870 Atlantic club.

In 1880, a new ballclub was born in Brooklyn—the first incarnation of the Mets. The founders were two men still in their twenties—John B. Day, a Manhattan tobacco merchant and would-be pitcher, and Jim Mutrie, a Chelsea, Massachusetts, native who had played on minor league teams in Fall River and New Bedford and had visions of becoming a sports promoter.

The squad played a few times in New Jersey, but most of its early games were in Brooklyn at the Union or Capitoline Grounds.

Day soon realized, however, that Brooklyn was something of a backwater for a man with high baseball ambitions. The construction of a long dreamed-of bridge linking Brooklyn with Manhattan had finally begun, but completion of this marvel was still years away. Day wouldn't wait.

One morning, a bootblack shining Day's shoes near his office on Maiden Lane off Wall Street is said to have told him about a field at 110th Street near Fifth Avenue used for polo games. Polo today, baseball tomorrow. Day investigated, liked what he saw, and leased the field from its owner, James Gordon Bennett, Jr., the son of the founder and owner of the *New York Herald.* Day moved the Mets to Manhattan before the 1880 season was over, and on September 29, he staged the first professional baseball game played in New York City. The Mets won it over a squad from Washington.

The Metropolitans played through 1881 as an independent team, meeting National League clubs in exhibition games. Soon after the 1881 season ended, so did the League's monopoly on big-time baseball. A circuit called the American Association was created, offering a sprightly alternative to the staid National Leaguers.

The League banned beer at its ballparks, but the Association was happy to quench a thirst. It also permitted Sunday baseball, cut the admission charge from the standard fifty cents to twenty-five cents, and cast aside the traditional flannel uniforms in favor of flamboyant silks.

To the dismay of fans from Brooklyn and New York City, the Association had one deficiency in common with the National League—no New York area franchise.

But in December '82, the Mets moved into the big time. The franchises from the two smallest cities in the National League—Troy, New York, and Worcester, Massachusetts—dropped out. To fill the gap, the League accepted two new owners, John Day of the Mets and Al Reach, the ex-Brooklyn Eckford ballplayer who was then running an independent club in Philadelphia.

While Day made it to the National League, the ballclub he founded in Brooklyn three years earlier did not. Instead of taking his Mets into the League, Day created an entirely new team, signing many of the best players from the defunct Troy club.

But the Mets were not dead. Day dispatched them to the American Association and sent Jim Mutrie along as the manager. There was still some leftover talent from Troy to help stock their roster.

So the New York City area, which had been without a major league team since the Mutuals of Brooklyn were thrown out of the National League in 1876, now boasted two big league ballclubs.

It had only one owner, however, and he had one ballpark. No problem. Day's Mets had been playing on a large tract of land extending from 110th to 112th Street and from Fifth to Sixth Avenue. Now, where there had been one diamond, there would be two. Day put his new National League squad onto the existing field, near the more desirable Fifth Avenue end. The grounds were well-manicured and there was a fine grandstand. He shifted the Mets to the Sixth Avenue side, where he concocted a shabby ballfield that he leveled by using raw garbage as landfill. To keep the Mets' second-rate operation entirely separate from his first-class National League entry, Day erected a canvas fence down the middle of the grounds between the two fields.

National League baseball made its debut in New York on May 1, 1883, when more than 12,000 fans, among them former President Ulysses S. Grant, saw Day's new club score a 7–5 victory over Boston at the original Polo Grounds.

On May 12, the Mets got around to making their home debut—at the poor man's side of the Polo Grounds—and suffered an 11–4 drubbing by Philadelphia.

Across the East River, at a new ballfield called Washington Park, there was another opener that Saturday afternoon. This one was merely a minor league game. But a band tooted away, fans jammed the wooden grandstand, and excitement was in the air again for Brooklyn baseball fans.

5

Minor League Ballclub, Major League Bridge

George Washington had slept there. Brooklynites had gone skating there. Now, on the frosty afternoons of January 1883, construction workers were toiling against a May deadline at a shallow basin in South Brooklyn.

Soon there would be a ballpark on the site and a brand new team—the franchise that would ultimately become the Brooklyn Dodgers.

It all began with four men: George J. Taylor, a newspaper editor; Charles H. Byrne, a real-estate investor who owned a gambling casino; Byrne's brother-in-law, Joseph J. Doyle, and another gambling hall proprietor, Ferdinand A. Abell.

At age 30, Taylor had risen to become the night city editor of James Gordon Bennett's *New York Herald.* But the years in the newsroom had taken their toll on his health, and his doctor suggested he seek some outdoor work. He decided to become a baseball promoter.

Taylor turned to Charles Byrne, a fellow alumnus of St. Francis Xavier College and a man nine years older. Byrne, too, had been a journalist and had studied law, but he had discovered a more lucrative calling outside the law. He operated a gambling house on Ann Street in Manhattan with Doyle as his partner. Byrne and Doyle agreed to join Taylor in starting a baseball team in Brooklyn. Soon they found a fourth partner in Abell, the owner of a gambling house in Narragansett, Rhode Island.

They selected land between Fourth and Fifth avenues and Third and Fifth streets for their new ballpark. It was historic ground. A stone home on the site built in 1699—the Vechte-Cortelyou House—had been George Washington's headquarters in the Revolutionary War during the Battle of Long Island. To honor him, the ballfield would be called Washington Park. But sentiment yielded to practicality when it came to Washington's old sleeping quarters. Byrne converted it into a ladies' rest room.

As work on the field progressed, the budding owners advertised for ballplayers. There would be many a free spirit in a Brooklyn uniform over the seasons to come, but at the beginning, it was all serious business.

"They want men of intelligence and not corner-lot toughs who may happen to possess some ability as players," warned a writer for the sporting journal *New York Clipper*. "Players whose habits and ways unfit them for thorough teamwork need not trouble themselves to apply for positions on the new Brooklyn club's team."

Forty players who presumably had sterling character references applied for jobs, and sixteen made the squad. Byrne was named club president and Taylor became the field manager. Assisting in everyday chores from hawking scorecards to working the turnstiles was a young man named Charles H. Ebbets from whom more would be heard.

Byrne placed the team in the Interstate Association, a minor league, and made sure that his troupe would open in fine style: He purchased polka-dot stockings for the players.

As Washington Park opened its gates, there were other signs of a new day. An announcement was made that the old Union Grounds—baseball's first enclosed field—would be redeveloped for housing and commercial use.

Brooklyn was indeed growing at a furious pace. The census of 1880 found that nearly 600,000 people called it home, a rise of more than 40 percent over the previous decade. Only New York City, with a population of 1.2 million, and Philadelphia, with 875,000, were larger.

On the Heights—really a suburb for the Wall Street financial crowd—Brooklyn's "old stock" still thrived on fine blocks lined with brick and brownstone row houses and a sprinkling of mansions.

But Brooklyn was well on its way to developing a rich ethnic mix. By the beginning of the 1880's, some 30 percent of its people were immigrants, most of them from Germany or Ireland. Soon huge numbers of Russian Jews would arrive, fleeing the persecution of the Czar.

The Brooklyn of the early 1880's was still considered a bedroom community overshadowed by New York City, but it had 5,000 factories of its own employing 49,000 people. Stretching along the East River were the huge Astral Oil Works, a division of Standard Oil; the Union Porcelain Works, producing some of the country's finest china, and D. Appleton & Company, a mammoth printing and binding plant. Grain elevators, five and six stories high, lined the waterfront, and shipments of sugar, coffee and flour passed through the docks. Some 2,000 workmen were needed daily at the Brooklyn Navy Yard, the largest facility of its kind in the nation.

There were fine shops, too, most of them along a short stretch of Fulton Street in downtown. Ovington's, at Fulton and Clinton streets, offered the best in imported glass, chinaware and ornamental pieces.

Brooklynites took great pride in Prospect Park, which was attracting some 5 million visitors a year. In the summers, tennis was the fad with more than 125 clubs using eighty courts laid out on the park's Long Meadow. In the winter, when the lake froze, thousands flocked to the park for skating.

Two new boulevards leading from the park—Eastern and Ocean parkways—provided fine routes for a Sunday carriage ride. For those seeking more vigorous exercise, the Kings County Wheelmen sponsored bicycle races at the Williamsburgh Athletic Grounds.

The steamy summer days brought millions to Coney Island. By 1883, nine steam railroads and a horsecar route were carrying Brooklynites to the beach, and the Iron Steam-Boat Company had just begun service to Coney from the Battery in Lower Manhattan.

For the workingman and his family, Coney Island meant simply a day at the beach and its amusement area. For those who could afford it, extended stays at luxury hotels were a way to beat the heat. The Manhattan Beach—the most ornate of the Coney hotels—could serve 4,000 people at a single setting. On one mid-July day in 1883, the menu included "Soft Shell Crabs in cases a l'Oriental" along with "Croquettes of English Snipe, Chasseur" and "Omlette à la Espagnole."

Rich and poor alike at Coney enjoyed Gilmore's World Renowned Band or perhaps Buffalo Bill and Dr. Carver's Wild Exhibition. There were the more disreputable elements too. Three-card monte dealers did a thriving business swindling the unwary at the beach.

As America roared into a marvelous age of inventions, Brooklyn tried to keep pace. The old ways did not, however, die so easily. Thomas Edison had invented the incandescent bulb in 1879, but four years later—when the team that would be the Dodgers was born—Brooklyn's roadways were still being lit with 15,000 gas lamps. And most of the streets remained unpaved. When the street sweepers came through to clear away the horse dung and the rotting food that had fallen from open carts, choking clouds of dust filled the air.

More than a dozen ferries linked Brooklyn with New York City. Within Brooklyn, most people traveled on the fourteen horsecar lines. Running on an iron rail and pulled by a single horse, each car could seat about thirty customers at five cents a head. The more prosperous Brooklynites maintained their privacy in horse-drawn cabs. In May 1883, roomier-than-ever horse cabs, painted a bright yellow, went into service on Montague Street, where one day the Dodgers would have their executive offices.

Elevated steam railroads carried some 93 million passengers in Manhattan during 1883, but Brooklyn had yet to discover the overhead railway. The first franchise for a Brooklyn "el" was not awarded until December '83, when the Kings County Elevated Railroad Company was given the right to build a line between Fulton Ferry and the Bedford section.

That "el" was unlikely to have trouble attracting riders. The Fulton Street waterfront area was crowded with tourists gawking at the great technological feat of the age—the Brooklyn Bridge.

There had been talk of an East River bridge linking New York City and Brooklyn since the beginning of the nineteenth century. Then came the savage winter of 1866, when ice covering the river stranded ferries at their docks. Action would soon replace wishful thinking.

In April 1867, the New York Bridge Company, a private corporation with the power to issue stock, began searching for a bridge-builder. The businessmen found a man with a vision. He was John Roebling, a German immigrant who had perfected a means of weaving wire like rope to produce the strongest cables ever created.

"The contemplated work, when constructed in accordance with my design, will not only be the greatest bridge in existence, but it will be the greatest engineering work of this continent, and the age," Roebling promised. "Its most conspicuous features, the towers, will serve as landmarks to the adjoining cities, and they will be entitled to be ranked as national monuments."

Roebling received the commission to build the bridge, and his prophecy would be fulfilled. But he would not live to see the completion of his great work. In June 1869, his foot was crushed when a ferryboat slammed against it at the Brooklyn waterfront, and he died of lockjaw. His son, Washington, took over and directed construction until he, too, was felled, suffering the "bends" while supervising the digging of the Brooklyn tower's underwater foundation. From then on, Washington Roebling remained in his apartment on Brooklyn's Columbia Heights, watching the workmen through a spyglass as his wife, Emily, who had taught herself engineering, became his emissary on the site.

Finally, fourteen years after construction had begun, after the deaths of at least twenty construction workers, the loss of John Roebling and the crippling of his son, after Boss Tweed and other grafters had grabbed their loot, the bridge was a reality.

On the afternoon of May 1, 1883, the fortunes of the fledgling Brooklyn baseball team were hardly noticed in the press. The thrilling bridge that was about to open dominated the news. And on this particular Tuesday, Brooklynites had personal matters more pressing than baseball to contend with. It seemed that everyone was up and about. May 1 was traditionally moving day in both New York City and Brooklyn. Every type of horse-drawn vehicle could be seen plodding through the streets and jamming ferries to bring the people and their possessions to new homes.

But it was also a new day for Brooklyn baseball. That afternoon, Charlie Byrne's team made its debut, taking the field in Wilmington, Delaware, for its Interstate Association opener against a club called the Quickstep. It was not a happy beginning. The Brooklyns—no nickname yet— were beaten, 9–6.

The team then headed back for its first appearance before the home folks. But the finishing touches had not yet been completed at Washington Park. A ballfield in Newark, New Jersey, and the Parade Grounds at Prospect Park would have to serve for a while as homes away from home. So the club made its Brooklyn debut at Prospect Park, taking on a squad from Harrisburg, Pennsylvania. The Brooklyns emerged with a 7–1 victory, but the opener was a box office flop. All 1,000 spectators were admitted for free since the game was being played on public land.

The Harrisburg team got things off to a surly start. The visitors' pitcher, a disagreeable fellow named Jack Schappert, abetted by Henry Myers, the manager-shortstop, and John Shetzline, the captain-second baseman, spent the afternoon making life miserable for the umpire, a Mr. Fleming.

The *Brooklyn Eagle* told how "this noteworthy trio began kicking against the decisions of the umpire on matters in which his judgment alone was concerned, Schappert exclaiming, 'You make me sick,' when balls were called on him instead of strikes."

Aside from the howling, the Harrisburg pitcher did little for his teammates.

"Schappert's wretched throwing of the ball to the bat contributed largely to their defeat," the *Eagle* noted.

As for the hometown heroes, "the conduct of the Brooklyn team was commendable under the circumstances, they playing a gentlemanly game throughout."

On Saturday, May 12, Washington Park was finally ready, and the Brooklyn team made its real home debut, facing the Trentons of New Jersey. More than 6,000 fans turned out, some 4,500 filling the grandstands, the others standing or seated in chairs they brought along. At three o'clock, the 23rd Regiment Band took its position before the crowd for an hour of music. The spectators, appreciative of the fine show and the chance to once again savor pro baseball, displayed a generosity that would not be a trademark of Brooklyn crowds in the years to come. When the Trenton players, clad in gray jerseys and red stockings, took the field for practice, they were greeted with applause.

The first two innings told the story.

"The Brooklyn team were a little nervous at appearing before the local crowd and the result was some errors in their fielding, which enabled the visiting batsmen to open the game with a score of three runs," the *Eagle* reported.

But Brooklyn came back with two runs in its half of the first inning, added another six runs in the second inning and came away with a 13–6 victory.

None of the rancor of the Prospect Park opener was repeated.

"The Trentons presented a most favorable contrast to the rough behavior of the Harrisburg team," the *Eagle* noted. "The visiting team behaved throughout like gentlemen, not a word being heard in disputing the decisions of the umpire, and the same credit is due the home team."

Despite the auspicious debut, Charlie Byrne's ballclub probably did not linger long in the thoughts of Brooklynites for the grandest celebration in Brooklyn's history was at hand. On Thursday, May 24—a perfect day with cloudless skies, a bright sun and a gentle breeze—the Brooklyn Bridge was opened to the people.

The Navy's Atlantic Squadron boomed its big guns and steam whistles blew from every tug and ferry on the East River as President Chester A. Arthur, to the strains of "Hail to the Chief," marched across the bridge from Manhattan to Brooklyn.

Thousands of Brooklynites and New Yorkers jammed the bridge for their own strolls during the afternoon, and prayers and speeches dragged on for hours. At nightfall, a spectacular fireworks display illuminated the skies, bathing the bridge in a shower of red light.

To conclude the celebration, President Arthur was treated to a grand reception at Brooklyn's Academy of Music.

A member of his Cabinet was overheard remarking, "Why I thought that Brooklyn had one hotel and a shipyard or two, but it's quite a town."

As spring turned to early summer, the new ballclub settled into third place. But then another team's misfortune provided a break for Brooklyn. The Merritt squad of Camden, New Jersey, although holding down first place, was forced to disband in July when it ran out of money. Byrne moved quickly, signing up five of Camden's top players—Sam Kimber, a pitcher; John Corcoran, a catcher, and three infielders, Bill Greenwood, Charlie Householder and Frank Fennelly.

The Brooklyns had been struggling with a 15–17 record when the new men arrived, but then they started to gain ground. The pennant race came down to the final two games of the season, at Washington Park. The Harrisburg team, which had provided such a contentious opener at Prospect Park, was back, trailing first-place Brooklyn by a game and a half.

On Friday, Jack Schappert, the chief complainer from that opening day, got a bit of revenge by pitching Harrisburg to an 8–5 victory, setting up a pennant-deciding game on Saturday.

This time, the Brooklyns struck early, getting a 7–1 lead by the third inning, and Adonis Terry, who had been recruited in June from his native western Massachusetts, pitched them to an 11–6 victory.

It was the climax of a wonderful year. Brooklyn had its great bridge at last and, on a less momentous note, it had a pennant winner.

6

American Association Days

New Yorkers might sneer, but Brooklyn's boosters never considered their town to be second rate in anything. So, after having won a minor league championship in his first season, Charlie Byrne looked for a larger challenge.

He found it in the American Association, which, while not having the prestige of the National League, was decidedly big-time baseball.

On May 1, 1884—exactly one year after making their debut—the Brooklyns began play in the thirteen-team Association. The introduction to the major leagues was a rough one. They were clobbered, 12–0, in Washington.

A happier result came four days later when Jim Conway, a right-hander making his first appearance in a Brooklyn uniform, pitched the team to an 11–3 victory over Washington in its home-opener. Brooklyn-born John Cassidy, the right fielder, whose career went all the way back to the 1875 Brooklyn Atlantics of the old National Association, provided the power with a home run.

The high point of the season for Brooklyn came in the final days when Sam Kimber, one of the players who had been picked up in July 1883 from the defunct Camden club, pitched a ten-inning no-hitter against Toledo. He did not, however, win the game. Brooklyn managed four hits off Toledo's Tony Mullane, but play was halted by darkness with neither team having scored.

Kimber's frustration was perfectly in tune with Brooklyn's season.

The team finished with a 40–64 record, landing in tenth place. To make matters worse, the rival New York Mets, in their second year in the Association, captured the pennant and finished 33½ games ahead of Brooklyn.

Charlie Byrne was not about to have Brooklyn remain at the wrong end of the standings from Manhattan, so he began to search for new ballplayers. He would get some from the Cleveland team, which had dropped out of the National League following the 1884 season. But corralling the new talent would take a bit of maneuvering that skirted the spirit, if not

♦ *The original New York Mets in an 1886 game at their home park, the St. George Cricket Grounds on Staten Island. The Mets would disband after the 1887 season and Brooklyn would pick up their few good players. (National Baseball Library, Cooperstown, N.Y.)*

the letter, of baseball's rules.

Knowing his club was about to go under, the Cleveland manager, Charlie Hackett, made a deal to manage Brooklyn in 1885. He then took a wad of cash and went visiting. Over a three-week period, Hackett met with his top players at their off-season homes, dispensing with his payroll in return for promises that each player would join him in Brooklyn the following spring. There was one little formality to be dealt with. When a player was released, he was required to wait ten days before signing with another team. The interval was designed to give all clubs a chance to bid. But Hackett was not about to have any competition. So when the Cleveland players were formally set free upon their club's dissolution, Hackett became a baby-sitter. He rounded up the players and kept them under watch at a Cleveland hotel so no one else could approach them. A few moments after midnight on the tenth and final day of the waiting period, they signed to play for Charlie Byrne.

It was, said the *Times,* "the biggest sensation ever made in Brooklyn."

Beyond baseball, there would be another sensation in 1885. Out at Coney Island, the first roller coaster—LaMarcus Thompson's Switchback Railway—went into operation. And in downtown, the St. George Hotel, later famous for its saltwater pool, opened its doors.

Despite the successful scheming, Hackett didn't last long in Brooklyn.

The team got off to a slow start as the former Cleveland players and the holdovers formed separate cliques. By June, Hackett had quit. But things only got worse. The dissension reached its climax on June 18, a week after Hackett left, when the team committed fourteen errors at Washington Park in an 18–5 loss to St. Louis. The Brooklyn pitcher, John Smith, who had just been brought up from Allentown of the Eastern League, was done in by his teammates.

It was partly a case of one Smith sabotaging another. George (Germany) Smith, the shortstop and an ex-Cleveland player, made seven errors.

The next morning, Byrne called the players together, fined the culprits a total of $500, and threatened that anyone pulling such a stunt again would be thrown out of baseball. Hours later, there was a miraculous turnaround as the ballclub beat St. Louis, 3–1, without making a single error.

But it was too late to salvage the season. The team finished in sixth place with a 53–59 record.

Amid the travails, Byrne had done his best to get Brooklynites behind the team. He enticed women to Washington Park by making all games, except those on holidays, Ladies' Day specials. It was hardly a financial sacrifice. With women close by, the men were less likely to brawl in the stands. So Byrne saved money he would otherwise have had to spend for hiring special police.

After the divisive 1885 season, Brooklyn climbed to third place, but by 1887 Byrne's men were back in sixth again.

Though the '87 club wound up in the second division, the World Series, which had been inaugurated in 1884, came to Brooklyn, at least for two afternoons. The St. Louis Browns, winners of the American Association title, and the Detroit Wolverines, the National League champions, staged a traveling show, playing a 15-game Series in 10 different cities. Games 5 and 12 were held at Washington Park.

After games in St. Louis, Detroit and Pittsburgh, the Browns and Wolverines journeyed to the East Coast, arriving in special railroad cars at Jersey City on Friday, October 14. The teams would be playing at Washington Park the next afternoon, but Brooklyn's hotels apparently weren't fancy enough for their night's lodging. They slept in Manhattan, the Browns staying at the Grand Central Hotel and the Wolverines at the Oriental.

On Saturday, the players crossed the Brooklyn Bridge in carriages and were cheered by fans lining their route to Washington Park. A crowd of 8,500 that included Brooklyn's political elite—Mayor Whitney and "Boss" McLaughlin—turned out to see the Browns beat the Wolverines, 5–2. The winning pitcher was Parisian Bob Caruthers, who had agreed to continue toiling for St. Louis after having spent the 1885–86 winter in France with his catcher, Doc Bushong, vowing to stay put until his salary demands were met. The European ploy eventually got Caruthers a new contract and a nickname in the bargain.

After the one-game stand in Brooklyn, the World Series moved on, and by the time it returned, the Wolverines had already clinched matters, 8 games to 3. Only 700 fans showed up at Washington Park on a chilly afternoon for a meaningless Game 12.

Though the Browns had now captured the American Association pennant three years in a row, their owner, Chris Von der Ahe, was enraged by the World Series defeat and accused his players of carousing when they should have been concentrating on baseball. His unhappiness was soon complemented by the chance to make a considerable buck. When Charlie Byrne offered to buy some of his top players, Von der Ahe was happy to cash in.

Parisian Bob Caruthers and Dave Foutz, two of the Browns' top pitchers and both outstanding hitters as well, were sold to Brooklyn along with Doc Bushong, Parisian Bob's batterymate and traveling companion.

Caruthers cost Byrne $8,250 while Foutz's price tag was $6,000, no small sums for the 1880's. But they seemed worth it. Caruthers, only five feet seven inches tall but possessing a muscular physique, had pitched four of the Browns' five World Series victories in 1887, and both he and Foutz had won ninety-nine games over the three previous seasons. Bushong was a journeyman catcher, but no dope—off the field he was a practicing dentist.

In another big move, Byrne picked up the Mets' players after the squad—by now toiling in obscurity at an old cricket grounds on Staten Island—went out of business following a seventh-place finish in 1887. Three Mets—Dave Orr, their first baseman and one of the club's trio of managers in '87; Paul Radford, the shortstop, who would be switched to center field, and Darby O'Brien, the left fielder—would become starters for Brooklyn in 1888. The ballclub was in first place at midsummer, but then the Browns, despite selling off most of their top players, came on to win a fourth straight pennant.

Although Brooklyn was getting closer to a championship, Manager Bill McGunnigle was frustrated. He vowed that if the team didn't catch the Browns the following season, he would jump off the Brooklyn Bridge.

The threat didn't provide any immediate inspiration as Brooklyn started slowly in 1889 and trailed the Browns for most of the summer. But then McGunnigle's men got hot and caught up with St. Louis by the end of August. On September 7, the Browns came into Brooklyn for the start of a two-game series. It was a day to remember.

The game began at four P.M. under overcast skies and dragged on as both teams bickered tirelessly with Umpire Fred Goldsmith. With darkness approaching, the Browns took a 4–2 lead in the late innings. Then they began to stall in hopes that Goldsmith would have to call the game.

◆ *Dave Foutz, a pitcher-first baseman who starred with the pennant-winning Brooklyn teams of 1889 and '90 and later managed the club with considerably less success. (Los Angeles Dodgers)*

That was the cue for Chris Von der Ahe—"Der Boss President" of the Browns as he was known—to spring into action. The St. Louis owner, a German-born saloon keeper with a huge nose and full mustache, had an enthusiasm for baseball matched only by his ignorance of the game. Having accompanied his team east, he decided to drop a not-so-subtle hint for Umpire Goldsmith.

To impress the lateness of the hour upon the umpire, Von der Ahe lit some candles and set them down in front of his players' bench. The Brooklyn fans promptly fired away with beer mugs, knocking a few candles over and starting a small fire. Umpire Goldsmith was unmoved and ordered that play continue. Finally, the Browns' captain, Charlie Comiskey, pulled his team off the field in the ninth inning with St. Louis still ahead by two runs. The fans now opened up with a bottle-throwing barrage, hitting Tommy McCarthy, a St. Louis outfielder, in the mouth and smashing windows in the Browns' clubhouse. The afternoon ended with Goldsmith awarding the game to Brooklyn on a forfeit since the Browns had refused to play until the final out.

Von der Ahe would not let his team take the field the next day so that game was also forfeited to Brooklyn.

Two weeks later, the American Association board reversed the forfeit of the game that was played, holding that the umpire should have called it because of darkness with the Browns ahead. But it upheld the forfeit arising out of the Browns' failure to appear the next afternoon. The compromise satisfied neither team and, by taking one game away from Brooklyn, left the club with a margin of three and a half games over second-place St. Louis.

With the pennant race coming down to its final days, the Brooklyn players now took some extreme personal action to keep the lead from slipping away. The team had become known as the Bridegrooms, or simply Grooms, during the 1888 season in tribute to four players who had married within a few weeks of each other the previous winter. But now the ballplayers decided to avoid their wives, hoping that energy conserved by staying out of the bedroom could be put to use on the ballfield. Caruthers even refused to see his new baby.

The sacrifices paid off as Brooklyn won its first American Association pennant, finishing two games ahead of the Browns. Caruthers went 40–11 while Adonis Terry had a 22–15 record. Oyster Burns, the right fielder, supplied batting punch with a .304 average and 100 runs batted in. Another big contribution at the plate came from Dave Foutz, who concentrated on playing first base instead of pitching. At six feet two inches and 160 pounds, Foutz was known as "Mr. Scissors" and "The Human Hairpin" and found it difficult to bend for throws. But he made up for the shortcoming of being too long by driving in 113 runs.

Over in the National League, it was an eventful season for the New York ballclub. In mid-July, the New Yorkers moved to a new Polo Grounds, at Eighth Avenue and 155th Street, and they went on to win the pennant by one game over Boston. (By now the team was known as the Giants. Back in 1885, the manager, Jim Mutrie, the ex-Met, inspired by the fact that two of his players were over six feet tall, had taken to marching around the Polo Grounds stands chanting the nonsensical, "Who are the people? The Giants are the people." The nickname stuck.)

With Brooklyn the American Association champion and New York the National League winner, the stage was set for the launching of baseball's greatest rivalry.

Just before the World Series got under way, the *Brooklyn Eagle* set the tone of brashness that would ripen among Dodger rooters in the decades to come. "We have the biggest Bridge, the biggest Burying ground and the biggest Base Ball club in this blessed land of big things," it puffed.

Set for a maximum of eleven games, the Series opened at the Polo Grounds on the afternoon of Friday, October 18.

It didn't take long for a controversy to erupt. The first dispute occurred, in fact, before the first pitch was thrown. Tom Lynch, who had been selected as one of the two umpires, demanded an $800 fee, more than twice what he had been offered. When he was turned down, he simply didn't show up. Bob Ferguson, the old Brooklyn Atlantic player, was pressed into service to replace Lynch and worked Game 1 along with Umpire John Gaffney.

The teams took the field before a crowd of 8,445 "cranks"—as fans were then known—many having come up from Brooklyn to see the blossoming of an intercity rivalry going back to the Brooklyn vs. New York all-star game of 1858.

Brooklyn struck for five runs in the first inning against Tim Keefe, the Giants' top pitcher, then lost the lead but rallied to go ahead by 12–10 after eight innings. With darkness approaching, the Bridegrooms then tried the same tactic the Browns had used against them only a few weeks before. They began to stall. With the game dragging, impatient fans got out of the stands and milled around on the field. The slowdown succeeded as the umpires called the game before the Giants had a final opportunity to catch up. Brooklyn's victory may have been tarnished by less-than-sportsmanlike behavior, but its fans were thrilled. A dozen of them lifted the captain, Darby O'Brien, on their shoulders and carried him to the clubhouse.

John Day, the Giants' owner, took out his anger on Ferguson's umpiring and threatened to boycott the rest of the Series if the former Brooklyn ballplayer was allowed to work another game.

Game 2 was played the following afternoon at Washington Park, where

16,100 fans jammed into a ballfield that seated some 4,500, the overflow standing along the foul lines or behind ropes in the outfield. Among those on hand was Umpire Lynch, who had ended his boycott after wrangling a $600 fee for working the remainder of the Series. The big crowd was disappointed as the Giants scored a 6–2 victory with Cannonball Crane outpitching Parisian Bob Caruthers.

That evening, the Giants belatedly celebrated their pennant victory with a banquet at the Broadway Theater. It almost cost them their star pitcher. While Manager Mutrie was engaging in oratorical flourishes, a huge overhead sign proclaiming the team's strange slogan, "We Are the People," came crashing down when a restraining rope snapped. The sign narrowly missed Tim Keefe.

The Series returned to the Polo Grounds, and Brooklyn took an 8–7 lead late in the game. The Grooms then went into another stalling routine in hopes that the dwindling light would soon be gone. In the last of the ninth inning, the Giants loaded the bases and seemed poised for a dramatic victory. It wouldn't happen. At that moment, John Gaffney, umpiring at home plate, killed the rally by deciding it was too dark to continue. Brooklyn had another tainted victory.

The Grooms took a 7–2 lead at Washington Park in Game 4 amid the customary delays brought by numerous arguments with the umpires. The Giants then tied it with five runs in the top of the sixth inning. By the last of the sixth, it was so dark that Orator Jim O'Rourke, the Giant left fielder, couldn't see a fly ball hit by Oyster Burns with two men on. The ball dropped and three runs scored to give Brooklyn a 10–7 lead. Umpire Gaffney then called the game, the third time he had ended play because of darkness with Brooklyn ahead.

Buck Ewing, the Giants' catcher and captain, groused afterward that the umpires were stealing the games from his club. As for the Grooms, he lamented, "Their work throughout has been of the sneaky order."

Brooklyn seemed in great shape with a lead of 3 games to 1. But the Giants came back the next day at Washington Park with an 11–3 victory as Crane bested Caruthers in a repeat of the Game 2 pitching matchups.

The Grooms' spirits were undaunted. That night, they gathered at the Brooklyn Academy of Music on the Heights for their own pennant-celebrating banquet, dining at linen-covered, perfume-scented tables. Perching overhead was not an inspirational sign but an ornamental eagle with spread wings, bearing a pennant in its beak and holding two crossed bats and a gold ball.

Conterno's band played "See, the Conquering Hero Comes," Charlie Byrne praised "the brave boys who brought the pennant to this town, the greatest baseball city in the world," and, on a final happy note, the eagle did not come crashing down.

◆ *The 1889 Brooklyn team, winner of the American Association pennant but loser to the Giants in an argument-filled World Series. (Brooklyn Public Library-Brooklyn Collection)*

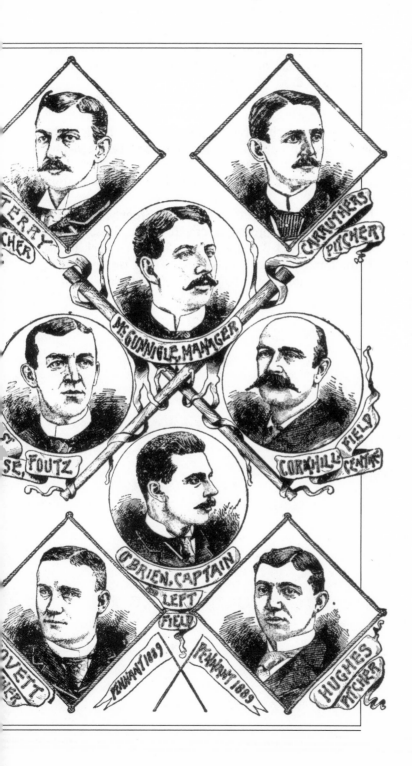

Both teams' banquets dispensed with, it was back to the Polo Grounds for Game 6. The Giants won that one, then captured another two games to take a lead of 5 games to 3.

The end arrived for Brooklyn on a cold, rainy Tuesday afternoon at the Polo Grounds.

An error by Doc Bushong, the Grooms' catcher-dentist, brought the winning run home in the seventh inning as the Giants scored a 3–2 victory to capture their second straight World Series championship. Exuberant Giant fans chanted the fight song "We Are the People" and rang a victory gong.

It was the first of many frustrating Octobers for Brooklyn fans. But the Grooms' supporters were appreciative despite the collapse. Darby O'Brien, the captain of the 1889 Brooklyn team, did not go back to his Peoria, Illinois, home for the winter empty-handed. The fans presented him with a gift that presumably would be the talk of the town—a pair of parrots.

7

Three Teams for Brooklyn

One week before the 1889 World Series opened, the Giants' short-stop, John Montgomery Ward, paid a visit to John Day, the club's owner. Day was popular with his ballplayers, but he was about to hear some very bad news: a revolt was at hand. Ward and most of the Giant players would be starting their own team in New York the following spring, playing on a field they had already leased adjoining the Polo Grounds. And financial backing had been arranged for ballclubs in seven other cities. Players from both the National League and American Association were launching a new league.

Ward concluded the meeting by offering Day an executive position if he would join with his players in abandoning the National League. The owner turned him down.

Three weeks later, the baseball world would be shaken by formation of the Players League. Ahead was a tumultuous season that would see three ballclubs in Brooklyn—one of them managed by Ward—and two more in Manhattan in a war that would bring much of organized baseball to the brink of financial ruin.

The revolt was rooted in long-standing anger over the reserve clause, which prevented a player from selling his services to the highest bidder, and in frustration over salary limitations, arbitrary fines and blacklisting of players who made trouble for management. The ballplayers had despaired of finding a way within the system to assert their rights against the tyranny of the owners.

The first step in baseball's great uprising of labor against management had come with creation of the Brotherhood of Professional Base Ball Players in October 1885. Founded by nine members of the Giants—among them stars like Ward, Roger Connor, Buck Ewing and Tim Keefe—the Brotherhood proclaimed the general goals of promoting the players' interests and fostering high standards of professional conduct.

Ward had been named the Brotherhood's president. A most uncommon baseball figure, he was one of the few nineteenth century ballplayers to be an educated man, having graduated from Penn State, where he played baseball before turning professional in 1877. The following season, he joined Providence of the National League, and in 1879 won forty-seven games in pitching the club to the pennant. An arm injury eventually forced Ward to switch to shortstop, where he became a mainstay of the New York Giants in the 1880's. While playing with the Giants, he obtained a law degree at Columbia University and he went on to be a successful attorney and businessman, serving in his later years as lawyer for the National League and president of the Boston Braves. And Ward was a sophisticate in an era of untutored ballplayers who came to the diamond from farm or factory. He was at home among New York's theater crowd, having married Helen Dauvray, a Broadway actress.

◆ *John Montgomery Ward, a key man behind the ballplayers' revolt of 1890 after having starred for the Giants. He went on to manage and play for the Players League team in Brooklyn and then the Dodgers. (Los Angeles Dodgers)*

Ward's Brotherhood began to grow, and during the late 1880's it tried to persuade the baseball owners to agree to contract reforms. But in an age where the capitalist was supreme, the worker could gain little by persuasion.

On November 4, 1889—just six days after the Giants had beaten Brooklyn in the World Series—several dozen baseball players gathered in New York City to bid goodbye to their bosses. They announced formation of the Players League, joining together with liberal-minded businessmen who would provide financial backing.

To underscore their rage, the players issued the Brotherhood Manifesto denouncing the National League owners. Said the Manifesto:

———

There was a time when the League stood for integrity and fair dealing. Today it stands for dollars and cents. Once it looked to the elevation of the game and an honest exhibition of the sport; today its eyes are on the turnstile. Men have come into the business for no other motive than to exploit it for every dollar in sight.

Players have been bought, sold and exchanged as though they were sheep instead of American citizens.

———

The new league would give the players a voice in their destiny. Each club would be controlled by a board divided equally among representatives of the players and the men financing them. The reserve clause was to be discarded in favor of three-year contracts for each player, generally at the 1889 salary level. Players would be able to purchase stock in their teams, and they envisioned sharing in some of the clubs' profits.

Ten days after the players' revolt was proclaimed, Brooklyn's Charlie Byrne staged a rebellion of his own. The National League and American Association clubowners had gathered for separate annual meetings at the Fifth Avenue Hotel in Manhattan. On the morning of Thursday, November 14, Byrne and Aaron Stern, the president of the Cincinnati team—both tired of feuds among their circuit's owners—walked out of the Association's meeting in Parlor DR and entered the National League's Parlor F a few doors away. Three wicker baskets of wine were opened, and Arthur Soden, the president of the Boston team, offered a toast "welcoming Brooklyn and Cincinnati to the League and wishing them prosperity among their new associates."

The Players League—known informally as the Brotherhood—decided to battle directly with the National League in seven cities, among them Brooklyn and New York. The new circuit began to raid the rosters of clubs in both the National League and the American Association and emerged victorious in breach-of-contract lawsuits filed by the established clubs.

The struggle in court was only one part of the war. Just as important was a propaganda battle that would see each side lie about attendance figures in an effort to bolster its image.

Years later, the deceit was recalled by Albert Spalding, once a great pitcher but by 1890 a wealthy sporting goods executive and a champion of the National League's struggle against the rebels.

"In place of powder and shell, printers' ink and bluff formed the ammunition used by both sides," Spalding remembered. "If either party to the controversy ever furnished to the press one solitary truthful statement . . . a monument should be erected to his memory."

The Brotherhood's effort to win over newspapermen brought mixed results.

That old Brooklynite Henry Chadwick, the father of sportswriting and still the editor of the National League's semi-official *Spalding's Guide,* blasted the Brotherhood players as "ingrates" and "seceders" who "had no sense of shame."

O. P. Caylor, editor of the pro-National League paper *Sporting Times,* denounced the rebels as "drunken knaves."

But the St. Louis-based *Sporting News* rallied to the players' cause while delighting in potshots at such established figures as Brooklyn's Charlie Byrne and the Browns' buffoonish owner, Chris Von der Ahe, whom it called Von der Haha.

As the season moved along, the *Sporting News* claimed that Byrne's Bridegrooms were losing money in the war but that it didn't really matter to the owner because "he is in baseball simply for his health and a position in society."

The Brotherhood squad in Manhattan called itself the Giants. Adoption of the existing National League team's nickname was not so brazen as it might appear. All of John Day's stars with the exception of pitcher Smilin' Mickey Welch and right fielder Silent Mike Tiernan defected to the new league. Playing for the new Giants next door to the Polo Grounds on a ballfield called Brotherhood Park would be such old Giants as Buck Ewing, the catcher-manager of the new squad; Roger Connor, Cannonball Crane, Tim Keefe and Orator Jim O'Rourke.

Day's Giants suffered the most serious personnel losses of any National League team. But Byrne's Brooklyn squad—newly arrived in the League—remained virtually intact. Byrne's practice of paying top salaries had kept his men loyal. Joe Visner, an undistinguished catcher-outfielder who jumped to the Pittsburgh Brotherhood team, was the only Bridegroom to depart.

While Day was faced with one directly competing team—the new Giants next door to him—Byrne had to vie for public support with two other ballclubs in Brooklyn. Not only would he be confronted with a Brooklyn club in the Players League, but there would also be a new Brooklyn team in the American Association he had just abandoned.

A Flatbush businessman named George W. Chauncey financed the Players League team in Brooklyn and built a ballpark in the rural East New York section at a cost of $100,000. Called Eastern Park, the field stood on what had been farmland, but it was easily reachable via an elevated railroad line.

The manager of the team—and its shortstop as well—was none other than the popular John Montgomery Ward, who had decided to cross the East River instead of accompanying his old Giant teammates to the new Giants.

On first base was Dave Orr, who at five feet ten inches and 240 pounds presented a formidable target for the infielders. Orr's bulk had, however, made him a target of ridicule when he played with the American Association Mets a few years back. As one newspaper account of an 1885 game put it: "The fat ballplayer from New York showed considerable animation in St. Louis today. Orr made a three-base hit, a homer for anyone else. Then he

◆ *The Brooklyn team that captured the 1890 National League title after leaving the American Association. Top row (l. to r.): Oyster Burns, Parisian Bob Caruthers, Adonis Terry, Darby O'Brien, Dave Foutz, George Stallings and Tom Daly. Bottom row (l. to r.): George Pinkney, Mickey Hughes, Manager Bill McGunnigle, Germany Smith, Charlie Reynolds and Hub Collins. Seated: Bob Clark. (Brooklyn Public Library-Brooklyn Collection)*

had to sit down on the bag, panting with exhaustion. . . . [The Mets] are nice fellows and good ballplayers when not too fat to play."

Out of shape or not, Orr was a tremendous hitter. He led the American Association with a .354 batting average in helping the Mets win the 1884 pennant. And he was a hero after the season had ended. When a train he was riding was involved in a wreck near Poughkeepsie, New York, on December 16, he freed a trapped child and carried the boy to safety. In December 1887, he saved a woman from an assailant in a Manhattan apartment building by throwing the attacker down a flight of stairs, then suffered a broken elbow and hand when he came tumbling down as well.

The Brooklyn Brotherhood team's second baseman was Louis Bier-bauer, who had jumped from Philadelphia of the American Association. At third was "Scrappy Bill" Joyce, a major league rookie. The outfielders— Emmett Seery, Jack McGeachey and Ed Andrews—all came from the National League's defunct Indianapolis club. Sharing the catching load were Tom Kinslow, Paul Cook and Con Daily, all with big league experience.

Ward's club opened the season with two proven pitchers, Gus Weyh-ing, a thirty-game winner for the American Association's Philadelphia team the previous season, and George Van Haltren, who had won thirteen for the National League's Chicago club while batting .309 as a part-time outfielder.

Rounding out the crowded 1890 scene was a new American Association club called the Brooklyn Gladiators, who were founded by William A. Wallace, a printing craftsman for the *New York Press*. The fledgling baseball entrepreneur hired a former player named Jim Kennedy as manager and put the team into Ridgewood Park, which was actually in Queens, just over the Brooklyn city line. The lineup consisted mostly of youngsters and castoffs from other Association clubs. There was a Peltz (John, an outfielder) and a Pitz (Herman, a utilityman), and dotting the lineup were a few colorful nicknames, Candy Nelson at shortstop and Jumbo Davis at third. But it was a forgettable bunch.

Byrne's Bridegrooms (the players who had taken their marriage vows in '88 were hardly newlyweds anymore but the nickname was surviving) made their National League debut on April 28, 1890, with appropriate fanfare. Conterno's 47th Regiment Band gave a concert in front of a brightly decorated Washington Park grandstand, floral bouquets were presented to Captain Darby O'Brien and a pair of teammates, and dignitaries ranging from Mayor Chapin to prominent judges and clergymen were on hand in the crowd of 2,870. It was a hugely successful afternoon as Parisian Bob Caruthers, scattering four hits, shut out Philadelphia, 10–0.

A couple of miles away, the Brotherhood team—known simply as the Brooklyns—opened in more dramatic fashion. After eight scoreless innings, Ward's club broke through against the new Philadelphia team for three runs in the top half of the ninth (the home club didn't necessarily bat last in those days) and hung on for a 3–1 victory.

But the formal home-opener didn't come until the following afternoon when Brooklyn played host to the Brotherhood Giants following a ceremony displaying fine comradeship.

At the sound of a gong, the 23rd Regiment Band assembled in front of the grandstand. Then the Brooklyn players, in blue and white uniforms, formed a line behind the musicians. The Brooklyns marched around the diamond to where the New Yorkers were waiting outside their dressing room, and the rival players raised their caps to each other and shook hands. As the crowd cheered them on, the teams paraded twice around the diamond behind the band and a platoon of policemen before winding up at home plate.

When Ward, batting cleanup, came to the plate for the first time, he was greeted with wild cheering. Connie Murphy, a Brooklyn pitcher, then presented him with two large floral horseshoes from the fans.

Behind Van Haltren's pitching, Brooklyn whipped New York, 10–5.

Murphy's talents went beyond the ballpark. Besides being a pitcher and a florist's middleman, he was a handy man with a razor. Noted the *Eagle*:

_____

Connie Murphy, the talkative pitcher of the Brooklyn P.L. team, is quite a useful man to have round. He is a machinist by trade, but can turn his hand to many things. When the boys first came to this city they engaged accommodation at the Pierrepont House. One day the barber of that establishment went to his dinner and forgot to lock the door of his shop. Connie, for a lark, took possession, and putting on an apron, shaved two customers to their entire satisfaction. The real barber and Murphy are now bad friends, as Connie refuses to give up the money he received for the work.

_____

Murphy had another distinction: He was the only man to play for both of Brooklyn's new teams. After going 4–10 with the Players League club, he moved over to the American Association's Gladiators, where he was at least consistent, compiling a 3–9 record.

The Gladiators got an eleven-day head start on the other two Brooklyn clubs, opening their season at Ridgewood Park on April 17 with a 3–2 loss to the Syracuse Stars. A lovely spring day was spoiled by Joe Gerhardt, the Gladiator second baseman, who made a pair of errors.

Both the run totals and the winds picked up the following afternoon as the Gladiators outlasted the Stars, 22–21, on a day when pop flies were blown all over the place. Gerhardt was 50 percent improved: He made only one error this time.

But the opening-day performance was indeed an omen. Gerhardt and his mates proved to be a flop, and they would have a brief life in Brooklyn. In the last week of August, the franchise was shifted to Baltimore and it staggered to a 41–92 record.

◆ Bill McGunnigle, who managed Brooklyn to pennants in 1889 and '90 and then was fired. (Los Angeles Dodgers)

The Brotherhood team in Brooklyn had a happier time on the diamond, finishing with a 76–56 record that was good enough for a second-place finish, six and a half games behind pennant-winning Boston.

The club's leading hitter was Dave Orr, the rotund first baseman, who tied for the Players League batting title with Cleveland's Pete Browning, hitting .373, and finished second in runs batted in with 124.

It would, however, be Orr's final season. During an October exhibition game in Pennsylvania, he suffered a stroke that left him, at age thirty-one, paralyzed on his left side. Orr would work in later years as a stonecutter and a stagehand in New York theaters, and in 1914 there was a return of sorts to baseball. He was put in charge of the press box at Washington Park when the new Brooklyn Federal League team moved in.

The other big man in the Brotherhood lineup was John Montgomery Ward, who batted .337 and stole sixty-three bases. The pitching staff was led by Gus Weyhing, who compiled a 30–16 record and hurled 390 innings.

Over at Washington Park, the Bridegrooms' Bill McGunnigle now took on the National League after having managed the team to an American Association pennant in his first season with the club. McGunnigle had plenty of talent since his players had resisted offers from the Players League, but he was looking for any edge he could find. The man who had threatened to jump off the Brooklyn Bridge if his team didn't win the pennant in 1889 showed he was not finished with imaginative methods to spur his club on.

McGunnigle was skilled in picking up the opponents' signs. But how to convey the fruits of his talent to his players? He hit upon a plan to install a small metal plate in the batter's box that would be connected via an underground wire to a button on the Brooklyn bench. When a Brooklyn player came to bat, he would place one foot over the plate. McGunnigle would press his button, setting off an electric shock that would tip off the batter on what was coming. Presumably, a sustained shock could signal a fastball while a short one or no shock at all could mean a curveball was about to arrive. It was, however, an idea whose time would never come. An electrician consulted by McGunnigle suggested that the plan might leave his players burned out before their time.

The manager turned to another scheme to make use of his sign-stealing. The center-field fence at Washington Park had a large cigarette advertisement featuring the head of a dog. McGunnigle proposed putting in one white eye and one black eye. He would operate the eyes by electricity. The Brooklyn batters would watch the dog's head after the pitcher had received his signal from the catcher. If McGunnigle decided that a fastball was coming, he would activate a current that would move the white eye. For a curveball, the black eye would blink.

Unlike the plan for the home-plate shocks, the electric-eye project seemed harmless enough. But the players laughingly turned a deaf ear.

It wasn't that McGunnigle's men balked at finding clever ways to better themselves. An 1890 scorecard advertisement by the Schwalbach Cycle Company of Brooklyn told why the Grooms were in the habit of winning:

The members of the Brooklyn Base Ball team desire to express to you their satisfaction and appreciation of Bicycle Riding as an exercise, it tones up the muscles, strengthens the legs and helped us win the pennant last year. It is the most pleasant exercise and best mode of training we have ever tried.

Presumably invigorated by some more bicycle riding, the Bridegrooms continued their winning ways in 1890. On Labor Day, they were victorious three times—once in the morning and twice in the afternoon—taking a rare tripleheader from Pittsburgh at Washington Park. With Oyster Burns, the center fielder, slugging thirteen home runs and Tom Lovett winning thirty games, the Grooms went on to capture the National League pennant their first year in the league by a margin of six and a half games over Chicago.

In mid-October, the Bridegrooms met the American Association's Louisville Cyclones in a five-of-nine-game World Series. The Cyclones didn't have a particularly fearsome lineup, but they were no dummies. Harry Taylor, the first baseman, was a Cornell graduate, and Tim Shinnick, the second baseman, had attended New Hampshire's Phillips Exeter prep school. (Harry Raymond, their third baseman, may not have gone to college, but neither did a certain Missourian of the next century with whom he had something in common. Raymond's real name was Harry Truman.)

The first four games were played in Louisville, with the Grooms winning two, dropping one and playing a tie.

The Series finally came to Washington Park on October 25 when Lovett's pitching and Burns's home run sent Brooklyn to a 7–2 victory.

A crowd of only 300 turned out for Game 6 on a raw and windy day. The Grooms didn't do anything to warm up their sparse rooting section, losing by 9–8. It was a cheerless afternoon as well for Ed Daily, a Louisville outfielder, who was fined $25 for what was described as "ungentlemanly talk to Umpire Curry."

The Cyclones evened the Series in Game 7, winning by 6–2 before another turnout of only a few hundred.

With the raw weather in Brooklyn getting no better, and spectator interest low, the teams decided to forget about the final two games of the Series. So it ended in a draw.

The poor turnouts reflected what had been a disastrous year at the box office for all of baseball. The three leagues each lost money since there were simply too many teams around. Soon after the World Series ended, the Players League collapsed, leaving the National League supreme and the American Association alive but in desperate shape.

George Chauncey, the chief stockholder in the Brooklyn Players League team, and Wendell Goodwin, the club's president, agreed to have their franchise absorbed by Charlie Byrne's National League Bridegrooms. But before capitulating, Chauncey made two demands. He insisted that the Grooms move from Washington Park to his ballfield in the East New York section and that they hire Chauncey's manager, John Montgomery Ward, to run the club. Since Chauncey would be supplying the funds to keep Byrne afloat, he got what he wanted.

The wondrously creative Bill McGunnigle had managed the Bridegrooms to two straight pennants. But when the ballclub packed up and went to the wilds of eastern Brooklyn, he was cut loose, a victim of the maneuvering that brought the great baseball war to an end.

CHAPTER

8

Moving East

The 1891 home opener for the Brooklyn team that emerged from the wreckage of the previous season's battles proved to be a frenzied occasion. Eastern Park, the field Charlie Byrne's men had been transplanted to, seated only 12,000. But a crowd of 17,892—several thousand spectators standing on the edges of the field—journeyed to east Brooklyn on April 27 to see the club debut against the Giants.

"Old men, young men and small boys took part in the applause bestowed upon the players and their shouts could be heard for a radius of half a mile," the *Times* reported. "The shouting was by no means confined to the male sex. Several thousand pretty and healthy looking ladies were present and they rendered all the aid in their power to transform Eastern Park into a modern Bedlam."

The Bridegrooms had not only changed ballparks, but they had acquired another nickname. They were now also known as Ward's Wonders, in tribute to their new manager. There was nothing wonderful, however, about their first game at Eastern Park. The Giants rallied for two runs in the ninth inning on a throwing error by Tom Kinslow, the Brooklyn catcher, and emerged with a 6–5 victory.

Eastern Park may have been out in the country, but it was no garden spot. On many an afternoon, the field was enveloped in thick black smoke emerging from the chimneys of a chair factory across the street. Each time the smoke belched out, the umpires would have to call time and wait for the air to clear.

And the fans were risking their lives for the dubious privilege of savoring the baseball atmosphere. After arriving in the vicinity of the ballpark by either trolley or elevated railway, they had to walk across the heavily used tracks of the New York and Manhattan Beach Railroad, which ran excursion trains from a ferry dock in Greenpoint to hotels at Jamaica Bay and Coney Island.

The railroad tracks were simply one more hazard for Brooklynites amid the march of progress. They paled as a danger in comparison with the terror wrought by trolley cars. By 1890, Brooklyn's population had grown to more than 800,000, an increase of some 200,000 over the 1880 census. To serve the needs of a city on the move, trolleys had been introduced, and they were an immediate hit—in more ways than one. By 1895, they were killing an average of one person a week.

According to one press account, the trolley motormen—most of them former horse-car drivers—did not realize they now had "the power of fifty horses under their control," were driving recklessly and "ere long the country rang with horror at the holocaust of victims sacrificed to the reign of electricity in Brooklyn."

◆ *One of the electrified trolley cars that terrorized pedestrians during the 1890's. Brooklynites were forced to dodge the trolleys if they were to survive. Soon their ballclub became known as the Trolley Dodgers. (New-York Historical Society)*

A restaurant owner in Yellowstone Park told his guests he had fled to the West from Brooklyn after trolleys had killed off his whole family. Admiral Robert Peary, the first man to reach the North Pole, was said to have considered Brooklyn's trolleys as dangerous as an Arctic expedition.

An 1890's visitor to Brooklyn from Providence wrote to Mayor Charles A. Schieren: "The people of your city ought to organize and form a vigilance committee and smash every dynamo in Brooklyn. Away with the trolley juggernauts."

And a Brooklyn clergyman, the Reverend A. W. Mills, urged the trolley companies to recognize the commandment, "Thou Shalt Not Kill."

But some good did come from the trolleys' onslaught: it provided yet another nickname for the Brooklyn team, and this one would stick. Since Brooklynites were forever dodging trolley-car drivers seemingly intent on mowing them down, their ballclub would come to be called the Trolley Dodgers, then simply the Dodgers.

The customers who braved the trolley tracks and railroad right-of-way outside Eastern Park in 1891 were not so well rewarded.

After having won pennants in the American Association in 1889 and the National League in 1890 under Bill McGunnigle, Brooklyn slipped to sixth place under John Montgomery Ward.

Eastern Park was repainted and renovated in 1892, but Ward's ballclub was only slightly invigorated, settling for second and then third place in an experimental split season.

Ward had not been especially successful managing Brooklyn in 1891 and '92, and Eastern Park's rural setting was far removed from the glamorous Manhattan scene he had known as a famous athlete married to an actress. So after the 1892 season, he crossed back to New York City, taking over as the Giants' manager.

Dave Foutz, who had been with Brooklyn since 1888, first as a pitcher, then a first baseman and outfielder, replaced Ward as manager. The move did not improve the club's fortunes, but it did produce yet another nickname. The team would occasionally be referred to as Foutz's Fillies.

In July, the Dodgers acquired a five-foot-four-inch Brooklyn native whose manipulations with the bat would easily make up for his lack of size. Wee Willie Keeler, a twenty-one-year-old rookie, was obtained from the Giants to play third base and the outfield. But the man who would be remembered for his ability to "Hit 'em where they ain't" saw only brief action with Brooklyn in 1893. He was sent to Baltimore after the season along with Dan Brouthers, an aging star, for two unexceptional players. It was a trade Brooklyn would regret as Wee Willie would go on to star with the swashbuckling Oriole teams that would dominate the National League through the 1890's.

While the Orioles flourished, the Dodgers would wallow in mediocrity.

They finished in sixth place in 1893, then were fifth in both 1894 and 1895. The following year, things got worse. The club slipped to ninth place, and finally Charlie Byrne had had enough of Dave Foutz as manager. After four disappointing seasons, Byrne fired the popular former player and replaced him with Bald Billy Barnie who, he hoped, would prove more of a disciplinarian. Barnie had never been much of a player, but he had managed in Baltimore some years before.

There had been a few bright spots during Foutz's years running the Dodgers. The 1895 season opened on a hopeful note with a 7–4 victory over the Giants at the Polo Grounds before more than 24,000 fans, many of them squeezed behind outfield ropes. The extraordinary turnout prompted a sportswriter named W. F. Koelsch to ask: "Where is the individual that said baseball is on the wane? Bring him out so that we can pity him, and also direct him to the Bloomingdale Asylum."

The winning pitcher was Bill Kennedy, a right-hander known for succumbing to fainting spells after drinking enormous amounts of ice water. Variously nicknamed Roaring Bill for his booming voice and Brickyard for his hometown of Bellaire, Ohio, a brick-making community, Kennedy evidently was wide awake that day. But a couple of years later, in another game against the Giants, he pulled a boner that did not speak well for his mental processes.

On the afternoon of August 1, 1897, Kennedy took a 2–0 lead into the ninth inning before a crowd of some 12,000 at Eastern Park. Then the Giants rallied for three runs and had George Davis on second base.

"On the field the New York players were turning handsprings and acting like a lot of maniacs," the *Times* reported. One man who kept his head amid the excitement was George Van Haltren—the former Brooklyn Brotherhood player now a Giant—who was coaching at third base. Van Haltren made a dash for home, pretending he was a baserunner. At that moment, John Grim, the Brooklyn catcher, was busy arguing with Umpire Hank O'Day over the previous play. Van Haltren had pulled an old trick, but Brickyard fell for it and fired the baseball home. It

◆ *Brickyard Kennedy, winner of 177 games for the Dodgers and their top pitcher during the 1890's despite an occasional mental lapse. (Los Angeles Dodgers)*

◆ *The 1895 Dodgers.* Top row (l. to r.): *Hunkey Hines, Buster Burrell, Ad Gumbert, Bert Abbey, George Treadway, Billy Shindle, Tom Daly, Dan Daub and George Shoch.* Middle row (l. to r.): *Joe Mulvey, Con Daily, Candy LaChance, Dave Foutz, Mike Griffin, John Grim, John Anderson and Oyster Burns.* Bottom row (l. to r.): *Ed Stein, Tommy Corcoran and Brickyard Kennedy. (National Baseball Library, Cooperstown, N.Y.)*

got past Grim and rolled to the backstop, enabling Davis—the real runner—to sprint to the plate and make it 4–2. That run proved the difference as the Dodgers went on to score once in their half of the ninth. Following Brooklyn's 4–3 loss, Manager Barnie showed he was made of sterner stuff than his predecessor, Foutz. The *Times* reported that he "fined Kennedy for his stupid work."

Kennedy was an outstanding pitcher, but illiterate and something of a hayseed. One story had him setting out for a game at the Polo Grounds from his Brooklyn home and winding up in the Middle West. Instructions had been posted in the Dodger clubhouse telling the players to take an elevated train across the Brooklyn Bridge and then transfer to an uptown train. Kennedy got lost and asked for directions from a policeman, explaining he was from Ohio and none too familiar with big-city transit. The police officer, about as confused as Kennedy, directed him to a railroad train going back to his home state.

If Brickyard seemed none too clever, he was hardly alone. The ballplayers of the late nineteenth century were an ill-educated, brawling, hard-drinking and hard-loving lot.

"The saloon and the brothel are the evils of the baseball world," anguished Henry Chadwick, that gentleman of the old school.

Beyond John Montgomery Ward, there were few ballplayers who read anything except the sports pages. Many couldn't put together more than a few words without a profanity. A Saturday evening's entertainment generally meant a poker game or a visit to a whorehouse. Madames often threw lavishly catered parties for entire ballclubs.

In Philadelphia, a ballplayer who years later would become the well-loved Brooklyn manager known as Uncle Robbie had a special role with the hero-worshiping ladies. Large busts being the vogue, the Athletics had an auxiliary known as the Big Bosom Girls. Wilbert Robinson was the A's official scorer in such matters, wielding a tape measure to determine which lady could be proudest of her figure.

With jobs scarce after the demise of the Brotherhood and then the American Association a year later, the baseball of the 1890's was rowdier than ever. The ballplayers, most of them Easterners of Irish or German background, out of families working in farms, factories and mines, were a tough bunch. They wouldn't hesitate to unleash a beanball, spike an opponent or splatter an umpire with tobacco juice.

Bill Dahlen, the man who would precede Uncle Robbie as Dodger manager, fit the perverse mold of the 1890's ballplayer quite nicely. A fine shortstop with the Chicago White Stockings, Dahlen sometimes liked to throw the ball in the dirt just to anger his manager, the famed Cap Anson.

A dedicated horseplayer, Dahlen sometimes got himself thrown out of games so he could get to the race track. Umpire Tim Hurst is said to have once told him: "Bill, this day it won't work. You call me anything, and I'll go you one better, but you don't get to the track this afternoon."

After stumbling along with few bright spots through the 1890's, the Dodgers closed out an unhappy era on October 2, 1897. Their 15–6 victory that afternoon over Boston, the National League champion, marked the final game at Eastern Park.

Three months later, Brooklyn would cease to exist as a city. Its ballclub would enter a new era as well. The Dodgers would go back to South Brooklyn, get a new club president and then forge an alliance with the Baltimore Orioles to bring a happy change in fortunes.

9

The Baltimore Connection

Outside the Brooklyn City Hall, a heavy rain pelted the downtown streets. Inside, a who's who of Brooklyn had gathered in the Common Council chamber amid freshly cut flowers and ferns from the Prospect Park Conservatory.

Mayor Frederick Wurster was there with five of his predecessors. Members of the Society of Old Brooklynites, wearing their blue and gold badges, had joined them.

At nine o'clock—three hours before the arrival of the new year—a silk American flag was dipped in tribute to the flag of the City of Brooklyn. And then the speechmaking began.

St. Clair McKelway, the editor of the *Brooklyn Eagle,* urged his fellow Brooklynites to march into the future proudly: "Let our institutes be Brooklyn institutes, our banks Brooklyn banks, our libraries Brooklyn libraries, our churches Brooklyn churches . . . and our boys and our girls Brooklyn boys and Brooklyn girls."

A poet named Will Carleton read from his work, "The Passing of Brooklyn." Its final lines:

You are no corpse, fit for tears or for pity;
You are the soul of the great coming city!

As midnight approached, a decidedly less melancholy evening was coming to a climax on the other side of the Brooklyn Bridge. A parade and a singing contest were winding down, and a crowd had braved the stormy night to assemble in New York's City Hall Park. Red, white and blue lights hanging from trees bathed the park in a patriotic glow, and searchlights from the tops of nearby skyscrapers—some as tall as eighteen stories— threw beams of white light onto the revelers.

Upon the stroke of midnight, whistles blew from waterfront factories, from steam-driven elevated trains, from ships throughout the harbor. A one-hundred gun salute boomed, and colored skyrockets soared high into the night.

At that moment, a new flag moved up the poles above the City Halls on both sides of the East River: the flag of the City of Greater New York.

With the arrival of the year 1898, Brooklyn was no longer an independent city. The pride of its leading citizens gathering at the Brooklyn City Hall might well be undiminished, but the building they had assembled in would now be known as Brooklyn Borough Hall. Brooklyn had become merely one of five boroughs in the mighty City of New York.

The loss of Brooklyn's independence had its roots in the opening of the Brooklyn Bridge fifteen years before. That technological marvel eroded what isolation Brooklyn had retained and tied it commercially with New York City, then consisting of Manhattan and the Bronx.

Brooklyn had continued to grow at a frenetic pace during the late nineteenth century. Elevated steam railways running from downtown had begun to service once-rural areas like East New York, the Dodgers' home in the 1890's. No longer dependent on slow horse-car service, outlying communities were now linked to Brooklyn's commercial hub and to New York City as well.

Brownstone, brick and frame homes sprang up on what had been farmland. New Lots, off to the east toward Long Island, was absorbed by Brooklyn in 1886. Flatbush, Gravesend and New Utrecht were annexed in 1894 and Flatlands in 1896 as Brooklyn assumed its current shape, covering the entire County of Kings.

As Brooklyn grew, it needed additional revenue to provide municipal services. By the 1890's, it was exhausting its ability to borrow. If additional public improvements like the projected Williamsburgh Bridge to Manhattan, and new streets, parks and sewers were to be built, Brooklyn would have to draw on the credit resources of New York City.

And so a coalition supported by the New York Chamber of Commerce began a drive for consolidation of Brooklyn with New York. The state legislature approved a revised charter in 1897, and the new city—Manhattan, Brooklyn, the Bronx, Queens and Staten Island—was born on that rainy New Year's Eve of 1898.

◆ *Charlie Ebbets in the 1890's. (Los Angeles Dodgers)*

The following evening, news came of another reshaping. Newspaper-men were invited to a Saturday night dinner at Brooklyn's Clarendon Hotel to meet the man who would be taking control of the Dodgers.

The new boss, at age thirty-eight, was Charles Hercules Ebbets, a dark-haired, mustachioed man who had been associated with the ballclub

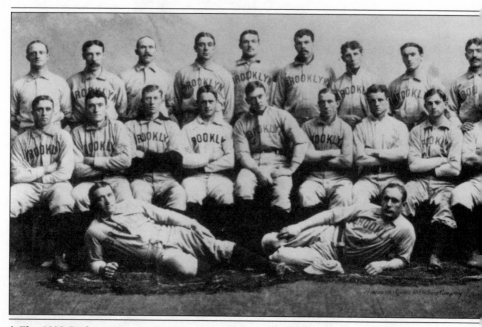

◆ *The 1898 Dodgers.* Top row (l. to r.): *Broadway Aleck Smith, Tom Daly, John Ryan, John Grim, John Anderson, Candy LaChance, Fielder Jones, Jimmy Sheckard and George Magoon.* Middle row (l. to r.): *Kit McKenna, Ralph Miller, Brickyard Kennedy, Welcome Gaston, Mike Griffin, Jack Dunn, Lefty Hopper, Joe Yaeger and Harry Howell.* Bottom row (l. to r.): *Bill Hallman and Butts Wagner. (National Baseball Library, Cooperstown, N.Y.)*

since its birth. Ebbets revealed that the previous afternoon, he had bought up the minority interest in the team and had also purchased an option on stock held by Ferdinand Abell, one of the franchise's original owners.

Most of the remaining shares were owned by Charlie Byrne, who was still the team's president. But he had taken ill the previous month, and as Ebbets played host to the press, Byrne lay in a coma.

Charlie Ebbets had dabbled in various enterprises before finding his niche in baseball. Born in New York City, he attended the public schools and then became a draftsman with the firm of William T. Beer, helping to draw up plans for Niblo's Garden, one of New York's more popular amusement centers, and the Metropolitan Hotel. Then he ventured into publishing, printing inexpensive editions of novels and textbooks and even selling some door-to-door when his salesmen's efforts lagged. In the spring of 1883—when the Dodgers debuted as a minor league team—he turned up at Washington Park, hawking scorecards he had printed and doing odd jobs. Quickly he became the team's secretary, and as the years went by, he was relied upon to oversee the details of running the franchise.

A man of great energy, Ebbets realized it wouldn't hurt for a baseball businessman to be politically well-connected. He ran successfully for the State Assembly as a Democrat in 1895, then tried for a State Senate seat the following year but was defeated. Later, he served as a municipal councilman.

A sportsman and socially ambitious, Ebbets was an avid cyclist and bowler and quite a joiner, belonging to the Old Nassau Athletic Club, the Good Roads Association, the Prospect Club, the Carleton Club, the Royal Arcanum League and what were termed "secret societies."

When he took control of the Dodgers, he was living with his wife, Grace, in a fine home on First Street in South Brooklyn, not far from the original Washington Park, and was the father of three daughters and a son.

Three days after Ebbets met with the press, Byrne died at his home on West 11th Street in Brooklyn, and now Ebbets was in full control, moving up from secretary to club president.

He quickly abandoned eastern Brooklyn, returning to the old neighborhood from the days before the Players League. A new Washington Park was built on a site between Third and Fourth avenues and First and Third streets, virtually across from the old Washington Park tract, which had been sold since the club had departed. The new home, ready for opening day, boasted a grandstand with a capacity of 12,000. It would obviously be an improvement over Eastern Park, where many fans who had paid for seats had to stand to see the action—the rear rows were curiously slanted so they faced away from the infield.

The Dodgers unveiled their new ballpark on Saturday, April 30, taking on Philadelphia before an overflow crowd of 14,000. But the festivities were overshadowed by the frenzy of a national military adventure. Spain's heavy-handed efforts to suppress a revolt by Cuba against its rule—sensationalized by the "yellow journalism" of the Hearst and Pulitzer papers—had inflamed America. Then, on February 15, 1898, the U.S.S. *Maine* (built at the Brooklyn Navy Yard) had been blown up in Havana harbor with a heavy loss of life. A naval inquiry found that a submarine mine had set off the explosion, and Spain was held responsible. In mid-April, Congress declared what would be known as "the splendid little war" against the Spanish Empire.

A patriotic glow enveloped Washington Park for the opening-day ceremonies. Ebbets unfurled an American flag and presented it to his young daughter May as the Brooklyn and Philadelphia players lined up alongside home plate. Miss Ebbets, dressed in red, white and blue, pulled at a halyard. The Stars and Stripes began to ascend as the 23rd Regiment Band played the national anthem amid a roar from the crowd and the waving of thousands of tiny flags.

That was the high point of the season.

The Dodgers lost the game, 6–4, and floundered as the spring moved along. On June 7, Ebbets fired Manager Billy Barnie and replaced him with Mike Griffin, the center fielder and captain. The team lost three of its next four, and then Griffin quit the managing job to concentrate once again on playing ball. Now Ebbets took over as manager though he relied on Griffin for his on-the-field strategy. Ebbets couldn't get the club going either, and Brooklyn wound up tenth in the twelve-team league.

The season was a flop for Ebbets at the box office as well. The public's preoccupation with the Spanish-American War and the team's dismal performance resulted in a drop of more than 40 percent in home attendance. Only 122,514 fans came out for the first year back in South Brooklyn.

Having decided that being the owner didn't necessarily make him a genius as manager, Ebbets left the bench and agreed to give Mike Griffin a real shot at managing for 1899. Then an interlocking arrangement between the Brooklyn and Baltimore Oriole ownerships saw the managing job taken away from Griffin before the season began. He refused to report as a player, sued for breach of contract and was eventually awarded $2,250.

The financial stakes were considerably higher in the deal arranged by Ebbets and the management of the Orioles, a franchise that would be legendary.

The Orioles played brainy baseball and they changed the game. Under their shrewd manager, Ned Hanlon, they perfected the hit-and-run play, the bunt and the art of base-stealing. What they didn't accomplish by pure skill, they managed through trickery and intimidation. As the *Sporting News* put it, the Orioles were accustomed to "playing the dirtiest ball ever seen in this country."

Baltimore had won pennants in 1894, '95 and '96, but then came second-place finishes behind Boston the next two seasons. By 1898, the Orioles' long-time owner, Harry Vanderhorst, was, like Ebbets, losing money.

Eyeing the New York metropolitan area as a potentially more lucrative market than Baltimore, Vanderhorst bought into it while continuing to run the Oriole franchise. He sent most of his best players to Brooklyn and in return obtained stock in the Dodgers and some second-line players for his Baltimore team. Ebbets, in addition to getting top talent from the Orioles, was allowed to purchase some Baltimore stock. Ned Hanlon, who had been president of the Orioles in addition to managing them, became the Brooklyn manager while retaining the presidency of the Baltimore club, and he received some stock in each team. It was an obvious conflict of interest, but perfectly legal so far as baseball's code of conduct went. By the end of the 1890's, interlocking ownerships would, in fact, be common. It was the era of "syndicate baseball."

Going to Brooklyn with Hanlon were Dan McGann, the Orioles' first baseman; Hughey Jennings, a tough little red-headed shortstop; two of the

◆ *Ned Hanlon, who managed the 1899 Dodgers to a pennant while also serving as president of the rival Baltimore Orioles. (Los Angeles Dodgers)*

league's top-hitting outfielders, Wee Willie Keeler—the Brooklyn native traded from the Dodgers to Baltimore in 1894—and Joe Kelley; and pitchers Doc McJames and Jay Hughes.

Two Oriole regulars remained together in Baltimore. One of them was John McGraw, the combative third baseman who could beat a foe with his speed and his bat or with a brief tug on a runner's belt when he tried to take off from third base for home plate. The other—his bosom-measuring days as an Athletic far behind him—was Wilbert Robinson, the catcher and the only man to have made seven hits in a single game.

In the years to come, McGraw and Robinson would confront each other as managers in a long and bitter personal rivalry. But back in 1899, they jointly owned a Baltimore saloon called the Diamond Cafe. Business there was too good to pack up for Brooklyn. McGraw replaced Hanlon as the Baltimore manager while remaining the third baseman, and Robinson, continuing to catch, became his chief coach.

The Brooklyn team had new vigor and, it developed, a new nickname as well. A popular acrobatic vaudeville troupe of the day was Hanlon's Superbas. Since Ned Hanlon—no relation to the performers—was now the Brooklyn manager, the club became known as the Superbas.

The ex-Oriole players made a big difference in the Dodgers'—or Superbas'—fortunes in 1899. Jennings, Keeler and Kelley all batted well over .300 while Hughes won twenty-eight games and McJames won nineteen. The ballclub captured the pennant by eight games over Boston while Baltimore fell to fourth place.

Brooklyn's pennant triumph was, however, overshadowed by a more thrilling event. Admiral George Dewey, the "hero of Manila" for his destruction of the Spanish fleet in the Philippines, brought his flagship into New York Harbor as the season neared its end. The excitement left the Dodgers' accomplishments as a tepid afterthought. There was, of course, no World Series since the National League had long since driven competing circuits out of business.

In 1900, the league streamlined itself to eight cities, taking the shape it would maintain for half a century. The Louisville, Washington and Cleveland franchises were dropped along with Baltimore, the glory team of the 1890's but now just another ballclub.

Some of the remaining good players on the Oriole roster joined their former teammates in the exodus to the Dodgers, foremost among them Joe McGinnity, who won twenty-eight games as a rookie in 1899. But McGraw and Robinson still refused to go to Brooklyn and were sold off to St. Louis.

McGinnity, who would be known as "Iron Man" (he pitched an extraordinary number of innings but had, in fact, been an ironworker in the Oklahoma territory), hurled brilliant ball as Brooklyn took over first place in late June. Possessed of a gentle expression and a small, round face with heavy eyebrows, McGinnity did not exactly strike fear into the hearts of opposing batters at first glance. And his pitches—rising, almost underhand deliveries that began near his shoetops—seemed eminently hittable. Yet the batters invariably topped the ball or swung under it. McGinnity finished the 1900 season at 28–8 and won six games on six straight days, a feat that earned him a $700 bonus to go with his $1,800 salary.

The Dodgers finished four and a half games ahead of runner-up Pittsburgh for their second straight title. Charlie Ebbets was indeed proud of his men. The club had, however, lost money that season and so his generosity of the previous year would not be duplicated. After the team won the pennant in 1899, the owner gave every player a $160 bonus. For the heroics in 1900, he came up with cufflinks.

The ballplayers did have an opportunity to make some extra cash when the season ended. The Pirates had taken the season series from Brooklyn, 11 games to 8, and they boasted a shortstop named Honus Wagner who had hit .381. Their supporters were convinced the team was really better than the Dodgers. So the *Pittsburgh Chronicle-Telegraph* challenged Brooklyn to meet the Pirates in a three-of-five-game playoff series—all the games to be played in Pittsburgh—with the winner receiving a silver trophy cup.

McGinnity faced Rube Waddell—later notorious for his zany days with the Philadelphia Athletics—before an opening-game crowd of 4,000. The Iron Man encountered little difficulty with the Pittsburgh bats: It was Waddell's knee that almost did him in. In the eighth inning, McGinnity was being chased by Waddell in a rundown between third and home. In trying to elude his pursuer, he was struck in the temple by Waddell's knee and was knocked out for a few minutes. After being revived, he insisted on continuing. The Pirates got a pair of runs in the ninth when the shaky McGinnity hit a batter and gave up a walk and two hits, but Brooklyn held on for a 5–2 victory.

Frank Kitson hurled the Dodgers to a 4–2 triumph in Game 2, but Pittsburgh came back to take the next game by 10–0. McGinnity returned to the mound the following afternoon. Yielding nine hits, he pitched the Dodgers to a 6–1 victory that gave them the series.

The next evening, the Brooklyn players were invited to Pittsburgh's Alvin Theatre, where Mayor Diehl turned the Chronicle Cup over to them before a packed house. Joe Kelley, the Brooklyn captain, delivered a victory speech in response to the gracious capitulation.

The Brooklyn and Pittsburgh players divided proceeds from the gate receipts, but there was something extra for McGinnity. In gratitude for his two victories, his teammates gave him the silver cup—valued at $500— and Ebbets kicked in with a $100 bonus.

The Chronicle Cup series was a pale imitation of the old World Series days when the National League winners met the victors in the American Association. Nevertheless, after having lost to the Giants in the 1889 World Series and tied Louisville in the abortive 1890 Series, the Dodgers could now consider themselves the undisputed champions of baseball.

Soon, however, another challenge would arise. It would be leveled not simply at Brooklyn but at all the big league franchises. The National League's monopoly on major league baseball was about to end.

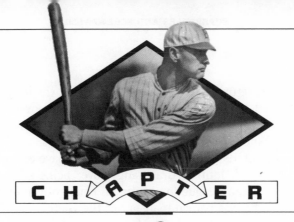

10

Nap and Zach

T he silver trophy cup and the $100 bonus did not keep Iron Man McGinnity contented for long. By the spring of 1901, he was gone from the Dodgers and had deserted the National League as well.

During those October days of 1900 when the Dodgers were capturing the Chronicle Cup in Pittsburgh, a minor league that had been formed only eight years before was getting ready to enter the big time.

Originally called the Western League, the circuit had been molded by a former college baseball player and Cincinnati sportswriter named Ban Johnson, who had developed it into the strongest league below the majors. In 1900, Johnson moved into several Eastern cities and shed the regional image, renaming his circuit the American League.

In February 1901, Johnson proclaimed, "The American League will be the principal organization of the country within a very short time— mark my prediction."

Now it was time to go raiding, and there would be few problems in getting talent. The prospect of bigger salaries along with the players' resentment of the National League owners' continued repression after the death of the old Players League and American Association brought Johnson and his associates a flock of good ballplayers.

The Dodgers were hit hard by the raids. They lost Fielder (his real name) Jones, an outfielder, who jumped to the Chicago White Sox, and Lave Cross, a third baseman, who went to the Philadelphia Athletics. The fabulous McGinnity went back to Baltimore, joining a resurrected franchise managed by his old teammate John McGraw. After two straight pennants, the Dodgers faded to third place in 1901.

The next year, there were more defections. Joe Kelley, after three

.300-plus seasons, returned to Baltimore. Tom Daly, the long-time second baseman, followed Jones to the White Sox. Brooklyn moved up to second place, but the Pirates were in a league by themselves, winning the pennant by twenty-seven and a half games.

Midsummer of 1902 saw a move that would have enormous impact on New York baseball. John McGraw, angry over being suspended indefinitely by the American League for continual abuse of umpires, left Baltimore. On July 9, he was named manager of the Giants.

The club had been floundering for years, but McGraw brought the makings of a fine team with him, taking McGinnity and several other Orioles to New York. The Giants would finish last that summer, but under McGraw they would be the class of the National League for years, leaving a bumbling Brooklyn team far behind most of the time.

In January 1903, a peace accord was reached between the National and American leagues. There would be no more raids. Players whose contracts were in dispute were simply assigned to various clubs by mutual agreements of the owners.

The Giants received a huge boost while the Dodgers suffered a blow when the contract arrangements were untangled. Christy Mathewson— destined to be the first baseball hero of the twentieth century—had signed with the American League's St. Louis Browns after pitching two seasons at the Polo Grounds. Now he was awarded back to the Giants. But Wee Willie Keeler, the Brooklyn native who was the Dodgers' most popular player, became an American Leaguer. Following the 1902 season, Ban Johnson had moved the Baltimore club to upper Manhattan. The franchise was taken over by Frank Farrell, a big-time professional gambler, and Bill Devery, a former police precinct captain with powerful political connections. A 15,000-seat wooden ballpark was built at 168th Street and Broadway in Washington Heights. Since the property was on hilly ground, the team was called the Highlanders. And so the Yankees-to-be were born, and in the peace accord, they got Willie Keeler.

The Dodgers opened the 1903 season at the Polo Grounds with a rookie from California named Henry Schmidt opposing Mathewson. Schmidt outpitched the Giant star, then went on to throw three consecutive shutouts.

Out in Coney Island, there were exciting doings as well. A new amusement area—Luna Park—opened on the site of what had been Sea Lion Park, famous for its shoot-the-chutes splashing thrill-seekers into a pool containing some friendly sea lions.

The chutes had been rebuilt, and now elephants slid down them in specially designed cars. Luna Park claimed to have the nation's largest elephant herd while also boasting forty camels who trudged through the Streets of Delhi exhibit. And dotting the complex were hundreds of towers, all of them magnificently glowing with electric light when the sun went down.

Henry Schmidt finished the season in a blaze of glory himself with a record of 22–13, and Brooklyn's Jimmy Sheckard led the National League in home runs, with a grand total of nine, and in stolen bases with sixty-seven. But the Pirates won their third straight pennant as the Dodgers slid to fifth place.

Things would get worse.

Following the season, the Dodgers made a curious deal. Bill Dahlen, a fine shortstop and a popular player who had been with the club since 1899—his horseplaying days in Chicago long behind him—was shipped to the Giants. Brooklyn received little in return, getting journeyman infielder Charlie Babb along with pitcher Jack Cronin, who had won only six games in 1903.

"It has always been my ambition to play in New York City," Dahlen exulted. "Brooklyn is all right, but if you're not with the Giants, you might as well be in Albany." He may have been happy with the deal but the Dodger fans were not.

And Schmidt, the star rookie pitcher, decided to call it a career after one season. He returned his 1904 contract unsigned, explaining, "I do not like living in the East and will not report." He was never heard from again.

Coney Island, vying with the Dodgers for Brooklynites' entertainment dollars, had another new attraction in 1904—Dreamland, an oceanfront amusement area designed to outdo Luna Park. It featured a one-armed lion tamer (he was rumored to be having an affair with the actress Marie Dressler, who ran a popcorn concession stand there); the Hall of Creation, where the first chapter of Genesis was replayed through the day, and Fighting the Flames, an extravaganza involving an hourly hotel blaze doused by firemen rushing on cue to the scene.

The 1904 season marked the first efforts by Charlie Ebbets to bring Sunday baseball to Brooklyn. Games had been played on Sundays in the National League's Western cities for more than a decade, but the New York State legislature banned Sabbath entertainment at which an admission fee was charged. Ebbets tried to beat the prohibition with a bit of creativity. On Sunday, April 17, he scheduled a game against Boston at which there was no formal admission charge. All fans were, however, required to buy scorecards. They were color-coded according to their price and, depending on how much a patron was willing to shell out for a card, he could sit in either the box seats, grandstand or bleachers.

The game was completed without incident, but Ebbets was not so fortunate when he tried the subterfuge the following Sunday for a game against the Phillies. After two pitches had been made, the police arrested the starting battery for Brooklyn—pitcher Ed Poole and catcher Fred Jacklitsch—along with Philadelphia's leadoff man, center fielder Frank Roth. The ballgame was, however, allowed to proceed. Ulysses Grant Thatcher was substituted as the Brooklyn pitcher, Lew Ritter went in to catch, and Hugh Duffy replaced Roth at the plate. Brooklyn won by 8–6 in what would be Thatcher's only appearance of the season.

The three arrested ballplayers were later acquitted by Justice William Gaynor—a future mayor of New York—who found "no evidence that the religious repose of the community was broken." Ebbets then felt free to continue with his Sunday games. But they didn't go on for too long— Gaynor's decision was overturned.

The 1904 season was otherwise forgettable as Brooklyn fell to sixth place, fifty games behind the pennant-winning Giants. The next season was a disaster as the Dodgers finished in last place with a 48–104 record, the only time in their history they had been at the bottom. To make matters worse, the Giants took the pennant again.

Whatever aggressiveness the Dodger ballplayers lacked was, at least, made up for by the fans. When the Giants would come to Washington Park, bringing sellout crowds, residents of the Ginney Flats neighborhood over- looking the field from across the street would rent out space on their fire escapes at ten cents a head. Their customers would fortify themselves with pails of beer hauled up to them on ropes by saloon owners and, their spirits enlivened, would fashion spears out of umbrella ribs and hurl them at Giant outfielders.

At the end of the 1905 season, reports surfaced that Ned Hanlon was scheming to have the National League drop the Brooklyn franchise and replace it with a club in Baltimore, the site of his great days with the Orioles.

Nothing came of it and in December, Hanlon was out as Dodger manager after seven seasons running the club. He took over the Reds and was replaced in Brooklyn by Patsy Donovan, who had played briefly for the Dodgers in 1890 and had managed Pittsburgh, St. Louis and Washington with little success while seeing action in the outfield.

Despite trading Jimmy Sheckard, a fine outfielder, to the Cubs for four ordinary players, the Dodgers improved in 1906, moving up to fifth place. They even boasted a pair of sluggers by dead-ball era standards. Tim Jordan, a left-handed batting rookie first baseman, led the league in homers with twelve while outfielder Harry Lumley had nine.

Two Dodger pitchers had no-hitters that year, the first ones for the club since Tom Lovett accomplished the feat against the Giants back in 1891. Mel Eason held the Cardinals hitless on July 20 in a 2–0 victory at St. Louis. But the other no-hitter was simply a hard-luck afternoon. Harry McIntire pitched ten hitless innings against Pittsburgh in a 0–0 game on August 1 at Washington Park, then had retired two batters in the eleventh

◆ *Nap Rucker, an outstanding pitcher for some poor Dodger teams. (Los Angeles Dodgers)*

when a shower arrived. After a brief delay, the Pirate second baseman, Claude Ritchey, bounced a single to center on a 2–2 pitch. The Pirates got three more hits and a run off McIntire in the thirteenth inning to win the game.

It was another fifth-place finish for the Dodgers in 1907, but that season marked the arrival of a pitcher who would rank among the league's best.

One afternoon in July 1904, a Vanderbilt University shortstop named Grantland Rice batted against a nineteen-year-old lefthander pitching for an Atlanta athletic club. The future sports columnist was so impressed with the teenager from Crabapple, Georgia, that he played scout, recommending him to Abner Powell, manager of the minor league Atlanta team. Powell signed the pitcher, then sent him to his Sally League affiliate in Augusta, a club that happened to have a right fielder by the name of Ty Cobb.

The young pitcher would eventually be promoted to Atlanta, and in the spring of 1907, George Napoleon Rucker—better known as Nap—was bought by Brooklyn for $500, one of the best investments Charlie Ebbets ever made.

On April 20, Rucker made his Washington Park debut. He yielded just three hits in a complete-game effort against the Philadelphia Phillies but was beaten, 2–0. The Dodgers would go on to lose sixteen of their first seventeen games. It was symbolic of events to come. Rucker had a 15–13 year and would pitch

◆ *Zach Wheat shows the form that will take him to the Hall of Fame. (National Baseball Library, Cooperstown, N.Y.)*

superbly for almost a decade, compiling a record of 134 victories and 134 losses. But he was usually with a bad ballclub.

The Brooklyn fans did some pitching themselves during the 1907 season with an unfortunate outcome. A favorite sport of the Washington Park faithful was throwing pop bottles at the enemy. One day, Frank Chance, the Cubs' first baseman-manager, picked up some bottles thrown at him and tossed them back into the crowd. One struck a youngster, badly injuring him. Chance, known as "The Peerless Leader" for his sterling qualities, expressed remorse, and Ebbets took action within the limits of commercial expediency. He stopped selling soda pop—for a single afternoon.

The Dodgers didn't create much excitement in 1908—finishing seventh—but September brought some remarkable pitching performances. After the club lost seven straight, Rucker pitched a no-hitter against the Braves on September 5 in the second game of a doubleheader at Washington Park, striking out fourteen. Thus inspired, Brooklyn went on to lose its next nine. Then, on September 26, the Dodgers were shut out twice in a doubleheader by the Cubs' Ed Reulbach, who yielded a total of eight hits over eighteen innings' labor.

While the Dodgers floundered, their owner was looking to the future. In September 1908, Charlie Ebbets took a first step—out of the public eye—toward truly bringing Brooklyn baseball into the twentieth century. He bought a small parcel of land in Pigtown, an area east of Prospect Park filled with garbage dumps and shanties. Some day, he hoped, he would accumulate enough property to build a grand ballpark there.

In December, Ebbets made another move that would pay off handsomely. At the National League meetings in the Waldorf-Astoria, a former printer's helper from Oswego, New York, named Larry Sutton who had once been a minor league umpire was hanging around looking for a job. Ebbets hired him as a scout.

Sutton spent the summer of 1909 touring minor league towns, and at Mobile, Alabama, he found a gem: Zachary Davis Wheat, a twenty-one-year-old left-handed batting outfielder with powerful wrists and a compact swing. Sutton persuaded Ebbets to buy the ballplayer's contract for $1,200.

Named for Zachary Taylor, a hero of the Mexican War and later President of the United States, and for Jefferson Davis, President of the Confederacy, Zach Wheat hailed, appropriately enough, from border country—rural southwest Missouri. He evidently descended from Huguenots who had emigrated to Virginia in the late eighteenth century, but was said to be part Indian. Wheat never denied having Indian blood, and the sportswriters loved the angle, but it may have been more fiction than truth. There was, however, no question about his ability with a bat.

Wheat made his debut at the Polo Grounds on September 11, 1909, going hitless against Christy Mathewson. But the next day he got two hits and he batted .304 in twenty-six games that season.

Wheat would become perhaps the National League's finest left-handed batter of his era. John McGraw was so wary of him that he ordered his pitchers never to throw him a curveball at the Polo Grounds, fearing he could easily drive the ball down the short right-field line. One day, the Giants' Jess Barnes served up a curve, and Wheat belted it into the seats. As he rounded the bases, Wheat could hear McGraw yelling at poor Barnes, "Pinhead! That stupid pitch costs you five hundred bucks."

Enormously popular with the Dodger fans and well liked by his teammates, Wheat would play left field in Brooklyn for eighteen seasons. He amassed 2,884 hits with a lifetime batting average of .317, and in 1959 he was elected to the Hall of Fame.

The 1909 team that Wheat broke in with had a new manager. After three second-division finishes with Patsy Donovan, Ebbets decided to change managers again. Harry Lumley, a Dodger outfielder since 1904 and the club's captain, got the job.

Lumley had been in right field when Brooklyn opened the 1909 season against the Giants at the Polo Grounds. The teams' aces—Rucker and Mathewson—were held out because of cold weather. But their replacements were sensational.

For the first nine innings, the Giants' Leon (Red) Ames didn't allow a hit, and the Dodgers' Irvin (Kaiser) Wilhelm was almost as good, pitching a no-hitter until George Schlei, the Giant catcher, singled with one out in the eighth. Whitey Alperman, the Dodger second baseman, finally broke up Ames's no-hitter with a double in the tenth and the Dodgers went on to win it, 3–0, in thirteen innings. The go-ahead run was scored by Manager Lumley, who tripled off Ames with one out and was driven home on a single by Eddie Lennox, the third baseman. Lennox, a rookie, would, however, be best remembered by his teammates for his prowess at the dinner table: He could devour three chickens at one sitting.

Things weren't so bright after that. Lumley broke his finger the next day in a 3–0 loss to the Giants and was sidelined for a month, and Kaiser Wilhelm would finish the season with only three victories against thirteen defeats. The late arrival of Wheat held promise, but the club finished in sixth place, losing ninety-eight games.

With the Dodgers continuing to go nowhere, Ebbets fired Lumley and hired Bill Dahlen, the former Brooklyn shortstop.

The high point for the 1910 Dodgers came on June 15 at Washington Park when right-hander Cy Barger pitched all fourteen innings and had four hits—including a game-winning double—in a 3–2 victory over the Cubs. The fans carried Barger off the field, and then Ebbets showed his gratitude by becoming an early-day Abe Stark: He bought his pitcher a new suit of clothes.

Exactly a week later, in a game against the Giants, there was more excitement at Washington Park, but it occurred in the stands. A fan had been heckling the Giant players, reserving some special taunting for Art Devlin, the third baseman. As the clubs changed sides in the third inning, Devlin struck back, punching a spectator named Bernard Roesler who he presumed was the guilty party. Josh Devore, a Giant outfielder, and Larry Doyle, the second baseman, joined in with some choice blows of their own. Then Ebbets came running over to yell at McGraw, who he figured was behind the retaliation. When it was all over, the fan was unconscious and the three Giant players were taken off to jail. The National League president, Tom Lynch, suspended Devlin for five days and fined Devore and Doyle $50 apiece.

Otherwise, it was another dreary season for the Dodgers. Rucker won seventeen games and pitched a league-leading 320 innings, but George Bell, a thirty-five-year-old right-hander, made up for Rucker's accomplishments by losing twenty-seven games. There was, however, a newcomer at first base who would star for the Dodgers over the next decade. Jake Daubert, a left-handed batter out of the Pennsylvania coal country, replaced Tim Jordan and led the club in homers with eight while batting .264. Daubert would hit over .300 for seven of the next eight seasons, winning the batting

◆ *Jake Daubert with trophy presented by Dodger fans in 1911 honoring him as the team's most popular player. (Courtesy of George Daubert)*

title in 1913 and 1914.

The Dodgers finished sixth for the second straight year. But they did get a break so far as the sports entertainment dollar went: thoroughbred racing disappeared from Brooklyn.

In years past, the blue-blooded types had assembled at Brooklyn's Sheepshead Bay racetrack for the Suburban and Futurity stakes and at the Gravesend course, where the Preakness was held. Brooklyn had become the racing capital of America, attracting socially prominent horsemen like William K. Vanderbilt, Leonard W. Jerome, August Belmont Jr. and Harry Payne Whitney. But in 1910, the state legislature passed tough anti-gambling laws, and the Sheepshead Bay, Gravesend and Brighton Beach courses all shut down. (The Sheepshead Bay track would play a part in aviation history the following year. On September 11, 1911, a pilot named Calbraith P. Rodgers, publicizing "Vin Fiz, The Ideal Grape Drink," took off from the track's infield in his Vin Fiz flyer and became the first person to fly an airplane coast to coast.)

Dahlen was given another chance despite the second-division finish in 1910. But beyond Wheat, Daubert and Rucker, the Dodgers still had little talent, and they dropped to seventh the following season.

The fans had a lively time the afternoon of July 8, 1911, when the Dodgers faced the Pirates at Washington Park. They took out their frustrations not on the floundering ballclub but on a newly hired umpire, Ralph Frary. The Brooklyn players had argued over Frary's ball and strike calls early in the game, and the fans lent their vocal support. In the fifth inning, the atmosphere became more heated when Frary called Daubert out at home plate on an attempted double steal. In the top of the ninth, with the game tied at 1–1 and one out, it got even hotter for Frary when he signaled "ball" on a pitch to Honus Wagner that the Dodgers and their rooters insisted was strike three. Moments later, the Pirates' star shortstop singled, stole second and scored on another hit. The heckling from the Brooklyn bench got louder, and Frary retaliated by throwing out Manager Dahlen, all the players sitting in the dugout, and the club's uniformed mascot, a youngster named Frankie Deery. After dallying a bit, the little group marched almost in lockstep to the outfield clubhouse, and then the fans really let loose with a barrage of pop bottles and a big lemonade tumbler that shattered a few feet from the umpire.

Eventually, the fans ran out of ammunition and, with two uniformed policemen and two detectives summoned to the front of the stands, the shower ceased. As it turned out, the crowd had shown little more throwing ability than the Brooklyn players were displaying these days: None of the missles hit the umpire. The Pirates' next batter, Jack Miller, picked up the broken glass, Pittsburgh went on to a 3–1 victory, and Frary, with policemen surrounding him, escaped from the field along with his fellow umpire, Bob Emslie. As Police Captain Hayes made a show of guarding the front door of the umpires' dressing room, they sneaked out the back way and fled to their hotel.

But Brooklyn got the last laugh: A week later Frary was fired.

Early in August, the Giants called Wilbert Robinson, John McGraw's old buddy from the Baltimore Orioles, out of retirement. Robbie was told to work with the pitchers and, being an easygoing sort, was called upon to lighten the tension under the hard-driving McGraw.

The Giants got hot, pulled away from the Pirates and Cubs, and clinched the pennant a week before the season ended.

On the season's final day, the Dodgers faced perhaps the strangest pitcher in baseball history. Back in June, a Kansan named Charles Victor Faust had turned up during the Giants' batting practice in St. Louis and had accosted McGraw. He told the manager that a fortune teller had prophesied he would pitch the Giants to the pennant, then would meet a beautiful girl named Lulu and sire a long line of baseball stars. McGraw gave the visitor a brief workout to humor him and quickly saw he could neither throw nor hit. The young man was then sent on his way. That evening, however, on the train to Boston, the Giants discovered that Charlie Faust was on board, determined to fulfill his destiny.

As a joke, McGraw allowed Faust to stick around and gave him spending money. Suddenly, the Giants began a winning streak. "Victory" Faust, as he became known, was bringing the club good luck.

Each afternoon, Faust would warm up and become convinced he would get into a game. But when play began, he would be back on the bench. Finally, with the pennant wrapped up, McGraw let Faust pitch the ninth inning in a game against the Braves. He gave up a run, then was allowed to bat in the bottom of the ninth after the Giants had, in fact, been retired in a 5–2 defeat. Faust grounded to the mound, but the Boston pitcher, Lefty Tyler, deliberately threw the baseball over his first baseman's head, and the Braves let Faust run all the way to home plate before throwing him out.

Faust was not quite finished. McGraw brought him in for the ninth inning against the Dodgers in the second game of a season-ending doubleheader at the Polo Grounds after he had been warming up since noon. The Dodger batters cooperated, and Faust, using a windmill delivery emulated by Joe E. Brown in the film "Alibi Ike," retired the side on one hit. In the bottom of the ninth, Faust came to the plate. Eddie Dent, the Brooklyn pitcher, hit him on the wrist with a slow curve to get him on base, and the Dodgers allowed him to steal second and third. Moments later, he scored on an out. The Dodgers went on to a 5–2 triumph, but "Victory" Faust had his moments in the sun.

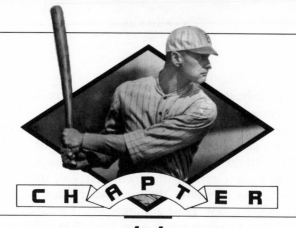

11

The House That Ebbets Built

For three years, he had been buying up land in secret. Now, on the evening of Tuesday, January 2, 1912—four days after filing the deed for the final parcel of property—Charlie Ebbets was ready to reveal his great plan.

The Dodger owner called sportswriters to a dinner at the Brooklyn Club on Pierrepont Street along the Heights.

Once, when asked whether he envisioned replacing Washington Park, Ebbets had remarked, "The question is purely one of business; I am not in baseball for my health."

He would now seek to forsake the image of hard-hearted capitalist for one of benevolent sportsman.

"Brooklyn has supported a losing team better than any other city on Earth," Ebbets told his dinner guests. "Such a patronage deserves every convenience and comfort that can be provided at a baseball park, and that is what I hope to provide."

Ebbets announced he was about to start construction on a fine new stadium of concrete and steel just east of Prospect Park.

The Dodgers' ballfield went back to 1898 and it was a firetrap. The original Washington Park—built on a site a few blocks away—had, in fact, been severely damaged by fire in May 1889. Beyond that, the ballclub had simply outgrown its home. Washington Park could seat only about 18,000, even with box seats that reached almost to the foul lines in spots, leaving the players little room for chasing down foul balls.

Ebbets's announcement made big news, but he was hardly the first to discard a nineteenth century ballpark. For all the old wood-construction ballfields were dangerous and antiquated.

Fire hit the Chicago White Sox's field in 1909 and the Washington ballpark in 1911. And just after midnight on April 14, 1911—a few days after the season got under way—flames erupted from the right-center field bleachers at the Polo Grounds. By the time horse-drawn fire apparatus arrived, the blaze had engulfed the horseshoe-shaped stands. All was lost except for a section of the bleachers. The Giants shifted their home games to the Yankees' Hilltop Park while their owner, John Brush, built with concrete and steel on what was left of his old ballpark. In August, the Giants unveiled the new, 40,000-seat Polo Grounds, the stadium that would survive into the early days of the Mets.

The age of the steel and concrete ballpark had been inaugurated by the Philadelphia Athletics a few months after Ebbets quietly began to buy up parcels for his own dream field. On April 12, 1909, the A's unveiled Shibe Park, named for Ben Shibe, their chief stockholder and Connie Mack's partner.

Ebbets estimated his new park would cost about $750,000 and he said it would be built entirely by the club's stockholders with no outside funding. The Dodger owner was a savvy operator, but that prediction proved to be wishful thinking.

After laying out the larger picture, Ebbets asked his attorney, Bernard J. York, to explain to the dinner gathering how the thirty or so parcels for the ballpark site had been acquired. It was, noted York, a tortuous and secretive operation. If the true purpose of buying up the property had been revealed, individual parcel owners would have demanded high prices. So Ebbets and York had set up a front—the Pylon Construction Company—to purchase the land.

The name was chosen haphazardly. When Ebbets and his associates in the scheme couldn't think of a title for the corporation, they opened a dictionary. The first word on a page selected at random was *pylon*. It would do.

Parcels were gradually bought up at the market value for property in the neighborhood—not a very high price since the area was essentially a dump. But then a snag developed. The owner of a tiny plot hedged in by the other parcels was believed off in Europe. Agents were sent to track him down, but they couldn't find him on the Continent. Finally, the man was reached in California. Since his pursuers had come a long way, the property owner figured something big was afoot and demanded $2,000 for a piece of land that ordinarily would have been worth about 100 bucks. Ebbets paid it.

His new ballpark was to be built on four and a half acres at the northern edge of the Flatbush section. It would be bounded by Bedford Avenue on the east, Sullivan Street on the south, Cedar Place (later renamed McKeever Place) on the west and Montgomery Street on the north.

He hadn't selected a name for the ballfield yet—at least publicly—but the best guess was Ebbets Park.

Designed by Clarence R. Van Buskirk of Brooklyn, the ballpark was to have the best of everything.

It would, said the *Times,* have "an immense grandstand which will have the afternoon sun in the rear and the Summer breezes in the front of the stand." The chairs would be "roomy and armless."

The spectators would be kept informed of who was who and what was what. No longer would they have to strain to hear the umpire shout out a lineup change.

"A megaphone device will inform the fans of every new face in the struggle, where he will play, his favorite author and what he thinks of the tariff," the *Eagle* explained. "That will be a tremendous advance over the old way of doing things, when you always asked the man beside you what the umpire said, the man always told you wrong, so that you did not know the difference until you read the papers next day."

For an efficient flow of fans into the ballpark, a semicircular rotunda with a mosaic tiled floor and white glazed brick side walls would be the major entrance.

A garage was to be built across from the park, and when a game neared its end, the rotunda would become a waiting area for motorists. Rugs would be placed over the tile floor and then folding chairs would be set down to allow fans to sit in comfort while attendants fetched their autos.

The park would be serviced by eight streetcar lines and the Brighton Beach "el."

"These connect with thirty-eight transferring lines. Even a bigamist could ask no more avenues of escape or approach," observed the *Eagle.*

Ebbets struck a patriotic note in announcing his plans for moving in. He hoped for Flag Day, June 14, and if the park wasn't ready by then, he would try for August 27, the anniversary of the Revolutionary War's Battle of Long Island.

The timetable would be wildly optimistic for it wasn't until March 4 that the groundbreaking ceremony was held. On that morning, with 500 guests looking on at a site once dotted with shanties and wandering goats, Borough President Alfred E. Steers got things started on a nostalgic note. He recalled how, as a boy, he had looked through a knothole to see the Atlantics play the Cincinnati Red Stockings in their famous 1870 game at the Capitoline Grounds.

Now came Ebbets's moment. Standing at a platform draped with bunting and flags and wearing a bowler hat and long overcoat, he grasped a silver spade with an ebony handle, dug up a bit of soil and tossed it into the air. Then the proud owner headed off to a celebratory luncheon at the Consumers' Park Restaurant as a crew of Italian laborers got to work at the site, described by the *Times* as a "howling wilderness."

If any doubts remained about the need for a new ballpark, they were dispelled when the Dodgers opened the 1912 season with the Giants at Washington Park.

The game brought out the largest crowd in Washington Park's history. By the time the Dodgers stopped selling tickets at 2:30 P.M.—two hours after the gates had opened and ninety minutes before game-time—25,000 fans had been allowed in, about 7,000 above capacity.

The overflow immediately swarmed all over the field, resisting efforts by the ballpark Pinkerton policemen to push them into the stands. Fans were knocked down, hats were smashed and coats torn, but the mob refused to budge, quite properly protesting that there was nowhere to sit. A frantic Dodger management pleaded with Deputy Police Commissioner Walsh to send in city policemen, but he maintained that anything happening within the ballpark grounds was the team's problem.

At 3:30 P.M., Mayor William Gaynor arrived for the customary opening-day festivities, managing to get inside only after the special police opened a lane through the jammed stands. The Dodgers urged the mayor to call in the regular police, but he decided to wait and see if the park policemen could get things under control.

They could not. So now the ballplayers from both teams decided to take matters into their own hands—literally. Wielding their bats as prods, they formed a long line and charged into the crowd. The fans refused to move back more than a few feet. Finally, Gaynor called out club-wielding policemen. But they were helpless as well. There was simply no place for the fans on the field to retreat to since even the aisles were choked with spectators.

Eventually, the infield was cleared, but when the game began fans were still on the outfield grass, coming as close as thirty-five feet from the infielders. Before the afternoon was over, thirteen ground-rule doubles would be hit into the throng. And the more brazen in the mob plunked themselves down on the clubs' benches, forcing the players to squat on the ground.

Some spectators who didn't have seats improvised by grabbing the movable chairs vacated by disgusted fans in the front rows. They took the chairs onto the field and stood on them along the baselines, making it impossible for anyone in the stands except those in the top rows to see the ballplayers. Even the mayor couldn't see anything from his box seat so he simply tossed the ceremonial first ball over the heads of the fans on the field, hoping it would land in someone's glove. Management eventually set up chairs along the first-base line so Gaynor and his party could figure out what was going on.

The frustrated patrons in the grandstand hissed Ebbets and the police, and they threw big wads of paper at the fans on the field. Numerous fights broke out.

The game, which began a half hour late, dragged on for 1 hour 45 minutes before Umpire Bill Klem mercifully called it at the end of six innings, citing darkness. What might have been a dandy pitching duel, with Nap Rucker facing Rube Marquard, ended in a farcical 18–3 Giant victory.

The hero of the day may have been Bert Maxwell, a rookie pitcher for the Giants who didn't even get into the game. He lifted three women over the New York bench so they could escape the mob and find refuge of sorts in the stands.

The chaos may have lent urgency to completion of the Dodgers' new ballpark, but the first date envisioned for its opening—June 14, or Flag Day—came and went with construction work barely under way.

On July 6, ceremonies were held for the laying of the grandstand cornerstone, a slab of Connecticut granite serving as a time capsule. Among the items placed in it by Ebbets was a photograph of—modesty aside—the Dodger boss. Also stuffed inside were issues of the *Brooklyn Eagle,* a congratulatory letter from President Taft, and a copy of Robert Peary's 1909 wireless message announcing he had raised the American flag at the North Pole.

Ebbets made a little speech promising he wouldn't rest until the Dodgers captured a pennant, something they hadn't managed since 1900. Then Monsignor Edward W. McCarty, once an aspiring catcher, blessed the great endeavor. Hailing Brooklyn as the spot where baseball had its roots, he pronounced the new ballpark "a crown of gold for the fair brow of the mother of the game."

As the summer moved along, it became clear that the alternate date for the park's opening—the August 27 anniversary of the Battle of Long Island—would pass with construction work still unfinished. Finally, Ebbets gave up on moving in during the 1912 season and set his sights on the following April.

Bill Dahlen, in his third season as Dodger manager, still couldn't pull the club out of the second division. He had, however, lost none of the contentiousness he was famous for. On April 20, Dahlen was at his obnoxious best at the Polo Grounds. But he met his match in Umpire Cy Rigler.

Dahlen had returned to the bench only the afternoon before, having served a three-day suspension for arguing with the umps. Not in the least

◆ *Bill Dahlen, a fine shortstop, a ferocious umpire-baiter but an unsuccessful manager. (National Baseball Library, Cooperstown, N.Y.)*

chastened, he stormed out of the dugout after Rigler signaled home run on a ninth-inning drive by the Giants' Art Wilson into the right-field upper deck with Heinie Groh on base, a shot that gave New York a 4–3 victory.

Insisting the ball had gone foul, Dahlen shook his fist in rage at Rigler. The umpire, evidently certain he was about to be pummeled, struck the first blow, punching Dahlen below the left eye. Dahlen then socked Rigler in the face, and a fine brawl erupted. The players rushed out, and Wilbert Robinson, the Giant coach, grabbed Rigler while Tex Erwin, catching that day for Brooklyn, got hold of Dahlen. The fans swarmed onto the field, yelling "smash him again, Rigler" or "soak him, Bill" depending on their allegiance.

Three days later, the league suspended Dahlen for ten days and fined both the manager and the umpire $100.

Wheat and Daubert were the main men in the Dodger batting order again, but there were some new faces on the 1912 ballclub. The powerfully built Otto Miller, better known as "Moonie" for his round face, began to take over the catching from anemic-hitting Bill Bergen. George Cutshaw, a fine fielder, had been drafted from the Pacific Coast League and was installed at second base. Red Smith, playing his first full season in the majors, was at third. As for the pitching, there still wasn't much after Rucker.

On Tuesday, September 17, a sun-splashed afternoon with the Pirates visiting Washington Park, Dahlen benched his center fielder, Hub Northen. The manager put into the

◆ It's April 5, 1913, the first afternoon at Ebbets Field. Mrs. Ed McKeever, wife of one of the Dodger owners, gets the honor of hoisting the flag. (National Baseball Library, Cooperstown, N.Y.)

lineup a twenty-three-year-old left-handed batter just arrived from the Southern Association with a reputation as both a solid ballplayer and something of an eccentric.

The outfielder had been spotted by superscout Larry Sutton on his travels through Illinois in the summer of 1911. He was playing for a ballclub in Aurora, thirty-five miles west of Chicago, in the Class C Wisconsin-Illinois League, and going to dental school in the offseason. Though the young man was only in the low minors, Sutton decided he was a hot prospect and persuaded Ebbets to draft him for $500.

In 1912, the ballplayer was moved up to Montgomery of the Southern

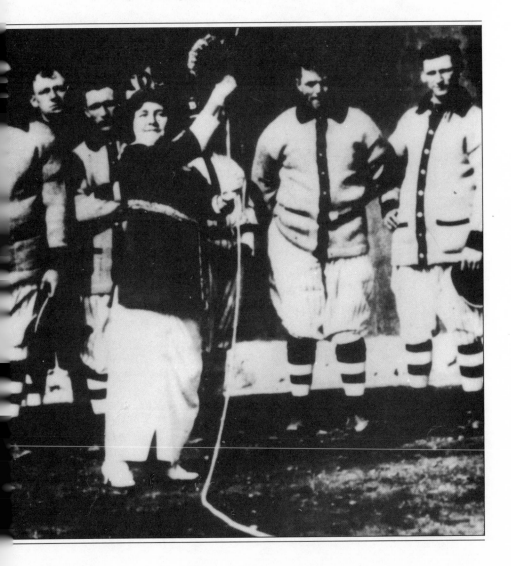

♦ *The house that Charlie Ebbets built, soon after its opening. (Brooklyn Historical Society)*

Association where he batted .290. He did not, however, take himself too seriously. One day during a spring training game, he hid in a small manhole crater. When a fly ball was lifted to his vicinity, he was nowhere in sight. Suddenly, he sprang from below the earth and grabbed the ball one-handed.

As soon as the Southern Association season ended, Charles Dillon Stengel was called up to Brooklyn.

His debut was spectacular. Batting against the Pirates' Claude Hendrix, a big right-hander, Stengel singled three consecutive times, drove in two runs and stole a base. Then, against a reliever named Jack Ferry, he singled again and stole another base. In the eighth inning, with the Dodgers ahead by 7–3 and the left-handed Sherry Smith pitching, the newcomer had a good time. Not normally a switch-hitter, he turned around to bat right-handed and drew a walk. When the afternoon had ended, the Pirates' twelve-game winning streak was over and an instant hero had emerged.

Stengel continued to hit in the waning days of the season, finishing with a .316 average over seventeen games. The *Brooklyn Eagle* ran a picture of him with the caption "New Superba Phenom."

And Charley (the Kansas City-

born Stengel was not Casey, for K.C., yet) lived up to his fun-loving reputation. One day at festivities before an exhibition game in Newark, he won
$10 for wrestling a greased pig to the ground.

On Saturday afternoon, October 5, the Dodgers played their final game
at Washington Park, Pat Ragan taking the mound against the Giants' Jeff
Tesreau before a crowd of 10,000. New York got the only run, Fred Snodgrass driving in Josh Devore with a seventh-inning single. Afterward, Charlie Ebbets held a reception, shaking hands with the fans and accepting
their good wishes for his new ballpark. Shannon's military band then concluded an era with "Auld Lang Syne."

The Giants, pennant-winners by ten games over the Pirates, headed
for the World Series against the Red Sox. For the Dodgers, it was another
dismal season: a seventh-place finish with a 58–95 record.

As springtime 1913 approached, the string of ten straight second-
division finishes and the mayhem at old Washington Park were consigned
to the past. The Dodgers' new home was ready.

The morning before St. Patrick's Day, Ebbets Field was opened for
inspection, and 15,000 Brooklynites took a look.

The most eye-popping feature that day was the rotunda, lit up in late
afternoon by a chandelier containing twelve arms simulating bats with
globes shaped like baseballs at their tips. The glow highlighted a ceiling
decorated with stars and clouds for a skylike effect. The rotunda floor was
magnificent as well, dotted with small white marble blocks inscribed with
a pattern resembling the circular stitching on baseballs.

Ebbets wasn't there to show off his ballpark. He had gone to New
Orleans for a brief vacation, pleading the strain of overwork in getting
things ready. At any rate, he no longer had sole control of the ballclub.
The reception committee for the preview was headed by two brothers who
had been taken in as partners.

The new co-owners were Edward J. and Stephen W. McKeever, prosperous and politically well-connected Brooklyn contractors who had res-
cued Ebbets when he couldn't come up with enough cash to finance the
new park. The previous August, Ebbets had bought out his partner, a
furniture dealer named Henry Medicus, in order to obtain all the outstanding stock. Then, in return for financial aid from the McKeevers, he sold
half the stock to them for $100,000.

Sons of an Irish immigrant shoe dealer, the McKeever brothers may
not have enjoyed Ebbets's prestige among Brooklynites but they had far
outstripped him in making money. Steve, who quit school at age ten,
became a plumber's apprentice, then went into business for himself, and
while in his twenties won a contract for the plumbing, gas and steamfitting
work on the Brooklyn Bridge. Ed, forsaking formal education at age fourteen, prospered with the Hudson River Broken Stone Company, which built

the roadbed for the New York Central Railroad's route from New York City to Buffalo in the 1890's.

At the turn of the century, the brothers joined forces as real estate developers, erecting more than a hundred houses in a section of Greenpoint they called McKeeversville.

Aside from their business interests, they were sportsmen. As youngsters, they had scurried for foul balls hit by the old Atlantics at a practice field near where the Brooklyn Bridge would one day rise. They had both been infielders for sandlot teams and, after making their fortunes, owned a string of outstanding trotters and pacers.

Though they shared a sharp business sense, the brothers were very different men. Ed, fifty-four when Ebbets Field opened—four years younger than Steve—stayed out of the limelight. But Steve loved people (Wilbert Robinson would be an exception) and became quite a character on the Ebbets Field scene. He would sit in the back of the stands behind home plate, his accouterments including a derby hat, thick gold watch chain, diamond stickpin and blackthorn walking cane. With a glass of milk in a specially built container beside him, he would enjoy the afternoons with his cronies.

Steve dabbled in politics as well, serving as a member of the Board of Aldermen—a forerunner of New York's City Council—from 1898 to 1901. He never spent a day on the bench—his perch at Ebbets Field excepted—but was known as Judge. That's what he called himself and everyone else.

Finally, the great day arrived: Ebbets Field opened on Saturday, April 5, with an exhibition game between the Dodgers and Yankees.

On that afternoon back in 1913, the ballpark only vaguely resembled the shape it would take from the 1930's on. It contained 24,000 seats in a two-tiered grandstand that ran from the right-field foul pole to a point midway between third base and the left-field pole. A concrete bleacher section ran adjacent to the grandstand along the left-field line. Wooden bleachers had been erected behind the left-field fence, but they would be used only for a sellout.

The right-field foul pole was about where it would always be, 298 feet from home plate. The scoreboard that would be so familiar a feature in right field was still years away, but the fence did have the traditional advertisement for Bull Durham tobacco. Anyone hitting it would win $50 and a supply of free ice, no small prize in the days before household refrigerators.

For right-handed batters, the distances were not as cozy as they would become. It was 401 feet down the left-field line and about 425 to dead center.

With memories of the ugly scene at Washington Park's opening-day game the previous April still fresh, Dodger management recruited a new

◆ *In 1931, the double-deck stands were extended to left field and center field and the scoreboard was moved from behind the left-field fence to right field. Here, the Ebbets Field that would be. (National Baseball Library, Cooperstown, N.Y.)*

corps of ballpark police. Some 100 strong, the unit was called the Doughertys and supposedly was composed entirely of former soldiers. The special cops certainly impressed the *Brooklyn Eagle,* which, in a wildly off-base prophecy, told its readers that "all kinds of disorder, from insulting remarks to bottle-throwing, will be unknown at Mr. Ebbets' new baseball park."

The morning hours of opening day brought clouds, but by afternoon the sun had broken through as a crowd estimated at between 20,000 and 25,000 filled the stands. A few thousand fans were turned away, but they could view the game for free from a bluff where the old Crow Hill penitentiary once stood. One entrepreneur erected a grandstand on the bluff, and 300 fans paid him fifty cents apiece for a seat two blocks from the field.

Ebbets was no doubt joyous as the fans streamed in. But moments after the gates were opened, it became obvious that his new ballpark was already obsolete.

Allen Sangree, covering the game for the *New York American,* told what happened:

Inspector Cohen and Captain Barney Gallagher, with twenty mounted "cops" and a regiment of foot, had all they could do to prevent a riot, principally because Charles Ebbets appears to have made a gross blunder in his architectural arrangements. The showpiece of his stadium is a huge rotunda. Mr. Ebbets spent many a restless night dreaming of this plan, and he went at it purely from his goodness of heart. He thought to shelter his patrons in event of rain. But yesterday's rush proved that Mayor Gaynor is likely to close up Ebbets Field if more space is not made at this opening. The first mad swirl found a thousand rooters swashed into the rotunda, capsizing a wonderful floral display sent by friends of the McKeever brothers, and only a quick closing of the gates saved a panic.

Once the fans made it to their seats, they were entertained by Shannon's 23rd Regiment Band. At about two o'clock, Umpire Tim Hurst handed the first ball to Genevieve Ebbets, Charlie's youngest daughter. She was to toss it to the other umpire, Bob Emslie, after the American flag was hoisted.

Then Mrs. Ed McKeever, accompanied by her husband and by Ebbets, marched to the center-field fence, Shannon's musicians trailing them, for the ceremonial flag-raising.

Now it became clear that the mad rush in the rotunda would not be the only snafu of the day.

"When they got over there, it was discovered that the flag hadn't arrived," the *American*'s Sangree reported. "One of the ground keepers was sent post-haste after Old Glory, which was snugly stowed away in the office."

Mrs. McKeever belatedly sent the flag aloft, the band played the "Star-Spangled Banner," Genevieve Ebbets threw out the first ball, and now it was time for the game to get under way.

Nap Rucker retired the Yankees, and then Casey Stengel came to the plate to face Ray Caldwell as the first Dodger batter in Ebbets Field. Casey bounced out sharply, and then George Cutshaw got the first hit at the ballpark, a single to center. Benny Meyer followed with a single to right, and next came the most exciting moment of the inning.

The *Brooklyn Eagle,* picking up the action, told how "that noble redman, Zach Wheat, advanced to bat and came mighty near putting a crimp in the band when he bounced a fly into the midst of the musicians. Hartzell ran over from third to nail it in, but he took a header right into the music, bumping his head on the bass drum and booming the G note, to the delight of the fans."

The Dodgers eventually took a 2–0 lead on an inside-the-park homer by Stengel and a home run over the center-field fence by Daubert. But the Yankees tied it in the top of the ninth on a throwing error by Frank Allen, who had relieved Rucker. Then came a dramatic ending to the big day. Wheat laid down a bunt and made it to second when Jeff Sweeney, the Yankee catcher, threw the ball away. Daubert sacrificed him to third and then Red Smith delivered a single to center field that sent Wheat home with the winning run.

The fans were thrilled—but exasperated as well. It proved to be just as hard to get out of the ballpark as it had been to get in.

The first regular-season game at Ebbets Field was played on April 9, the following Wednesday, when the Phillies' Tom Seaton stopped the Dodgers, 1–0. Rucker pitched superbly, only to be sabotaged, as usual, by his teammates' failings at bat and in the field. The Philadelphia run came in on a fly ball muffed by right fielder Benny Meyer in the first inning.

A floral horseshoe—the customary opening-day tribute—was presented to the team, and Borough President Steers threw out the first ball. But only 10,000 fans showed up on a cold, blustery day. The game was really an anticlimax to the ceremonial opener against the Yanks.

On April 26, the Giants came to Ebbets Field for the first time, and a capacity crowd saw Pat Ragan pitch the Dodgers to a 5–3 victory. But once again, the rotunda was the scene of a human traffic jam.

"Everybody who saw that rotunda, architects, baseball magnates and such, stamped it as the last word in baseball entrances, but that was only in theory," wrote Abe Yager, the *Eagle*'s sports editor. "When it came down to the practical use of the big circle, the owners quickly discovered that the average crowd, when turned loose, is very much like a Western roundup or a stampede. They piled into that enclosure like a leaderless suffragette army and ran in all directions for tickets. The result was that Ebbets got all the blame, and his pet rotunda is anything but popular."

Eventually, Ebbets created two new entrances to divert some of the rotunda traffic, and nobody was killed.

The Dodgers were within hailing distance of the top for the first half of the season, but then lost ten straight in July. They finished in sixth place, though Daubert hit .350 to win the batting title and received a Chalmers automobile as the outstanding player in the National League. The award ceremony was held in, of all places, the Polo Grounds, before a World Series game between the Athletics and the Giants, who had finished thirty-four and one-half games ahead of Brooklyn.

Although Ebbets had his ballpark, he obviously wasn't developing a decent team to play in it. And soon he faced far more serious headaches. A new league arrived in 1914 and with it another baseball team for Brooklyn.

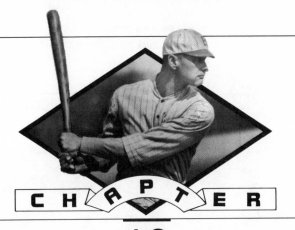

12

The Tip-Tops
Come to Town

After managing the Dodgers to four straight second-division finishes amid numerous arguments with umpires, Bill Dahlen was told by Ebbets to take his battles elsewhere. He was fired soon after the 1913 season.

Ebbets found his new manager at the Polo Grounds. It was Wilbert Robinson, John McGraw's teammate on the old Orioles, former Baltimore cafe business partner and, since late summer in 1911, a trusted coach who had turned Rube Marquard and Jeff Tesreau into top-flight pitchers.

It seemed that McGraw and Robinson would go on for many a year bringing pennants for the Giants. But they had a falling out during the 1913 season. Years later, Robinson maintained that the estrangement resulted from what should have been a minor set-to. He said he was coaching at first base when he spotted a steal sign from McGraw. The runner, Fred Snodgrass, was hobbled with a charley horse, but, obeying instructions, Robinson sent him down. Snodgrass was thrown out by a mile, and McGraw was livid, insisting he had never ordered the steal. One word led to another and, according to Robinson, McGraw told his long-time friend and baseball partner that he would be finished as a Giant when the season ended. They would, in fact, remain enemies for the rest of their lives.

Three days after he fired Dahlen, Ebbets called the press to the Clarendon Hotel to introduce Robinson.

Born in Bolton, Massachusetts, during the Civil War, the son of a

◆ *Robert B. Ward, founder of the Tip-Tops: white bread and baseball team. (National Baseball Library, Cooperstown, N.Y.)*

butcher, Robinson had made his major league debut as a catcher for the Philadelphia Athletics of the American Association in 1886. He stayed in Philadelphia until 1890, then moved on to Baltimore and caught for the great Oriole teams of the 1890's. His claim to fame as a ballplayer went back to the afternoon of June 10, 1892, when he had six singles and a double, going seven for seven, at Baltimore against St. Louis, setting a major league record for most hits in a game.

As a player, Robinson showed some speed, had in fact stolen 196 bases, and at five feet eight inches he had packed 180 pounds into a muscular physique. But by the time he arrived at Ebbets Field, he could charitably be described as rotund. "I haven't been feeding on oysters and wild duck all these years in Baltimore for nothing," he told the sportswriters at the introductory get-together.

Turning from the matter of his ample frame to the rather large needs of the ballclub, Robinson said his top priority would be to develop pitching beyond Nap Rucker.

But the Dodgers' prospects were complicated by a challenge to the major leagues that had brought another ballclub to Brooklyn. Ebbets was faced with losing his few good players to an upstart league's raids.

In 1913, a new league independent of organized baseball arose in the Midwest, invading big league cities with six franchises. It called itself the Federal League.

At first, the new circuit did not seek to sign players under contract to major league or minor league clubs, settling instead for free agents and youngsters. But in 1914, it emerged as a real threat, raiding the big league rosters and adding franchises in the East, including a team in Brooklyn. And it had wealthy backers. Convinced that baseball was entering a golden age of money-making—all those concrete and steel ballparks were clear evidence of faith in the future—rich men looking to own a ballclub but finding themselves shut out of the majors bought into the new league.

James A. Gilmore of Chicago, who had made his money in the coal business, was named the Federal League's president. Among the men he brought in for 1914 were Charles Weeghman, the owner of a chain of Chicago restaurants; Otto Stifel, a St. Louis brewer and bank director; Philip De Catesby Ball, also of St. Louis, who had become rich through the sale of ice-manufacturing plants, and—most ominous for Charlie Ebbets—Robert Boyd Ward.

Ward and his brother George were the owners of the Brooklyn-based Ward's Bakery Company, boasting thirteen plants around the country. ("From Baker to Consumer, Untouched by the Human Hand," its hygienic slogan.) They would be running the Federal League's team in Brooklyn.

The league wasted little time in making an impact on the Dodgers' fortunes. Following the 1913 season, the Cincinnati Reds sold their short-stop-manager, Joe Tinker, to Brooklyn for $25,000. Ebbets gave the Reds $15,000 and was to pay Tinker $10,000 of the purchase price. But Tinker never arrived in Brooklyn. Unhappy with the $7,500 salary Ebbets offered, he spurned the $10,000 bonus and signed to manage the Federals' Chicago club for a three-year deal that included stock in the franchise.

The big league teams went to the courts in an effort to fight the Federal League raids, but were rebuffed, and over the 1914 and '15 seasons,

81 major league players and 140 minor leaguers jumped to the Federals.

Among the better-known deserters besides Joe Tinker were Mordecai (Three Finger) Brown, once a top pitcher for the Cubs but then nearing the end with the Cincinnati Reds; Hal Chase, the long-time Yankee and then White Sox first baseman, and the Philadelphia Athletic pitchers Chief Bender and Eddie Plank.

Early in 1914, Casey Stengel was rumored to be considering a Federal League offer, and Pat Ragan, one of the Dodgers' starting pitchers, said he had received a bid from the Federals. It seemed that Ebbets might lose his star first baseman as well. Jake Daubert, who had signed a three-year contract the previous season, threatened to jump if he got a better deal.

Ebbets decided to act quickly and traveled around the country by train, offering good deals to his key players. Wheat and Rucker agreed to three-year contracts while Stengel, turning down a long-term pact, got $4,000, almost double his 1913 salary. Before the war with the Federal League ended, Daubert would wrangle a five-year contract from Ebbets at a spectacular $9,000 a season.

"I didn't let one of my good players get away," Ebbets later boasted.

The Dodgers did lose five players to the Federals for 1914—Benny Meyer, Bill Collins and Al Scheer, all outfielders; Fred (Mysterious) Walker, a pitcher, and Enos Kirkpatrick, a third baseman—but none were front-liners.

The Federals opened the 1914 season with teams in Brooklyn, Baltimore, Buffalo, Pittsburgh, Chicago, Indianapolis, Kansas City and St. Louis, all in new ballparks. The Chicago Whales played in a park on the North Side that would become the league's sole physical legacy: It was called Weeghman Park—for the team's owner—but would eventually be known as Wrigley Field.

Brooklyn's Robert Ward built anew on the site of the old Washington Park, tearing down the wooden framework and replacing it with cement and steel. The concrete for the main grandstand wasn't poured, however, until April 17, four days after the season started. Construction had been delayed by union laborers' refusal to work at the field because of the Ward brothers' reputations as employers of nonunion help in their bakeries.

Robert Ward installed himself as the club president, named his brother George as vice president and appointed brother Walter as secretary-treasurer. A fourth Ward was business manager: that one-time owners' nemesis John Montgomery Ward, no relation to the bakery brothers.

The team would go down in history as the only ballclub named for a brand of white bread: It was known as the Tip-Tops.

Presumably preferring the blander alternative nickname Brookfeds, Robert Ward disclaimed any responsibility for using the team to promote his bakery products.

"I am not in baseball as an advertising business," Ward told *Baseball Magazine* in July 1915. "My club was nicknamed the Tip-Tops by the sporting writers. They took the name from my favorite brand of bread, very true, but they did so without my knowledge or consulting me. As far as I am concerned I am sorry they did, for it lays me open to some criticism. But a nickname is like a disease. It comes without the consent or knowledge of the person who has it."

Ward's protestations to the contrary, his "official scorecard" cover for the 1915 season was emblazoned: "Brooklyn Federal League Base Ball Club: The Tip-Tops."

The 1914 Tip-Tops had several players with big league experience. Hap Myers, the first baseman, had played with the Braves in 1913. Solly Hofman, the second baseman, was formerly with the Cubs and Pirates. Among the outfielders, Steve Evans and Al Shaw had jumped from the Cardinals, Danny Murphy had played with the Athletics and Claude Cooper had seen action with the Giants. Grover Land, the first-string catcher, had been a substitute with the Indians. The key pitcher was Tom Seaton, who won twenty-seven games for the Phillies in 1913.

◆ *The Brooklyn Tip-Tops, followed by the Pittsburgh team, open the 1914 Federal League season at the new Washington Park in a burst of patriotic glory. (National Baseball Library, Cooperstown, N.Y.)*

Bill Bradley, a long-time third baseman for the Indians and their manager for part of the 1905 season, got the Tip-Top managing job. One of his coaches was a familiar face in Brooklyn: Wee Willie Keeler.

Some 15,000 fans—about 4,000 short of the new Washington Park's capacity—turned out when the Tip-Tops opened at home on May 11 against Pittsburgh. Before the game began, the Brooklyn players paraded with a huge American flag, accompanied by a brass band dressed in the uniforms of the Revolutionary War's Continental Army. Even the 200-foot-high flagpole provided a patriotic touch: Its uppermost section was the mast of the America's Cup defender, the yacht *Reliance*. Shannon's 23rd Regiment Band, which traditionally played at opening days in Brooklyn, was to have been on hand but its members stayed away out of loyalty to Charlie Ebbets.

James Gilmore, the Federal League president, helped kick things off by marching with the three Ward brothers and the players in the pregame festivities. Then Danny Murphy, who had been the Athletics' captain before seeking greener fields, was presented with a gold baseball, a chest of silverware and Killarney roses from old friends who had come up from Philadelphia.

Had Murphy poked a long drive in the right spot he would have had even more goodies to take home: a candy manufacturer's advertisement on the outfield fence promised a box of bonbons to any player who knocked a baseball over the sign.

The Wards put their own message on the right-field wall, spelling out a code of conduct for baseball fans. It read:

———

Baseball players are all human, and therefore love applause. If you want a winning team, root for them, speak well of them to your friends, and while we are here let us all be clean of speech—so that the ladies may find it pleasant to come often.

———

The Tip-Top fans didn't find much to root for in the home opener. Tom Seaton gave up two runs in the first inning, and that was it for the scoring. Howie Camnitz, a three-time twenty-game winner for the Pirates before switching to Pittsburgh's Federal League club, shut out the Tip-Tops on five hits.

Steve Evans, the left fielder, went on to bat .348—second in the league to the Indianapolis Hoosiers' Benny Kauff—and Seaton won twenty-five games, but the Tip-Tops wound up in fifth place, eleven and one half games behind pennant-winning Indianapolis.

Wilbert Robinson didn't work any magic with the Dodgers. The team was in last place as late as September 8, then showed some life and finished fifth with a 75–79 mark. Rucker, plagued by illness, appeared in just sixteen games with a 7–6 record, but the pitching got a boost from Jeff Pfeffer, a big right-handed rookie who won twenty-three games. Daubert captured the batting title for the second straight season, hitting .329.

This was the year of the Miracle Braves, who came from way behind to win the National League pennant and then shocked the Athletics with a four-game sweep in the World Series.

The Brooklyn that Wilbert Robinson found back in 1914 exuded a relaxed atmosphere in its residential areas, a contrast to the frenetic pace of the Manhattan he knew with the Giants. Uncle Robbie, as he would be fondly called for his easygoing ways, would fit right in.

Robbie and his wife—known to everyone as "Ma"—lived near Ebbets Field as did many of the Dodgers. It was all very cozy. The ballplayers might be spotted by their neighbors walking with their youngsters in Prospect Park or gathering in a cigar store at the corner of Flatbush and Parkside avenues, a favorite spot for an evening of baseball talk.

One of Uncle Robbie's less publicized moves upon joining the Dodgers was the naming of Jake Daubert's nine-year-old son, George, as a batboy.

Seventy-five years later, George Daubert, a retired business executive living in Columbia, South Carolina, would recall the atmosphere in Brooklyn in the days before America's entry into World War I.

By the time he got the batboy's job, young George was a veteran of sorts, having been around the Dodgers from the days before the first brick was laid for Ebbets Field.

"In 1911, at the age of six, my dad parked me on a wooden bench in front of the Brooklyn clubhouse in the old Washington Park," he remembered. "The clubhouse attendant was enlisted as a babysitter for the duration of the game. He explained to me that Pittsburgh was the visiting team and, as the players emerged from their clubhouse, he pointed out a player and told me his name was Honus Wagner. That bit of information meant nothing to me until a few years later, but I was intrigued by Wagner's bow legs and very long arms.

"I was fascinated by a large Bull Durham sign near the clubhouse in left-center field. A batter who hit the sign received a prize of fifty dollars. My dad's first base hit in the major leagues struck the Bull Durham sign for two bases."

The Daubert family lived year-round on Coney Island Avenue, not far from Ebbets Field.

"Brooklyn was like a big country town," Daubert recalled. "There were a lot of beer gardens on the corners with German brass bands playing and free lunch and nickel beers.

"When you went to New York, you went to 'the city.' Brooklyn wasn't considered a city in that sense. On rare occasions, dad would pack my sister, mother and I into the car and drive to New York City, an exhilarating and spine-tingling experience. It seemed that every street crossing was a challenge between car and trolley. The conductor rang his bell, dad honked his horn, but neither slowed, creating an unbearable period of bated breath, followed by a long sigh of relief from the passengers accompanied by a few shouted insults by the drivers of both vehicles directed at each other."

These were the days when a fan wouldn't hesitate to collar a ballplayer on the street to replay that afternoon's game.

"My dad commuted to the ballpark by trolley," the son recalled, "and for the longest time he would complain about some baseball nut who always waited for him when he got off the trolley after the game, usually tired and hungry. It was impossible to evade this portly, stuttering, nail-chewing baseball nut without being rude, so dad would listen."

Eventually, the star first baseman and the fan—an undertaker named Harry Blair—became partners in a real estate venture, and a lasting friendship developed. The admirer became known to the ballplayer's son as Uncle Harry.

"Uncle Harry would take me with him to ballgames, where he chainsmoked Between the Acts cigars, chewed his fingernails and fidgeted in his seat if Brooklyn was losing," George Daubert recalled.

George found the batboy's job exciting, but "there were also some bad moments" arising from the players' superstitions.

Rubbing the head of the batboy was considered a good-luck measure.

"A player would grab me and give me a barber's rub, rubbing my head hard with the knuckles."

At one point, Daubert recalled, one of the pitchers decided that temporarily getting rid of the batboy might end a losing streak.

"The team lost eight or nine games in a row, and I was chased off the bench by Jeff Pfeffer, a burly pitcher. I spent the day in the runway, playing back there by myself. My dad didn't interfere. He didn't say, 'Let him sit here.' He said, 'Go on back there,' so that's where I went. But they lost anyway so I reclaimed my spot on the bench the next day."

Daubert remembered how the players looked for signs of good fortune while striving to keep bad luck away.

"If there was a load of empty barrels from a brewery that passed in the street, that was always considered a good sign by the ballplayers. If any particular ballplayer had a good run of luck, he usually used the same uniform, the same shirt. The uniforms got very, very dirty. You wondered if they were ever gonna get washed. And all the players' wives usually sat together. Most of the time they sat with their fingers crossed."

By 1915, it seemed that good luck had entirely deserted Charlie Ebbets. Not only would he have to compete again with the Tip-Tops for the fans' dollars, but the new Federal League team just installed in Newark would presumably overshadow the minor league club Ebbets owned there.

The 1915 Tip-Tops were bolstered by the arrival of outfielder Benny Kauff. After hitting a league-leading .370 for Indianapolis, Kauff was transferred by the Federal League to Brooklyn when his club moved to Newark.

A former coal miner from Pomeroy Bend, Ohio, Kauff loved the nightclub circuit, was a big spender, and had a flamboyant taste in clothing, favoring loud checked suits. He was just the man to attract press coverage for the Federals in their battle for New York newspaper space with the established leagues.

After an abortive attempt to jump to the Giants, Kauff went on to lead the Federal League again in batting, this time with a .342 average. He was the league-leader in stolen bases as well with fifty-five while hitting twelve home runs.

Lee Magee, an infielder-outfielder, left the Cardinals to join the Tip-Tops, playing second base and getting the manager's job. He fared better at the plate than in the dugout. Magee would bat .323 for the season, but in late summer, with the club floundering, he was dropped as manager. John Ganzel, a former first baseman who had managed the 1908 Reds, took over but couldn't do much better as the Tip-Tops finished seventh. Joe Tinker's Chicago Whales won the pennant by a single percentage point over St. Louis.

Shortly before the season ended, the Tip-Tops were preparing to offer their fans something no big league team could feature: night baseball. Five steel poles, each eighty feet high, were to be erected at Washington Park with a large light atop each of them. But when Brooklyn played its final game on October 1, losing to Buffalo by 3–2 in what would be the finale in the club's brief history, construction of the light towers had not been completed.

The Dodgers lost a few more players to the Federal League for the 1915 season, among them Jack Dalton, who made headlines back in 1910 by getting four hits against Christy Mathewson in his first major league game. After batting .319 as an outfield regular, Dalton was lured to Buffalo by an $8,000 contract.

Ed Reulbach, who had come to the Dodgers in the summer of 1913 after a splendid pitching career with the Cubs, also went to the Federal League and would win twenty-one games for the Newark club. But his departure was forced on him for he had been released by Ebbets after the 1914 season.

In a May 1915 article in *Baseball Magazine,* the sportswriter F.C. Lane maintained that Reulbach had been cut by Ebbets purely out of vindictiveness. According to Lane, Ebbets had retaliated for Reulbach's activities on behalf of the Players' Fraternity, a protective association. Beyond that, Lane wrote, the owner suspected the pitcher had instigated a movement against Wilbert Robinson that Jake Daubert was, in fact, behind.

Reulbach's bitterness was undisguised. When Lane asked him whether he would want his son, then six years old, to follow in his path, Reulbach responded: "Never. I would rather he would be a hod carrier."

The 1915 season began on an embarrassing note for Wilbert Robinson. A few years before, Gabby Street, a catcher for the Senators, caught a baseball dropped from the top of the Washington Monument, 500 feet above the ground. When a young female aviator offered to take thrill-seekers up over Daytona Beach while the Dodgers were training there in the spring of '15, Robbie—an old catcher—set out to prove he was every bit the man Gabby Street had been. He resolved to snare a ball dropped out of the plane from about the same altitude as in Street's feat.

George Daubert, who was there in his miniature Dodger uniform, recalled what happened:

―――――

The girl who flew the plane was named Ruth Law. The engine was in the back; it was a biplane. You just sat on a board and put your feet on a rod that ran across and she took you up over the ocean and back. She landed on the beach, that was her runway. I think it was ten dollars a ride.

Robbie tried to catch the ball dropped from the airplane— but it wasn't a baseball. I think it was Casey who gave 'em a grapefruit instead and it came down and Robbie missed it—it hit him in the chest. It frightened the daylights out of him. The juice splattered all over him. He thought he was dead.

―――――

It was just the sort of stunt Casey Stengel would be likely to pull. But he evidently wasn't the culprit. Years later, Ruth Law revealed that just before taking off, she realized she had forgotten to bring a baseball with her and so she substituted a grapefruit from a crew member's lunch box.

Daubert recalled that Robbie "was angry for the time being but later he got over it because everybody was kidding him. The ballplayers had a big laugh about it and he joined in and took it in stride."

Robbie was never particularly tough on his players, Daubert remembered.

"If they lost a game, he'd sympathize with them. If the pitcher was down in the dumps, he'd say, 'Well, now, get yourself a couple of highballs and forget it.' He always said a little drink now and then would solve a lot of problems."

By the time the 1915 season began, George Daubert had retired as batboy. A Brooklyn youngster named Hank LeBost got the job, and he too would discover—to his profit—what an easygoing sort Uncle Robbie was.

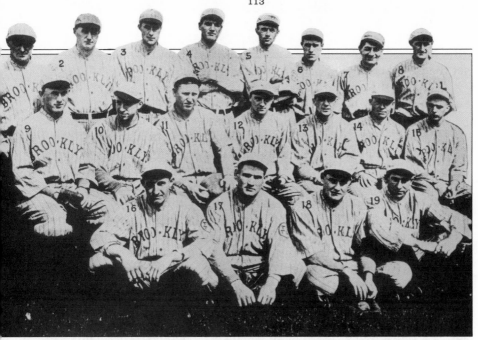

◆ *The 1915 Tip-Top club.* Top row (l. to r.): *Benny Kauff, Hugh Bradley, Bill Upham, Jim Bluejacket, Hap Myers, Fred Smith, Mike Simon and Hooks Wiltse.* Middle row (l. to r.): *Claude Cooper, Happy Finneran, Grover Land, Manager Lee Magee, Harry Smith, Andy Anderson and Al Holt.* Bottom row (l. to r.): *Ty Helfrich, Mysterious Walker, Don Marion and Tom Seaton. (National Baseball Library, Cooperstown, N.Y.)*

A retired sales manager still vigorous and still a Brooklynite as he approached his eighty-eighth birthday, LeBost reminisced about his batboy days one spring afternoon from his home in the Marine Park section.

"My dad owned a cigar and candy store at the corner of Eastern Parkway and Troy Avenue," he recalled. "There were beautiful homes, beautiful apartment houses on Eastern Parkway, it was one of the finest areas. But you could walk down the hill on Troy Avenue and for ten or twelve blocks, it was desolated. There were squatters' huts and nanny goats.

"It was a walk of about twelve minutes, and you'd be at Ebbets Field. The Dodgers were my idols—I used to hang out at the players' entrance. There'd be a mob of kids there asking the players to take them in. Casey Stengel befriended me. I had bright red hair, so he called me Carrot Top. He took me in, he got to like me."

In those free and easy days, a few youngsters would be allowed on the field during batting practice, and soon Hank LeBost was lucky enough to be one of them. He quickly found out that his heroes had feet of clay, at least so far as running down fungoes was concerned.

"There was no discipline," he remembered. "For exercise, the players supposedly would roam the outfield and catch fly balls. Well, they were a little lazy, and if it went over their heads, they'd say, 'Go get it, kid. Go get the ball.' I'd throw it back. I kept doing that for the longest time."

Finally, the young man parlayed his outfield errands into a little business operation.

"I got my mother to sew big pockets into my baseball uniform pants. Every time I went to chase fly balls, I would throw one back, and one I kept. I was selling those balls for a quarter apiece to the industrial league in Prospect Park."

Hank eventually got the batboy's job, spending the summers of 1915 and 1916 at Ebbets Field, where his main duties had little to do with bats. He was in charge of satisfying the players' eating and drinking appetites.

"The manager was manager in name only," he recalled, noting how rotund Uncle Robbie set a poor example for his men. "He didn't create the atmosphere with regard to having the athletes get away from their paunchy bellies.

"They used to drink terrific amounts of beer. I would shop for four or five ballplayers, get them beer and sandwiches all the time. Sometimes during a game, they'd say, 'Kid, go up and get a hot dog.' They didn't care about weight. I'd have to stand in line and get a hot dog. And it usually wasn't one, it was four or five. If one got the fever for a hot dog, they all got it.

"I had no salary," he remembered. "They used to tip me one penny. If I went out for five ballplayers, I got five cents. Wilbert Robinson was a big tipper. He gave me two cents on occasion."

But the tips could go a long way.

"When you had two cents and one of the other kids had three cents, you got into the movies—two for a nickel."

Casey Stengel may have been well served by his young admirer turned small-scale caterer, but he had a sub-par season in 1915, having suffered over the winter from what was said to be typhoid. Zach Wheat had an off year, too, hitting just .258. Jeff Pfeffer won nineteen games, but Nap Rucker was no longer a dominant pitcher.

Among the new faces on the pitching staff was an old hand, Jack Coombs, picked up from the Athletics at age thirty-two. He gave Robbie fifteen victories.

To go with that newly arrived old-timer were the promising rookie pitchers Wheezer Dell and Sherry Smith. Near the end of the season, the Dodgers picked up the Giants' Rube Marquard, who had tailed off after pitching a no-hitter against Brooklyn in April. They also obtained the Cubs' Larry Cheney, another good pitcher. Robinson was beginning to live up to his reputation for developing pitching staffs.

The team was in the race through early September, then fell back to finish third, ten games behind the Phillies, who won their first pennant thanks to a thirty-one-victory season from Grover Cleveland Alexander.

By the time the 1915 season was ending, the war between the established major leagues and the Federal League had proved a drain on everyone's pocketbook. Then, in October, Brooklyn's Robert Ward, a leading force among the Federals' owners, died unexpectedly. The Federal League was ready for a peace conference.

In December owners from all three leagues gathered in Cincinnati. When their work was finished, the Federal League was dead. The Ward interests were paid off by the majors at the rate of $20,000 a year for twenty years.

As 1915 came to a close, Charlie Ebbets had reason to be optimistic. For the first time since 1902, his men had finished ahead of the Giants. John McGraw's once mighty ballclub had fallen to last place. And now the Dodgers were once again the only baseball show in Brooklyn.

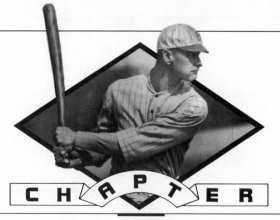

13

A Pennant
for Uncle Robbie

The salaries commanded by the Dodger squad assembling at Daytona Beach for spring training in March 1916 could not have made Charlie Ebbets very happy. Many players were still in the midst of long-term contracts—at a hefty pay increase—wrangled while casting their sights on the Federal League. But as the season got under way, it appeared that this team might be worth the money.

The pitching staff had been reshaped. A couple of years back there had been Rucker and little else, but now Uncle Robbie could choose among six starters. Jeff Pfeffer, the ace of the staff, was still in top form, and to back him up were five returning pitchers—a blend of experience and youth—who had arrived in Brooklyn just the year before: Rube Marquard, Larry Cheney, Jack Coombs, Wheezer Dell and Sherry Smith. Rucker was only thirty-one years old, but was plagued by bursitis and would seldom get into a game.

Jake Daubert, in his prime as one of the league's top hitters, returned at first base, and George Cutshaw would again provide outstanding defense at second. Ivy Olson, obtained from the Reds late in the 1915 season, showed admirable spirit in spring training, once throwing sand over an umpire to earn the rare distinction of being ejected from an intrasquad game. He would share the shortstop job with Ollie O'Mara.

At third base, the 1916 Dodgers had a new face, Mike Mowrey, a veteran National Leaguer who had played with the Pittsburgh Federal League club the year before. Mowrey replaced Gus (Gee-Gee) Getz.

Otto Miller, the regular catcher the season before, would now share the spot with thirty-six-year-old Chief Meyers, who was picked up from the Giants. Meyers, a member of the Cahuilla Indian tribe, had caught for McGraw's top pitchers—Mathewson, Marquard and Tesreau—and would bring an experienced hand to help Uncle Robbie mold the Brooklyn pitching.

The outfield looked strong with Zach Wheat in left, Hi Myers in center and Casey Stengel in right. Jimmy Johnston, a right-handed batter with some major league experience, was signed out of the minors and would see lots of playing time.

Near the end of the season, Robbie would again look to his old ballclub for help, getting Fred Merkle, the long-time Giant first baseman, who filled in for Daubert when he developed leg problems.

With Wheat, Daubert and Stengel bouncing back from off-years and the pitching tough, the Dodgers were in the pennant race from the outset.

It would prove to be a landmark year for the Dodgers—and also for Coney Island. Nathan Handwerker, a newcomer to the beach, opened Nathan's Famous in 1916, getting himself started by cutting the price of a hot dog from the customary ten cents to a nickel. But Casey Stengel would not have very fond memories of that summer at Coney. He got into a brawl one evening with Whitey Appleton, a Dodger pitcher, after a bunch of Brooklyn players had savored a few beers at the beach. Stengel and Appleton, each bandaged up the next day, concocted a tale of falling down a flight of stairs together, but the very proper Ebbets wasn't fooled and didn't take kindly to the fisticuffs.

Chief Meyers would later credit Stengel with having a big hand in the Dodgers' 1916 success, observing: "Robbie was just a good old soul and everything. It was Casey who kept us on our toes. He was the life of the party and kept us old-timers pepped up all season."

Over at the Polo Grounds, a hero was gone. In mid-season, the Giants sent Christy Mathewson, washed up as a pitcher at age thirty-five, to the Cincinnati Reds so he could fulfill his ambition to be a manager. Buck Herzog, the Reds' playing manager, came to New York in return. It was a rebuilding year for McGraw, but the Giants suddenly became unbeatable late in the season, winning twenty-six straight games—the longest winning streak in major league history—before losing to the Braves on September 30. They had started out too far back, however, and were headed for a fourth-place finish.

On Tuesday, October 3—two days before the end of the season—the Dodgers met the Giants at Ebbets Field with a chance to clinch the pennant. If they beat New York while the second-place Phillies lost a doubleheader to the Braves that day, they were in.

The Giants scored three runs in the first off Sherry Smith, but the

◆ *(L. to r.) Casey Stengel, Jimmy Johnston, Hi Myers and Zach Wheat, the outfielders for the 1916 National League champions. (National Baseball Library, Cooperstown, N.Y.)*

◆ *Casey Stengel and Zach Wheat together again in 1963 for Mets' old-timers' day at the Polo Grounds. (National Baseball Library, Cooperstown, N.Y.)*

Dodgers routed McGraw's starter, Rube Benton, who was relieved by Pol Perritt. The Giants then went into a swoon. Easy ground balls went through their infield, they ran the bases brainlessly, and Perritt, disregarding McGraw's orders, kept going into a full windup with runners on base. By the fifth inning, with the Dodgers leading, 6–5, McGraw had seen enough and left the field in a rage. The Dodgers went on to win, 9–6, as Jeff Pfeffer, in relief, got his twenty-fifth victory. The Phillies, meanwhile, lost both their games that day. Brooklyn captured its first pennant since 1900.

Many of the Giant players had good feelings toward

Uncle Robbie from his days coaching for McGraw, and there had been ill will between the Giants and Phillies stemming from several brawls over the previous few years. So had the Giants dumped the game to give Brooklyn the title over Philadelphia?

McGraw didn't cry fix but he came close.

"I do not say that my players did not try to win, but they simply refused to obey my orders, and they disregarded my signals," he said after the game. "Such baseball disgusted me."

Robinson dismissed any suspicions McGraw may have had as "ridiculous" and an alibi for the Giants' poor play after their long winning streak.

The next afternoon, instead of returning to the dugout at Ebbets Field, McGraw ended his season early in favor of an afternoon at Laurel racetrack near Baltimore. The Phillies' manager, Pat Moran, demanded an investigation, but the suggestions of a fix were discounted by Harry N. Hempstead, the Giants' president, and by John K. Tener, the president of the National League, who maintained that every Giant player "was fighting tooth and nail."

So, under a slight cloud, the Dodgers headed for the World Series against the Boston Red Sox, who had won their second straight pennant.

The Brooklyn fans gave their heroes quite a sendoff, lining the streets as the players rode in a procession of eighteen touring cars from Ebbets Field to Grand Central Terminal, and turning out 5,000 strong to see them off at the station.

Boston's hitting was nothing special, but the Red Sox had a strong corps of starting pitchers, led by a twenty-one-year-old left-hander named George Herman Ruth who had won twenty-three games while leading the American League with a 1.75 earned run average.

For no evident reason, Robbie decided to go with left-handers, leaving his two winningest pitchers, the righties Jeff Pfeffer (25–11) and Larry Cheney (18–12), on the bench.

With Rube Marquard, a thirteen-game winner, opposing Ernie Shore, who had gone 16–10, the Series opened on October 7 at Braves Field, borrowed by the Red Sox because it could hold larger crowds than Fenway Park. A few hundred Brooklyn fans came up by train, but they were drowned out by Boston's famed cheering section, the Royal Rooters, known for their endless renditions of the pep song "Tessie." The Rooters marched in pregame ceremonies, Mayor Curley threw out the first ball, and Brooklyn finally got a taste of World Series play.

Boston took a 6–1 lead into the ninth inning, but then the Dodgers rallied for four runs and loaded the bases with two out. Jake Daubert came to the plate with a chance to win the game. He hit a grounder to deep short, but Everett Scott made a fine pickup, threw to first just ahead of Daubert's diving slide, and the Dodgers were done.

Their fans back home got the bad news almost instantly. In those days before radio, scoreboards would be set up at busy intersections, providing the play-by-play via telegraph reports. At Times Square, the *New York Times* reported on the action with a 12-by-30 foot scoreboard displaying a white baseball diamond on a green background. Some 10,000 people massed in the street, following the plays by watching light bulbs moving around on the mock-up field.

"If Zach Wheat goes to bat at 3:35 P.M., the Times Square spectators will know it before 3:36," the *Times* boasted.

Following the game, there was a bit of nastiness between the owners of the two clubs. Ebbets, having just seen his team lose a close one, was not made any happier upon learning that the Boston management had given the Dodger fans poor seats. To make matters worse, he was suffering from vertigo. So his wrath was indeed kindled when Joseph J. Lannin, the Red Sox president, approached him at the Dodgers' Hotel Brunswick headquarters and asked if arrangements had been made yet for the Royal Rooters' seating in Brooklyn for Game 3.

"No, but I will make it now," Ebbets responded. He telephoned to Brooklyn in Lannin's presence and told one of his employees, "Save 250 of the worst reserved seats you have in the grandstand for the Boston rooters."

Game 2 produced the greatest World Series pitching duel ever with Sherry Smith and Babe Ruth vying for fourteen innings. The Dodgers scored in the first inning on an inside-the-park homer by Hi Myers, then the Red Sox tied it in the third on a triple by Everett Scott and a grounder hit by Ruth. That was all the scoring until the fourteenth when Boston won on a walk, a sacrifice and a pinch-single by a reserve first baseman named Del Gainer.

The teams then returned to Brooklyn with the Royal Rooters, undeterred by the prospect of miserable seats, accompanying the Red Sox. The zealots had played "Tessie" so many times during Game 2 that they got on Uncle Robbie's nerves and he persuaded Umpire Bill Dineen to make them stop. Now the band tooted away with a vengeance upon arriving at Grand Central Terminal after one A.M. Some 500 Royal Rooters, accompanied by the red-coated Fifth Massachusetts National Guard Band, blared their fight song while marching from the train station to the Red Sox's headquarters at the St. Andrews Hotel on upper Broadway.

The Dodgers came alive in Game 3 before a crowd of 21,000 bundled up in overcoats and furs on a chilly, windy day. They overcame the submarine pitching of Carl Mays in a 4–3 victory as Olson hit a two-run triple and Daubert got three hits. Coombs was the winner with relief help from Pfeffer.

Ebbets made good on his promise to give the Royal Rooters terrible seats: They were shunted to the extreme upper corner of the grandstand nearest left field. This time the Brooklyn fans had all the fun, snake-dancing on the field after the game. The revelers were led by a band of their own and two youngsters carrying aloft a large green banner (no one was bleeding Dodger blue yet) with a baseball emblazoned on it, the official pennant of the Brooklyn club.

The Red Sox took the next game, 6–2, as Dutch Leonard beat Marquard. The highlight that afternoon for Brooklyn was the farewell appearance of Nap Rucker, who had started only four games during the season and had announced he would retire after the Series. With the Dodgers trailing, Robbie yielded to sentiment and brought him in for the eighth inning. He held the Red Sox scoreless in the final two innings of his career.

The teams now went back to Boston where the Red Sox wrapped up the championship in Game 5 with a 4–1 victory before 42,620, the largest crowd that had ever turned out for a World Series game. Ernie Shore, the winner in the opening game, stopped Brooklyn again while Jeff Pfeffer, finally getting a start, took the loss.

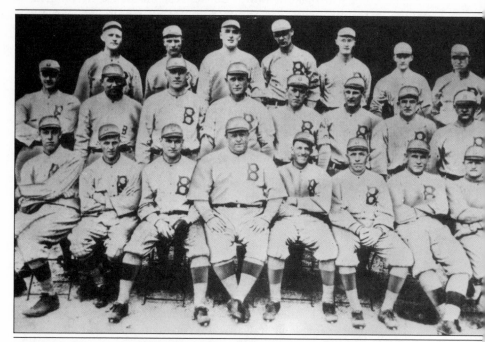

◆ *The 1916 pennant-winning Dodgers.* Top row (l. to r.): *Casey Stengel, George Cutshaw, Duster Mails, Rube Marquard, Sherry Smith, Artie Dede and Wheezer Dell.* Middle row (l. to r.): *Whitey Appleton, Chief Meyers, Jeff Pfeffer, Larry Cheney, Nap Rucker, Ivy Olson, Gus Getz and Zach Wheat.* Bottom row (l. to r.): *Jack Coombs, Ollie O'Mara, Hi Myers, Manager Wilbert Robinson, Jake Daubert, Jimmy Johnston, Hack Miller and Mike Mowrey. (Los Angeles Dodgers)*

When it was all over, the Royal Rooters, growing tired of "Tessie," switched to "Glory, Glory, Hallelujah!" as they marched onto the field, trailed by thousands of fans. They stopped at Charlie Ebbets's box seat and brought him forth to meet the Red Sox's Lannin. The two owners, burying their dispute over seating arrangements, shook hands and paraded arm in arm.

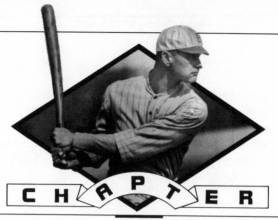

14

Wartime Wrangling

Having exulted over a rare pennant for his boys, Ebbets got back down to business: He slashed the salaries of eleven players whose long-term contracts, won during the Federal League war, had finally expired.

Attendance had increased by 600,000 in the National League and by more than one million in the American League in 1916 over the previous year, yet the owners voted at their annual meetings in December to cut salaries across the board. With no rival league to turn to, the players would be at management's mercy again.

Although Stengel had a fine season, Ebbets mailed him a contract calling for a cut from $6,000 down to $4,600. Casey sent his contract back unsigned with a "Dear Charlie" note, hardly the kind of salutation likely to endear himself to the self-important Ebbets. To further inflame the owner, Stengel advised Ebbets that his salary offer suggested he had probably gotten him confused with Red Hanrahan, the assistant clubhouse custodian.

But Ebbets was determined to maintain a hard line. Terming Stengel's response "a most impudent letter" and citing his "disgraceful brawl" with Whitey Appleton the previous year, he sent Casey a second contract calling for an even greater salary reduction. The owner's thrift crusade also angered Zach Wheat and Hi Myers, the rest of his outfield, and they refused to sign as well. The infielders fared even worse. When Ollie O'Mara, the shortstop, and Mike Mowrey, the third baseman, held out, Ebbets sent them to the minors.

If nobody showed up at spring training, the newspapermen wouldn't have anything to write about. So the *Eagle*'s sports editor, Abe Yager, decided that at the least, the squabble with Wheat had to be settled. He sent a wire to the outfielder at his Polo, Missouri, farm near Kansas City reading "Report at Once" and signed it "C.H. Ebbets." Wheat set out for the Hot Springs, Arkansas, training camp. When he confronted Ebbets, the puzzled owner denied writing any such note, but once the two men sat down, they reached an agreement. Wheat finally signed for what he maintained was the same salary he had earned in 1916.

Hi Myers didn't benefit from any chicanery on the part of sportswriters: He cooked up a scheme on his own. The outfielder had a small farm near Kensington, Ohio, with a cow, a horse and some chickens. One day he hired a printer to put together a letterhead reading "Myers's Stock Farm" and wrote Ebbets he was so prosperous that "at the terms you offer me, I cannot possibly afford to play baseball anymore." When Ebbets decided to visit him and presumably call his bluff, Myers had a friend loan him some cattle and horses for the day. Ebbets was certainly no fool, so it's questionable whether the ruse worked, but they did come to terms.

As spring training moved along, Stengel remained the only holdout. But two weeks before the season began, he capitulated, settling for the 23 percent pay cut Ebbets demanded in his first contract offer.

By the time the Dodger players opened the season, their individual salary squabbles were being overshadowed by events far removed from baseball. Europe had been at war since August 1914. America had managed to keep out of the fighting for almost three years, but Woodrow Wilson's peace efforts finally fell victim to the Zimmermann telegram, proposing a German-Mexican alliance against the United States, and to the sinking of American merchant ships by German submarines. On the evening of April 2, 1917, proclaiming "the world must be made safe for democracy," the President asked Congress to declare war against Germany. On Good Friday, April 6, the United States entered World War I.

The war proved to have little impact on big league ballplayers during the 1917 season. The draft machinery didn't get into gear until midsummer and few players were called into military service. Not many volunteered either.

Organized baseball found a way, however, to go to bat for America—literally. In a drive led by Clark Griffith, the manager and future owner of the Senators, the big league teams sent kits containing balls, bats and gloves to the armed forces. The clubs also contributed to the Red Cross and urged players to invest in Liberty Bonds financing the war effort.

Ebbets seized on wartime conditions to promote his long-frustrated bid to bring Sunday baseball to Brooklyn. He arranged a game with the Phillies for Sunday, July 1, announcing that the gate receipts would go to the Militia for Mercy, a war-related charity organization, and to the Red Cross. Ebbets staged a band concert before the game in an effort to cir-

◆ *Building another pennant winner? Not this year. Enjoying 1917 spring training at Hot Springs, Arkansas, are Jimmy Johnston at apex, Jim Hickman (l.) and Zach Wheat in middle row, and (l. to r.) Hi Myers, Chief Meyers and Ivy Olson. (National Baseball Library, Cooperstown, N.Y.)*

cumvent the state legislature's prohibition against Sunday games at which an admission fee was charged. The fans ostensibly were buying tickets for the musical entertainment, then would be allowed to stick around and watch the game for free. It was a variation on Ebbets's 1904 bid to get around the Sunday law by charging for scorecards while not actually selling tickets.

The Navy gave its blessings to the affair since servicemen would be benefiting, and it sent 1,500 sailors to parade on the field before the game. Admiral Usher, commandant of the Brooklyn Navy Yard, proudly looked on from a box seat.

Some 15,000 fans turned out, about half of them paying for the early concert and the other half simply walking in without charge after the music was over. They saw an exciting game, the Dodgers edging the Phillies, 3–2, on a pair of runs in the ninth inning. But Ebbets didn't fool the authorities. Both he and Wilbert Robinson were arrested. The following September, a Brooklyn court ruled that the band concert was merely a subterfuge and that the team had violated the Sunday laws. Imposition of a fine was, however, suspended.

Sunday baseball would finally come to Ebbets Field in 1919 when the New York State legislature passed a measure sponsored by State Senator James J. Walker—the playboy mayor of New York City during the 1920's— allowing ballgames on the Sabbath by local option.

The 1917 season was a sour one for both Ebbets and his players. The pennant-winning lineup of 1916 was virtually intact and a promising right-hander named Leon Cadore won thirteen games. But Jake Daubert's hitting fell way off, Zach Wheat's productivity was down, and Jeff Pfeffer went from a 25–11 season to a mark of 11–15. The Dodgers fell from first place to seventh while the Giants, climaxing their revival, won the pennant by ten games.

Evidently still angry over Stengel's cavalier response to his salary-cutting, Ebbets got rid of his colorful outfielder in January 1918, sending him to the Pirates along with George Cutshaw, the second baseman, for three players.

Stengel would not be the only familiar face missing in 1918. The starting lineup lost no one to World War I, but three of the leading pitchers—Pfeffer, Cadore and Sherry Smith—departed for military service.

In the winter of 1917–18, Ebbets decided upon a token of gratitude to Pfeffer who, the owner understood, had joined the Navy. Using proceeds from a fund he had set up to aid the dependents of ballplayers taken into the service, the Dodger owner bought a wristwatch, had it engraved, and sent it to his pitcher. But when the Dodgers opened spring training at Hot Springs, there was Pfeffer, proudly displaying the watch. He had not joined the regular Navy but a unit called the Naval Auxiliary Reserve Force. Ebbets's gesture did not, however, go for naught. Soon Pfeffer was indeed a real sailor, stationed at the Great Lakes training center in Illinois.

Early in May 1918, there were reports that Brooklyn pitcher Al Mamaux, one of the players obtained in the Stengel deal, had enlisted in the Army. Then it was learned he had, in fact, taken a draft-exempt job at a Quincy, Massachusetts, shipyard, thus avoiding possible combat. Mamaux justified his action by saying he had to support his mother and younger brother. But mom revealed she had no need for financial help. As for Al's decision to begin a career as a ship-worker, mother Mamaux exclaimed to a reporter: "My goodness, has Albert done that? He never said a word to me about it."

Another of the Pittsburgh players who came to the Dodgers for Stengel—Chuck Ward, a short-stop—had been drafted just as Brooklyn opened spring camp. So now Ebbets was left with only one of the three men he had traded for, a twenty-four-year-old pitcher named Burleigh Grimes. The previous year, his first full season in the majors, the right-hander had compiled a dismal 3–16 record. But he would quickly blossom as a Dodger, winning nineteen games his first year with the club.

"Ol' Stubblebeard," as he would be known, went on to four twenty-game seasons with Brooklyn, dominating batters with his spitball. He would pitch for the Dodgers through 1926 and would win 270 games over a nineteen-year career, then return to Brooklyn for an unhappy stint as manager. In 1964, Burleigh Grimes—the last pitcher to throw legal spitballs—would be elected to the Hall of Fame.

In mid-May of 1918, Casey Stengel was back in Brooklyn for the first time as a Pirate. He used the occasion to pull a stunt for which he would long be remembered.

Providing laughs for the fans was nothing new to Stengel. George

◆ *Burleigh Grimes, ace Dodger spit-baller. (National Baseball Library, Cooperstown, N.Y.)*

Daubert recalled from his 1914 batboy days how Casey once upstaged Uncle Robbie to display his unhappiness over being on the bench:

He'd been on the disabled list with a pulled leg muscle but felt he was ready to play and was anxious to get into the lineup against the Giants. Robbie and the club physician thought otherwise. Robbie told Casey he could serve as third-base coach in Robbie's place.

He finally agreed but he was put out about it. If he was going to be disabled, he was going to show the public that he was really disabled. He went into the clubhouse and had both hands bandaged almost to the elbow. Robbie fumed but went along with the deception. Casey stood there in the coach's box waving the players around with his bandaged hands. It drew a lot of comment in the stands because the fans didn't hear that he was burned or anything.

Robbie felt Casey's antics were unbecoming to a ballplayer so he ended the sideshow by calling on Casey to hit for the substitute right fielder. Casey stood in the coaching box and unwound all the bandages, then trotted over and got his bat. Before he could step into the batter's box, the fans were almost hysterical.

Now, in 1918, though no longer a Dodger, Casey could still entertain the Ebbets Field fans with a madcap antic.

While out in right field for the Pirates, he picked up a sparrow and brought it with him into the dugout. Years later, Stengel recalled what happened next:

Those Brooklyn fans were riding me. They cheered you as long as you were playing for them, but when you went away you weren't any good, see.

I walked up to the plate swinging three bats very hard. And the crowd yells, everybody gets excited, and they're booing me to death. Then I threw the bats down and grabbed my eye as if something was in it, and said, "Time." Cy Rigler was umpiring behind the plate, and he called time. Then I turned around to face the crowd and lifted my hat off and made a big bow. And when the bird flew out, the crowd just went, "Oh-h-h-h-h-h-h."

Early in June, Umpire Rigler was more directly involved in some excitement at Ebbets Field. With the Dodgers and Cardinals tied at 1–1 and the bases loaded in the top of the thirteenth inning, Marty Kavanagh of St. Louis hit a drive down the left-field line. Zach Wheat, convinced the ball was foul, didn't bother to run it down, but Rigler called it fair, and Kavanagh wound up with a grand-slam, inside-the-park homer. The Dodger players, tossing their caps into the air with disgust, argued fiercely with Rigler, who was no stranger to altercations with Brooklyn, having been involved in that fist fight with Bill Dahlen a few years back. Ollie O'Mara and Jimmy Johnston were ejected, and then the fans poured onto the field and surrounded the umpire. Finally, the St. Louis players formed a protective cordon around Rigler, threatening to bash the fans with their bats if they harmed the source of the Cards' good fortune.

When play resumed, the Dodgers tried to stall in the hope that darkness would arrive and the game would revert to a twelve-inning tie. Jack Coombs grooved the ball to the St. Louis batters and his infielders made no effort to stop grounders. But the Cardinals finally were retired with an 8–1 lead, the ballgame was completed and Rigler got away in one piece.

Otherwise, there wasn't much to arouse Brooklyn fans during the 1918 season—or what was left of it once the war had made its inroads.

Fearful over baseball's fate, the owners drew up a schedule cutting back from 154 games to 140. It turned out that far fewer games were played.

The Federal Government proclaimed baseball, along with other sports, to be nonessential activities in terms of the war effort. On May 23, General Enoch Crowder, the provost marshal of the armed forces, issued a "work or fight" order setting July 1 as the deadline for men in nonvital occupations to obtain war-related jobs or go into the armed forces.

The owners tried to get the edict delayed until October so that the already-shortened regular season and the World Series could be completed as planned. War Secretary Newton Baker did extend the deadline, but only until September 1. The ballclubs could have played into October anyway, using men who were draft rejects or too young or too old for military service, but baseball ended the season on Labor Day with the teams having played about 125 games apiece. The Cubs then met the Red Sox in a September World Series.

The Dodgers finished in fifth place with a 57–69 record, twenty-five and one-half games behind Chicago, despite Grimes's big season and a batting title for Zach Wheat, who hit .335.

For Jake Daubert, there was unfinished business. The clubowners had forfeited the players' final month's salaries because the season had ended early. But the way Daubert figured it, baseball could have kept going, in part using players too old for the draft, as was Daubert at age thirty-four.

So, he claimed, Ebbets had no right to deny him his September paychecks.

Soon after the World Series, the first baseman sent Ebbets a letter demanding $2,150, that portion of his salary for the period from Labor Day, when the season ended, to October 14, when his five-year contract expired. Ebbets refused to pay. Daubert appealed to the National Commission—the three-member owners' body overseeing baseball—and was again turned down. Then he got himself a lawyer—the leader of the old Players League revolt, John Montgomery Ward—and sued for the money.

Daubert eventually settled out of court for $1,500, but when the following season opened, he was no longer a Dodger. Ebbets sent his unhappy ballplayer to the Reds in February '19 for Tommy Griffith, an outfielder nowhere near a hitter of Daubert's caliber but a few years younger.

Baseball had put the war years behind it when the 1919 season arrived, but Daubert was still angry over his salary dispute. He got even with Ebbets on two occasions.

A baseball rule barred anyone not directly involved in a game from sitting in the dugout. Daubert's son, George, recalled that "Ebbets had a habit of sitting on the bench in his civilian clothes. He did that out in Cincinnati in 1919, the first time that Brooklyn played Cincinnati. My dad had the umpires chase him off the bench. So Charlie had to sit in the stands."

When he came to Brooklyn with the Reds, Daubert gave Ebbets grief in a more direct manner: by pounding the baseball. The Dodger owner couldn't retaliate directly, so he took out his frustrations on his pitcher that afternoon.

Years later, Burleigh Grimes recalled being the victim of Ebbets's wrath:

====

I pitched Jake a slow ball, and he hit it off the right-center field wall for an inside-the-park home run. Ebbets had a direct phone from his box to the bench, and he used it to order them to pull me out of the ballgame.

Mr. Ebbets fined me one thousand dollars. I didn't say anything about it till the next spring. I started off that next season with eight or ten wins in a row, and then I went on strike. I said, "Gimme back that one thousand dollars or I ain't gonna pitch anymore." I was gonna go home, and Ebbets knew it.

I got the thousand back.

====

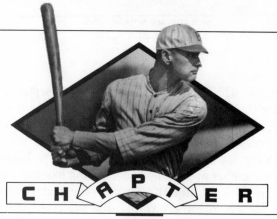

15

Everything Happens in Cleveland

After a poor season at the gate in 1918, the owners looked at their post-war prospects and decided to move full speed ahead: cutting costs. They kept the 140-game schedule in place, slashed salaries and reduced rosters from twenty-five players to twenty-one.

Uncle Robbie went into the 1919 season with a pitching staff that was reasonably deep once again. Jeff Pfeffer, Leon Cadore, Sherry Smith and Al Mamaux (he entered the armed forces after that abortive shipbuilding career) returned from military service to join Burleigh Grimes and Rube Marquard. Ed Konetchy, a thirty-three-year-old right-handed batter who would never be confused with Jake Daubert as a hitter, came from the Braves and replaced the disgruntled and now departed first baseman.

Grimes displayed remarkable endurance early on, pitching a twenty-inning complete game against the Phillies April 30. But he didn't get a victory for his trouble. It ended in a 9–9 tie called by darkness. His pitching opponent, Joe Oeschger, also went all the way.

In mid-May, Mamaux turned in a brilliant performance before finally coming apart. He vied with the Reds' Hod Eller through twelve scoreless innings at Ebbets Field, but then Cincinnati walloped him for ten runs in the thirteenth inning to win it, 10–0.

On the bright side, Sunday baseball had finally arrived. With everything perfectly legal, thanks to Jimmy Walker's efforts in the state legislature, there would be no more need for ruses like specially priced scorecards or charity band concerts. On May 4, the Dodgers played for the first time on a Sunday without Ebbets worrying he might spend the afternoon in jail. They celebrated by beating the Braves, 6–2.

The season ended with the Dodgers in fifth place, about where they usually finished. Pfeffer showed he hadn't left his stuff in the Navy, winning seventeen games, but Grimes had a sub-par season and Marquard did little. Wheat, with a .297 average, was the only real threat in the lineup.

The following spring the Dodgers played the most tortuous string of three games in baseball history: They plodded through fifty-eight innings without a single victory.

It started at Braves Field on Saturday, May 1, a chilly, overcast day, with only 3,000 fans on hand. Joe Oeschger, having been traded from the Phillies, took the mound for Boston, opposing Leon Cadore. Some 3 hours and 50 minutes later, Oeschger had shown that his twenty-inning stint against Brooklyn a year and a day earlier was no fluke. But Cadore was hardly faint-hearted either. Both went twenty-six innings, Oeschger blazing away with fastballs and allowing no hits over the final nine innings, Cadore frustrating the Braves with his change of pace. Finally, the umpires called it a 1–1 tie as darkness arrived.

Cadore was put to bed and the Dodgers grabbed a midnight train to Brooklyn. On Sunday, they went thirteen innings against the Phillies, losing 4–3, as Burleigh Grimes was bested by Columbia George Smith in another pair of complete-game efforts. On Monday, the Dodgers returned to Boston via another overnight train. This time they went nineteen innings, dropping a 2–1 game. Brooklyn's Sherry Smith and the Braves' Dana Fillingim turned in yet a third set of extraordinary route-going performances.

The three frustrating afternoons did not leave the Dodgers discouraged for long. They went on to stage a remarkable revival from the second-division finishes of the two previous seasons.

The pitching was outstanding, led by Grimes, baseball's finest spitballer, who went 23–11. The spitter had been outlawed early in the season, but Grimes did not have to dry up. The seventeen pitchers who were then throwing it—also among them Brooklyn's Clarence Mitchell, the majors' only left-handed spitballer—were allowed to continue wetting the ball for the remainder of their careers.

The batting order also showed new life, with Zach Wheat, Ed Konetchy and Hi Myers hitting over .300.

That left only poor Ivy Olson for the fans to pick on. The Dodger shortstop's habit of fumbling easy groundballs inspired torrents of booing. One day it got so bad that he was driven to stick wads of cotton in each ear.

"Brooklyn fans, particularly on a week day, foregather at Ebbets Field with two fell purposes in view," wrote F.C. Lane in *Baseball Magazine*. "One is to ride the ball players of the opposing team, which is more or less legitimate rooting. The other is to ring execration and vituperation on the hapless head of Ivan Olson."

When Ivy wasn't ignoring the fans by turning a deaf ear or two, he was dismissing them as ignorant. "I sometimes wonder how many games a spectator has to see before he learns something about baseball," he huffed.

Ivy's transgressions weren't severe enough to sidetrack the Dodgers that summer. Brooklyn swept to the pennant by seven games over the second-place Giants and drew a franchise-record 808,722 fans.

But the Dodgers were hardly the sensation of the season. The lively ball had been introduced in the American League in 1920—it would arrive in the National League the following year—and a national hero emerged. Babe Ruth, sold to the Yankees by the Red Sox after leading the league in homers with twenty-nine, slugged an unbelievable fifty-four home runs.

The Babe could not, however, carry the Yankees to the pennant single-handedly. The Cleveland Indians, led by their star center fielder and manager Tris Speaker, edged out the White Sox by two games and the Yankees by three.

Cleveland hung on despite being shaken by the only fatality in baseball history. On August 17, the submariner Carl Mays of the Yankees, pitching against the Indians at the Polo Grounds, struck the Cleveland shortstop, Ray Chapman, on the head with a fastball. Chapman collapsed, and at five A.M. the next day, he died.

As the 1920 season entered its final days, there was more shocking news. This time, the story would be too big for confinement to the sports pages. On September 27, the day the Dodgers clinched the pennant, the *Philadelphia North American* ran a front-page headline, "Gamblers Promised White Sox $100,000 to Lose." The next day, a grand jury in Chicago indicted eight White Sox players on charges of conspiring to throw the 1919 World Series to the Cincinnati Reds.

The scandal was a national sensation, and it came on the eve of another World Series. Now the Brooklyn District Attorney, Harry E. Lewis, garnered a few headlines for himself. The *New York Evening Sun* had cited rumors that the same clique of gamblers involved with the White Sox was trying to get the Dodgers to throw the 1920 Series. Lewis promptly announced he would summon all the Dodger players and Ebbets to his offices and ask them what they knew about another fix.

The district attorney asked the infielder Chuck Ward whether he would throw a game for $10,000.

"I wouldn't throw a game for my father," Ward shot back.

Ebbets professed faith in his players, declaring, "The boys of the Brooklyn baseball team are as clean-cut and as honest fellows as can be found anywhere in the world of athletics."

That may have been faint praise in view of the Chicago scandal unfolding, but after questioning the Dodger players, District Attorney Lewis pronounced them pure.

"My investigation has not disclosed a single suspicion that there has been any attempt to fix the coming Series," he announced.

Set for best of nine games, the World Series opened at Ebbets Field on Tuesday, October 5. Mayor John Hylan, carrying a Dodger pennant—his entrance heralded by the trumpets of a policemen's band—emerged from the center-field gate to march to the infield for the first-ball ceremony. The Dodgers, in pinstriped cream uniforms, went with Rube Marquard. The Indians, wearing mourning bands on the left sleeve of their visiting grays in memory of Ray Chapman, started the spitballing Stanley Coveleski.

Bundled in overcoats, a capacity crowd of 23,573 braved a chilly, windswept afternoon. Among the spectators was a poignant figure: Eddie Collins, the second baseman of the White Sox and a future Hall of Famer. One of the few first-line Chicago players uninvolved in the fix, Collins had gone earlier to the Indians' headquarters at the Pennsylvania Hotel in Manhattan to wish them luck. Spotted in the lobby, he had been congratulated by fans—for being honest. A few weeks back, Collins had envisioned playing in the World Series for a second straight October. Now he would sit and watch from the Ebbets Field stands.

Coveleski had little trouble with the Brooklyn hitters as the Indians

◆ *The 1920 pennant-winning Dodgers:* Top row (l. to r.): *Jack Sheridan, George Mohart, Ray Schmandt, Otto Miller, Rube Marquard, Bill Lamar, Leon Cadore, Burleigh Grimes, Johnny Miljus and Tommy Griffith.* Middle row (l. to r.): *Ernie Krueger, Pete Kilduff, Jimmy Johnston, Zach Wheat, Manager Wilbert Robinson, Hi Myers, Ed Konetchy, Sherry Smith and Ivy Olson.* Bottom row (l. to r.): *Bill McCabe, Zack Taylor, Bernie Neis, batboys Bennett and Cloude, Rowdy Elliott, Jack Sheehan and Clarence Mitchell. (Los Angeles Dodgers)*

won the opener, 3–1. But Grimes evened things in Game 2, yielding seven hits in spitballing his way to a 3–0 victory over Jim Bagby. The next afternoon—finally a warm, sunny day—Sherry Smith's southpaw curveballs frustrated the Indians as the Dodgers won again, 2–1. The fans had been subdued during the first two games, and speculation had it that the shock of the White Sox scandal had muted their enthusiasm. But perhaps they had simply been too cold to exert themselves. In Game 3, Ebbets Field came alive with the clamor of cowbells, foghorns and full-throated cheers.

Then the Series moved into Cleveland's League Park, and suddenly the Dodgers couldn't do anything.

Coveleski stopped Brooklyn, 5–1, on a five-hitter Saturday afternoon to even the Series at two games apiece.

Leon Cadore, the Dodger starter, lasted only an inning, but it was an even worse day for Rube Marquard. That morning, the Dodger lefty was arrested in the club's hotel lobby as a ticket-scalper. The police said he was overheard trying to sell eight box seats—original cost $52.80—for a total of $350. Marquard was released on his own recognizance pending a hearing set for the following Monday, and he even got into that afternoon's game, pitching three innings in relief. But an embarrassed Ebbets was steaming.

♦ *Rube Marquard, who in 1920 became the only man in major league history to be arrested for ticket scalping at the same World Series he pitched in. (National Baseball Library, Cooperstown, N.Y.)*

On Sunday, Grimes again opposed Bagby in what would be one of the most memorable games in World Series history.

In the opening inning, Elmer Smith, the Indian right fielder, hit the first bases-loaded home run in Series history, driving the ball over the right-field fence.

"Fate tried to conceal this lucky boy by naming him Smith, but with that tremendous slap, Elmer shoved his commonplace identity up alongside the famous Smiths of history, which include Captain John, the Smith Brothers, and the Village Smithy," chuckled the *Times*.

In the fourth inning, Bagby walloped a three-run homer off Grimes into the temporary seats in right-center field, the first home run ever hit by a pitcher in a Series game.

But a far more remarkable feat

◆ *Uncle Robbie with Tris Speaker, the Indians' star center fielder and manager, before the 1920 World Series. Black band on Speaker's sleeve is in memory of Ray Chapman, the Cleveland shortstop killed by a pitched ball the previous August. (National Baseball Library, Cooperstown, N.Y.)*

◆ *Indians' Bill Wambsganss tags Dodgers' Otto Miller to complete the only unassisted triple play in World Series history. (Los Angeles Dodgers)*

came moments later. Pete Kilduff, the Dodger second baseman, and Otto Miller, the catcher, led off the fifth with singles. With the Dodgers trailing by 7–0, Uncle Robbie let Clarence Mitchell, who had relieved Grimes, bat for himself. The hit-and-run was on, and Mitchell hit a liner toward center field. Bill Wambsganss, the second baseman, leaped and speared the ball one-handed. Kilduff was far down the line toward third and Miller was almost at second base. Wambsganss's momentum carried him toward second and he touched the bag. Then he tagged Miller and completed the only unassisted triple play in World Series history.

Joe Sewell, a future Hall of Famer who was playing shortstop that day, later claimed some credit for the rarity, recalling: "He turned around to throw the ball to first to double Miller—I should say triple Miller off— but I noticed Miller was just a few steps away from him, so I hollered, 'Tag him!' 'Tag him!' which Bill did."

Wambsganss, in reliving the play long afterward, remembered that "Otto Miller, from first base, was just standing there with his mouth open, no more than a few feet away from me. I simply took a step or two over and touched him lightly on the right shoulder."

His next time at the plate, Clarence Mitchell improved some: He hit into a mere double play.

The Indians went on to an 8–1 victory and moved two games away from taking the Series. Then Cleveland's Duster Mails, who had pitched briefly for the Dodgers in 1915 and '16, stopped them, 1–0, on a three-hitter in Game 6. In the process, he got revenge on Charlie Ebbets. Mails claimed that in his days at Ebbets Field, he liked to keep in shape by donning overalls, taking a brush in hand and helping the painters decorate the outfield walls. But when he had gone to Ebbets for some extra cash to reward his artwork, he was turned down. Now he had his payback.

The following afternoon, the Indians wrapped it up, 5 games to 2, as Coveleski stopped the Dodgers, 3–0, outpitching Grimes for his third World Series victory.

Marquard, who maintained he had only been joking in discussing the sale of his tickets to a fan, learned of his fate in court the day the Series ended. A municipal judge found the pitcher guilty of scalping, but merely fined him $1 and court costs, observing, "He has been punished enough by being written up more than any Presidential candidate."

But Ebbets promised further retribution, asserting, "Marquard will never again put on a Brooklyn uniform." He never did. Ebbets traded him to the Reds in December for Dutch Ruether, another left-hander.

Marquard was not the only Dodger to run afoul of the law during the Series. The other was that epitome of propriety—the Squire of Flatbush as the newspapermen called him—Charlie Ebbets himself. During Game 1, Ebbets had given out half-pint bottles of rye to the sportswriters to help them persevere amid the frosty weather. It was a kindly enough gesture, but quite illegal: Prohibition had arrived. One reporter hinted at the largesse in his story the next day. That brought out a troupe of Federal agents who prowled through the club's executive offices, looking for the booze. The Dodger owner had, however, been tipped off, and he hid the liquor in an attic.

Whether Ebbets eventually returned to the cache to drown away the sorrow of a second World Series defeat in five years is lost to history.

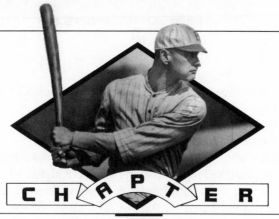

16

Dazzy Arrives,
Charlie Departs

The Dodgers couldn't stand prosperity. Just as the 1916 pennant-winners turned into a seventh-place club the following season, so the 1920 champions sank into the second division in '21.

At least the fans remained in high spirits as Umpire Cy Rigler was to learn. Still hanging in there after the Bill Dahlen fistfight of 1912 and the riotous Dodger-Cardinal game back in '16, Rigler was a target again at Ebbets Field one afternoon in late May.

The newest uproar came after Rigler ruled that Turner Barber, the Cubs' right fielder, had not trapped the ball when he turned in a somersault catch on a drive hit by Dodger pitcher Dutch Ruether with two on and two down. His "out" signal was a cue for the Dodger fans to unlimber their arms when the Cubs came to bat. Their pop-bottle barrage aimed at Rigler was so fierce that Zach Wheat momentarily took shelter from his outfield spot to avoid being beaned. The Cubs went on to win it, 6–4, in twelve innings and Rigler made a familiar exit: via police escort.

By that point in the season, the Dodger rooters were indeed frustrated. The club had launched an eleven-game winning streak in April, but was careening down to the .500 mark. Grimes went on to win twenty-two games and there were four .300 hitters—Wheat and Tommy Griffith in the outfield; Ray Schmandt, the first baseman, and Jimmy Johnston at third base—but the Dodgers wound up in fifth place.

The baseball spotlight shifted to the Polo Grounds, shared by the Giants and Yankees. McGraw's men won the National League pennant while the Yanks, with Ruth smashing fifty-nine homers, finally captured an American League title. In October, the first of three consecutive Subway Series was played.

As baseball recovered from what would be known as the Black Sox scandal, there was reform at the top. The ineffectual three-man National Commission, supposedly overseeing the game, was swept away, the owners anointing Kenesaw Mountain Landis as the first commissioner. The stern former Federal judge would rule baseball for two and a half decades.

When the ballplayers assembled for spring training in 1922, a new pitcher who could hardly be termed a fresh face was on the scene. The previous summer, Larry Sutton, doing some scouting for Ebbets in New Orleans, had recommended a powerfully built right-hander from Iowa named Clarence Arthur Vance. At age thirty, Vance did not seem a bright prospect. He had been knocking around the minors for three years after brief stints with the Yankees and Pirates, had suffered arm trouble and was plagued by wildness. But Ebbets was eager to get Vance's catcher, Hank DeBerry, and New Orleans insisted he pay for both of them or get neither. So the Dodgers bought Vance and DeBerry for $10,000.

At six feet two inches and 200 pounds, the blond, florid-faced Vance—to be known from then on as Dazzy—could throw the ball hard. He would rear back, kick his

◆ *Dazzy Vance shows his stuff. (Brooklyn Public Library-Brooklyn Collection)*

left foot high in the air, and deliver a devastating overhand fastball and outstanding curve. And he was wily. By slitting the sleeve of his white undershirt—causing the tattered cloth to flap as he wound up—he would make it doubly tough on batters to pick up the ball. Under Uncle Robbie, Vance conquered his wildness and arm trouble, winning eighteen games and losing twelve in his first year with Brooklyn. He would go on to lead the National League in strikeouts for his first seven seasons and win 197 games—all but seven for the Dodgers—en route to the Hall of Fame.

Hank DeBerry would never become a front-line player, but he remained Vance's favorite catcher and so would stick around with Brooklyn through the 20's.

Ebbets had extended himself financially to build the ballpark that bore his name, and he had just parted with $10,000 for the Vance-DeBerry duo, but he could not overcome a reputation for penny-pinching that the sportswriters reveled in.

When the Dodgers opened the 1922 season at the Polo Grounds with Mayor Hylan leading the traditional march to the flagpole, W.O. McGeehan told his *New York Herald* readers:

———

President Ebbets was in the parade but dropped a dime just before the band signaled the start of the procession, and the parade moved on while he was searching for it.

———

Ebbets didn't take the quip seriously, but fearing that some of the Brooklyn fans might, he protested to McGeehan. That brought the following retraction:

———

I was in error when I wrote that Squire Ebbets held up the Opening Day parade by searching for a dime he had dropped. The president of the Brooklyn club has informed me that the amount involved was fifteen cents.

———

The Dodgers were in the '22 pennant chase through early July, but then dropped eight straight. In August, there was some nastiness between Uncle Robbie and one of his pitching mainstays. Burleigh Grimes had been rocked by the Cincinnati Reds in a game at Ebbets Field. His first reaction was a barrage of invective at his infielders for waving at groundballs heading their way. Finally, in evident disgust at the prospect of being out in the sun any longer, he grooved a pitch to Jake Daubert, who belted it out of the park, climaxing a six-run inning. When Grimes got to the bench, he and Robbie exchanged choice words amid mutual finger-pointing.

Ebbets fined Grimes $200, suspended him and humiliated the pitcher with a public letter saying he would lift the ban when Grimes promised to "discontinue the use of insulting language" and "pitch as Manager Robinson advises." A few days later, Grimes was back, and he went on to win seventeen games to go with Vance's eighteen victories and Dutch Ruether's twenty-one. The Dodgers also had six .300 hitters. But somehow they managed to wind up in sixth place.

It didn't take long for Uncle Robbie's gang to set the tone for 1923. One day during spring training, the team went by bus to Lakeland, Florida, to play the Indians, only to find the Cleveland players relaxing on the veranda of their hotel. The game had been scheduled for the following day.

When the '23 season got under way, the Dodgers had a new first baseman who could hit like Jake Daubert. He was Jack Fournier, a left-handed batter who had been in the majors for a decade, most recently with the Cardinals. Fournier hit .351 with twenty-two homers in his first year as a Dodger.

Fine season that he had, Fournier was outdone by Zach Wheat, who at age thirty-six came through with a .375 average. And the pitching was decent with Grimes, Vance and Ruether again effective. But the Dodgers once more wound up in sixth place as the Giants won their third straight pennant.

If it wasn't much of a year for the Brooklyn ballclub, it was certainly a magnificent summer at Coney Island. The eighty-foot-wide Boardwalk opened, providing an almost two-mile wooden surface for strolling, watching the ocean from benches or getting a ride in wickerwork rolling chairs.

Four express subway lines—the Brighton, Sea Beach, West End and Culver routes—had finally linked Manhattan with Coney. The 1920's were, in fact, bringing a boom to much of Brooklyn. The subway system had been extended to the Flatbush and New Lots areas, and residential communities sprang up along their routes.

The 1924 season got off to a controversial start for Ebbets over that old issue of Sunday baseball. It had been legal for five years, but when the Dodgers scheduled their home opener with the Phillies for Easter Sunday, Protestant clergymen howled.

Ebbets went ahead with the game, declaring, "We are law-respecting and God-fearing people and won't do anything to offend the churches, but we doubt if the majority would regard the game on Easter as an offense against the Church."

Some 22,000 fans showed up on a rainy afternoon, but the usual opening day hoopla was dispensed with, apparently to appease the churchmen.

As the summer moved along, the Dodgers surprisingly found themselves in a pennant race for the first time since 1920, winning fifteen straight before dropping the second game of a doubleheader against the Braves on September 6. The next afternoon, a Sunday, the Giants came to Brooklyn, leading the league by a half game over the Dodgers. It was to be the most frenzied day in Ebbets Field's history.

The surrounding streets were packed as thousands of fans—a horde far beyond the park's capacity—tried to get inside. Many of those with reserved-seat tickets never made it through the gates while others forced their way in, far outnumbering the few dozen city policemen on hand. The center-field gate was broken open by a telephone pole used as a battering ram, the gate between the covered grandstand and open bleachers was torn from its hinges and the sliding doors to the rotunda were ripped open as fans stormed the turnstiles. Scores more leaped over the fences and the grandstand walls. The beleaguered Dodger management was forced to put up ropes stretching all the way across the field to pen in spectators standing on the grass. Eleven ground-rule doubles would be hit into the crowd.

The game was a thriller. The Giants took an 8–3 lead in the top of the eighth but the Dodgers stormed back with a run in the bottom of the inning and three more in the ninth, their last-ditch rally aided by the mob on the field. Eddie Brown, a Dodger outfielder, sent a fly ball to center. Hack Wilson retreated, then disappeared into the crowd. He emerged without the ball and claimed interference, but it was ruled a ground-rule double. The Giants held on, however, for an 8–7 victory as Dodger pitcher Dutch Ruether, strangely pinch-hitting for the shortstop, Jimmy Mitchell, struck out with two on to end the game.

The Dodgers stayed close, but the Giants clinched their fourth consecutive pennant on the final Saturday. Brooklyn finished in second place, a game and a half out.

The windup was disappointing, but Dodger fans finally had something to cheer about after three lackluster years. They showed their gratitude a few days before the season ended, turning out 30,000 strong for festivities at a National Guard armory. A band played "Sweet Rosie O'Grady," the Police Department glee club showed its stuff, and the players received gold watches, individually initialed, from the Brooklyn Chamber of Commerce.

Jack Fournier had a terrific season, leading the league in homers with 27, finishing second in r.b.i.'s with 116 and batting .334. Wheat hit .375, though it wasn't enough for the batting title, won by Rogers Hornsby with a .424 average. Vance was superb, leading the league in victories with a 28–6 mark, strikeouts with 262 and earned run average at 2.16. Grimes turned in twenty-two wins.

That year, a touch of nineteenth century Brooklyn passed from the scene when the Fulton Ferry, having long ago been rendered obsolete by the Brooklyn Bridge, made its final trip.

When springtime 1925 arrived, the man whose roots in Dodger baseball went back to the club's very first days—the spring of 1883 when the great bridge opened—was fading rapidly.

Charlie Ebbets had been suffering from heart troubles for several years, and his friends and doctors had advised him to cut back on his activities or to sell the team.

He would do neither. During the winter of 1924–25, Ebbets subjected himself to tiring railroad trips and the demands of speechmaking as he journeyed to major league and even minor league meetings around the country. The McKeever brothers offered to relieve him of his executive duties with the club, but he insisted he was strong enough for the annual contract battles with the players.

By the time Ebbets arrived at his off-season home in Clearwater, Florida—the site of the Dodgers' training camp—he was near collapse, and the warm weather would prove no help.

"When the end comes, I'd like to be out there in the grandstand, watching the game and hearing the cheering of the fans—that would be a fitting place to die," he once mused in a chat with Joe Vila of the *New York Sun*.

Not only would the end not come at a ballpark, but Charlie Ebbets's last days weren't even spent in Brooklyn.

Upon returning north with the ballclub in early April, Ebbets had taken to his bed at a suite he maintained in the Waldorf-Astoria. A few moments after six o'clock in the morning on Saturday, April 18, with his wife, Grace, and their children at the bedside, he died at age sixty-five. The senior club official in the National League, he had been with the Dodgers, from scorecard hawker to club president, for forty-two years.

Later that morning, the great names of Brooklyn baseball arrived at the Waldorf to pay their respects. Uncle Robbie was weeping as he entered an elevator to go up to the family quarters. Zach Wheat was there too along with Burleigh Grimes and Dazzy Vance.

They couldn't stay too long, for there was a ballgame that afternoon at Ebbets Field: the home opener against Ebbets's long-time rival, the Giants. The game would indeed go on, the Dodger players wearing mourning bands on their sleeves and joining with the Giants in a moment of silence at home plate before the first pitch. Shortly after five P.M., while the game was still in progress, the hearse carrying Ebbets's body passed by the ballpark he had built en route to the family's Flatbush home on Glenwood Road.

On Tuesday, the day of the funeral, all National League games were called off. The flags at the ballparks were dipped to half mast and would remain that way for thirty days.

Blanketed in violets and white sweet peas, the bronze coffin was taken from the Ebbets house on a cold, wet morning. After passing through a

◆ *Charlie Ebbets, the Squire of Flatbush. (Brooklyn Public Library-Brooklyn Collection)*

lane formed by the Dodger ballplayers, it was placed in a hearse, and the cortege wound its way around Ebbets Field and then past the site of the old Washington Park.

Long before the procession arrived at Holy Trinity Episcopal Church downtown, crowds had gathered in the area. Despite the foul weather, the onlookers massed for several blocks around the church in every direction. Scores more glanced down from the windows and roofs of office buildings.

At about two o'clock, the cortege arrived at the church, at Clinton and Montague streets. As the funeral party entered, the strains of Chopin's "Funeral March" were played by Shannon's band, a familiar presence at Ebbets Field and before that at Washington Park.

Some 2,000 people crowded into the church, from the baseball world and simply from Brooklyn. Commissioner Landis, Uncle Robbie and the sportswriters who covered the team served as honorary pallbearers.

There was no eulogy. The choir sang "Nearer My God to Thee" and a few other hymns, then it was on to Greenwood Cemetery.

Ebbets was buried about 700 feet from the grave of the Brooklyn sportswriter Henry Chadwick, another baseball pioneer.

Some years before, learning that the Chadwick grave had fallen into disrepair, Ebbets had persuaded the National League to vote funds for a monument at the site and for perpetual care.

Every April 20, the anniversary of Chadwick's death, Ebbets had come to the gravesite to place flowers. It was said that on one of those occasions, he had picked out the spot for his own grave. And now, on the crest of a hill, he was buried seventeen years and one day after Henry Chadwick was laid to rest.

Ebbets would be hailed in the sports columnists' eulogies as a man devoted to Brooklyn and to the larger interests of baseball as well. His often-cited remark "baseball is in its infancy"—greeted with ridicule when he made it back in the century's first decade—was recalled as evidence of his foresight.

Amid the plaudits, there was an issue to be confronted: the image of a tightwad. At Ebbets's death, his son, Charles, Jr., said his father had been a millionaire. Yet the ballclub had traditionally been reluctant to spend big money for a star.

The *Brooklyn Eagle* emphasized that Ebbets was a man of great charity despite what his detractors said. The paper noted that he had established a day each season at which hundreds of orphans were admitted free to Ebbets Field. That bit of good-heartedness did, however, have an unfortunate outcome, as the paper could not help but observe.

"He was obliged to give up his charity when the youngsters grew so unruly that they endangered their own safety," the *Eagle* lamented. "On one occasion one of them fell to the concrete floor, fractured his skull and died soon after. This put a stop to orphans' day."

W.O. McGeehan, the sportswriter who had indulged himself at Ebbets's expense a few years back with the tale about the dropped dime, now let the sentiment pour out.

———

Professional baseball will always owe much to the abiding faith of Charles H. Ebbets in the game, the kindly Squire who was misunderstood to the last.

The first game of baseball near New York was played on grounds known as the Elysian Fields. It is pleasantest to think of the Squire of Flatbush passing on to those other Elysian Fields, where the shades of some of the founders of the game are playing it for all eternity. There you will find Doubleday, the inventor of the game; Spalding, Chadwick, and all of the others who arrived before him.

They will welcome the Squire of Flatbush and take him into their spectral league, no doubt as president, as befits his understanding and dignity.

———

Upon Ebbets's death, sixty-six-year-old Ed McKeever took over the club presidency. He would not have it for long.

The Ebbets grave had been dug too narrowly to accept his oversized bronze coffin, so more spadework had to be done while the mourners stood around in the rain.

McKeever caught a cold from the long day in the wet and the chill, then developed influenza and finally suffered heart failure. Eleven days after Ebbets's funeral, Ed McKeever was dead as well.

Steve McKeever, the club's treasurer, was named acting head of the franchise. When the shareholders met in May, he sought the club presidency, but Ebbets's heirs—controlling 50 percent of the team—backed Wilbert Robinson for the post.

Uncle Robbie had suffered from pleurisy over the previous winter, and there had been rumors just the past January that he would be replaced as manager. But the Ebbets faction prevailed, and Robbie would have two jobs. On May 25, he was named club president to go along with the managing job.

Robbie named Zach Wheat as his assistant manager and picked Jack Fournier to succeed his star outfielder as captain. But Wheat's authority was never really clear. Some days Robinson would be on the bench, but often he would watch from the press box or grandstand. The essentially leaderless club was in second place during June, but then began to flounder.

September proved an eventful month. Dazzy Vance pitched a one-hitter at Philadelphia on September 8, winning by 1–0, then came back five days later at Ebbets Field to throw a no-hitter against the Phillies. That time, however, he didn't get a shutout. A double-error in left field by Jimmy Johnston in the second inning allowed a run to score, and Vance would end up with a 10–1 victory.

Fournier had another great year, hitting .350 with twenty-two homers, but in mid-September, while the team was in Pittsburgh, he announced he would quit baseball.

"The Brooklyn fans have hurled ugly epithets at me all season for the usual run of errors and for failing to do what they expected me to do," the first baseman complained. "I have been called vile names. Mrs. Fournier gave up attending games in Brooklyn some time ago because she could not stand the language that was hurled from the grandstands."

Fournier's anguish struck a sympathetic note among the fans. The next time he took the field in Brooklyn—a game against the Giants—his every move was cheered. He responded with a pair of singles to tie the game twice and then got a hit in a ninth-inning rally, bringing a 5–4 victory. The threat to retire would be forgotten.

But by then the Dodgers had given up hopes of challenging again for the pennant. Vance led the league in victories with a 22–9 mark and in strikeouts with 221, but Grimes fell to 12–19, and beyond those two, there wasn't much to the pitching. The club wound up in a sixth-place tie with the Phillies. The 1925 season proved disappointing for the Giants as well. After four straight titles, they settled for second place behind the Pirates.

John McGraw's fall from the top may have provided some glee in Brooklyn. But the deaths of Charlie Ebbets and Ed McKeever followed by the battle between ownership factions for control of the ballclub had made for a most unhappy year.

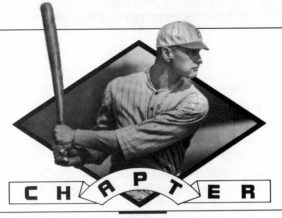

17

The Daffiness Boys

Uncle Robbie was not amused. The cartoon in the *New York Sun* twitting the Dodger brass went too far. So Robbie grabbed a telephone and let loose a tirade at one of the newspaper's top executives.

It was the most unfortunate phone call of his career. What began as a harmless drawing ended up with Wilbert Robinson, the president and manager of the Brooklyn ballclub, becoming a nonperson to the *Sun*'s readers and incurring the undying enmity of his rival for power, Steve McKeever.

The feud between Robinson and McKeever paralyzed operations. For years to come, the Dodgers would stumble along with castoffs and characters on the field and few signs of intelligent life in the executive offices.

In the words of newspaperman Westbrook Pegler, the era of "The Daffiness Boys" was born.

The *Sun* cartoon, drawn by Feg Murray and appearing in the editions of June 5, 1926, depicted several of Uncle Robbie's better-known ballplayers. Alongside their respective likenesses, the captions read: "Wheat is paid $16,000 a year," "Fournier draws down $15,000," "Vance gets over $15,800," and "Grimes, $15,000."

Next to a caricature of Jesse Petty, a left-handed pitcher in his second year with Brooklyn, Murray wrote: "Petty, who started the season off as the bright star of the Brooklyn club, but who doesn't begin to draw the pay that these other four get."

A gremlin-like character at the lower left observed, "Four out of five get big salaries."

Below the cartoon, Murray added:

If on the last April 12 you had broadcast the fact that Brooklyn would be leading the league when the season was a month old and that the great Dazzy Vance would still have his first victory of the season to look forward to and that he would not win one game in April or May, you would have immediately been tagged with the word cuckoo and sent off to some sanitarium.

Thanks to the sensational pitching of southpaw Jess Petty, and the two tall right-handed aces—McGraw and McWeeny— the Robins' pitching staff went on doing its stuff in spite of Vance's inability to get going. Petty became the first Robin of spring by pitching a one hit shutout game against the Giants on opening day. So far this year his sharp curves and control have been worth far more to the club than Vance's, yet you'll not notice Jess's name included among the quartet who draw the big salaries.

Next year he probably won't overlook such a petty detail.

An enraged Uncle Robbie phoned the *Sun*'s managing editor, Keets Speed, to bluster it was nobody's business how much money his players made.

The newspaper was hardly intimidated. It responded by running a "box" likening Robinson to the lowliest member of the ballclub. The item read:

THE BAT BOY'S SALARY

Wilbert Robinson of the Brooklyn baseball club called up THE SUN Monday to protest violently because the paper printed correctly the salaries paid to several Brooklyn players. He said maybe the salary of the bat boy would interest the public.

THE SUN doesn't care what Robinson earns.

That wasn't the end of it so far as Joe Vila, the *Sun*'s sports editor, was concerned. He ordered that Robinson's name never again appear in the paper's sports pages. Not only that, but the *Sun* would no longer call the team the Robins, the nickname commonly used in honor of Uncle Robbie. It would stick with the Dodger nickname.

On Tuesday, June 8, a headline in the *Sun* had read:

M'WEENY HURLS AGAINST SONGER
ROBINS AND PIRATES CONCLUDE SERIES TODAY

The editions of the following afternoon—the day the Vila order went out—carried the headline:

DODGERS DROP
A PEG IN RACE

Steve McKeever, already irked at being passed up for the club presidency in favor of Robinson, was furious at him for making the team a laughingstock and angering an important newspaper. The incident provided fuel for a feud that would grow more and more bitter over the years.

Things got so nasty that the president-manager of the ballclub became a man on the run. In order to get to his office at Ebbets Field, Robbie had to pass McKeever's big desk. Going through that area was an open invitation to a torrent of abuse. So Robbie would transact most of the team's business from the Ebbets Field clubhouse or the suite he kept at the St. George Hotel.

The *Sun,* as promised, was ignoring Robbie by name—he was the mysterious "manager of the Dodgers" in print—but it would not miss an opportunity to ridicule him. One day during the '26 season, Robinson told his players that for every mental miscue, they would have to contribute $10 toward a pot to be divided up after the season. That very afternoon, Robbie fouled up his batting rotation by not following the lineup card given to the umpire. The *Sun*'s Eddie Murphy wrote: "The manager of the Dodgers formed a Bonehead Club before yesterday's game and promptly elected himself a charter member."

The ultimate in bonehead plays came at Ebbets Field on August 15, 1926. It would spawn what became a well-worn gag:

First Fan: *"The Dodgers have three men on base."*
Second Fan: *"Which base?"*

The Dodgers were tied with the Boston Braves, 1–1, but had loaded the bases with one out in the seventh inning of a doubleheader opener. Chick Fewster, an infielder, was the runner at first base, Dazzy Vance was on second, and Hank DeBerry, Vance's catcher, was at third. George Mogridge, an aging lefty, was the pitcher. At the plate was a six-foot-four-inch left-handed batting rookie with blond hair, buck teeth and slumping shoulders giving him a distinctive ungainliness. His name was Floyd Caves Herman, but he called himself Babe. He was about to take a jaunt that would make him a legend.

The twenty-three-year-old Herman wasn't the only novice on the field for the Dodgers at that moment. Otto Miller, the former Brooklyn catcher who was the regular third-base coach, had decided to take a breather and had let Mickey O'Neil, a catcher, go on the coaching lines.

Mogridge delivered and Herman drove his pitch to right field. For a moment it appeared the ball would be caught, but it bounced off the wall. DeBerry scored easily. Vance, after holding up, came around the third-base bag and got halfway down the line to home plate. Fewster, having hesitated as well, rounded second base and headed for third. As Fewster approached the bag, right behind him was a speeding Babe Herman.

O'Neil shouted "back, back," meaning that Herman should retreat to second. Vance, possibly doubtful he could make it home and perhaps thinking that the fill-in coach was yelling at him, headed back toward third base.

Fewster took a few steps back toward second. Vance then slid into the third-base bag from the home-plate side while Herman, disregarding the coach's shouting, came sliding in from the second-base side. A totally confused Fewster then scampered to third. The Dodgers now had three men on a single base.

The Boston third baseman, Eddie Taylor, got the baseball after it had been thrown to the plate. He tagged Vance and Herman but missed Fewster. As the lead runner, Vance was entitled to third base so the tag meant nothing. Herman was actually already out for passing Fewster on the basepaths. So at this point, one out had legitimately been made on the play, meaning there were two men down in the inning.

Now Fewster, assuming a double play had been made to end the inning (two men had been tagged), started for his spot as the second baseman when he should have tried to make it back to the second-base bag. Doc Gatreau, the Braves' second baseman, called for the ball and set out after Fewster. Finally realizing he was fair game, Fewster ran into right field, but Gatreau caught up with him and tagged him on top of the head.

So Herman had, in effect, doubled into a double play. Understandably overlooked in the folklore born that day was the fact that DeBerry scored what would be the winning run, the Dodgers taking the game by 4–1.

That play—and Babe Herman himself—would symbolize the age of "The Daffiness Boys."

Babe defended his baserunning years later by pointing a finger at fellow miscreants in an interview with J.G. Taylor Spink of the *Sporting News*.

"I knew I made my share of skulls, but I wasn't as bad as they said," Herman maintained. "I remember one time I was on first when Glenn Wright hit a ball that I was afraid was going to be caught alongside our wall at Ebbets Field. I stood halfway between first and second and Wright charged past me. Hell, he wouldn't have had to run at all if it went over. Well, it went over, all right. I said to him, 'Hey, Capt., what's your hurry' as he charged past me. He was out for passing me on the bases, and who was blamed? Old Babe, of course."

"The next week the same thing happened again," Herman went on, "but this time Del Bissonette was the hitter. I stuck out my hand to stop him as he charged past me on a high fly near the right field wall, but he brushed me off and ran on. He was out, and I was blamed again."

Both boners came in 1930, and the details are pretty much the way Herman remembered them. The incident involving Bissonette actually came first, on Memorial Day. He hit a ball over the fence, then passed Herman after Babe had held up, fearing the drive would be caught. The second gaffe came after Wright hit a ball that bounced into the wooden bleachers in left-center field.

Herman grew up in southern California, supposedly getting his nickname early on by touting himself as the Babe Ruth of the Imperial Valley. He flunked chances with the Tigers and Red Sox and knocked around the minors for five years, then was bought by the Dodgers from the Minneapolis team. When first baseman Jack Fournier suffered a severe ankle injury, Herman got his chance. He played first base for a while, proved to be a terrific hitter, then was moved to the outfield, where further adventures were to come.

The three-men-on-a-base snafu provided Babe Herman with his main claim to immortality. But the litany of his misadventures also includes his being hit on the head trying to catch a fly ball.

There's no proof it ever happened. But one day during the 1928 season, Herman was removed late in a game at Ebbets Field. A ballplayer named Al Tyson took his place in right field. Tyson lost a line drive in the sun and it landed on top of his head and bounced to the wall. Herman, nowhere near the scene of the crime, would come to be blamed.

According to an often-told story, Herman made it clear to the sportswriters that if a fly ball ever hit him on the head, he'd quit.

"How about on the shoulders?" he was asked.

"On the shoulders don't count."

In a *Collier's* profile titled "The Great Hoiman," Kyle S. Crichton described the quintessential scene when a fly ball came Babe's way:

―――――

It was an even bet that Babe would either catch it or get killed by it. His general practice was to run up when the ball was hit and then turn and run back and then circle about uncertainly. All this time the ball was descending, the spectators were petrified with fear and Mr. Herman was chewing gum, unconcerned. At the proper moment he stuck out his glove. If he found the ball there, he was greatly surprised and very happy.

―――――

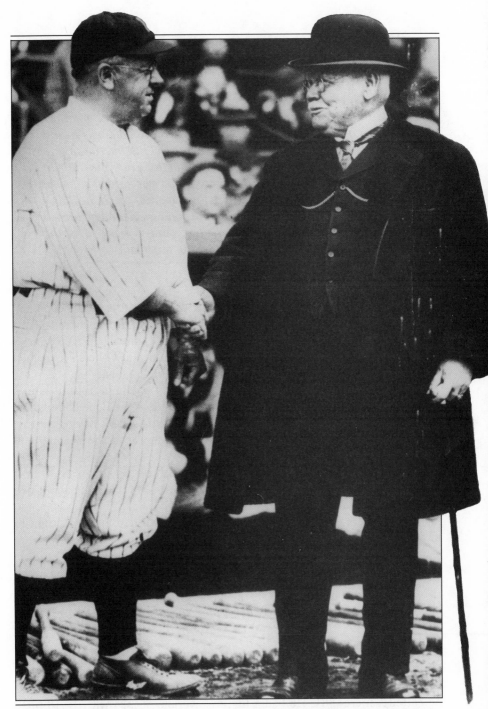

♦ *Wilbert Robinson and Steve McKeever take a break from their monumental feud.*
(Los Angeles Dodgers)

Al Lopez, then a young catcher, was Herman's teammate for a couple of seasons. Recalling those years one morning from his home in Tampa, Lopez maintained that Babe was not as bad an outfielder as legend has it.

He got a bad rap on that. He came up as a first baseman. In the spring of '28, the year I reported there, Robbie was trying to make him an outfielder because he had Del Bissonette coming up, who had a tremendous year at Buffalo. They put him in right field, and he was new out there. Babe was kind of a gawky guy, all legs and arms, and even making a great catch, he didn't look good. But he had a good arm and good speed and he turned out to be a damn good right fielder. And right field is the toughest position in the outfield to play, especially in Brooklyn with that wall.

But the legend of Babe Herman extends beyond the ballfield.

There was the time Babe supposedly took a lighted cigar out of his pocket. "Well, just the tip of it was lit," he later claimed.

And what about the day he left his son stranded at Ebbets Field when he hurriedly left to visit his wife, who was having a baby?

"The story about my leaving my oldest boy at the park until late at night because I forgot him, that was all wrong, too," the Babe complained in that interview with the *Sporting News.* "My wife wasn't having a baby. Our second boy had a mastoid operation, and she was at the hospital and I was rushing there."

But had he forgotten to take the child with him?

"Well, yes. But I remembered him as soon as we had gone about two and a half blocks."

Then there was the story that, in the words of Red Smith, "ought to be true":

Woman meeting Babe wearing white linen suit: *"Oh, Mr. Herman, you look so cool."*

Babe, gallantly: *"You don't look so hot yourself, ma'am."*

But there was no joking about Herman's hitting. In 1930, he set six Dodger records while batting .393 (Bill Terry of the Giants won the league batting title at .401) with 241 hits, 94 for extra bases. The season before he batted a mere .381. He had a lifetime average of .324 with 1,818 hits.

Image aside, Babe was nobody's fool. He was a tough negotiator at contract time, went on to run a ranch in Glendale, California, and his family was hardly uncultured. Babe's son Robert became the assistant to Rudolf Bing at the New York Metropolitan Opera and later a major figure in the Miami performing arts world.

The year of Herman's arrival, change was in the air at the Brooklyn ballclub. Max Carey, a star outfielder and superb baserunner for many seasons with the Pirates, was purchased in August. Carey was thirty-six years old and near the end as a ballplayer, but rumor had him as the next Dodger manager if Steve McKeever ever succeeded in dumping Uncle Robbie.

Soon after the Dodgers finished the '26 season in sixth place, seventeen and a half games behind the pennant-winning Cardinals, three fixtures were gone from Ebbets Field.

Zach Wheat, hampered by a pulled leg muscle suffered while running out a home run, was released. He signed on with the Athletics, then called it a career a year later.

Uncle Robbie, who had been having his problems getting along with Burleigh Grimes, now vowed to be rid of him. Since Grimes wasn't nearly washed up, Robbie certainly did not want to see him spitballing the Dodgers in a Giant uniform. So, a week after dropping Wheat, he dealt Grimes to the Phillies for a catcher named Butch Henline. The very next day, Philadelphia made Robbie look like a dunce by sending Grimes to the Polo Grounds in a four-player deal.

Another familiar face departing after the '26 season was Jack Fournier. The first baseman was released, then caught on with the Braves for one year before retiring.

For baseball, 1927 is the year of Babe Ruth's sixty home runs. For the rest of mankind, it is remembered for Charles Lindbergh's solo flight across the Atlantic. The Dodgers had more modest achievements, and yet 1927 brought not a little satisfaction for them.

In a sensational deal, the Giants had obtained the Cardinals' Rogers Hornsby, one of the greatest right-handed batters ever, in return for Frankie Frisch. And they got a fine season from Burleigh Grimes, who would win nineteen games. On September 25, they came into Ebbets Field battling for the pennant with the Pirates. The Dodgers were headed for a sixth-place finish, but now they were inspired. With Jesse Petty pitching before a packed house, Brooklyn played the Giants to a 0–0 tie in a game called by darkness after seven innings. A week later, in the makeup game, Dazzy Vance beat McGraw's men, 10–5, and eliminated them.

The Dodgers bested the Giants in an off-the-field maneuver that year as well.

The machinations centered on Overton Tremper, a Brooklyn boy who, after graduating from Erasmus Hall High School, became a fine outfielder at the University of Pennsylvania. McGraw thought he had Tremper all but delivered upon graduation, but then Brooklyn took him away.

Many years later, living in Clearwater, Florida, and retired from a career as a secondary school administrator, Tremper recalled what happened:

Back in my junior year, there was a man named Howard Berry, who was a scout for the Giants. He lived in Philadelphia. I had a good year. They were gonna take me up to the Polo Grounds for the summer. I'd work out in the morning and sell tickets in the afternoon for fifty or a hundred bucks a week. But toward the end of the spring I had a bad slump so they canceled out on me, which left me a little bitter. I went down to the shore and played under another name.

The next year I had a swell spring and that's the year the Giants paid me a hundred bucks a month for the first chance at signing me—the first offer. I'd been getting a hundred dollars a month from Howard. In May, the Dodgers offered me $6,000 to sign, so I told Howard, and he said, "Get it in writing." Well, you couldn't get something in writing because it was during the school year, it would jeopardize your amateur standing.

Skeptical that Tremper really had a bid from the Dodgers, the Giants waited.

"As a consequence, I never, to this day, received an offer or a contract from the Giants," Tremper went on. "I signed with Brooklyn for an $8,000 bonus. McGraw hadn't registered me with the National League in any way so I was free to do what I wanted. He was just covering me up. McGraw spilled the beans about what happened and it got in the papers."

Tremper joined the Dodgers in June 1927, then repaid the undercover money the Giants had given him, with interest.

The Dodgers got their man, but he never fulfilled expectations. Tremper played in a handful of games in 1927 and '28, then was sent to the Macon, Georgia, farm club. He never made it back to the majors.

Playing for Uncle Robbie presented quite a contrast to what Tremper might have encountered under the hard-driving McGraw.

"Robbie would spend his days arguing with the cabmen over the dugout—what plays to make, whether to bunt or hit. He'd poke his head over the top and they'd banter back and forth. It was a free and easy lifestyle.

"I enjoyed playing for him. He was nice, agreeable. It was very laissez faire—you'd do what you want."

Tremper recalled that except for Jay Partridge, the second baseman, he was the only college man on the team. He didn't encounter any razzing from his less learned teammates, but didn't get any special help either.

"I was twenty-one, I just kept my mouth shut," he explained. "Dazzy Vance and a lot of the older fellas were all very friendly, but there was no desire to show you anything or help you do anything. You were just on your own."

By the time Tremper joined the Dodgers, he had already encountered hazing—under the directive of a fellow collegian who would eventually make quite a name for himself in Brooklyn and points west.

"Walter O'Malley was a classmate of mine at Penn," Tremper noted. "He was an operator back then in college, a political man. He was a year ahead of me. He was the head of the sophomore vigilance committee. I was a freshman and happened to come up before him because I didn't wear my beanie cap one time. You were supposed to wear it all the time. I proceeded to get paddled by the committee."

With the Tremper dispute having blown over, the Dodgers conducted business as usual in 1928, finishing sixth for the fourth year in a row.

The Dodgers may not have been flourishing, but downtown Brooklyn certainly was booming in the late 20's. The Brooklyn Paramount and Fabian's Fox movie palaces opened their doors in 1928 with stage shows and top films. A year later, the Williamsburgh Savings Bank building arose, its 512-foot tower making it the tallest building in Brooklyn.

While the team was getting no better, the squabbling between Steve McKeever and Uncle Robbie grew worse.

Robinson had been given a new three-year contract as manager at the end of the 1926 season by Joe Gilleaudeau, a son-in-law of Charlie Ebbets and representative of the Ebbets heirs. McKeever was seriously ill then. By the time he recovered, the deed had been done.

In August '28, McKeever began grousing in public about Robinson. Soon after the season ended, Robbie told newspapermen he might give up the managing job while staying on as club president and building up the scouting system, which had a grand total of two employees. Robbie observed that Max Carey, the club's captain for the past two years, might be a good choice as his successor, and he envisioned quitting as manager at the board of directors' meeting in December.

The session was scheduled for the morning of December 11, but it never came off. McKeever and Frank York, a club director allied with him, wanted the showdown to be held at the club's Ebbets Field offices. But Robbie ensconced himself at the Waldorf-Astoria, where the National League meetings were being held, and refused to budge. Since he still had the backing of the Ebbets heirs, there was nothing McKeever could do.

The Dodgers had five .300 hitters in 1929, but Vance was fading a bit

◆ *Babe Herman admires Hack Wilson's woodwork in August 1930. Hack would hit 56 homers for the Cubs that season, then find himself in a Dodger uniform two years later. By then, Herman would be with Cincinnati. (National Baseball Library, Cooperstown, N.Y.)*

and failed to lead the league in strikeouts for the first time since joining the club in 1922. Watty Clark, a left-hander in his third season with the ballclub, was the workhorse, pitching a league-leading 279 innings with a 16–19 mark.

On May 17, a right-hander named Alex Ferguson who had been kicking around the majors since 1918 arrived in Brooklyn, another in a long line of retreads. Ferguson's teammates celebrated his debut by making four errors against the Phillies in the first inning at Baker Bowl. It was to be that kind of year once again. But the Dodgers were at least consistent. For the fifth straight season, they finished in sixth place.

By December '29, with the feuding in the Dodger hierarchy turning the franchise into a joke, baseball's power structure tried for a peace treaty.

John Heydler, the National League president, persuaded the four directors—Joe Gilleaudeau and Wilbert Robinson on one side and Steve McKeever and Frank York on the other—to sit down with Commissioner Landis at his suite in Manhattan's Roosevelt Hotel where the two leagues were holding their annual meetings.

Half an hour after the session began, Landis emerged mopping his brow. "In all my experience on earth I've never seen anything like it," he told reporters. After a break, he went back inside. A few minutes later, the four directors emerged, one by one, and it was clear that Landis had gotten nowhere.

The next day, Uncle Robbie returned to his winter home at the Dover Hall hunting preserve in Georgia. Asked "How is the big fight coming along?" he playfully poked the writers and responded: "Fight—what fight? Do I look like a fighting man?"

Robinson's contract as manager and Dodger president was to run out on January 1. It was understood that if the deadlock continued, he would remain as president under the club constitution. But no one knew if he could stay as manager. It was, in short, a mess.

Finally, Heydler and the National League clubowners worked out a way to keep the franchise functioning. In February 1930, at the league's meeting in Manhattan's Hotel Commodore, the warring sides agreed that Robbie would get a two-year contract as manager but would step down as club president. Joe Gilleaudeau, Robbie's chief supporter, would stay on as a director and would name another director to replace Robbie on the board.

Heydler then appointed Frank York, the club director allied with Steve McKeever, as Dodger president. A Manhattan attorney, York had roots in the Brooklyn franchise. His father, Bernard York, had been Charlie Ebbets's lawyer and had arranged for the secretive purchase of land to build Ebbets Field. The York law firm had been handling the club's legal work for decades.

Heydler also got both sides to accept a fifth director whose vote would break the inevitable deadlocks. He selected Walter F. (Dutch) Carter, a lifelong Brooklyn resident and a star pitcher at Yale in the 1890's who happened to be the brother-in-law and former law partner of the newly appointed Chief Justice of the United States, Charles Evans Hughes.

Chubby, red-cheeked Steve McKeever, now seventy-one years old, would remain as treasurer. He could continue to sit in his big chair in the last row of the grandstand, a glass of milk beside him and, in back of his perch, a cabinet with locked glass doors containing his prized possessions: rows of battered baseballs from the era after the Civil War, passed on by the departed owner of a Brooklyn saloon. He would once again be calling out "Hello, Judge" to all he met, ask his familiar "How's yer heart?" and be greeted as Judge in return.

The franchise had survived. But with York—a lawyer who knew little baseball—theoretically running the club, McKeever lazing away the afternoons with his cronies, and Robbie stripped of half his authority, it seemed that 1930 would be yet another year of bumbling. Surprises were, however, about to be sprung.

The Dodgers would once again have five .300 hitters in the starting lineup, led by Babe Herman's .393, and they finally had a fine shortstop in Glenn Wright. After many outstanding seasons with the Pirates, Wright had been traded to Brooklyn in 1929. He was a disappointment his first year at Ebbets Field, getting into only twenty-four games because of a sore shoulder. But he had an operation in the off-season, was able to throw again and batted .321 in 1930.

Al Lopez, who would eventually set a major league record for games caught, took over the catching at age twenty-one and went on to hit .309.

Lopez had been up briefly in 1928 while still in his teens. Some sixty years later, he recalled how he was literally measured against the veteran catcher Hank DeBerry before he could convince Uncle Robbie that he had enough size to stand up to the rigors of big league ball.

"He liked big guys that could throw hard," Lopez explained. "He didn't like the little fellas. We had a guy named Watson Clark, a left-hander. He weighed about one eighty, he was about six foot one, but he was kind of bowlegged. He looked smaller than he was. Robbie thought he was going to be too small. But Watty turned out to be a good pitcher.

"He thought I was going to be too small also when I first came to spring training in '28 in Clearwater. He wondered, who in the hell brought that kid? I was only eighteen or nineteen at the time. I weighed 155 pounds. Finally, he called DeBerry over. He said, 'Hey Hank, get next to this kid. I wanna see how big he is.' I didn't know what it was all about. Finally, he said, 'You're gonna be all right.' "

DeBerry, it turned out, was the same height as Lopez, though he had forty pounds on him.

By 1930, when Lopez was ready for the starting lineup, the Dodgers were finally making a run for the pennant again with their corps of .300 hitters and some good pitchers. Ray Phelps, a sidearmer, and Dolf Luque, who came over from the Reds at age thirty-nine, bolstered the pitching. Luque, a Cuban, teamed up with Lopez, a Floridian, to form what was said to be the major leagues' first Spanish-speaking battery.

Dazzy Vance won seventeen games with a league-leading 2.61 earned run average after suffering the season before from what was reported to be neuritis and sciatica. His turnaround was publicized for all of America by the national magazine *Literary Digest*, which marveled at the club's revival in a July article titled "What Makes the Robins Soar?" The magazine quoted the *New York Evening World*'s Forrest Cain, who observed that "the waving, tattered sleeve of Vance for years has been the symbol of Robin fortunes. It means to the Robins what the white plume of Henry of Navarre meant to the hosts of France. Now he is in splendid shape again."

The Dodgers were atop the league for most of June and July and held an edge of three and a half games on August 8. But they couldn't quite make it, fading in late September to fourth place, six games behind the pennant-winning Cardinals.

"We had a couple of injuries," Lopez remembered. "Johnny Frederick in center field came up with a torn muscle. Rube Bressler came up with a broken finger. Neither of them could play."

Still, the 1930 season had been a huge success, not only on the field but at the box office. Though the stock market had crashed in October '29, home attendance went over the one-million mark for the first time.

The team had done so well at the gate that a little generosity was in the offing. Following his fine season, Lopez never asked for a raise, but he got one nonetheless.

"I had a pretty good year, I hit over .300," he noted, "but I didn't go up to the office. I didn't know about things like that. At the end of the year, they gave me a bonus. And they doubled my salary from the first year to the second year."

Presumably expecting the ballclub would remain good enough to keep the customers coming, what passed for Dodger management now set out to enlarge Ebbets Field. In mid-February 1931, Steve McKeever, spade in hand and three-year-old grandson in tow, broke ground for an extension of the double-deck grandstand. The concrete bleachers down the left-field line and the wooden seats beyond the left-field fence would be gone by 1932, replaced by a grandstand wrapping around the entire ballpark except for right field, where heavily traveled Bedford Avenue proved a barrier to construction work.

Then Uncle Robbie started off the '31 season like old times. In the words of the *Brooklyn Eagle*'s Tommy Holmes, the Dodgers opened up in Boston "impersonating nine or more Marx Brothers."

After the club lost the opener to the Braves, Robbie lost his way in the batting order.

Alta Cohen, a rookie outfielder awaiting banishment to the Hartford farm club later in the week, got into the second game of the season as a replacement for Ike Boone who in turn had replaced Babe Herman in right field. Robbie had taken the Babe out for dropping a fly ball he claimed to have lost in the sun.

A pitching change was made as well, and now Robbie was thoroughly confused amid a double switch. Cohen batted in the No. 3 spot when he should have been No. 9 in the order. He hit a single. The Braves didn't realize at first that Cohen had batted out of turn so the hit stood, and when they finally caught on, he was switched to the No. 9 spot. He hit another single before bouncing into a double play and was terrific in the outfield, making a fine catch and two great throws in a 9–3 loss. After the game, Robbie allowed as how Cohen would stay with the club after all. But his debut also proved his farewell for the season: He was kept around for three weeks but then was dispatched to the minors and didn't play another game for Brooklyn all year.

The Dodgers lost their first five, then rallied in midsummer but fell back to finish in fourth place as the Cardinals won another pennant. The only new face who helped was outfielder Lefty O'Doul, picked up in a trade with the Phillies after hitting .398 and .383. O'Doul batted .336 for Brooklyn, but Babe Herman dropped from .393 to .313 and Glenn Wright was hobbled by an ankle injury. Uncle Robbie outdid himself in picking up pitching castoffs by getting spitballer Jack Quinn, at age forty-seven the oldest player in the game and an alumnus of the 1909 Yankees. On the debit side, Robbie also came up with Clyde (Pea Ridge) Day of Pea Ridge, Arkansas, whose main claim to fame was his hog-calling from the mound. Robbie coaxed some more life out of Quinn, who—in a statistic figured out retroactively—led the league in saves with fifteen. Day did little beyond the bellowing.

On October 23, 1931, the Dodger directors held a long meeting at Ebbets Field. When it was over, so was the era of Uncle Robbie. Having been forced to step down previously as club president after his drawn-out battle with Steve McKeever, he now was fired—by unanimous vote, it was said—after eighteen seasons as manager. The job went to Max Carey, whom Robbie had suggested as his successor a few years back before deciding he couldn't be dispensed with.

Robbie had had his triumphs in Brooklyn. He won pennants in 1916 and 1920 and battled John McGraw's Giants—a far better team most of the time—on almost even terms with a record of 190 victories and 197 losses. And he could get something out of a pitcher when many another manager wouldn't even try. If he was often the butt of a joke, well, so were many of his fellow Brooklynites.

In announcing the firing, the Dodger directors issued a statement extending to Robbie "wishes for his health and happiness," and they dispatched a telegram to his winter home near Brunswick, Georgia, to give him the news. But the reporters got to Robbie's Dover Hall hunting preserve before the telegram did. He said he was surprised, hadn't even known the board was meeting. "If the directors want Carey as manager it's all right with me," was about all he was willing to say that day.

The forty-one-year-old Carey, an Indiana native whose real name was Maximilian Carnarius, had studied for the Lutheran ministry at Concordia

College in Missouri, then turned to baseball. Breaking into the majors with the Pirates in 1911 at age twenty-one, he went on to become a fine outfielder and hitter and a super baserunner, winning the National League base-stealing title ten times. After finishing out his career with the Dodgers in 1929, he had taken a coaching job with the Pirates, then had gone into private business in St. Louis in 1931.

Carey might have put quite a personal stamp on the team if the *Eagle*'s Tommy Holmes had had his way. The ballclub couldn't very well be called the Robins anymore with Uncle Robbie gone. Since the new manager's real name was Carnarius, Holmes figured why not the Brooklyn Canaries? Instead, the other newspapers joined the *New York Sun* in reviving the Dodger nickname. The association with birds would linger, however, with the tabloid press occasionally calling the team The Flock into the 1950's.

Carey quickly brought in Casey Stengel, who had been his teammate on the Pirates in 1918 and '19. Casey had just been dropped after six years as manager of the American Association's Toledo Mud Hens. Now he would be a Dodger coach, but really the assistant manager.

When the Dodger players showed up for spring training '32, they would encounter a sharp change in the dugout.

Instead of trying to out-think the opposing manager, Robbie had let his men play their own game.

As the *New York Times* columnist John Kieran put it: "He knew baseball as the spotted setter knows the secrets of quail hunting, by instinct and experience."

Carey, by contrast, was a practitioner of "inside baseball"—brainy play, lots of speed and bunting. A serious student of baseball techniques, he wanted to be a teacher.

After eighteen years of laissez-faire rule by Uncle Robbie, could the Dodger organization now produce players who knew they had something to learn?

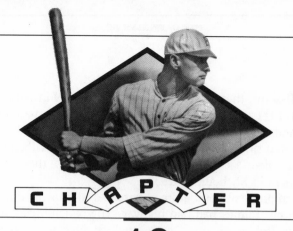

18

Max Carey
Meets His Match

The era of "The Daffiness Boys" was surely over. Not only had Uncle Robbie been sacked, but Babe Herman—his accomplice in entertaining and exasperating the Dodger fans—was finished in Flatbush as well by the time the 1932 season got under way.

Herman had balked over a salary cut from $19,000 to $15,000 and had refused to report to the Clearwater, Florida, spring-training camp. While he was sulking at home in southern California, the Dodgers got rid of him. The Babe was sent to the Cincinnati Reds along with Ernie Lombardi, a young catcher who would become a terrific hitter, and Wally Gilbert, Brooklyn's starting third baseman for the three previous seasons. The Dodgers got a pair of infielders, Joe Stripp and Tony Cuccinello, and a catcher, Clyde Sukeforth.

Max Carey figured the Dodgers could dispense with Herman since they had acquired one of baseball's greatest power hitters. Back in February, they paid the Cardinals $45,000 to get Hack Wilson, who had come to St. Louis from the Cubs in a trade a few weeks earlier. Just five feet six inches tall, but 190 pounds with a powerful torso, Wilson had slugged fifty-six homers—a National League record—in 1930. He tailed off to thirteen home runs the following season, but the Dodgers gambled on his revival.

Wilson had an outstanding though not spectacular '32 season for Brooklyn: 23 homers, 123 runs batted in and a .297 average. His outfield mate Lefty O'Doul led the league in batting with a .368 average, and Johnny Frederick delivered six pinch-hit homers, a major league record. As for the pitching, Watty Clark had his best season with a 20–12 mark, but Dazzy Vance, in the twilight of his career, went just 12–11. A twenty-year-old rookie right-hander from South Carolina with a blazing fastball and the intriguing name of Van Lingle Mungo showed promise of becoming a star, posting a 13–11 record.

The ballclub spent most of the summer around the middle of the pack, then finished strongly to wind up in third place, nine games behind pennant-winning Chicago.

◆ *Max Carey, successor to the easygoing Wilbert Robinson,* *will find that the no-nonsense approach to running the Dodgers doesn't work either. (National Baseball Library, Cooperstown, N.Y.)*

Joe Stripp, replacing Wally Gilbert at third base and filling in at first base for an injured Del Bissonette, was the key man for Brooklyn in the Herman deal. He would give the Dodgers a dependable bat during the 1930's, hitting .303 for the '32 season and then having three more .300-plus years before being dealt to the Cardinals.

Like Babe Herman, "Jersey Joe" Stripp—he was from Harrison, New Jersey—wasn't shy about voicing salary demands. But with the Depression cutting into attendance and, in some cases, bringing ruin to a ballclub owner, the battles were especially tough.

A half-century later, living in retirement in Orlando, Florida, Stripp would recall the struggles of a Depression-era ballplayer, first in Cincinnati and then in Brooklyn.

———

The Reds' owner, Sidney Weil, had made a barrel of money. He had big garages, he owned everything in Cincinnati.

It doesn't seem fair like almost in a week's time a guy can get wiped out, but that's what happened to Sidney. They tell me he lost over $30 million in the market.

So before the '32 season, he wanted to cut my salary. I said, "I hit .324, what do you want to take money from me for?" And he said, "I don't have any money. I lost it all in the stock market. I'm broke." The receivers had control of the club, and later the radio people, Crosley, took over.

I said, "I hate like hell to say this to you, Sidney, but I want off the ballclub." So they got rid of me.

Anyway, I went to Brooklyn, and they were always trying to cut me there. Every year it used to be the same thing: I'd hit .300 or better, and instead of giving me a raise, they'd want to cut me $2,000 or $3,000. They'd say, "Well, what are you going to do?" I'd say, "You don't want to give me the money, I'll stay out of baseball." Of course, I didn't have any intention of staying out. I had to work like hell to get the money I did.

One reason I held out was I knew I was in good condition. I thought, why the hell do I have to go to spring training where we used to work out four or five hours a day? Why did I have to suffer because of the guys that drank a lot of beer and came down with big pot bellies? I was living in Orlando then, and I liked to go fishing and enjoy myself. I figured I'd join the ballclub the day they left Florida, and I'd be in as good condition as the fellas that were there.

———

Stripp recalled the contract battle before his second season in Brooklyn:

——

In March '33, Joe Gilleaudeau, the Brooklyn vice president, calls me and says, "Joe, if you don't come down here, how are we gonna talk? Why don't you come down to Miami?"

So I went down there. The Miami Biltmore was the hotel we stayed at, but we had no right to be at that hotel. It was all millionaires there. I reported to him, and he said, "Well, let's have breakfast together." The breakfast was $18, and then he put a $10 tip down.

He finally raised the offer a couple of thousand dollars, but I said, "I gotta have more money than that," and we couldn't get together. I could drive home to Orlando in about three hours, so I said, "I'm just gonna go back home." I said, "I'm not paying this big hotel bill." I think it was about a-hundred-odd-dollars a day. Hack Wilson had held out, and they made him pay his own bill. I told all the newspapermen I was gonna leave, that they only wanted to give me a $2,000 raise. They said, "What does that make your salary?" I said, "A lousy $15,000. It ain't worth it for me. I'm a better ballplayer than that." I named a few of the guys that I felt were getting more money than me—and I found out later that I was getting more than they were. So I came home and we dealt over the telephone.

——

Just as an era had ended in Brooklyn with the firing of Wilbert Robinson, so too would a fixture depart from the Polo Grounds. John McGraw, suffering from a prostate condition, had been forced to leave the Giants during their first Western trip of the '32 season. His doctor told him he would have to limit himself to managing the club at home games. That was unacceptable. On Friday, June 3, the Giant game with the Phillies at the Polo Grounds was rained out. But there would be big news that day. The man who had brought the Giants ten pennants since rescuing the franchise from oblivion in 1903 announced his retirement. Bill Terry, McGraw's star first baseman, took over.

Soon after the season ended, the Dodgers' old man became their new president. Steve McKeever, fast approaching his seventy-eighth birthday, finally got the top post when Frank York, installed in February 1930 to replace Uncle Robbie, announced his resignation.

In February 1933, the last great name from "The Daffiness Boys" was gone. In a deal that brought scores of angry phone calls from fans, the

◆ *Hack Wilson, delighted   for the moment to be in a Brooklyn uniform.*
(National Baseball Library, Cooperstown, N.Y.)

Dodgers traded Dazzy Vance, a month shy of his forty-second birthday, to the Cardinals. They also sent along Gordon Slade, a reserve infielder, and got in return Ownie Carroll, a pitcher who had been around since 1925 with only a single outstanding season. Sentiment aside, it wasn't a bad trade for Brooklyn. Vance did little for St. Louis in '33, but Carroll turned in a 13–15 record for the Dodgers. That would not, however, be the last of Vance so far as Flatbush was concerned. He returned to the Dodgers in 1935, his final season, appearing in twenty games as a reliever.

In June, the Dodgers traded both the previous season's batting champion and their twenty-game winner, sending Lefty O'Doul and Watty Clark to the Giants for Sam Leslie, a first baseman. The deal was not so silly as it might have seemed since O'Doul was thirty-six years old and Clark had been struggling early in the season while Leslie, only twenty-seven, had been hitting at a .321 clip. Yet the trade left the Dodgers little in the way of proven talent. The one big name remaining, Hack Wilson, had put on the pounds and would manage only nine homers in 360 at-bats.

In August, the Dodgers made a move off the field. McKeever fired Dave Driscoll, the general manager, and replaced him with Bob Quinn, a former owner of the Red Sox. By then the ballclub was floundering again. Van Lingle Mungo had blossomed and would go on to a 16–15 record and Al Lopez would hit .301. But aside from those two, there was no young talent. The team finished sixth as the Giants won the pennant for the first time since 1924.

The Dodgers came up with a twenty-game loser in Walter Beck, who was picked up from the Browns and promptly weighed in with a record of 12–20. He would be better known as Boom-Boom for pitching that produced a double thud: first the crack of the bat and then the crack of the baseball slamming into an outfield fence.

In 1934, Boom-Boom would team up with Hack Wilson on a play that didn't count in the record books but showed that the spirit of "The Daffiness Boys" lived on.

Beck was off to another lousy season and was about to be yanked out of a game at Philadelphia's Baker Bowl, a decrepit and tiny ballpark only 280 feet down the right-field line to a high tin fence.

What happened next remained vivid long afterward for one of Beck's teammates, Ray Berres, then a rookie catcher.

"It was a real hot day in that little bandbox," Berres would recall. "Geez, they started hitting Boom-Boom and hitting him hard. Finally, Casey went to take him out and Boom-Boom got mad and wheeled around and threw that ball up against the fence.

"Hack, in the meantime, had been leaning along the rail where the fans would sit. He had been running the ball down all day long. Here comes that crash against the fence. Hack took out after the ball, ran and grabbed it and threw it back to the cutoff man—and discovered the joke was on him.

"He felt so silly. Later he came in and told Walter, 'I hope to hell they send you to Jersey City tomorrow.'"

The '34 season would be Wilson's last in the majors. A hard drinker, he may have been done in by liquor, or perhaps the years and an expanding waistline just caught up with him. In mid season, at age thirty-four, he was sent by the Dodgers to the Phillies. It was his last stop.

Berres remembered Wilson as "a lovable character, a big-hearted guy" who would go out of his way to do someone a kindness.

———

We had a clubhouse man by the name of Comerford, who had a boy going to military school outside of Philadelphia. And Hack had promised to visit the kid on a certain day, when we had an off day in Philadelphia.

On that day, he had forgotten about it, and I said to him, "Hey, you were supposed to meet Comerford's boy." And he said, "Oh gosh, yes." Damned if he didn't get a cab and go all the way out to the military school. It had to have been fifty or sixty miles.

———

The final years for Hack Wilson would be sad ones. Long after Wilson's death, Joe Stripp, who had played alongside him in Brooklyn for two and a half seasons, recalled the aftermath to Wilson's baseball career and also the painful last days of another famous ex-Cub, Joe Tinker.

———

You'd be surprised at the amount of guys that were broke after they quit playing. They always thought they were gonna keep making that good money, and as fast as they got the money, they spent it.

When Hack Wilson broke the home run record, a guy in Chicago offered him $30,000 for the bat he set the record with. But he wouldn't take it. Here's a guy, with all the money he made, he died broke.

My last year in Brooklyn, he was tending bar right across the street from Ebbets Field. The last time I remember him, he came right here to Orlando. It was 1940 or '42. He was looking for ballplayers to hand him out some money. He borrowed $100 from me. And I was taking care of Joe Tinker at the time. I helped him for three or four years. He'd been with the Cubs and was part of that famous double-play combination: Tinker to Evers to Chance. He was living in Orlando. A fella used to have a soda fountain down on Church Street and Central, and I used to send him money to give Joe every month. Well, when Wilson came to me, he'd already got twenty-five bucks from Joe Tinker. I saw Tinker and I said, "What the hell are you giving Hack Wilson money for?" And Tinker said, "He's broke." I said: "What are you? You're broke too, and you're giving my money to him."

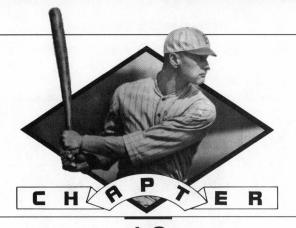

19

Still in the League

Having led the Giants to a pennant and World Series victory in 1933—his first full season as manager—Bill Terry was feeling upbeat when he met with sportswriters at the club's 42nd Street offices one Wednesday the following January to preview the coming season.

Terry ticked off his assessment of the other ballclubs, predicting that the Pirates, Cardinals and Cubs were the teams to beat. He seemed not to notice that gang across the river. So Roscoe McGowan of the *Times* inquired, "How about Brooklyn?"

"Brooklyn?" Terry responded. "Is Brooklyn still in the league?"

Things had been quiet over at the Dodger offices, but now Brooklyn came alive.

"It doesn't take much to start a baseball war in Brooklyn," wrote Dan Daniel in the *New York World-Telegram*. "In so far as Flatbush, Red Hook, Gowanus, Brownsville, Bushwick, Coney Island, and Bath Beach are concerned, Bill Terry's remark the other day about the Dodgers was like the shot that rang out on the bridge at Concord."

Bob Quinn, about to begin his first full year as the Dodger general manager, turned purple over the harmless quip. He demanded that the National League president discipline Terry for conduct "detrimental to baseball." Then, presumably to prove the Dodgers were indeed doing something in the off-season, he made a move. But instead of getting some good players, Quinn fired Max Carey and hired Casey Stengel to replace him.

At his introductory press conference on February 23, Stengel kept the war of words alive. "The first thing I want to say is that the Dodgers are still in the National League," he told reporters. "Tell that to Bill Terry."

◆ *Casey Stengel, about to debut as Dodger manager, gets a good-luck greeting from Brooklyn Borough President Raymond V. Ingersoll, who will be throwing out the first ball of the 1934 season. Mrs. Ingersoll, beside him, lends moral support while co-owner Steve McKeever sizes up his new man. (National Baseball Library, Cooperstown, N.Y.)*

Two days later, the silly dispute was overshadowed by news coming from a hospital in New Rochelle, New York. John McGraw, stricken with uremic poisoning, had died at age sixty.

"This is one of the saddest messages that has ever come to me," said his old foe, Wilbert Robinson, reached at his home in Georgia.

As the season moved along, Terry's remark added fuel to the Brooklyn fans' hatred for the Giants. On Memorial Day, a crowd announced at 41,209—some 5,000 were turned away—filled Ebbets Field to jeer Terry, who brought in a Giant team fighting for first place. The Dodgers, as usual, were well down in the second division, and Terry had the last laugh that day as his club swept a doubleheader.

The Dodgers were, however, still in the league, as Van Lingle Mungo showed on Wednesday, August 8, when he shut out the Giants, 2–0, at the Polo Grounds.

Late that afternoon, having taken over the presidency of the Southern Association's Atlanta club, Wilbert Robinson was in the lobby of his Atlanta hotel. Suddenly, he felt faint. He went to his room and then collapsed, suffering a broken arm in the fall. He was rushed to a hospital without regaining consciousness and was found to have suffered a stroke. At ten-thirty that night, Robbie died at age seventy-one.

And so, within less than half a year, John McGraw and Wilbert Robinson—the two long-time allies and then enemies who had spiced the Dodger-Giant rivalry for so many years—were both gone.

With two of his old Oriole teammates—Joe Kelley and Steve Brodie—paying respects at the funeral, Robbie was buried on a hillside in Baltimore's Bonnie Brae Cemetery. The grave was not very far from the mausoleum of John McGraw.

The Giants seemed headed for a second straight pennant under Terry, taking a seven-game lead over St. Louis during the first week of September. But that colorful ballclub to be known as the Gas House Gang—the Cardinals of Pepper Martin, Joe Medwick, Leo Durocher and, especially, the Dean brothers—wouldn't give up.

On Friday, September 21, the Cards came into Ebbets Field for a doubleheader. Brooklyn could do nothing to hurt Bill Terry that day. In the opener, Dizzy Dean shut out the Dodgers, 13–0, on a three-hitter for his twenty-seventh victory. Then Diz's brother, Paul, pitched a no-hitter—yielding only a walk to Len Koenecke in the first inning—for a 3–0 victory.

"If I'da known that Paul was gonna throw a no-hitter, I'da thrown one too," Diz remarked.

At the end of the afternoon, the Cardinals had drawn to three games back of the Giants. They kept gaining, and going into the final two days of the season they had tied the Giants for the league lead. Terry's team was at home for the last Saturday and Sunday, but the Giants hardly had an edge. For coming into the Polo Grounds were the Dodgers, and it seemed they had brought all of Brooklyn with them.

The *Brooklyn Eagle* egged the Dodger fans on, its front-page Saturday headline reading:

DODGERS SET TO KICK
GIANTS OUT OF RACE AT
POLO GROUNDS TODAY

On the eve of the games, John Kieran had some fun with the Giant manager in his *New York Times* column, composing the "Ballad of Bitter Words." Its opening stanza:

Why, Mister Terry, oh! why did you ever
Chortle the query that made Brooklyn hot?
Just for the crack that you thought was so clever,
Now you stand teetering right on the spot!
Vain was your hope they forgave or forgot;
Now that you're weary and bowed with fatigue,
Here is the drama and this is the plot:
Brooklyn, dear fellow, is still in the league.

Settled in sixth place, the Dodgers went into the two-game set as if they were fighting for the pennant. Stengel sent Mungo, his ace, to the mound against Roy Parmelee for Saturday's game. When the teams took the field, Brooklyn fans roared their support, clanged cowbells and waved defiant posters reading "We're Still in the League."

The Dodgers had beaten the Giants only six times in twenty games during the season, but Mungo was in top form that afternoon though suffering from a cold. The teams were scoreless through four innings. In the fifth, Mungo led off with a single and went to second on a passed ball. Then, after Buzz Boyle struck out, Lonny Frey delivered a single to center, and the Dodgers were ahead. They went on to a 5–1 victory, Mungo's eighteenth win of the season. The Cards' Paul Dean defeated the Reds that day, 6–1, at Sportsman's Park, and so the Giants fell out of first place for the first time since June 5.

"YES, INDEED, MR. TERRY, THE DODGERS ARE STILL IN THE LEAGUE," read the front-page headline in the next morning's *Brooklyn Times-Union*.

Now, the Giants had to win on Sunday while the Cards lost, and even if that happened, there would be a playoff.

Stengel started his second-best pitcher, fourteen-game winner Ray Benge, on Sunday while the Giants went with knuckleballer Freddie Fitzsimmons. Terry's men scored four runs in the first inning, but the scoreboard soon posted two runs for the Cardinals in their first inning against the Reds. Worse, Dizzy Dean was pitching. It seemed that hope was gone for the Giants, and perhaps the spirit was knocked out of them. The Dodgers came back to tie the game at 5–5 in the eighth. By then, the Cards were ahead by 8–0, so the Giants were done. Delivering a final insult to match Terry's crack of the previous winter, the Dodgers won the game in the tenth. They took the lead when Blondy Ryan, the Giants' shortstop, kicked a ground ball hit by Al Lopez, then added two more runs and won it 8–5. Dean finished off with a 9–0 victory—his thirtieth win of the season—and the Cards were National League champions.

In the Dodger clubhouse, Casey Stengel, clad in a bath towel draped diaper-fashion around his hips, gloated over knocking the Giants out of World Series paychecks. But he did display a bit of sympathy.

"The Giants thought we gave 'em a beating Saturday and today. Well, they were right," Casey said. "But I'm sorry for them when I think of the beating they still have to take. Wait until their wives realize they're not going to get those new fur coats. I've been through it, and I know."

Bill Terry had the answer to his question.

But according to Al Lopez, the Brooklyn ballplayers didn't require any special incitement from an inflammatory remark.

"They made a big thing of it, but we didn't need to have any remarks to stir it up when we played the Giants," Lopez observed years later in recalling that frantic finish. "It didn't make any difference whether we were in a pennant race or not, the Brooklyn Dodgers and New York Giants were bitter rivals—they always wanted to beat each other real bad."

And the fans wanted it badly, too, Lopez noted, in recounting an unwanted ride to the clubhouse after the final out of the '34 season.

———

They lifted me up and they were running like mad over there, like a bunch of wild horses. I kept hollering, "Put me down, put me down." I thought they were gonna drop me and break my neck or step all over me. They were just crazy. They just picked me up and ran all the way to center field.

Stengel felt great. I understand Stengel went to Terry in the winter to tell him he was gonna come into his clubhouse and tell him how sorry he was.

Terry told Stengel, "I'm glad you didn't because you'd have got thrown out on your butt."

———

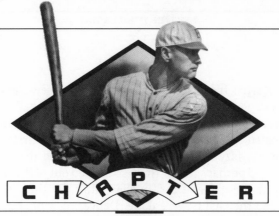

CHAPTER

20

Depression Days
with Casey and Burleigh

Having proved in 1934 they were still in the league, the Dodgers
showed once again in '35 that they were still a bad ballclub.

Perhaps unduly encouraged by the heroics against the
Giants, General Manager Bob Quinn made no major moves after a sixth-
place finish.

Sam Leslie at first base, Joe Stripp at third and Jimmy Bucher, a
utilityman, all hit over .300 in 1935, but the lineup would scare few pitchers.
The Dodgers wound up in fifth place, thirteen games under .500.

At least there were a few laughs as the ballclub languished in the
second division through the mid-1930's.

An outfielder named Stanley Bordagaray arrived from the White Sox
in '35. Everyone called him Frenchy and everyone noticed when he appeared
one spring training with a black mustache. That may have been fine for
the 1890's out at Eastern Park, but no one was sporting facial hair these
days. The mustache brought a stir and then, at Stengel's insistence, came
a shave.

Frenchy became legendary for his misadventures. He was picked off
second base while tapping his foot on the bag. Once he stopped to retrieve
his cap while chasing a fly ball.

Another bit of craziness saw Stengel as the victim.

"We had been losing, losing, losing," recalled Ray Berres. "One day,
we were in Cincinnati. To instill a little life into the guys, Casey decided
to hit infield practice and whoop it up a little bit.

"The players were out in front of the dugout and on the sidelines warming up. Casey grabbed an infield fungo stick and he said, 'Come on my little chitlins, let's go.' As he ran out of the dugout, Frenchy, who was warming up with me, fired a ball, and just about that time Casey crossed his path and it hit him in the ear and knocked him cold.

"We all ran to see what we could do. And Casey said, 'Don't tell me, you don't have to tell me. It was that god-damned Frenchy cracked me in the ear.'

"We went on to win the ballgame. And the next day we had a pregame meeting and Casey concluded by saying, 'Well, does anybody else got anything to say?'

"Frenchy piped up and said, 'Yeah, I have, Case.'

"Casey said, 'Frenchy boy, let's hear it.'

"Frenchy said, 'Let me hit you in the other ear and maybe we'll win a ballgame again today.'"

Casey also had his moments with an outfielder named Nick Tremark, out of Manhattan College. After five-foot-six-inch Hack Wilson was released, the Dodgers brought up Tremark, who was an inch smaller. Tremark had neither Wilson's physique nor his ability to pound a baseball. He did possess a wonderful nickname: Mickey Mouse. When he got on first base, Stengel would peer over from the third-base coaching box and cup his hands over his eyes, pretending he needed a pair of binoculars to locate his tiny baserunner.

Tremark presumably had some speed since at five feet five inches he wasn't likely to boast of many other physical assets. It developed, however, that he was not quite as quick as the biggest man on the team.

The Dodgers had a right-handed pitcher named Les Munns who went six feet five inches and 212 pounds, exceptional size for a 1930's ballplayer.

From his home in Wahoo, Nebraska (birthplace of the Hall of Fame outfielder "Wahoo" Sam Crawford), Munns recalled the time Stengel arranged a race between the biggest and smallest Dodgers.

===

One day, along about the seventh inning, Casey put Tremark in to run for somebody.

I said, "Hell, I can beat him."

Casey said, "You can? You two be down here tomorrow morning about ten o'clock and we'll find out. We'll have you run a hundred yards." So the bets started in. They must have had 300, 400 bucks bet on the deal. Danny Taylor, an outfielder, I think it cost him fifty bucks. We had a guy, Larry Barton, who saw me run in spring training. He bet on me.

I knew doggone well I could beat him. Running alongside

him in the outfield, he looked like he was flying with those short legs. But I ran the 100 in 10.3 seconds, which back in those days was pretty good for a man my size.

So they measured off a hundred yards and I must have beaten him by five or six yards. All I got out of it was about twenty-five bucks.

◆ *Casey Stengel and Athletics' Connie Mack presumably commiserating on their respective down-and-out Depression era teams. (Los Angeles Dodgers)*

When Stengel wasn't carrying on with his ballplayers, he was razzing the umpires.

"One day we're leading the Giants and it started to rain like heck," Ray Berres recalled. "Casey wanted to get the game called. He went out there with striped stockings and a big umbrella to coach third base. It didn't take long, he was chased."

Les Munns recalled the time Casey got the last laugh on an umpiring crew.

We used to get Moran, Quigley and Rigler—we called them The Three Blind Mice—for the umpires. They put the three lousiest umpires together.

This one day, they'd had a bad afternoon. One of the New York papers had a zoom camera. They showed a picture at first base where Sam Leslie had Mel Ott out by about two steps and the umpire called him safe.

The next day, Casey went ahead and pinned the newspaper picture on home plate before the umpires came out. The umpires just crumpled the picture up, never said anything. Judge Landis sent a telegram to the club: There'd be no more of it.

Soon after the 1935 season ended, Bob Quinn left to become president of the Boston Braves, and John Gorman, the road secretary, took his place as the club's dealmaker. It did not seem to be a step heralding spectacular changes.

When springtime 1936 arrived, the Dodgers did have a new first baseman. In a three-way trade, Buddy Hassett, a New York City native, was purchased from the Yankee farm system.

The Dodger season opened on a riotous note at the Polo Grounds, and in the middle of it—celebrating his major league debut—was Hassett.

Reminiscing from his home in Hillside, New Jersey, he recalled that day:

Lonny Frey had got hurt the year before—Dick Bartell had either slid high or did something to him. Mungo still had it in his craw. He was a tough competitor. I'm at first base. Bartell comes up to hit, and Van threw one behind his ear. The next one, Bartell bunted between first and the pitcher. Luckily, he bunted it far enough toward the line that I could make the play myself without getting Van involved. But Van ran over anyhow. I ran across the bag to make the out. By the time I turned around, Van and Bartell were about ten feet beyond the bag toward right field and they were on the ground scuffling.

I got in the middle of it, and the next thing I knew, I had Bartell under me, and luckily I had both my hands on the ground because I looked up and there were all white uniforms around me. I said, "C'mon, get up, Dick." I wanted to get out of there. All my people were taking care of Van.

⸻

Hassett would be one of the Dodgers' few decent ballplayers over his three years with the team, batting .310, .304 and .293 before being traded to the Braves.

He also lightened things up as the team floundered in the second division. Nicknamed "The Bronx Thrush," Hassett would serenade his teammates and fans with his Irish tenor crooning.

"I did a little singing in the Paulist church choir on Fifty-ninth Street when I was growing up and then we moved to the Bronx," he recalled. "My father ran the Shamrock Democratic Club, and he'd have parties up there and I used to sing. I didn't take any formal lessons, I just fooled with it, it seemed I was able to carry a tune."

Hassett first combined baseball and ballads as a member of the semipro Bay Parkways, who played at the Erasmus Hall High School field in Brooklyn. His specialty was keeping the folks in the house when the skies grew grim.

"If it got a little threatening and some drops came down before game time, Joe Press, the manager, used to grab me. He had a little megaphone. He'd get me up there and say, 'Hey, sing them a couple of songs to keep them in the park.' Once in a while, it worked."

When he got to the Dodgers, Hassett turned to big-time entertainment, singing in stage shows between movies at the downtown Brooklyn Strand.

"We did a little vaudeville, Stan Lomax and I," Hassett recalled. "Stan was then broadcasting and writing for the *New York Journal*. We had a little act for several weeks, little songs and witty sayings, around '36 and '37. And I'd sign autographs in the lobby."

His specialties?

"Mostly Irish songs—'When Irish Eyes Are Smiling,' 'Take You Home Again Kathleen.' "

Hassett's first year in the majors was the last one for a Dodger infielder named Jimmy Jordan, whose sometime nickname was "Lord." Royalty in Brooklyn? Absolutely.

"There was a character," Hassett remembered. "He was a practical joker. He was liable to sidle up to you and say something that would really shake you up. If you knew Jimmy Jordan, you figured he'd be the last guy in the world to marry a titled Englishwoman. But he married a gal with an English peerage: Lady Eaves."

Making his Dodger debut in 1936 along with Hassett was a thirty-four-year-old rookie outfielder from Texas named Oscar (Ox) Eckhardt, whose constant companion was a Saint Bernard.

"He was a fella that hit .400 in the Coast League, but he didn't make it because he just couldn't pull the ball," Hassett recalled. "He was a left-handed hitter and he hit everything to the left side of the diamond."

A man like that was not in a position to issue demands, but, as Hassett remembered, Ox Eckhardt would not be parted from his Saint Bernard.

"He said, 'If the dog goes, then I go with the dog.' He did. He went with the dog."

Eckhardt lasted for sixteen games, hit .182, and was never heard from again.

In June '36, two months after his ruckus with Bartell, Mungo was in the middle of another row. But now the target wasn't a Giant ballplayer but his own teammates. The temperamental pitcher had simply grown disgusted with the bumbling cast kicking the ball around behind him.

After getting knocked out by the Pirates in Pittsburgh, Mungo got hold of Stengel in the lobby of the Schenley Hotel and demanded a trade. When Casey told him the owners had to decide about something like that, Mungo flew back to Brooklyn and promptly informed the newspapers he was tired of playing with "a gang of semipros." A few days later, he was persuaded to come back, and he wound up with a record of 18–19 and a league-leading 238 strikeouts.

While the Dodgers may not have been semipros, there was just one professional team they finished ahead of in 1936. They sank to seventh place, better only than the Phillies.

But amid the hijinks and the characters of the middle 1930's came a dark affair.

One ballplayer the Dodgers had high hopes for was outfielder Len Koenecke. After breaking in with the Giants, Koenecke came to Brooklyn in 1934, won a regular job and batted .320 with 14 homers and 73 runs batted in. But he tailed off in 1935 to .283, showed little power, and played erratically. In mid-September, he left the ballclub along with two pitchers, Les Munns and Bob Barr.

"We were in St. Louis," Munns remembered, "and Casey Stengel said, 'We've called up some young guys. We'll send you back to New York, by plane if you want to go.' "

The three players took an American Airlines flight with a stopover in Detroit.

"Len must have had a few snoots, because when we got to Detroit, the pilot came back and told me, 'We're going to have to put him off, he's getting hard to handle and obnoxious,' " Munns recalled.

"They had a couple of security guys there, and I told them who he was, and one said, 'Oh, great. My kid's a ball fan.' He had his kid come down to meet him."

As Munns remembered that flight, Koenecke "was getting up and bothering people. He wasn't roughing anybody up or being foul-mouthed."

But a stewardess, recounting the trip for reporters a day or so later, said that an evidently drunken Koenecke hit her after she intervened when he had argued with another passenger.

Munns and Barr continued on to New York via commercial airliner.

That evening, Koenecke chartered a small plane to take him to Buffalo. But he never arrived there. The plane made an emergency landing on the infield of the Long Branch racetrack in Toronto. The pilot, William Mulqueeney, told the police that Koenecke had been drinking, then had grabbed the controls and fought with him and the pilot's companion when they tried to restrain him. The plane was rocking dangerously as the battle went on for perhaps fifteen minutes, and finally Mulqueeney grabbed a fire extinguisher and hit Koenecke over the head. By the time he brought the plane down, Koenecke was dead of a brain hemorrhage. He was thirty-one years old and left a wife and three-year-old daughter.

Munns recalled: "The next morning, somebody came up to our apartment door about six o'clock and said: 'Len Koenecke's dead. He was killed by a couple of guys in a plane.' I couldn't believe it."

Afterward, Munns and his wife went to the Koenecke home in Wisconsin, one of them driving the Munns's family car and the other transporting the Koenecke car back from Brooklyn.

What had driven Koenecke to go out of control?

"His dad could never figure it out," said Munns.

Stengel was too upset to give the reporters a comment. The Dodger management, fearing Casey would be viewed as callous if he had nothing to say, turned to one of the sportswriters for help. Roscoe McGowan of the Times was persuaded to call the Associated Press, impersonate Stengel's gravelly voice and issue a few appropriate expressions of grief. The remarks went out over the wires and no one was the wiser.

Koenecke's pilot and the flier's friend were jailed by Canadian authorities on manslaughter charges, but were released a few days later when a coroner's jury found they had acted in self-defense.

Although the Dodgers sank to seventh place in 1936, there was a major victory for some Brooklynites. The Schechter brothers, poultry dealers on East Fifty-second Street in Flatbush, took the Roosevelt Administration to the Supreme Court, challenging the New Deal's regulation of business through the National Recovery Administration. Joseph Schechter's

detailed explanation of chicken slaughter techniques "sent the usually sol-
emn justices into gales of laughter," observed the *Times*. But he won. The
court unanimously found the legislation setting up the N.R.A. to be
unconstitutional.

Mrs. Joseph Schechter—perhaps symbolizing every Brooklynite who
had prevailed against a hostile, sophisticated world—penned a poem entitled "Now That It's Over."

=====

No more excuses
To hide our disgrace;
With pride and satisfaction
I'm showing my face.

For a long, long time
To be kept in suspense,
Sarcastic remarks made
At our expense.

I'm through with that experience
I hope for all my life
And proud again to be
Joseph Schechter's wife.

=====

Casey Stengel didn't fare nearly as well. He was fired a few days after
the '36 season ended. Like Max Carey before him, he was dumped with a
year remaining on his contract.

Casey paid for the shortcomings of the players. And what the Dodgers
lacked in skill, they evidently did not make up for in concentration, as a
Brooklyn pitcher named Harry Eisenstat would recall.

"One time a lot of the fellows were playing the stock market and
weren't paying too much attention to what was happening on the field,"
Eisenstat remembered from his Shaker Heights, Ohio, home. "I guess we
lost about eight or nine straight.

"Casey held a meeting and said he's got a good tip for the ballplayers.
The Pennsylvania Railroad would be a good stock to buy because half the
team was gonna be sent out and be riding to other teams."

Eisenstat was that rarity on any big league ballclub: a boy from the
neighborhood. His family lived at Bedford Avenue and East Twenty-sixth
Street and he had pitched schoolboy baseball in Flatbush.

"Al Lopez came to see me play when I was pitching for James Madison
High School," Eisenstat recalled. "He was the captain. Somebody had sent
him to check me out.

"I pitched a no-hit game that day. So they invited me to Ebbets Field, I worked out, and after I graduated I was sent to Dayton in the Mid-Atlantic League."

In 1935, Eisenstat made it to the Dodgers, and he brought something special to that ballclub.

"The Dodgers were anxious to see me make good. Especially being a Jewish ballplayer, they thought it might help the attendance. The sportswriters kept writing about it—'the only Jewish player.' Goody Rosen came on a little later."

The '35 Dodgers were either too young or too old. "I still have pictures I took with Dazzy Vance," Eisenstat noted, recalling the once-great pitcher's second tour with the ballclub. "I was sitting on his lap and they said, 'The youngster with the old-timer.' "

Another grand name from the Dodger past—that spitballer of yesteryear, Burleigh Grimes—was brought back to succeed Stengel in 1937. That presented a curious situation: The Dodgers would be paying more money to a man not to manage than to the fellow actually doing the job. Stengel was paid $15,000 for the final year of his pact. Grimes's salary wasn't revealed, but it was estimated at $8,000 to $10,000.

Grimes had ended his pitching career with the '34 Yankees, then turned to managing in the minors. He presumably would feel at home with a Dodger team that had finished seventh the season before since that's the spot he led the Louisville Colonels to in 1936.

It didn't take long for Ol' Stubblebeard to get the feeling he was back with "The Daffiness Boys" again.

Among the Dodger pitchers was a strapping right-hander named Max Butcher who had arrived in the '36 season, managing a 6–6 record. He would get his second year off to a shaky start with the new manager. Buddy Hassett recalled the scene:

———

It happened in spring training in Clearwater. Burleigh Grimes was coaching at first base. Our clubhouse was off the left-field foul line. We got behind three or four runs and a little outfielder—Gib Brack—got on first base. The phone rang in the clubhouse, and Dan Comerford, the clubhouse man, yelled, "Hey Burleigh, they want you on the phone." I guess there was a deal pending or something. Somebody got up and coached at first base.

Now, the steal sign was if you blinked your eye. Max Butcher blinked all the time—I don't know how he pitched between blinks.

First thing you know, Brack took off to second base and

he got thrown out from here to the wall. Grimes came out of the clubhouse and he saw what was going on and he stopped the game and came screaming, "Who gave that steal sign?" He came running across first base, he was looking at the bench.

Butcher said, "I didn't give any steal sign." And he's blinking away a mile a minute.

———

Notwithstanding the blinking Butcher, Grimes was determined to have a no-nonsense training camp.

"Everything is deadly serious since Manager B. Grimes first marshaled his Flatbush flock here and gave the crushing order: 'No laughing in ranks,' " observed the *Times*'s John Kieran.

Dedicated to applying the latest techniques, Grimes called in Percy Beard, a former hurdling champion, to teach his men how to negotiate the basepaths.

Beard "put the Dodgers through their paces for a few days and then solemnly departed," noted Kieran. "Either he had taught them all he knew or all they could learn."

The '37 season opened at Ebbets Field the same way the previous year had begun in the Polo Grounds: with an uproar involving the Giants' Dick Bartell. Once again Mungo was facing him. They wouldn't be rolling around on the grass, but Bartell would nonetheless be in for a rough time. Mungo's first pitch was a called strike. Bartell promptly dropped his bat and began to argue with Umpire Beans Reardon. As he turned around— plop. His gray jersey was suddenly gushing red.

Sitting upstairs behind first base was a teenage fan named Jack Kavanagh and a friend. More than a half-century later, by then a writer living in Rhode Island, Kavanagh would remember how his friend vented his anger against the Giants.

"Bartell stepped up. He was batting leadoff. Here from the upper deck came a high arcing tomato—got him right in the chest. It was a remarkable throw.

"He went back in the dugout, wiped himself off and went to bat again."

Kavanagh said his friend was an instant hero.

"There were people congratulating him on *A,* his accuracy, and *B,* his choice of target."

The story did not quite end that afternoon. There would be a reminder for Bartell in connection with his memoir *Rowdy Richard,* written in the 1980's.

"When Bartell was on a promotion tour for his book he was in Providence," Kavanagh recalled. "We have a Brooklyn Dodger fan club up here.

We made a presentation to him—a picture of a tomato and a kind of a proclamation.

"We granted him amnesty. With the passage of time, we forgave him."

Bartell wasn't the only ballplayer with a strange coloring to his uniform that opening day in 1937. The Dodgers were attired for the first time in green trim. Otherwise, they were a familiar bunch. After taking a three-run lead, they were beaten by the Giants, 4–3.

Casey Stengel, having watched from a box seat, remarked afterward, "Those spiffy new uniforms had me fooled for a while, but I recognized the boys in the late innings."

The managing chores seemed to be unnerving Burleigh Grimes early on. By the fifth game of the season, he had been ejected by the umpires twice.

In May, it was Mungo's turn to grow ornery.

"Mungo was a nice fellow," recalled Al Lopez. "When he had a few drinks in him, he just went crazy, but he wasn't a bad guy. He was a nice individual."

Jimmy Bucher probably wasn't feeling so benevolent that spring after being awakened with a jolt at four A.M. in the St. Louis hotel room he was sharing with fellow Dodger infielder Woody English.

Mungo invaded the room, one word led to another, and then the agitated pitcher swung at Bucher, who retaliated with a right hand to the eye. Eventually, Mungo was carted off to bed. The next day, he was fined $1,000 and suspended for three days, a period he probably needed anyway to recuperate.

It would be a lost year for Mungo. He hurt his back, then strained his arm in the All-Star Game, had his tonsils out and finally was suspended by Grimes in late August for disobeying the trainer's instructions on getting back in shape. He went 9–11 and would never have another decent season with the Dodgers.

A week after Mungo's escapade in St. Louis, the Dodgers enjoyed a moment of glory. Before a Memorial Day doubleheader crowd of 61,756 at the Polo Grounds—some 25,000 were turned away—they snapped Carl Hubbell's winning streak at 24 games with a 10–3 victory. To add a bizarre touch, the two-run single that virtually put the game away was stroked by a catcher named Paul Chervinko making his major league debut. Chervinko would appear in only 42 big league games, but for one afternoon he was a hero against the great left-handed screwballer.

In June, the Dodgers acquired two aging pitchers with big years behind them in New York uniforms. They obtained Fat Freddie Fitzsimmons from the Giants for a young pitcher named Tom Baker and got Waite Hoyt, the Yankee star of the 1920's, from the Pirates.

Having spent thirteen seasons at the Polo Grounds, Fitzsimmons

◆ *Van Lingle Mungo, who starred for the Dodgers of the 1930's when he wasn't brawling, walking out or under suspension. (National Baseball Library, Cooperstown, N.Y.)*

could hardly imagine becoming a Dodger. "I'll never forget riding across that bridge in a cab that afternoon," he would tell an interviewer long afterward. "More than once I was tempted to tell the driver to turn around and go back." But the knuckleballer would go on to have a great 1940 season and would pitch for Brooklyn into the war years. Hoyt, a product of Brooklyn's Erasmus Hall High School and briefly a Dodger back in '32, went 7–7 over the rest of the summer. But the following year, he called it quits at age thirty-eight.

The Dodgers had a new second baseman in '37, a promising Californian named Cookie Lavagetto. But with Mungo variously inflamed and injured, there wasn't much pitching.

The second division beckoned again, this time sixth place. It may have been the accustomed spot for Brooklyn, but running a losing team did nothing for Grimes's disposition. He had pitched under an easygoing manager in Uncle Robbie, yet would prove a tough man to work for.

Joe Stripp, who was still holding down third base in 1937, would not have fond memories of his old boss.

"Burleigh Grimes was a rough one," Stripp recalled. "In '37, my teeth went bad on me, and the infection went to my shoulder. I couldn't even throw a ball to second base from third. But Burleigh said, 'Go out there and play.' A lot of them thought you could play and didn't want to play. A couple of years, I used to play with all my injuries, but I found out it didn't pay. Here you were sacrificing, but if you didn't have a good year, they wanted to cut you the next year. So I said to myself, 'The hell with this, I'm not playing anymore when I'm hurt.'"

Stripp appeared in only ninety games, and the next year he was sent to the Cardinals.

Grimes was none too popular with Buddy Hassett either.

"Burleigh and I always seemed to have problems," Hassett recalled. "In '37, I guess it was, it was a man on first and second, we were playing the Cubs. It was a bunt-play situation. I was playing first base. I charged in for the bunt to make the play at third base if I could. I reached for the ball, but as I reached I looked and dropped the ball and everybody was safe. So Grimes stopped the ballgame. He came out on the field and indicated toward Johnny Cooney to come in and play first base and took me out of the game right then and there, which I thought was not very nice.

"In '49, we were both working for the Yankees. I had been managing Newark and he was scouting. At the Yankee victory dinner, he came over in a corner and said, 'Hey, do you remember that day around '37?' I said, 'Yeah, I remember.' He said, 'Well, I want to tell you, I'm sorry.' I said, 'Yeah, so was I.'"

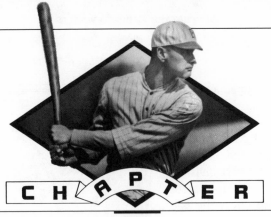

21

MacPhail to the Rescue

By the beginning of 1938, the Brooklyn Dodgers were, in a sense, America's team: Like so many others throughout the nation, they were down and out.

Having last turned a profit in 1930, the franchise owed a half-million dollars to the Brooklyn Trust Company, which was trying to keep it afloat since the bank happened to hold the Ebbets Field mortgage. Telephone service had been shut off at the team's Montague Street office for non-payment of bills, and process servers representing various creditors flocked to the waiting room. Ebbets Field was a mess. The seats were falling apart and desperate for a paint job, the ceiling of the once ornate rotunda was peeling and mildewed, the outer walls were dangerously crumbling, and the playing field was pockmarked. The average daily home attendance during 1937 had been about 6,300. The few diehards who braved the Ebbets Field elements encountered ushers with reputations as roughnecks.

It was a ragtag operation that yielded devotion mainly from young boys—who could find heroes on any diamond—but also, happily, inspired a certain sports cartoonist. This was the era that produced the Brooklyn Bum, a symbol that perfectly captured the times, yet would endure through the triumphant and prosperous years to come.

"The Bum was born one day in the 30's," its creator, Willard Mullin of the *New York World-Telegram,* would recall decades later.

"The Dodgers were losing then, but won the first game of a doubleheader one day and momentarily moved into fourth place. It was their peak and it lasted about seventeen and a half minutes. The other team scored seven runs in the first inning of the second game and the Dodgers lapsed back into the second division.

"When I hopped a cab back to the office, the driver asked me: 'What did our bums do today?' So when I got to the office, I drew the Bum—stepping into the first division, then putting his feet into a cuspidor, knocking down the door, stumbling all over the place and never really making it."

A tattered tramp with a four-day growth of beard, patched clothing and flapping soles, chewing on a cigar stub and mangling English, the Bum would appear in some 2,000 Willard Mullin drawings.

And when the Dodgers traded in the old neighborhood for the glamour of Los Angeles — surely inhospitable territory for the Bum — it was he who would underline the sorrow.

In one of Mullin's best-remembered drawings, holding bat in hand and expressing the ultimate in despair, the Bum anguished: " 'member me? I used t'reside in a jernt called 'Ebbets Feel' . . . in Flatbush . . . Bedford Avenuh . . . ain't there no more."

While the Dodgers were collapsing in the days Willard Mullin brought the Bum to life, their management sat in the sun and did little.

Fearing the franchise was plunging toward bankruptcy and desperate to protect his precarious investment, George V. McLaughlin, the president of the Brooklyn Trust Company, set out to find a forceful

◆ *Willard Mullin's Brooklyn Bum.*
(National Baseball Library,
Cooperstown, N.Y.)

leader for the ballclub. He asked Ford Frick, the National League president, for a recommendation.

After consulting with Branch Rickey, who was running the Cardinals, Frick suggested a name, and on January 19, 1938, the Dodgers called a news conference to introduce Leland Stanford MacPhail to Brooklyn.

A man of enormous energy, great imagination and a thunderous temper, Larry MacPhail would shake up the franchise and ultimately bring the Dodgers to the top of the National League.

Born into a Michigan banking family, MacPhail showed his restlessness early on. He attended Beloit College in Wisconsin, then moved to the University of Michigan and finally George Washington University, where he got a law degree at age twenty. During the school years, he played varsity baseball, and in the summers he played for pay, using an assumed name to keep his eligibility intact.

Following college, MacPhail practiced law, became credit manager for several national concerns, and at age twenty-seven was named president of a large Nashville department store. When World War I arrived, he helped form the 114th Field Artillery, a Tennessee volunteer outfit, joining as a private. He rose to captain, fought at Saint-Mihiel and in the Argonne, and was wounded and gassed. Then came the exploit he would be famous for. After the armistice, MacPhail and seven other Americans piled into Cadillac and Winston touring cars and drove from Paris to the Netherlands in a bizarre scheme to kidnap Kaiser Wilhelm of Germany, who was living in a castle in the town of Amerongen. They fled when Dutch troops were reported en route to intervene, but MacPhail came away with one of the Kaiser's ashtrays—embossed with the imperial coat of arms—a memento that would adorn his offices for years to come.

Returning to civilian life, MacPhail went into business in Columbus, Ohio, and refereed Big Ten football games, then bought the financially ailing Columbus team of the American Association in 1930. He later sold the club to the Cardinals, who could supply him with players from Branch Rickey's vast farm system, and stayed on as club president.

The autumn of 1933 brought a move providing a harbinger of MacPhail's arrival in Brooklyn. A Cincinnati bank, upon Rickey's recommendation, selected MacPhail to revive the Reds' franchise, which was in hock following the financial ruin of its owner, Sidney Weil.

Three months later, MacPhail persuaded Powel Crosley, Jr., the radio and refrigerator manufacturer, to buy the club. MacPhail began to acquire young ballplayers and, in a move to bring the fans back, introduced night baseball to the major leagues in 1935. But he couldn't stay in one spot for too long. In 1936, MacPhail left after a falling out with Crosley and went into the investment business in Grand Rapids, Michigan, with his father and brother.

When he arrived in Brooklyn, MacPhail was a month short of his forty-eighth birthday. He had bright red hair, a face filled with freckles, and a flamboyant taste in clothing running to loud check suits, wide-striped ties and custom-made silk shirts. He cut a colorful figure indeed.

He was abrasive and he was loud—in the words of the *New York Daily Mirror*'s Dan Parker, "The Great Mouthpiece."

"MacPhail's voice is one of the most important parts of his equipment," Robert Lewis Taylor would observe in a profile for *The New Yorker*. "Raspy and carrying, it has often been compared, with scientific accuracy, to the call of an adult male moose. On a wall of his office is the stuffed head of a giant elk which was killed by Curt Davis, one of the Dodger pitchers. Listening to MacPhail talk when he is standing under the specimen gives many people an eerie sensation."

Signed to a three-year contract as executive vice president, MacPhail was given a free hand in running the ballclub. He immediately set out to build a farm system. But the franchise couldn't wait for young players to develop if it was to offer anything to the fans. So MacPhail persuaded George McLaughlin and his bank to open its pocketbook for experienced talent.

As the '38 spring training season arrived, MacPhail made his first big move, buying the slugging first baseman Dolph Camilli from the Phillies for a reported $75,000. It was a huge price tag for those days, an unheard of one for the Dodgers. But Camilli, a holdout when the deal was struck, looked to be worth it. His 27 homers in 1937 were only 10 below the total for the entire Brooklyn team, and the short right-field wall at Ebbets Field would provide an inviting target.

The day after Camilli was purchased, the arrival of a new age for the Dodgers was underlined by the death of Steve McKeever. The "Judge," still the club's president, succumbed to pneumonia in his home on Brooklyn's Maple Street at age eighty-three.

When opening day arrived, Cedar Place, one of the four streets surrounding Ebbets Field, had been renamed McKeever Place. But MacPhail never looked back after that. With $200,000 for improvements cajoled from the Dodgers' bank, he worked a transformation on the old ballpark. The seats were repainted in varying shades of blue and the exit corridors redone a bright orange. New concession stands were built and bathroom fixtures refurbished. The grass was resodded with turf from a Long Island polo field. Even the sportswriters were taken care of with a roomier press box and their own bar.

Courteous young men were hired as ushers and outfitted in spiffy green and gold uniforms in an effort to overcome a disreputable past. Back in 1922, an Ebbets Field usher had been convicted of beating up two fans who happened to be disabled World War I veterans. In the summer of '37, a sportswriter witnessed three ushers dragging a fan down a ramp and slugging him. "He stoled a ball," they explained.

The ballplayers would be color coordinated with the seats, trading in their Kelly green uniforms for what would henceforth be known as Dodger blue.

Only three of the '37 regulars still held starting jobs: Babe Phelps, a hard-hitting catcher; Buddy Hassett, moved from first base to left field to make room for Camilli, and Cookie Lavagetto, who shifted from second base to third. There was a new man at shortstop. Leo Durocher, a light hitter but a flashy fielder and pugnacious leader on the field, had been obtained from the Cardinals just before the '37 World Series for four players.

"Leo may be past his prime as a player, but if the Dodgers are looking for a 1939 manager mebbe the trade wasn't such a bum one at that," observed the *Brooklyn Eagle*.

It would take at least a few years to build a winner. But MacPhail had to get the fans out in order to justify his big spending. Following up on his Cincinnati innovation, which proved a sure way to boost attendance, he persuaded the Brooklyn Trust Company to put up $100,000 for a lighting system. Seven night games were scheduled for the '38 season.

On Wednesday, June 15, night baseball came to Ebbets Field. A crowd of 38,748 turned out, jamming the aisles beyond the park's capacity, to see the Dodgers take on MacPhail's old ballclub. First came a fireworks display and then a stunt featuring Jesse Owens. The track champion spotted the Dodgers' and Reds' fastest men ten yards, then finished just behind the Dodger outfielder Ernie Koy in a 100-yard dash.

A brief ceremony followed in honor of the Reds' starter that night, a twenty-three-year-old left-hander from Midland Park, New Jersey, named Johnny Vander Meer. His family and 700 townspeople were at the ballpark, and they presented him with a watch just before the first pitch.

Four days earlier, Vander Meer—once a Dodger farmhand—had pitched a no-hitter against Boston in a 3–0 victory at Crosley Field. As the Dodger game moved along, he was a bit wild but the string of hitless innings continued. Gradually, the crowd began to cheer him on. Relying at first on his fastball and then mixing in curves, Vander Meer went to the bottom of the ninth inning with a 6–0 lead and his no-hitter intact.

Hassett led off with a topped grounder toward first base. Vander Meer ran over, grabbed the baseball and tagged him. Then his control went haywire. First he walked Phelps, then Lavagetto and finally Camilli.

"What I was doing was forcing myself, trying to throw the ball harder than I could," he would recall.

The Reds' manager, Bill McKechnie, went to the mound in an effort to calm the young pitcher's nerves. "Just get it over the plate," he advised.

Ernie Koy, having beaten Jesse Owens in that foot race, came up

◆ *The Reds' Johnny Vander Meer pitching his second consecutive no-hitter as the Dodgers inaugurate night baseball at Ebbets Field. (Los Angeles Dodgers)*

◆ *The Reds' Johnny Vander Meer pitching his second consecutive no-hitter as the Dodgers inaugurate night baseball at Ebbets Field. (Los Angeles Dodgers)*

next with a chance for even greater glory. But he grounded to the third baseman, Lew Riggs, who threw to the plate, forcing out Goody Rosen, who had run for Phelps. Two down. Now Durocher was at bat. The count went to one ball and two strikes. He lifted a drive into center field, Harry Craft caught the ball, and an extraordinary evening was over. Johnny Vander Meer had inaugurated night ball in Brooklyn by becoming the first man in baseball history to pitch two consecutive no-hitters.

The following Sunday afternoon, a big crowd turned out at Ebbets Field for a doubleheader with the Cubs. Part II of MacPhail's plan to get the fans back had been unveiled. Clapping his hands on the coaching lines was the most recognizable face in baseball. Fat and forty-three, Babe Ruth had become a Dodger.

Ruth had last been in uniform during the 1935 season when he ended his playing career with the Boston Braves. Now MacPhail had brought him back as Brooklyn's first-base coach. The Babe wasn't hired to keep three men from stranding themselves on the same bag. His real mission was to boost attendance with exhibitions of home-run hitting in batting practice.

Readers of the *New York Daily Mirror* couldn't be blamed for gaining the impression there were two Ruths the afternoon he made his Dodger debut.

Edward Zeltner, the *Mirror* sportswriter covering the doubleheader, found that Ruth had instantly solved the Dodgers' baserunning problems. But Bob Considine told *Mirror* readers the new first-base coach simply didn't know what he was doing.

Zeltner saw it this way:

Babe Ruth's presence on the coaching lines had an inspiring effect on the Flatbushers yesterday. While 28,013 lusty throated citizens cheered the Bambino in his new role, the Dodgers massaged the Cubs into a 6 to 2 defeat in the first game and then went down fighting in the nightcap, 4 to 3.

Ruth worked both games, coaching behind first base. It was held highly significant that there was a noticeable lack of lopsided base running by the Dodgers. They ran with daring agility. Babe showed no wear and tear for the long afternoon. Admittedly, he lost a few pounds.

In his "On the Line" column, Considine described Babe's day rather differently:

Here's how the Babe coaches.

He slaps his fat hands together a lot, and his full fat lips holler encouragement in a resonant bass. He paces up and down on his impossible legs. Once he nearly fell down on a particularly close play at first base. The first man he "sent down" to second—Kiki Cuyler in the fourth—was thrown out by three yards. In the fifth inning, with the bases clogged, an infielder's throw went through Collins at first and rolled over toward the Dodger dugout. Babe excitedly waved all the runners on, but they all disobeyed him, and it was just as well, because the ball bounded off the wall of a sideline box and Collins could have thrown out any man by 10 feet.

But as the summer moved along, Ruth may have become a better baserunning director than the Dodger manager.

"They tried to make out that he was stupid in baseball, but he wasn't the way they pictured him," maintained Dolph Camilli in recalling Ruth's coaching days in Brooklyn. "I remember one day in the Polo Grounds. We were behind four or five runs. In those days, hell, you'd never run unless it was either the tying or winning run, and I got the sign to steal. What the hell, I wasn't that kind of a baserunner. I would steal a base on occasion but I wasn't a guy who could go out and run, run, run and be successful. And I looked over to Babe and I says, 'Hey, Babe, they give me the steal sign.' He says, 'Don't go.' Of course, Burleigh Grimes ate my butt out. He said, 'Didn't you see the sign?' I said, 'Yeah, I saw it.' He said, 'Well, why didn't you go?' I said, 'Because it's lousy baseball.'"

Ruth brought his forty-two-ounce bats with him for pregame slugging and was putting 240 pounds of fat into his swings by his own admission. His legendary eating and drinking had hardly diminished with the years.

"Me and Babe became good friends," Camilli noted. "He didn't have many people that he liked on the club. He kind of stayed away from most of them socially. But there were four or five that he liked—Cookie Lavagetto, Buddy Hassett, myself, Merv Shea and maybe one more. And when he threw a big party in St. Louis, he just invited the five of us. He had friends there that had a basement rathskeller type of place and he ordered a big barrel of beer and all the food. He paid for the whole thing. We killed the whole barrel. Babe says after it was over, 'Hell, I didn't think we'd finish that barrel of beer.' He was quite a beer drinker."

Hassett recalled how one Friday, his religious obligations forbidding meateating proved no obstacle to Ruth's desire for a hearty culinary start to the day along with some companionship.

♦ *Buddy Hassett wasn't called the Bronx Thrush for nothing. A Dodger quartet of (l. to r.) Tuck Stainback, Hassett, Kiki Cuyler and Babe Ruth belts out an unidentified tune. (National Baseball Library, Cooperstown, N.Y.)*

MacPhail had got him to play in these exhibition games. We got into Buffalo about seven A.M. The Babe had the first cab from the train to the hotel. I got in around seven-thirty, a quarter to 8, and I was paged. It was the Babe, and he said, "Come on up and have breakfast with me in my room."

I went up, and it's a Friday and I'm a Catholic. He said, "I'll order breakfast." I said, "Well, wait a minute." He said, "Yeah, I know, you're gonna tell me you're a Catholic." I said, "Yeah." He said, "I know, I'll order." He had to go in the other room to get to the phone. When it came up, it was lobster à la Newburgh omelet for breakfast. I've never had it before or since.

Ruth had been seeking a big league managing job, and MacPhail supposedly had considered giving him the Dodger post if he dumped Burleigh Grimes. But the Babe wasn't the only one MacPhail was eyeing. Leo Durocher was also a candidate. Friction would develop. In August, Durocher and Ruth got into a fight in the Dodger locker room at the Polo Grounds after Leo accused the Babe of botching the signs.

◆ *It's the summer of 1938. Babe Ruth, Dodger coach and would-be manager, is flanked by Burleigh Grimes (left), who had the managing job, and Leo Durocher, who would get it the following season. (National Baseball Library, Cooperstown, N.Y.)*

Later that month, after a pregame home-run hitting contest with teammate Babe Phelps in Pittsburgh, Ruth became convinced he could still clout the ball against major league pitching. He asked for a chance to play.

"If he can hit, I can pitch," Grimes responded. "And I know I'm too old for that."

Thus rebuffed, Ruth stayed away from batting-practice performances for the rest of the season. By the following spring, he would be gone from the Dodgers.

The Babe wasn't the only one to arouse Grimes's ire as he suffered with another bad ballclub. In July, a jury ordered Grimes to pay a sixteen-year-old Brooklynite named Harold Greenberg $124 in damages stemming from an unpleasant moment the previous spring.

The boy had sued Grimes, contending the manager punched him in the stomach during an Ebbets Field game against the Giants on April 23 when he asked for an autograph on a scorecard. According to the youngster's lawyer, the Dodgers were hopelessly trailing at the time, driving Grimes to "bad temper." The circumstances may have been mitigating enough to arouse sympathy for Burleigh, but he offered no defense.

That summer, the Dodgers' fortunes provoked far more serious mayhem.

A thirty-three-year-old Brooklyn postal clerk named Robert Joyce spent the evening of July 12 at a South Brooklyn bar. Joyce was a big Dodger fan. Since Brooklyn had whipped the Giants, 13–5, that day, he presumably was in a mood for celebrating. He began drinking about nine o'clock and would later tell the police he had consumed eighteen glasses of beer.

The talk at the bar got around to the Dodgers' acquisition of outfielder Tuck Stainback from the Phillies. The other patrons contended that Stainback's arrival would make little difference since the team was virtually beyond repair that season. Ridiculed for his devotion to the Dodgers, Joyce left in a rage and supposedly warned he was "going to get two guns and shoot up the place."

He went to the post office where he had worked for the past nine years with an unblemished record, found the key to a weapons bin, took two pistols, and returned to the bar about 2:30 A.M. He walked up to twenty-eight-year-old William Diamond, a friend of his and the son of the owner, pulled out one of his guns and shot Diamond twice in the left side. Two other men, one of them thirty-nine-year-old Frank Krug, jumped Joyce, and the gun he used on Diamond was wrestled from him. Joyce then pulled his second pistol and shot Krug in the heart as he sought refuge inside a telephone booth, killing him instantly. Joyce fled, but the police picked him up a few blocks away.

Two days later, William Diamond died of his wounds. The following February, Joyce was convicted of murdering Diamond, and a month after that he pleaded guilty to the murder of Frank Krug.

The Dodgers were in sixth place the day Robert Joyce went berserk. They finished the season a notch lower. Camilli came through as advertised, hitting 24 homers and driving in 100 runs, but MacPhail had only begun to reshape the team.

The day after the Yankees swept the Cubs in the World Series, MacPhail fired Burleigh Grimes. In short order, he named Durocher as manager. Introducing Leo at a luncheon in the Hotel New Yorker, MacPhail said that Babe Ruth had informed the club he would "not be available" to return as a coach.

Durocher, taking over at age thirty-three, was cast in the same mold as MacPhail. Dubbed "Lippy" early on, he was brash and ambitious, a sharp dresser and a big spender. He had broken in with the Yankee ballclubs of the late 20's, then was banished to Cincinnati in the winter of '29 when he told off Ed Barrow, the general manager, with some choice language at contract-haggling time. Traded by the Reds to the Cardinals in 1933, Durocher had become the captain of the Gas House Gang. Soon after taking over as the Dodger shortstop in '38, he had been made captain by MacPhail.

In the years to come, the volatile MacPhail and the equally tempestuous Durocher would make a combustible duo. MacPhail would fire Durocher, then rehire him instantly, then fire him again.

"There is no question in my mind that Larry was a genius," Durocher would say in his autobiography. "There is that thin line between genius and insanity, and in Larry's case it was sometimes so thin that you could see him drifting back and forth. . . .

"During my four years as his manager, there wasn't one dull moment."

Having broken the taboo against night baseball in New York, MacPhail now moved to end the ban on radio coverage. An agreement among the Dodgers, Giants and Yankees to bar radio broadcasts of their games had another year to run. But in December '38, MacPhail announced that the Dodgers were going on the air. He accepted an offer from General Mills to sponsor the games over WOR for the princely sum of $1,000 a game.

When the 1939 season arrived, Brooklyn fans were introduced to a strange sound: the gentle southern tones of thirty-one-year-old Red Barber. Born in Columbus, Mississippi, Barber had started out at the University of Florida radio station, then moved on to Cincinnati and broadcast the Reds' games when MacPhail was running the club. Now MacPhail brought him to Brooklyn.

Meticulous in his preparation, Barber earned the respect of Dodger fans with his knowledge of the game. He gained their affection with his colorful phrase-making. An argument was a "rhubarb." When a rally was in progress, "the boys are tearin' up the pea patch." When the bases were loaded, they would be "F.O.B." for full of Brooklyns.

In Barber's early years with the Dodgers, only the games at Ebbets Field were broadcast from the ballpark. Barber would be in the WOR studio for road games, providing an account based on telegraph reports.

Many a youngster would huddle by the radio late at night to hear Barber describe a game in the Middle West that Red wasn't even watching. One of the listeners was a boy named Philip Roth. Years later, the writer would recall how "my feel for the American landscape came less from what I learned in the classroom about Lewis and Clark than from following the major-league clubs on their road trips and reading about the minor leagues in the back pages of the *Sporting News*. The size of the continent got through to you finally when you had to stay up to 10:30 P.M. in New Jersey to hear via radio 'ticker-tape' Cardinal pitcher Mort Cooper throw the first strike of the night to Brooklyn shortstop Pee Wee Reese out in 'steamy' Sportsman's Park in St. Louis, Missouri."

It seemed that Barber's voice was everywhere in Brooklyn. And a fan could hear the play-by-play even when a radio wasn't personally at hand.

In the 1950's, Dave Anderson would be covering the Dodgers for the *Brooklyn Eagle*. In the early 40's, as a youngster in Bay Ridge—a neighborhood of mostly two-family homes near the Narrows waterway—he could hear Barber simply by taking a stroll.

"When you were a kid, you always went to the street corner where the newsstand was, or the movies," Anderson would recall. "Then you would decide to go somewhere.

"Those were the years there was no air conditioning. People had their windows open. You could walk down a street—I'm thinking of Seventy-second Street between Third Avenue and Ridge Boulevard—and never miss a pitch. It was amazing. Everybody had Red Barber on the radio."

Each evening, there would be small crowds around the newsstands awaiting the first editions of the tabloid papers and their accounts of the games Barber had described.

"Those were times when you had early editions of the *News* and the *Mirror*," Anderson remembered. "They were each two cents. They'd come in between eight and eight-thirty. They'd throw them off the big trucks. We would wait for that."

In this pre-TV era, a trip to the ballpark and the ensuing eyewitness account made a youngster a celebrity on the block for a few hours.

Decades later, living in Dave Anderson's old neighborhood, Tom Knight would bring back the memories by helping to form a Brooklyn Dodger Hall of Fame. Back in the 1930's, his devotion to the Dodgers first stirred on the streets of Park Slope and soon took shape in the Ebbets Field pavilion.

If a youngster was lucky, he might spot a Dodger player—perhaps even the manager—around Park Slope. And even though the Dodgers were perennially stumbling, they were the stuff of heroes for some.

"There was a cigar-candy store on the corner of Ninth Street and Third Avenue owned by a man named Jacob Wolf," Tom Knight remembers. "I went in one day, and there was a Coca-Cola glass on top of the cash register. Somebody said, 'What's the glass doing there?'

"One of Jacob Wolf's sons said, 'Casey Stengel drank out of it.' So they put the glass on top. It was there for quite a while.

"He probably was up at the Greater New York Saving Bank, which was a block away. A lot of the ballplayers had accounts there.

"And there was a saloon on Fifth Avenue—a speakeasy during Prohibition days—called Felzman's, and a lot of the ballplayers hung out in that place. It started when they were in Washington Park. This was right in the neighborhood. But even when they moved to Ebbets Field, a lot of the players would continue going over there because it was a really good restaurant."

◆ *A stormy pair: Larry MacPhail and Leo Durocher. (Los Angeles Dodgers)*

Soon, young Tom Knight was experiencing the excitement of a day at the ballpark and then reporting to his fellow Dodger fans on what he had seen.

"There was no television, of course. When you came back to the neighborhood and told your friends you were at a ballgame, you were the most important guy around. They were asking about different plays, how did so-and-so do, and how did this guy look? Going to a game was really a big deal, it was quite an experience."

The game was the thing in the days before exploding scoreboards and giveaway gimmicks.

"You didn't go for bat days or glove days or hat days," Knight noted. "None of this promotional stuff. You just went because you wanted to see a baseball game.

"When you went into the ballpark, the only thing you might buy would be a scorecard for a nickel. But they'd sell the *Eagle* outside for three cents, and you'd get a special wrapper over the regular paper with the lineup and the pictures of some of the players who were going to play that day. And they'd give you a pencil. And, of course, you'd have your regular sports stories inside, by Tommy Holmes and Harold Parrott and Harold Burr. That way you'd save two cents than if you got the scorecard at the ballpark."

For young fans, the upper deck in center field provided a cheap but wonderful view.

"The Polo Grounds and Yankee Stadium had the regular bleacher seats," Knight recalled. "There was no covering overhead. There were no backs or arms to seats, there were benches.

"Brooklyn didn't really have bleacher seats in center field. They called that the pavilion. You had a very good comfortable seat for fifty-five cents. It was beautiful sitting up there on a sunny day when there was a nice breeze. You could look out on Bedford Avenue and see the whole ballpark in front of you. The only thing you couldn't see were catches made against the wall in center field."

By the time the 1950's had arrived, a trip to Ebbets Field, while still a thrilling event for a youngster, could never be quite as special. For the Dodger heroes could be seen with a flick of the television switch.

Late in the 1939 season, Red Barber became a television pioneer.

On the final Saturday afternoon in August, Americans were preoccupied with the grim news from overseas. Before the following week would be over, Europe would be at war.

But in Brooklyn, there was a respite of sorts from the headlines telling of Hitler's threats. The Dodgers took on the Reds in a doubleheader, and 33,535 fans jammed Ebbets Field.

The outcome of the games would hardly be remembered a few days later. Yet an item below a story detailing the hits, runs and errors would herald a communications revolution.

"Major League Baseball Makes Its Radio Camera Debut," read the modest headline in the *New York Times*.

The "radio camera" was television.

On the afternoon of August 26, the National Broadcasting Company's experimental station W2XBS inaugurated TV coverage of major league baseball by carrying the first game of the Dodgers-Reds doubleheader.

The ballpark crowd, of course, vastly outnumbered the home viewing audience: There were only a few hundred TV sets in the New York metropolitan area.

The NBC station, located in the Empire State Building, installed two cameras for the pioneering effort. One was placed behind home plate, the other in the upper deck over third base, where space had been cleared for Barber. He did the telecast from an open box, using earphones that put him in touch with the director, who was stationed in a truck outside the ballpark.

"There was no monitor—this was before anyone ever dreamed of a monitor," Barber would recall in his memoirs. "Burke Crotty was the director, and every once in a while he would holler at me through the earphones that the camera was on second base now or it was on the pitcher."

The sponsors of the Dodger radio broadcasts—Wheaties, Mobil Oil and Ivory Soap—were given one free TV commercial apiece. Barber pitched the products without a script. For the Wheaties advertisement, he held up the cereal box, taking out what he called a "breakfast-size sample" while confessing it was rather late in the day for such a treat. Barber dropped the flakes into a bowl, sliced a banana, poured some milk and touted "The Breakfast of Champions."

The Dodgers' Luke (Hot Potato) Hamlin had a 2–0 shutout going into the eighth inning, but then his catcher, Babe Phelps, became the first "goat" of a televised sports event. Phelps dropped a pop-up, allowing a rally to begin, and later fumbled a throw from the outfield as Bucky Walters, the Reds' pitcher, barreled into him with the inning's third run. Cincinnati eventually won by 5–2.

When the game was over, Barber interviewed Durocher and the Reds' Bill McKechnie. He also asked Walters to show how he gripped a baseball and had Dolph Camilli display his exceptionally large hands for the camera.

Although the telecast was a milestone for the major leagues, it was actually the second baseball game to be seen on TV. The previous May 17, NBC had televised the Columbia-Princeton game from Baker Field in Manhattan, with Bill Stern doing the announcing, supported by only one camera.

NBC got the rights to the Brooklyn game free in return for installing a TV set in the Dodger press room so Larry MacPhail could view history in the making.

MacPhail allowed occasional telecasts during the following two seasons, but then World War II put the experiment on hold.

The Dodgers would be involved in two other television "firsts." The 1947 Dodger-Yankee World Series was the first one to be telecast. In 1951, CBS chose a game between the Dodgers and Braves for the debut of major league color telecasting.

The team that Red Barber reported on during his first summer in Brooklyn wasn't "tearin' up the pea patch" with regularity, but MacPhail had stepped up the pace of buying ballplayers.

Before the '39 season, he took a chance on a couple of right-handed pitchers from Georgia who had been failures elsewhere in the big leagues. Hugh Casey, who hadn't done much with the Cubs back in '35—his lone major league season—was drafted from the Memphis farm club. Whitlow Wyatt, plagued by arm problems and wildness, had floundered with the Tigers, White Sox and Indians, but he had won 23 games in the minors with Milwaukee the previous year so MacPhail bought him too.

In July '39, MacPhail purchased another Georgia native, a left-handed batting outfielder named Fred (Dixie) Walker. A decade earlier, Walker had looked to be a terrific prospect. He hit .401 in the Sally League in 1930, was fast and had a great arm. But he was hampered by shoulder, collarbone and knee injuries in his years with the Yankees, White Sox and Tigers, and now, at age twenty-nine, had been waived by Detroit for a modest $10,000.

Casey, Wyatt and Walker would prove to be wonderful pickups. But MacPhail got some clunkers as well. The Giants had bought a pitcher named Red Evans from New Orleans, where he won 21 games in 1938. In an oversight, they placed him on the roster of their Jersey City farm team, making him vulnerable to the draft process. MacPhail promptly grabbed him. But the joke was on the Dodgers. Evans went 1–8. Then there was Cletus Elwood (Boots) Poffenberger, a pitcher purchased from the Tigers in April. He was routed in a few appearances, was fined twice for breaking curfew, then jumped ship in May, explaining, "Where I belong is back home in Maryland, where I can get $15 for pitching a ballgame every Sunday."

Durocher, continuing to play shortstop, kept things lively. On July 2, in the second game of a Sunday doubleheader at the Polo Grounds, he spiked the Giant first baseman, Zeke Bonura, after hitting into a double play. Bonura fired the ball past Durocher's head, then chased him into right field where they briefly exchanged punches. Bonura was fined $50 and Durocher $25. Dodger fans collected 2,500 pennies to pay their manager's fine, the idea being that Durocher would dump them on the field. But Ford Frick warned he wouldn't look kindly on the stunt, so Leo anted up some bills.

◆ *Red Barber interviews Leo Durocher at Ebbets Field in August 1939 during the first telecast of a major league game. (Los Angeles Dodgers)*

The Dodgers struggled for most of the '39 season, but a late spurt brought them home in third place, the first time they had finished out of the second division since 1932. The pennant winners were the Cincinnati Reds, the team MacPhail had started building a few years before.

Camilli and Lavagetto supplied what little punch the lineup had. Camilli hit 26 homers, drove in 104 runs and batted .290. Lavagetto had 10 home runs, 87 r.b.i.'s and a .300 average. Dixie Walker saw a lot of action and hit .280. The big surprise was Hot Potato Hamlin, who went 20–13 in what would be his only outstanding season. Hugh Casey, both a starter and reliever his first year in Brooklyn, was 15–10, and Whitlow Wyatt helped out with an 8–3 mark.

While MacPhail was spending money, he also brought it in. The Dodgers drew 955,668 fans at Ebbets Field, double the turnout from 1937, the year before MacPhail arrived. The ballclub claimed a profit of more than $143,000, the first time it had made money since 1930.

The Dodgers were coming back, but 1939 proved a losing year for another Brooklyn outfit—the organized crime rubout squad known as "Murder, Inc." Based in Midnight Rose's, a candy store at Livonia and Saratoga avenues in the Brownsville section, the gangsters were reputedly responsible for hundreds of mob-ordered executions around the country. They rivaled the Dodgers in providing colorful newspaper copy with a roster including the likes of Abe (Kid Twist) Reles, Hershel (Pittsburgh Phil) Strauss, Mot'l (Bugsy) Goldstein, Abraham (Pretty) Levine, Philip (Little Farfel) Cohen, Irving (Knadles) Nitzberg, Anthony (the Duke) Maffetore and Albert (Allie Tick Tock) Tannenbaum. But on August 24, 1939, "Murder, Inc." suffered a big blow when its head man, Louis (Lepke) Buchalter, turned himself in to J. Edgar Hoover. A few years later, Lepke would be executed at Sing Sing.

"Murder, Inc." wasn't the only crew with colorful nicknames. The 1940 season brought the arrival in Brooklyn of Pee Wee, Ducky and Pistol Pete.

During the winter of '40, MacPhail purchased a slender young short-stop from Kentucky named Harold Reese, better known as Pee Wee since winning a marble tournament at age twelve. Reese had been playing for the Louisville Colonels, a farm team of the Red Sox. Since Joe Cronin, the Boston manager, wasn't ready to give up his shortstop job, Reese was expendable. For $50,000, the Dodgers found a wonderful replacement for the aging Durocher.

In June, looking for outfield punch, MacPhail forked over $132,500 and four players to the Cardinals for Joe (Ducky) Medwick, a star from the Gas House Gang days, and Curt Davis, a veteran right-handed pitcher.

Soon after that, the Dodgers called up a twenty-year-old with speed and power who showed promise of becoming a superstar. Back in March 1938, Commissioner Landis had declared seventy-three players in Branch Rickey's Cardinal farm system free agents because the club violated various regulations. MacPhail quickly signed fourteen of the emancipated prospects. One of them, picked up for $100, was Pete Reiser. In the spring of '39, Reiser had been a sensation in training camp. He was sent back to the minors, but in 1940 he arrived to stay.

The Dodgers won their first eight games of the '40 season and then Tex Carleton, an over-the-hill right-hander, captured No. 9 with a no-hitter against the Reds at Crosley Field. The next day, Cincinnati ended the winning streak.

Soon came the month of the beanballs.

On June 1, Reese was hit in the head by the Cubs' Jake Mooty at Wrigley Field and was sidelined for a few weeks. While the rookie shortstop was recuperating, Medwick arrived, but a couple of days after joining Brooklyn, he was beaned at Ebbets Field by the Cards' Bob Bowman and carried off on a stretcher. Certain that Medwick's old teammate had deliberately hit him, MacPhail raced over to the Cardinal bench and challenged the whole bunch to a fistfight. Pepper Martin and Johnny Mize held him back, and Bowman was hustled from the ballpark by a pair of detectives. MacPhail then demanded that Brooklyn District Attorney William O'Dwyer, who had been investigating "Murder, Inc.," turn his energies to what the *Brooklyn Eagle* called "Beanball, Inc." Burton Turkus, the O'Dwyer aide who was the chief prosecutor of "Murder, Inc.," did look into the Medwick beaning, but found no intent of assassination on the part of Bowman. Medwick returned to the lineup before long, but never again was the aggressive hitter he had been.

The Dodgers battled the Reds for the league lead into midsummer, but then Cincinnati began pulling away.

On September 16, the teams met at Ebbets Field in their last encounter of the season. The game was tied, 3–3, in the tenth inning when Umpire George Magerkurth made a call on the bases that helped keep a Reds rally going. Durocher stormed onto the field and was ejected. Moments later, a fly ball brought in what became the winning run. As Magerkurth was leaving the field, a twenty-one-year-old fan named Frank Germano came out of the stands and jumped him. At six feet three inches, Magerkurth towered over his assailant, but Germano got atop him and began pummeling away. With the help of the other umpires, he was finally dragged off and arrested. It turned out that the overly zealous young man was out on parole for a petty larceny conviction so he was quickly shipped back upstate to do his rooting behind bars again.

Was Germano denounced for misguided mayhem? Not in the *Brooklyn Eagle,* he wasn't.

"Come what may, the little man had his big day in Flatbush yesterday in the fading hours of sunlight," wrote Jimmy Wood, the *Eagle*'s sports editor. "Our Frankie will become ex-officio a member of the Hall of Fame, for he single-handedly defended the fair name of the Dodgers from what he considered to be grievous wrong.

"You didn't get hoited much, did you, kid?"

Magerkurth proved sympathetic as well. When the case came to court the following April, he dropped his complaint.

Cincinnati went on to its second straight pennant. The Dodgers finished second by 12 games but their 88–65 mark was the club's best since 1924. Camilli hit 23 homers, Medwick batted .300, and Freddie Fitzsimmons, at age thirty-nine, turned in a 16–2 season.

Dixie Walker hit .308, but his real heroics were saved for the Giants, against whom he batted .435. He punctuated his Giant-killing with two singles, a triple and home run at the Polo Grounds on August 7 when 53,997 fans turned out for Mel Ott Night, only to see an 8–4 Dodger victory.

Any Dodger who tormented the Giants deserved special adulation, and Walker got it. He became the Brooklyn fans' hero, "The Peepul's Cherce."

While building a contender, MacPhail continued to thrive as an innovator and promoter. His experiment with a yellow baseball didn't last long. But he saw the future when it came to aviation. On the evening of May 7, 1940, the Dodgers became the first big league team to fly en masse during the regular season, traveling in two planes from St. Louis to Chicago.

After playing the Cubs, the Dodgers flew on to Brooklyn's Floyd Bennett Field, again in two planes. It was quite an occasion. Arriving just before one A.M., the ballplayers were greeted by 10,000 fans, a huge sign reading "Welcome Home Brooklyn Dodgers," and a speech by Borough President John Cashmore.

In September, MacPhail brought the heroes of yesterday back to Brooklyn for an old-timers' game, an event that had yet to be commonplace. Zach Wheat made two nice catches in left field, Dazzy Vance pitched an inning, and Bill Dahlen, who had managed the Dodgers their first year at Ebbets Field, showed up too.

Wheat had played on the Dodgers' two previous pennant-winning teams. But that was back in 1916 and 1920. Another pennant was long overdue.

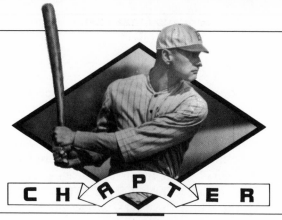

22

First-Place Finish, Third-Strike Sorrow

T he trade talk—and the whiskey—flowed freely into the early morning hours. Larry MacPhail was in the process of wearing down the Cubs' brass to get a ballplayer he wanted badly.

After long haggling inside a Hotel Commodore suite with Chicago's general manager, Jim Gallagher, and the field boss, Jimmie Wilson, the deal was done.

And what a deal it was. MacPhail gladly parted with Johnny Hudson, an undistinguished infielder; Charlie Gilbert, a reserve outfielder—both in the minors with Montreal—and a hunk of cash (perhaps $60,000) in exchange for Billy Herman, the perennial all-star second baseman.

MacPhail couldn't wait for daylight's arrival to pass on the news. He phoned Herman in his room to welcome him aboard.

"It was about two o'clock in the morning," Herman would recall. "He said, 'You were sleeping, weren't you?' I said, 'Yeah.' He said, 'Can you get dressed and come on down, I wanna meet you.' So I did. I was there maybe about thirty minutes. He said, 'I'm Larry MacPhail and you're my new second baseman.' "

"It was kind of a shock," Herman remembered. "I'd been with the Cubs so long. I'd been there ten years and I had no inkling I was being traded. But I thought, what the heck, I'm going to a better ballclub—so that's good enough for me."

Herman was in the lineup against the Pirates the next afternoon, his old teammates having gone up to the Polo Grounds.

♦ *Dixie Walker, The Peepul's Cherce.*
(Los Angeles Dodgers)

"The first game I played with the Dodgers, I was nervous as a rookie coming up, I was like a kid," he recalled. "I was so used to wearing that Cub uniform and playing in Chicago."

But he made the adjustment beautifully that afternoon of May 6, 1941, celebrating with a double, three singles and a walk.

The previous winter MacPhail had obtained Kirby Higbe, a fourteen-game winner with the lowly Phillies, and Mickey Owen, a fine catcher for the Cardinals. Now, with the arrival of Herman, the final pieces were in place from a building plan begun back in March '38 with the purchase of Dolph Camilli.

But before the '41 lineup was set, Durocher's maneuvering brought an uproar. At spring training, all eyes were on Pete Reiser. He had played mostly at third base after being called up during the summer of '40, but now Durocher was grooming him to play center field. When the season opened, Reiser had replaced Dixie Walker in center. Walker went to the bench, and the aging Paul Waner, recently obtained from the Pirates, was put in right field. The fans were furious. A telegram signed by 5,000 Dixie Walker fanatics demanded that the "Peepul's Cherce" return to the lineup.

Reiser stayed in center, but Walker was soon back. He went to right field, replacing Waner, who was sent to the Braves. With Joe Medwick still in left, the outfield looked just fine.

Camilli at first base, Herman

◆ *With Brooklyn two weeks away from clinching the 1941 pennant, a few of the Dodgers rehearse for the team's championship photo. (L. to r.) Manager Leo Duro-cher, Pee Wee Reese, Billy Herman, Dolph Camilli, Lew Riggs and Cookie Lava-getto. (National Baseball Library, Cooperstown, N.Y.)*

at second in place of Pete Coscarart, Reese at shortstop and Lavagetto at third gave the Dodgers a strong infield as well.

Having gotten the ballplayers he wanted, MacPhail, ever the innovator, now looked for a way to safeguard his investments. During spring training, he unveiled a plastic protector that could be sewed into the lining of caps. Reese and Medwick, both having been beaned the season before, were the first to try it. Designed by doctors at Johns Hopkins University in Baltimore, the protectors were forerunners of the batting helmet.

As the '41 season moved along, the Dodgers battled for the league lead with the Cardinals. The old Gas House Gang was gone, but Branch Rickey, the St. Louis general manager, had come up with the likes of Enos Slaughter, Johnny Mize and Marty Marion.

The tension grew as the Dodgers went west in September. In perhaps the biggest game of the season, Whitlow Wyatt outpitched the Cards' Mort Cooper in a 1–0 victory at Sportsman's Park, the only run coming home on Herman's eighth-inning double. On the Dodgers' next stop, they played sixteen scoreless innings with the Reds, but Pete Reiser led off the seventeenth with a homer and Brooklyn went on to a 5–1 victory.

Then came a stormy visit to Pittsburgh. On September 18, in the second game of that series, Hugh Casey was called for a balk bringing Vince DiMaggio home with a run, tying the game in the eighth inning. Furious at the home-plate umpire, George Magerkurth, Casey took up where that exuberant Dodger fan Frankie Germano had left off the previous September. He fired three straight fastballs aimed not at the catcher's mitt but at Magerkurth's head. The umpire naturally let Casey know how aggrieved he was. Durocher came out to inquire what Magerkurth was so upset about, and before long Leo had also incurred the ump's wrath and was ejected. On the way to his locker, he stopped long enough to smash all the lightbulbs in the clubhouse corridor and then hurled a chair through the transom of the umpires' dressing room. Moments later, Durocher's fury reached new heights when a puny-hitting rookie shortstop named Alf Anderson tripled home the winning run for the Pirates.

Now it was on to Philadelphia and more trouble for Durocher. The next day, he was fined $150 for the run-in with Magerkurth and got into a confrontation outside the Warwick Hotel with Ted Meier, an Associated Press reporter, who claimed Durocher landed three right hands to his jaw. But the stopover in Philly was a rewarding one as Wyatt and Higbe combined for a doubleheader victory.

A few days later—on the afternoon of Thursday, September 25—the Dodgers clinched their first pennant since 1920 on Wyatt's 6–0 shutout over Boston at Braves Field.

◆ *The 1941 pennant-winning Dodgers. Top row (l. to r.): Hugh Casey, Dolph Camilli, George Pfister, Jimmy Wasdell, Herman Franks, Coach Roy Spencer, Pete Coscarart, Freddie Fitzsimmons, Augie Galan and Dixie Walker.* Middle row (l. to r.): Joe Medwick, Curt Davis, Tom Drake, Larry French, Whitlow Wyatt, El Albosta, Luke Hamlin, Newt Kimball, Billy Herman and Johnny Allen. Bottom row (l. to r.): Wilton, trainer; Cookie Lavagetto, Pee Wee Reese, Pete Reiser, Coach Red Corriden, Manager Leo Durocher, Coach Charley Dressen, Kirby Higbe, Mickey Owen and Lew Riggs. (Los Angeles Dodgers)*

A happy gang of tie-snipping, champagne-guzzling ballplayers headed to Grand Central Terminal, where 10,000 fans mobbed them.

Most definitely not on hand for the celebration was Larry MacPhail.

MacPhail had taken a cab to the 125th Street station—the last stop before mid-Manhattan—intending to board the train there so he could join his players for the entry into Grand Central Terminal. But he watched the railroad cars whiz by. Unaware that MacPhail was waiting to climb aboard and fearful that some of his besotted players might get off in Harlem, Durocher had ordered the conductor to bypass the stop.

By the time MacPhail had taken a taxi back to midtown, the celebration was long over. He finally caught up with Durocher at his Hotel New Yorker suite later in the evening and promptly fired him. That lasted until the next morning, when Leo was rehired in time for the World Series.

Before the Series began, there was a wild celebration in the streets of Brooklyn. The players assembled at Grand Army Plaza and rode in a motorcade along Flatbush Avenue and Fulton Street to the Brooklyn Borough Hall as a crowd estimated at more than one million packed downtown. Confetti rained down as the throngs tried to grab at their heroes, one gray-haired woman scratching a policeman when he stopped her from kissing Durocher's hand as his car went by. Banners proclaimed "Lippy for Mayor" and "Moider Them Yanks." An infant in a stroller was bedecked with a sign reading "Our Little Bum Is Proud of All Our Brooklyn Bums."

When the fun was finally over, the Dodgers looked ahead to a formidable task. The Yankees had rolled to the American League pennant by 17 games over the Red Sox in the electrifying summer of Joe DiMaggio's 56-game hitting streak.

The Dodger team that went into the World Series had been almost wholly remade by Larry MacPhail. Only four men on the roster that January '38 day MacPhail arrived—Durocher, Fitzsimmons, Lavagetto and Hamlin—remained on the ballclub.

MacPhail's most spectacular acquisition—Pete Reiser—won the batting title with a .343 average. The other outfielders weren't bad either—Medwick hit .318 and Walker .311. Camilli led the league in homers with 34 and runs batted in with 120.

Higbe (22–9) and Wyatt (22–10) were the pitching aces while Casey, working mostly in relief, went 14–11. Freddie Fitzsimmons, after a 16–2 season, got into only 13 games with a 6–1 record, but he had an excuse. Early in the season, while coaching at third base, he picked up Medwick's glove when the Dodgers came off the field. A little later, trotting out to left, Medwick tried to grab the glove back. Fitzsimmons's fingers became tangled in the webbing and he suffered a torn muscle in his left arm, sidelining him for a month. That wasn't the only bizarre incident worthy of Uncle Robbie's days. Wyatt might have had an additional victory had he not swallowed mouthwash by mistake while taking a salt tablet during an outing against the Reds. The ensuing fiery belly forced him to depart from a game the Dodgers eventually won.

The Series opened at the Stadium with Durocher saving Higbe and Wyatt and going with Curt Davis, 13–7 on the season, against Red Ruffing. Trailing 3–1 in the seventh, the Dodgers came up with a run, but Reese killed the rally by foolishly trying to go from second to third after a foul pop. The Yanks won it, 3–2.

The Dodgers got even the next afternoon with a 3–2 victory, the winning run scoring on a sixth-inning single by Camilli off Johnny Murphy, who had relieved Spud Chandler. Wyatt, scattering nine hits, went all the way.

After a one-day rain delay, the Series resumed at Ebbets Field with Fitzsimmons starting against Marius Russo. The game was scoreless in the seventh inning, but then Fitzsimmons ran into hard luck that made the glove-grabbing misadventure pale in comparison. Joe Gordon walked with one out, then took second on a grounder. Next at the plate was Russo. He connected with a shot off Fitzsimmons's left kneecap that hit so viciously that the ball caromed into the air. Reese grabbed it on the fly to end the inning. But that also ended Fitzsimmons's afternoon—he was taken off with a broken kneecap. Casey, having to warm up quickly, came on in the eighth and was immediately touched for a pair of runs. The Yanks went on to win it, 2–1.

The Yankees knocked Higbe out early in Game 4, but the Dodgers came back against Atley Donald and took a 4–3 lead in the fifth inning on Reiser's two-run homer over the right-field scoreboard clock. It stayed that way until the ninth. Casey, the fourth Dodger pitcher of the day, retired Johnny Sturm and Red Rolfe and now needed one more out to even the Series at two games apiece. The count went to 3 and 2 on Tommy Henrich, and then Casey delivered a breaking ball. Henrich missed it by half a foot. The game was seemingly over. But to the Dodger fans' horror, catcher Mickey Owen missed the pitch as well. The ball got past him to the backstop, and Henrich was safe at first. DiMaggio followed with a line single to left and then Charlie Keller doubled off the right-field screen to put the Yanks ahead, 5–4. Two more runs crossed later and the Dodgers were done for.

Whatever else he did, Mickey Owen would always be remembered for that moment. The missed third strike would make him one of the "goats" of World Series history.

A few years later, Casey claimed the pitch was a spitball. But Owen and Henrich always said it wasn't so. Almost a half-century after that day at Ebbets Field, they were inducted together into the Brooklyn Dodger Hall of Fame in ceremonies outside the Brooklyn Museum. Linked together in baseball history, they lined up again on the same side of the story.

◆ *Mickey Owen chases the one that got away as Yankees' Tommy Henrich dashes for first base in Game 4 of the 1941 World Series. (Los Angeles Dodgers)*

"If Casey threw a spitball he threw it on his own. It never looked like a spitball to me," said Owen. "It was a curveball—that's what I called for." Owen said he had been looking for the quick curve Casey had been throwing for the previous couple of innings, but that Casey instead delivered a big overhand curve for the first time in the game and "it really broke big, down and in. Tommy missed it by six inches."

"I swung at a big breaking curveball," echoed Henrich.

The Dodgers remained alive despite Owen's calamitous miscue, but, as Billy Herman would recall, they might just as well have headed home.

"It was like being in a morgue," remembered Herman, conjuring up the scene in the clubhouse. "We were running them right out of the ballpark, we were running hard and sliding hard and knocking them down and we were just having a ball, and we were going to do all right until that thing happened and, of course, that took all the fire out of us and put some in them. We played a real good Series until that one play."

The Yankees wrapped it up at Ebbets Field the following afternoon with Ernie Bonham besting Wyatt, 3–1.

The next day, the *Brooklyn Eagle* sounded a rallying cry that would become the theme for frustrated Dodger fans over many an October to come:

"WAIT TILL NEXT YEAR."

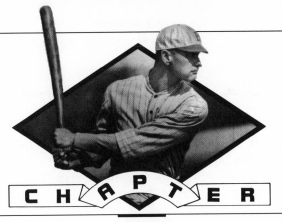

CHAPTER

23

At War with the Cardinals

In the first weeks of 1942, America's Pacific Fleet lay in ruins at Pearl Harbor, the Japanese were about to capture the Philippines, and Hitler was triumphant throughout Europe. The burdens on Franklin D. Roosevelt were enormous. And then a letter arrived on the President's desk asking him to turn briefly from his real worries.

Would it be okay for the national pastime to keep going in wartime?

On January 14, Commissioner Landis penciled a note to F.D.R.: "Baseball is about to adopt schedules, sign players, make vast commitments, go to training camps. What do you want us to do? If you believe we ought to close down for the duration of the war, we are ready to do so immediately. If you feel we ought to continue, we would be delighted to do so. We await your order."

Roosevelt quickly responded in what became known as his "Green Light" letter.

Citing the sport's presumed value as a morale-booster, the President wrote: "I honestly feel it would be best for the country to keep baseball going." But individual players eligible for the military "should go without question into the services."

And so baseball would carry on through the war years, eventually limping along with a collection of draft rejects, old-timers and teenagers.

For the Dodgers, the war had its first major impact on February 1 when Cookie Lavagetto, an all-star third baseman the four previous seasons, announced he had joined the Navy. But Larry MacPhail evidently was expecting the news. Two months earlier, he had obtained the outstanding third baseman Arky Vaughan from the Pirates for four players, none of them regulars.

The Dodgers began their first wartime spring training with several games in Cuba before settling in at Daytona Beach. One evening in Havana, a private war far removed from the real one erupted. The combatants were as unlikely a pair as ever confronted each other: Hugh Casey versus Ernest Hemingway.

Billy Herman, a witness to the battle, recalled it vividly many years later:

We met Ernest Hemingway, and he was a very gracious person and just a wonderful man—when he was sober. He was the type of man, he did not want to lose. I don't care what he did— pitch horseshoes—he'd fight you to beat you. He wanted to be a winner all the time.

He asked if any of us guys liked to shoot—he was a great skeet shooter. Four of us went out—Hugh Casey, Larry French, Augie Galan and myself. He invited us out to the skeet club after the workout. So we went out and shot skeet, and it's a real fancy club, and we were just having a fine time and doing some drinking too. They had a portable bar right behind where you stood to shoot. So every time you shot, you reached around and they handed you a drink. This goes on till late in the afternoon, almost dark, and he invited us to his house for dinner. He said his wife would fix up something. So, okay, we were feeling pretty good by then. So we went.

We had a few more drinks, and she had dinner. He was a huge man—about six feet three or four and weighed like 220 pounds—he was about the same size as Hugh Casey. So after dinner, his wife cleaned up the den and we sat around and we're talking and drinking. Now it's getting kind of late at night, and out of a clear blue sky he looks at Casey and he says, "You know something, Hugh, you're just about my size. Let's you and I box." Casey's a kind of slow, easygoing guy. He says, "Nah, I don't wanna box."

But they were both feeling pretty good by then, of course, so Hemingway finally went over and opened the closet door in the family room there and pulled out two pair of boxing gloves. He said, "Here, slip these on, we'll just spar a little bit, we'll just have a little fun." So Hemingway put his gloves on right quick and he wound up and hit Casey while he was putting his gloves on. But he wasn't getting the best of him right quick. So Casey got his gloves on and he wasn't near as drunk as Hemingway, so he hit Hemingway, and Hemingway flew into a little portable bar they had there, and there's bottles and glasses hitting on the terrazzo floor, made a helluva noise.

His wife comes running out of the bedroom and says, "What's going on here?" He says, "That's all right, honey, go on back to bed, we're just having a little fun." So she did, and he and Casey sparred for a couple of minutes and we saw it was gonna get pretty nasty so we stopped it. So okay, he said, "Let's have another drink." So we sat down and everything quieted down and finally it's getting pretty close to twelve o'clock and we're supposed to have a curfew at twelve, so we said we gotta go, and he said, "I'll call my chauffeur and he can drive you back to town."

His chauffeur came and we started for the door, and when he got to the door he grabbed Casey by the arm and he said, "Look, why don't you stay here and spend the night with me? You got the better of me tonight, but I'd like to try you again. In the morning we'll both be sober and we'll have a duel. You pick the weapons—pistols or knives or swords—whatever you want to use."

Of course, we got the hell out of there in a hurry. The next morning, about nine o'clock, his wife and him walked into the lobby of the hotel. We were all sitting around, talking, and she brought him over and made him apologize, and he was almost in tears, hanging his head. He was ashamed of what happened.

―――――

An armistice having been agreed to, the Dodgers soon headed for Daytona Beach. But before they could re-enter the country, the Brooklyn road secretary, John McDonald, had to do some explaining to an American intelligence officer.

Figuring Havana would be a treat for his more fun-loving players, MacPhail had hired a private detective to shadow the night owls. When the U.S. intelligence official checked McDonald's briefcase, he found the following notation:

―――――

Trailed No. 15 to the Florida, where he was joined by two others. He had two daiquiries. From there, he went to Sloppy Joe's, where he spent some time and had more drinks. No. 1 appeared and they walked together. No. 1 had a glass of beer. They left and walked toward Prado 86, but met No. 7 and No. 12 on the way. All of them got into a cab and they were driven to the Nacional.

━━━━━

Wondering whether he might have come upon an espionage operation, the intelligence officer demanded an explanation. McDonald told how the numerals corresponded to uniform numbers—No. 15 was Johnny Allen, a hot-tempered pitcher—and convinced the official there were no Axis agents in sight.

Finally, the Dodgers started to barnstorm north from Florida. Along the way, they got a taste of military life. First, they stopped for a ballgame at Camp Wheeler, Georgia, with several Brooklyn players treated to a Jeep ride from the Macon train station to the Army post. The Dodgers beat the servicemen, 7–5, before a crowd of 10,000 G.I.'s who were rewarded with vintage Durocher. Leo got himself into a mock argument with Joe Street, an Army private, who served as an umpire.

Entertaining the troops was one way baseball backed up its claim to be a morale-booster. There was a lot more it could do to support the war effort from the homefront.

The big league brass called on all ballplayers to put 10 percent of their salaries into war bonds. In February '42, Freddie Fitzsimmons, upon agreeing to a $12,000 contract, became the first major leaguer to sign up for bond purchases. He did it with considerable fanfare, posing alongside Larry MacPhail in front of a bond-drive poster.

When the Dodgers opened the season against the Giants, the Polo Grounds was enveloped in a patriotic glow.

Durocher and the Giants' Mel Ott—named the previous December to replace Bill Terry as manager—were handed war bonds by Mayor Fiorello LaGuardia in a home-plate ceremony at which they formally diverted 10 percent of their first paychecks to the bond drive. To the cheers of 50,000 fans, the mayor declared: "There are no more patriotic and loyal citizens in this country than ballplayers and ball fans."

Then the 17th Infantry band played the "Star-Spangled Banner" as players from both teams lined up at the outfield plaque honoring Eddie Grant, the former Giant captain killed in action during World War I.

The bond blitz was pursued from the broadcast booth as well. Years later, Red Barber would look back with great pride on his efforts to help finance the war effort.

"There were so many things to be done, every broadcaster did everything he could," Barber recalled. "In 1942, the general manager at WHN and two or three others up there came up with the idea that we'd go on the air. People would call in pledges for war bonds and we'd give their name. Then for every person who pledged, there was an acknowledgment card personally signed by me. I signed thousands. It was so successful, the Treasury Department in Washington asked me to come down and tell them how we'd done it."

The patriotic fervor at the Dodgers' season opener and home opener gave way to surliness in the stands when Brooklyn played its second game at Ebbets Field. At issue was a ball hit into the upper deck behind third base by the Phillies' Ron Northey. Fans at all parks had been asked to toss back foul balls so the baseballs could be sent on to military bases for recreational programs. But the spectator who grabbed Northey's foul refused to give it up. Another fan threatened to punch him. Ushers kept the pair apart and finally prevailed upon the reluctant ball-catcher to part with his souvenir.

Before long, the stands would be filled with men and women in uniform. When military personnel were on leave, they could attend ballgames without having to purchase tickets. Some 65,000 were admitted free at Ebbets Field during the 1942 season, nearly double the number at any other National League ballpark.

In May, the Dodgers stepped up the patriotic hoopla with a military spectacle. The two leagues had instructed each team to donate proceeds from one home game for a servicemen's charity, either the Army Emergency Relief Fund or the Navy Relief Society. MacPhail set May 8, a twilight game against the Giants, for the Dodgers' benefit affair.

In pregame pageantry, 2,000 sailors from the U.S.S. *Prairie State*—among them MacPhail's son Bill—marched on the field, an Army band played and the crowd sang "God Bless America."

A total of 42,888 tickets were sold—the 10,000 tickets beyond the park's capacity purchased by people who simply wanted to make a donation—and $60,000 was raised to benefit the Navy's welfare organization. With Dolph Camilli's bases-empty homer over the right-field wall in the seventh inning providing the margin of victory, the Dodgers capped the glorious evening with a 7–6 triumph.

The benefit game would be the first of many twilighters in Brooklyn during the '42 season. For night baseball in New York became a casualty of the war. In mid-May, Army officials and Dodger representatives took a boat a few miles out into the Atlantic as the lights were turned on at Ebbets Field. Their fears were confirmed: The glare from the light towers silhouetted ships, making them easy targets for torpedoes from Nazi U-boats lurking offshore.

The Dodgers had scheduled fourteen night games for 1942, but they were all converted into twilighters, and the Giants moved up the starting times of evening games at the Polo Grounds. The lights would remain on until an hour after sunset—when they would begin to take significant effect—and at that point, any twilight game still going on would be called. The score at the end of the previously completed inning would be the final result.

The shift to twilight games may have benefited the nation's war effort, but it only inflamed the enmity between Dodger and Giant fans.

On August 3, the largest single-game crowd in Polo Grounds history turned out to see the Giants play the Dodgers in a twilight game for the Army's serviceman relief agency. The Giants were trailing, 7–4, going into the bottom of the ninth, but they staged a rally. Bill Werber led off with a single against Whitlow Wyatt and then Mel Ott walked. That was it. As the clock struck 9:10 P.M.—the time designated for lights out—the umpires called the game. The Dodgers were declared the winners based on the score through eight innings.

War or no war, the Giant fans were enraged over their team's hopes being snatched away. As the Fred Waring Orchestra and a 150-member choral group began to conclude the evening's festivities with the national anthem, they were drowned out by booing. The fans quieted down only when a spotlight was shined on the American flag atop the center-field roof.

Dodger fans did some jeering of their own the very next evening when the teams played another twilight game at the Polo Grounds. Brooklyn had apparently been sent to victory on a bases-loaded inside-the-park homer by Pee Wee Reese off Fiddler Bill McGee that broke a 1–1 tie in the top of the tenth inning. But soon afterward, with Joe Medwick at bat, the moment for lights out arrived. The game became a nine-inning tie that would have to be replayed in its entirety. With their team's evident triumph taken away, the Dodger rooters let loose with a storm of boos. They did have a clear conscience, however, since this time there was no rendition of the national anthem to interrupt.

Notwithstanding the tempest over the twilight games, the season was going just fine for the Dodgers.

The war had made little impact on the team. Except for third base, where Vaughan had replaced Lavagetto, the lineup was unchanged from 1941, and the pitching staff was intact.

There had, however, been a scare in mid-July when Pete Reiser ran into the center-field wall at Sportsman's Park chasing an eleventh-inning drive by Enos Slaughter in the second game of a Sunday doubleheader. The shot went for an inside-the-park homer that gave the Cardinals a 7–6 victory. More importantly, Reiser had collapsed with a concussion. But he was back in the lineup by early August.

As the summer moved along, it seemed the Dodgers would run away from the Cardinals. As late as August 15, Brooklyn was in first place by nine and a half games over St. Louis.

But the margin brought no comfort to Larry MacPhail. In mid-August, he summoned his players to give them an unwelcome prediction.

"He called us up to his office in the ballpark," Billy Herman remembered. "He wanted everybody up there. I don't know what we were, about eight games out in front or something like that with about six or seven weeks to go. He said, 'You think you're gonna walk into this pennant; you're not gonna win it. Anybody wanna bet?' Dixie Walker says, 'Yeah, I'll bet ya.' I guess he could see something about us, a nonchalant attitude or something. He was trying to get us stirred up, to fight a little harder. Some of the players said, 'That old s.o.b.,' they didn't want to believe it."

But MacPhail was on the mark. The Dodgers dropped three out of four games to the Cardinals at Sportsman's Park in late August and left town only five and a half games in front. The Cards kept getting closer and gained a tie for first place after victories at Ebbets Field on September 11 and 12. The next day, St. Louis moved a game ahead by splitting a Sunday doubleheader with the Phillies while the Dodgers dropped two to the Reds.

The Dodgers played good ball as the season neared its end, but the Cardinals were even hotter, and by Sunday morning, September 20, they had moved ahead by two and a half games.

On the final Saturday, the Dodgers closed to a game and a half down. They won again on Sunday, but it was too late. The Cardinals captured the pennant with a 9–2 victory over the Cubs in the first game of a doubleheader as Ernie White pitched all the way.

After taking over first place on September 13, St. Louis had never given it back, winning 10 of 11 to close out the season. Despite MacPhail's warning, the Dodgers had not, in fact, collapsed. They took their final eight games. The Cardinals were simply too tough, winning 43 games while losing only 9 and tying 1 down the stretch.

Brooklyn finished with 104 victories. But St. Louis had 106. Mort Cooper's 22 wins and Johnny Beazley's 21 and a batting attack led by Enos Slaughter and Stan Musial put it away.

As the 1942 season came to an end, the Dodgers lost more than a pennant. Larry MacPhail, having built a winner after the futility of the Depression years, quit baseball to accept an Army commission.

The Cardinals won the World Series, defeating the Yankees in five games. But they too suffered a loss. On October 30, their general manager— perhaps the finest mind the game has ever known—left St. Louis to take MacPhail's place.

24

Few Heroes
on the Homefront

In some ways they were alike, and yet they were vastly different men.
Larry MacPhail and his successor in Brooklyn—Branch Rickey—
both were Midwesterners, both were innovators with enormous stores
of energy, and they both shared a talent for making money.

But where MacPhail was explosive and direct, Rickey bared his aims
with the greatest reluctance, seizing on biblical allusions and folksy stories
that might obscure rather than reveal. MacPhail was a heavy drinker, Rickey
a teetotaler and a religious man who seldom swore.

Wesley Branch Rickey was born on December 20, 1881, on a farm in
southern Ohio hill country near the town of Stockdale, the second son of
a devout Methodist family. (His first name, which he dispensed with as a
young man, was in honor of the founder of Methodism.) He attended a
one-room schoolhouse as a child and read voraciously when he could get
away from his farm chores. After a stint as an elementary school teacher
in rural Ohio, he went on to Ohio Wesleyan University, where he played
baseball and football and eventually coached the baseball team.

After a brief stay in the Texas League, Rickey was called up to the
Reds as a catcher in September 1904. But he never got into a game. As
soon as the ballclub discovered he wouldn't play on Sundays because of
religious principles, it released him. Rickey later caught on with the Browns
and in 1907 he played for the New York Highlanders, the forerunners of
the Yankees. Hampered by a sore arm, he set an unenviable record: thirteen
runners stole bases on him in a single game.

With his baseball career going nowhere and the obligations of a family man upon him—he had married Jane Moulton, the daughter of an Ohio merchant, in 1906—Rickey left the world of sports following his unhappy summer in New York.

He returned to school, getting a law degree at the University of Michigan, and then set up a private law practice in Idaho. But finding clients proved as tough as throwing out baserunners, and soon he returned to Ann Arbor, accepting a position as coach of the Michigan baseball team.

Rickey had been considered a brainy ballplayer, and now he found his true vocation: teaching the finer points of baseball. He did some scouting for the Browns while at Michigan, and soon he was back in the majors, named assistant to the president of the St. Louis ballclub in 1913. Before the summer was over, he had become the Browns' field manager, and he remained in the job through 1915, then took over as business manager.

In 1917, Rickey was named president of the Cardinals, and after service in World War I, he got the manager's job while continuing to work in the front office. He remained as manager until 1925, when Rogers Hornsby succeeded him, then was named general manager, flourishing in that role until he arrived in Brooklyn.

Since the Cardinals were perennially short of cash in Rickey's early years with the team, he was usually outbid in seeking to buy players. So he decided to raise them himself by developing a chain of minor league ballclubs. The concept of the farm system was born. Eventually, Rickey would build an empire: The Cardinals controlled thirty-two minor league teams at one point.

Between 1925 and 1942, Rickey's nurturing of prospects and shrewd dealing brought the Cardinals six pennants, four World Series titles and a pile of cash through the sale of surplus talent. Over the years, he attained a measure of personal wealth and gained renown throughout the baseball world for his intellect.

In contrast to his meticulous preparation in developing winners, Rickey's personal appearance seemed an afterthought. Extra-wide bow ties made to his order by Lord & Taylor and Brooks Brothers were his only bow to fashion.

"Rickey looks massive, benign and bucolic," wrote Robert Rice in a *New Yorker* magazine profile. "His hands are big, and several of his knuckles are swollen, a reminder of his career as a big-league catcher. At work, he is usually tilted perilously back in a swivel chair, his unshined shoes on his desk, a pair of spectacles on the end of his nose, a cowlick standing straight up on top of his head, and, in his hand, a tattered cigar describing eloquent conversational circles."

By the end of the '42 season, Rickey's long association with Sam Breadon, the Cardinal owner, had become strained. The Rickey family,

◆ *Larry MacPhail takes time from his Army chores to visit with Branch Rickey in August '43 as a team combining Dodger, Giant and Yankee players defeated a servicemen's club in a war-bond benefit game at the Polo Grounds. (National Baseball Library, Cooperstown, N.Y.)*

meanwhile, had developed ties to Brooklyn. Rickey's son, Branch, Jr., had been serving as the Dodgers' farm director since 1939. So when MacPhail went into the Army, Rickey decided to take on a new challenge. Two months before his sixty-first birthday, he was named president of the Dodgers.

In short order, Rickey found himself scrambling for talent as Brooklyn, along with the other big league teams, started losing men to the military.

Pete Reiser and Pee Wee Reese played ball during the summer of 1943, but their uniforms didn't bear the Dodger script. Reiser ran down fly balls at Fort Riley, Kansas, while Reese fielded grounders in Virginia for the Norfolk Naval Air Station. One of his teammates was Hugh Casey.

Larry French, one of the Dodgers' top pitchers the season before, also went into the Navy. He would eventually take part in the Normandy invasion, but in '43, French was a lieutenant junior grade at the Brooklyn Navy Yard. The proximity to Ebbets Field inspired him to ask the naval brass for a favor. Having compiled 197 career victories, French sought permission to pitch for Brooklyn while on leave so he could get No. 200. He offered to donate to the Navy Relief Society any Dodger salary he would get, but Rear Admiral W. B. Young turned him down, fearing "a flood of such requests" from ballplayers.

Springtime '43 brought a harsh contrast to the traditional sun-splashed training camps. With the railroads jammed by servicemen reporting to bases or overseas embarkation points, Federal authorities sought to curb nonessential travel.

The journeys of the 16 teams could have little impact on rail service. But baseball agreed to forgo training in Florida and California. It would hardly enhance the game's precarious wartime image to have the news-

papers display photos of players cavorting at the beach while the Marines were storming beachheads overseas.

On the mild, sunny morning of March 14, an advance party of Dodger players took a short boat ride from Manhattan to the west side of the Hudson River, then hopped a railroad train for a trip 45 miles upstate.

The Dodgers had planned to train at West Palm Beach, Florida, but they wound up at Bear Mountain, New York. They would work out at the foot of a ski jump on a ballfield that three decades before had been the site of a Sing Sing prison stockade.

Their training-camp home would be the Bear Mountain Inn, a rustic lodge providing game rooms with pool tables, roaring fires, and—in honor of the guests—a dessert menu featuring Stewed Mixed Fruits Fitzsimmons, Jelly Roll à la Higbe and Ice Cream Puff Medwick.

Bear Mountain had been chosen by Rickey not for its culinary delights but because it was a short bus ride away from the United States Military Academy. The heated West Point field house—complete with batting cage— was a wonderful find. It enabled the players to take their cuts and work up a sweat amid a succession of wintry afternoons.

Early in April, the Dodgers went south—to Brooklyn—for a few exhibition games. As opening day approached, the players also kept busy by touring defense plants to spur war-bond sales and trooping to donate blood for the war effort.

The chief publicist for the local Red Cross was the Ol' Redhead.

"I was the best-known fella in Brooklyn then, so somebody said Red is the fella to be chairman; he's a natural," Red Barber recalled. "I worked full time on it during the off-season. I had an office in Brooklyn and one in Manhattan. I worked day and night."

At the start of the baseball broadcasts, Barber appealed for blood donations.

"I would come into the booth a half-hour before the game. I'd call the Brooklyn Red Cross chapter and ask how many donors they needed and at what hour. On the air, I'd say, 'Here's the phone number and their needs.' And by the fifth or sixth inning, the center would call and say, 'We have all our appointments set for tomorrow.' "

The Dodger players donated blood en masse one April day, providing a thrill for Red Cross nurses, who stocked up on autographs. But the most exciting afternoon of the training season may have come when Hollywood arrived in Flatbush. Seven players were outfitted with fake beards for roles as members of the Battling Beavers team in the Red Skelton film "Whistling in Brooklyn" shot in part at Ebbets Field.

The war was beginning to leave the Dodgers short of bodies, but on the first Sunday of the season, Durocher managed to spare half his pitching staff for a worthy cause. Whit Wyatt, Kirby Higbe, Bobo Newsom, Max Macon and Ed Head circulated among the 12,503 fans during an Ebbets Field game with the Phillies in a personal appeal for war-bond purchases. The occasion even brought Rickey to the ballpark despite religious scruples forbidding him to attend games on Sundays. He accepted a Treasury Department certificate in recognition of the Dodger players having spurred war-bond sales via appearances at seventy-five industrial plants throughout Brooklyn.

On the afternoon of Saturday, July 10, the Dodgers found another way to aid the war effort: It was Kitchen Fats Day. Household greases could be converted by the military into glycerine, a key component of explosives, so the ballclub offered free grandstand seats to anyone bringing at least a half-pound of fats. More than 4,500 women accepted the invitation.

But there was almost no game that day. The Dodger players threatened to strike over Durocher's suspension of Bobo Newsom—the club's leading pitcher with nine victories—in a dispute over whether he had followed the manager's tactical instructions. At the last moment, the players took the field and then they took their anger out on the Pirates with a 23–6 walloping. A few days later, Newsom was banished to the St. Louis Browns.

The rest of the Dodger ballplayers were going nowhere in midsummer as the Cardinals moved way out in front. Rickey, however, was more concerned with the future. While other clubs were retrenching and waiting out the war, the Dodgers announced they were "engaged in the development of a vast expensive farm system" and that 20,000 letters had been sent to high school coaches asking that they recommend players.

"We are building for the future," explained Rickey, "and if the war is over within two years, we expect wonderful results."

In August, a *New York Times* story on a Dodger game in Philadelphia mentioned a nineteen-year-old shortstop who had been spotted at one of the tryout camps Rickey organized.

The teenager "worked with the Brooks and drew Durocher's admiring comment for the manner in which he belted the ball in practice," the *Times* reported.

The young man would soon go overseas with the Marines, but Rickey's master plan had already uncovered a gem. Gil Hodges would be back.

While waiting for the ballplayers of the future, Rickey turned to old-timers. He signed forty-two-year-old Johnny Cooney (a Dodger back in the mid-1930's) and thirty-nine-year-old Paul Waner—a future Hall of Famer on his last legs—to replace Reiser. With Reese gone as well, Durocher tried to come back at age thirty-seven. He went to shortstop in June, but survived for only six games before calling it quits again.

As the summer moved along, Rickey unloaded two top players who were nearing the end. First, he sent Joe Medwick to the Giants for the $7,500 waiver price. Then, on July 31, he traded the enormously popular Dolph Camilli to the Giants in a five-player deal. The Dodger fans were furious and they let Rickey know it with signs reading "We Want Camilli" and "We Want MacPhail."

But Camilli would never wear a Giant uniform. Reflecting decades later on the trade, he explained he couldn't see himself being a Dodger one day and then a Giant the next.

"The Giant thing is a historical rivalry from the beginning of time and always will be," Camilli emphasized. "It was real serious; this was no put-on stuff. Their fans hated us and our fans hated them. It was so bad that a couple of fans got in a beef in a bar and one guy killed the other because of it."

The hatred between the Dodgers and Giants even extended to Camilli's young daughter.

"My kids were small. The daughter, she was out playing and some little girl did something that she didn't like and she couldn't think of anything real nasty to call her so she called her a Giant fan. It even went down into the family."

When he got word of the trade, Camilli decided he would at least need a cooling-off period before reporting to the Polo Grounds.

"I hated the Giants. I couldn't change allegiance that quick, plus the fact that it was near the end of my career. I was getting tired and I needed rest."

Mel Ott tried to persuade Camilli to make the move.

"Mel said, 'Will you just come over and talk.' So I went in the clubhouse, sat down, and he tried to talk me into it. If he'd have said, 'Well, take a few days rest,' I'd probably have considered it. But oh, no. They wanted me to report and play right away to help fill the park because the Boston Braves were coming into town for a three-day weekend. I said, 'That's a helluva reason for me to go.' I said nuts to them and I quit."

"The Brooklyn fans, they were mad," Camilli recalled. "They carried signs to the ballpark. They were mad at Rickey because I was one of the favorites. Even today I can go into Brooklyn and even the grandchildren make a big fuss over me. It's been handed down. You'd think I was still an active ballplayer the way they treat me. I was put into the Brooklyn Dodger Hall of Fame about three or four years ago. They had a carnival-type thing under a tent and I signed autographs for two hours."

After refusing to join the Giants, Camilli went back to California and soon took a job managing Oakland in the Pacific Coast League. Two years later, he returned to the majors briefly, with the Boston Red Sox, before retiring for good. In 1960, his son Doug became a Dodger as well, joining Los Angeles as a catcher.

Dodger fans had little to cheer about in the weeks after Camilli's departure. Billy Herman, Arky Vaughan and Dixie Walker all hit over .300 for the season, but the Cardinals were in a league by themselves. They finished 18 games ahead of the second-place Reds while Brooklyn wound up third, 23½ games out. It was small consolation, but the Giants were dead last.

If the Dodgers were slipping in 1943, they were positively ridiculous the following season when fifty-three players took turns in a lineup of teenagers, old-timers and men unfit for military service or discharged because of war injuries.

On a Sunday afternoon in August '44, Chuck Workman, a Boston Brave outfielder, hit a drive against the right-field screen at Ebbets Field off an eighteen-year-old pitcher named Cal McLish. The baseball didn't bounce back—it went through the wire onto Bedford Avenue. The screen had developed holes, but the shortage of materials prevented a patch job. The result was a war-aided home run.

It would be that kind of season for the Dodgers.

Arky Vaughan stayed on his California ranch, Billy Herman joined the Navy and Kirby Higbe went into the Army. There wasn't much left.

Holdovers Dixie Walker, Augie Galan, Luis Olmo, Frenchy Bordagaray and Mickey Owen, along with Eddie Stanky, obtained from the Cubs' farm system, got the bulk of the playing time. Curt Davis, at age forty, Rube Melton and Hal Gregg handled the pitching load. Whitlow Wyatt was still around, but his arm was shot.

Cal McLish would develop into a fine pitcher after leaving the Dodger organization. But in 1944, he found himself in a Brooklyn uniform even before finishing high school in Oklahoma City. He had plenty of fellow teenagers to keep him company. Among the other Dodger youngsters who would make their mark in the post-war years were Duke Snider, Ralph Branca, Clyde King, Eddie Miksis, Tommy Brown and Gene Mauch.

"I was as green as you could possibly get," McLish would recall, reminiscing one morning from a Kansas City hotel room while on a trip as a pro scout for the Milwaukee Brewers.

"I had registered for the draft on my eighteenth birthday, December 1, 1943. But I didn't get my draft call until August 1944. I had played infield and different places, but Tom Greenwade [the scout who would sign Mickey Mantle] signed me as a pitcher because he saw me pitch in American Legion ball."

◆ *Branch Rickey is persuaded to permit a wartime Ebbets Field extravaganza titled "Here's Your Infantry" for promotion of bond sales. (Brooklyn Public Library-Brooklyn Collection)*

After going to spring training at Bear Mountain, McLish briefly returned to Oklahoma.

———

I hadn't graduated. Mr. Rickey had me go home to see if I could take correspondence courses. My teacher said, "No, you've missed too much time."

Then Mr. Rickey sent me a train ticket to St. Louis. The team was starting a fourteen-day road trip and I was in the bullpen. Rube Melton had started the game. Durocher had me warm up. In the seventh inning, I came in. The first time my foot ever hit the rubber in organized ball, I had the bases loaded and no outs in Sportsman's Park.

It was exciting to dream about being a big league baseball player, and all of a sudden you're there even though in your heart and mind you knew you didn't belong yet.

Danny Litwhiler was the hitter. I struck him out, but the next guy got a base hit.

———

One afternoon, McLish was given a starting assignment. It was then that he discovered he was probably the lowest paid pitcher in modern major league history.

———

Charley Dressen, who was a coach, said to me, "You're starting tomorrow, go home and eat a big steak."

I said, "Well, I don't have any money."

He said, "You just got paid."

I said, "I paid my hotel bill. I don't have any more money."

He said, "What in the world are you making?"

I told him I was making $150 a month. So he went in to Durocher and told him. The next day, I met Mr. Rickey at his office on Montague Street. He tore up my contract and wrote me one for $500 a month. It was just an oversight. I thought I was going into the service and he probably did too.

He took me down to a department store and outfitted me with a pinstripe suit. We stopped at a lunch counter and had a milk shake.

———

In these days before ballclubs had scores of specialized instructors, a young player simply learned as he went along.

"I didn't have a changeup, I didn't have a curve, I'd just rear back and throw one pitch," McLish remembered. "There was no pitching coach.

Charley Dressen was the only one who offered anything along those lines to me. He told me about keeping the ball down. I learned from the Whitlow Wyatts and Curt Davises. You watched them and asked questions."

After struggling to a 3–10 record, McLish was gone from Ebbets Field by late summer, and soon he was wearing a different uniform in Europe.

"I got drafted August 15. After fifteen weeks of basic training, I was overseas. Four days after I landed, I'm carrying a .30-caliber machine gun, No. 1 gunner on a machine gun squad with the Third Infantry Division. I carried it from Nancy, France to Salzburg, Austria."

One of McLish's teammates at the Dodgers' 1944 spring camp was seventeen-year-old Duke Snider. The young outfielder would be sent to the minors when the season began, but he enjoyed a moment of glory with a three-run homer against West Point. Another seventeen-year-old, a catcher named LeRoy Jarvis, saw his training camp end prematurely. He left Bear Mountain for his Atlantic City home to have his tonsils taken out.

Even Snider and Jarvis were a year older than Tommy Brown at the time he made his major league debut. A Brooklyn boy who had been discovered at the Parade Grounds along Prospect Park, Brown was called up to play the infield in July '44 at the age of 16 years 7 months.

Red Barber would remember: "We called homers Old Goldies. We'd run a carton of Old Golds down the screen whenever any ballplayer hit a home run. There was a hole in the screen, and the batboy grabbed them for the player. When Tommy Brown hit one, Durocher said, 'Give me the cigarettes, he's too young to smoke.' "

In this season of extremes, the graybeards were also well represented. Johnny Cooney and Paul Waner returned from the '43 team, and now Paul's brother was a Dodger as well.

Lloyd Waner had been obtained in a March 1943 trade with the Phillies but had stayed home in Oklahoma City, working in a draft-exempt job as a fireman at Will Rogers Army Air Base.

By 1944, Waner was thirty-eight years old so his draft board lost interest in him. The Dodgers didn't.

"Branch Rickey called me just before the '44 season opened and he said he's gonna lose two or three of his outfielders to the Army," Waner remembered many years later. "He wanted me for insurance and wanted to know if I could get in shape. I says, yeah, I thought I could, I had a little softball and a little handball and volleyball over at the fire department. So he offered me a pretty good contract and I went to Brooklyn. And Paul was there."

"We weren't reunited very long," Waner noted, "because Branch, before cutting-down time in June, called me into his office and told me he wasn't gonna lose any of his outfielders after all, so he's gonna have to release me."

Another outfield retread was
Goody Rosen, who had last seen big
league action as a member of the
1939 Dodgers. Ben Chapman, a
teammate of Babe Ruth in the Yankee outfield of the early 1930's,
found another life in the majors as
a pitcher. Obtained from the International League's Richmond Colts,
where he had been a pitcher-
manager, Chapman won five games
for the '44 Dodgers.

If they weren't too young or
too old for the military, they weren't
too physically fit.

Just before the '44 season, the
Dodgers made two moves that sym-
bolized their plight. They called up
Jack Franklin, a right-handed
pitcher, from Montreal and sent
Tom Sunkel, a lefty, to the Royals.
The pair had much in common:
Both were from Paris, Illinois and
both were blind in one eye. Clancy
Smyres, a twenty-one-year-old
shortstop, was missing one kidney.
Howie Schultz was a wonderful candidate for first base: At 6 feet 6½
inches he was both an easy target
for the infielders and a shade too tall
for the Army.

Tommy Warren, a pitcher, was
an ex-Navy commando who had
spent nine months in a military hospital after suffering a concussion in
the North African invasion. Elmer
(Red) Durrett, an outfielder, was a
veteran of twenty-one months with
the Marines on Guadalcanal. His
nerves had been so frayed by shelling
that he would hit the ground at the
Bear Mountain spring training field
when artillery rounds were fired at

◆ First baseman Howie Schultz (also
known as Stretch and Steeple) was a
fine target for the '45 Dodger infielders
but a shade too tall for the military at
six feet six and one-half inches. Lefty
pitcher Vic Lombardi was all of five feet
seven. Together, they provide a wonderful photo-cliché opportunity. (Brooklyn
Public Library-Brooklyn Collection)

nearby West Point. "I did it twice, and that's no joke," he confessed to reporters.

For Dixie Walker, who spent the previous Christmas visiting servicemen in Alaska and the Aleutians on a U.S.O. tour, the Bear Mountain camp was like the Arctic all over again. On March 20, a six-inch snowstorm hit camp.

When the Dodgers arrived in Brooklyn to complete spring training, Durocher looked around at his infield corps and grew desperate. So, at age thirty-eight, he gave it another try, playing second base in an Ebbets Field game against the Red Sox. The comeback didn't last very long. He broke his thumb taking a throw from a future manager, eighteen-year-old shortstop Gene Mauch.

The Dodgers brought some genuine star appeal to Brooklyn a few days later when they met the Phillies in an exhibition benefit for the Red Cross. The female fans were virtually in hysterics as Frank Sinatra, who had been wowing the bobbysoxers at the New York Paramount, sang three numbers at home plate.

The season wasn't far along before the Dodgers got a taste of things to come. On April 27, the knuckleballing Jim Tobin pitched a no-hitter against them at Braves Field and hit a home run in a 2–0 victory.

Three days later, it was even worse at the Polo Grounds where a crowd of 56,068 turned out for a Sunday doubleheader. The Waner brothers were together in the outfield for the first time in four years. But this wasn't the 1930's, when they were tearing up the league for the Pirates. The Dodgers were flattened, 26–8, in the opening game.

The Giants set a major league record with 26 runs batted in and tied a National League mark by getting 17 walks. But Durocher avoided having to stick around until the end. He was ejected after arguing with the umpires in the sixth inning. Joe Medwick, the ex-Dodger playing left field for the Giants, wasn't there for the second game. A frustrated Dodger fan hit him in the groin with a pop bottle as the opener ended.

The big star in the rout was Phil Weintraub, the Giants' first baseman. He connected for two doubles, a triple and a home run to drive in eleven runs, one short of the major league record set by the Cardinals' Sunny Jim Bottomley in 1924 against—of all people—the Dodgers.

Years afterward, Weintraub recalled that day.

"I remember Sinatra was sitting in back of our dugout, and every time I came around after hitting one, he kept crawling out on the top of the dugout trying to shake my hand. Babe Ruth was at the game and came in the clubhouse afterward, and in his big roaring voice said, 'Where is the guy who knocked in enough runs for a month?' And they brought him over to me at my locker, and I was thrilled beyond words. This was the great Babe. I'd watched him as a kid, coming from Chicago."

Weintraub might have driven in a few more runs that day if Luis Olmo, normally an outfielder, hadn't been playing the infield late in the game.

"I had a chance to knock in two more; I came up another time after I drove in eleven," Weintraub recalled. "There were two men in scoring position, and Olmo, who was brought in to play second base, was playing out of position. I hit a line drive over second that he made a one-handed stab of. If he hadn't been out of position, I would've had two more runs batted in and possibly something like that would never have been touched."

On May 23, with wartime lighting restrictions eased, night baseball returned to Ebbets Field. To celebrate, the Dodgers unveiled satin uniforms, then beat the Giants, 3–2.

But the Dodgers went from bad to simply dreadful. On June 28, they dropped a doubleheader to the Cubs at Wrigley Field. They didn't win again until the second game of a July 16 doubleheader against the Braves. Their 15-game losing streak was the longest in the club's history.

The season's high spot may have come on August 8. After five major league teams had lost to the Great Lakes Naval Training Station—a squad filled with former big leaguers—the Dodgers beat the sailors, 7–4, at their home field.

Dixie Walker won the National League batting title with a .357 average, but Brooklyn finished in seventh place with a 63–91 record. The Cardinals, winning 105 games, laughed their way to a third straight pennant.

November 1944 brought a reshaping of the Dodger ownership, which had been evenly divided between the Ebbets and McKeever heirs since Charlie Ebbets's death in 1925. The heirs of Edward McKeever sold their 25 percent interest to a group of four men that included Branch Rickey and a lesser-known club official, the team's lawyer, Walter O'Malley.

In February 1945, Pee Wee Reese and Billy Herman were reunited. But it wasn't on the Dodgers. They formed the double-play combination for the Navy's Third Fleet team in its Hawaii series against an Army Air Corps squad of ex-major leaguers.

The '45 season would find Brooklyn once again with few genuine major leaguers in their prime.

Soon after the Dodgers arrived for their third wartime spring training camp at Bear Mountain, Durocher prepared for yet another comeback. Rickey promised Leo an extra $1,000 if he could stay in the lineup for at least the first fifteen days of the season. He would last for two games, then go back to the bench for good.

Four days before the traditional season opener in Washington, the nation was shaken by the death of Franklin D. Roosevelt. Baseball went ahead with its schedule, and when the Dodgers opened at Ebbets Field with the Phillies, the American flag was flown at half-mast.

The Dodgers would fare a lot better than they had in '44, but at times they still seemed a comic imitation of a real major league team.

On June 7, they made eight errors and their pitchers yielded seven walks, threw three wild pitches and hit a batter in a 10–5 drubbing by the Giants at the Polo Grounds.

So when the Dodgers met the Phillies three nights later at Ebbets Field, Durocher was evidently not in the cheeriest of moods. As the game moved along, his temperament wasn't soothed any by the shouts coming from an upper-tier box behind third base. A twenty-one-year-old Army veteran named John Christian was enjoying his evening with a stream of heckling easily heard in the Dodger dugout.

At the end of the sixth inning, Joseph Moore, a burly park policeman, invited Christian to accompany him beneath the stands. At 5 feet 11 inches and 200 pounds, Christian, an ex-glider corps trooper, could presumably take care of himself. But he wound up at Kings County Hospital with a broken jaw. Christian told the police that Moore had slugged him with a blunt instrument on the dirt runway between the Dodger dugout and clubhouse and that when he got to his feet, Durocher began to beat him.

The next day, Durocher and Moore were arrested on assault charges, then released on $1,000 bail.

Rickey quickly came to his manager's defense, telling Dodger supporters at a Rotary Club luncheon that his players would stand "as a unit against unfair abuse, against indecent or vulgar remarks from fans in the stands." He saluted his troops as "ferocious gentlemen."

Durocher would have his day in court the following April.

As the season moved into midsummer, the Dodgers had visions of a pennant run. So Rickey reached back to a legend of yesteryear for pinch-hitting help: He summoned Babe Herman out of retirement.

After being traded by the Dodgers following the 1931 season, Herman played for the Reds, Cubs, Pirates and Tigers, then retired to his Glendale, California, ranch in 1938. But Babe wasn't ready to get out of uniform entirely so he found a spot with Hollywood of the Pacific Coast League. He stayed around through the 1944 season and then, age forty-one and hobbled by a bad knee, he called it quits, presumably for good.

But one day in July '45, the phone rang. Tom Downey, the Dodgers' West Coast scout, asked Herman if he'd like to get back into a Brooklyn uniform.

Years later, Herman recalled the moment: "I was up at the ranch; I had an orange grove up there and a house. On the back part, I had five thousand turkeys, which I had a hired man running. But I thought maybe I would just like to try it one year and see how it went."

There was virtually no time for him to get into playing condition.

"They were gonna give me two weeks to get in shape. I hadn't seen a ball since the past September. But Durocher wanted to know if I could hit, and I said, 'Sure, I'll go up.' "

Cheers from an Ebbets Field crowd of 36,053 drowned out announcement of his name as Babe stepped to the plate in the first game of a Sunday doubleheader against the Cardinals on July 8. Tape was wound around hands blistered from three days of batting practice. It was the seventh inning, Red Barrett was pitching and Luis Olmo was on third base.

"The first ball I swung at, I cracked the bat," Herman recalled. "I went back and got the other bat, and the next ball I got a hit to right."

And then, it was just like the old days. Babe fell down rounding the first-base bag.

Later in the season, after Herman got another pinch hit, a teammate's remark in the dugout brought home the absurdity of his being a Dodger again.

"I went up and hit with three men on," Babe remembered. "I hit it about six inches from the top of the screen. The ball came back to the right fielder's hands so I only got a single out of it, but I drove in two runs. I was hitting for Tom Brown.

"Durocher gave me a runner and I went back to the bench. When I got there, Tom said, 'Babe, when did you start playing in Brooklyn?' I said, '1926, Tom,' and he said, 'Gee, that's about two years before I was born.' So I said, 'Well, then, I think I'd better quit.' But I went on and finished out the season."

Babe's performance was nothing to be ashamed of. He hit .265 with 9 hits in 34 at-bats and even had a home run before going back to California for good.

Two weeks before the season ended, the Dodgers had a brush with disaster. Following a twilight-night doubleheader in St. Louis, the team split into two groups for the trip to Chicago, scrambling for scarce railroad accommodations. The regulars boarded the first available train and then Durocher, his coaches and the rest of the squad crowded into a later train.

In the early morning hours, the second train suddenly came to a halt and the sounds of an explosion jolted the ballplayers. The engine had smashed into a gasoline tanker-truck attempting to cross the tracks near the town of Manhattan, Illinois.

One of the Dodgers on the train was Tom Seats, a thirty-three-year-old lefty whose big league career had been resurrected in this final war year.

A half-century later, that moment of terror was still vivid for him.

"You didn't get too many sleepers," he recalled from his home in San Ramon, California. "We were on a coach that morning. It was just about daylight. I was sitting in the smoker with a bunch of newspapermen. I couldn't sleep.

Babe Herman brings the era of the Daffiness Boys back to life with the '45 Dodgers. (Brooklyn Public Library-Brooklyn Collection)

"We hit this tanker and we went through a ball of fire. We got clear of the flames before the engineer stopped.

"Somebody looked out the window, and the train's fireman was out there on fire. We got a bunch of blankets and put it out, but the poor guy passed away that afternoon.

"The second tank from the truck was wrapped around the engine, and it was a mess. The engineer died in the cab."

Ahead of the Dodgers, in sleeping cars, was a group of servicemen.

"They busted every window and came out through the windows," Seats remembered. "Smoke got in the cars. I'd been on planes that lost motors, but I thought, 'This is it.' "

The ballplayers scrambled to safety, however, with nothing worse than a bruised right knee suffered by Charley Dressen and a cut on the right arm of Luis Olmo.

By all logic, Seats should never have been aboard that train. That he was on a big league roster was graphic evidence of how the war had taken its toll on the ballclubs.

Seats had pitched just one year in the majors, going 2–2 with the Tigers in 1940, then went to the Pacific Coast League. By the late war years, he was pitching for the San Francisco Seals and working in a shipyard during the off-season with no thought of returning to the majors.

But Branch Rickey, desperate

for left-handed pitching, persuaded him to come to Brooklyn.

Seats remembered that he drove a hard bargain with a man famous for hating to part with a dollar.

As Seats recalled it, Rickey phoned with an offer of $600 a month.

"I believe I asked for $15,000 for the year. He liked to come through the phone on that. I said, 'Well, I won't come for any less.' "

Seats claims he got the money, and it wasn't such a bad deal for the Dodgers. He posted a 10–7 record. Only Hal Gregg, with an 18–13 mark, won more games for Brooklyn that season.

The Dodgers finished in third place, eleven games behind the pennant-winning Cubs, who ended the Cardinals' wartime dominance. St. Louis settled for second place, three games out.

The Brooklyn outfielders had fine seasons with Dixie Walker driving in a league-leading 124 runs and batting .300 to go with Goody Rosen's .325 average and Luis Olmo's .313. Augie Galan, switched from the outfield to first base, hit .307.

While the wartime stalwarts kept the club going, major changes were occurring again at the top of the Dodger organization. On August 13, Rickey and O'Malley joined with John Smith of the Pfizer drug company, who had participated with them in the 1944 stock purchase, to obtain the 50 percent of the team owned by the heirs of Charlie Ebbets. The three men now held 75 percent of the shares. The heirs of Steve McKeever retained the remainder of the stock.

On Sunday, September 2, 1945, General Douglas MacArthur accepted the Japanese surrender in Tokyo Bay on the deck of the U.S.S. *Missouri,* the 45,000-ton Pacific Fleet flagship launched at the Brooklyn Navy Yard on New Year's Day of 1944.

By the following spring, the players who had carried the Dodgers to the 1941 pennant would return from the war. In addition to the familiar faces, there would be a rookie outfielder, a strong-armed twenty-four-year-old named Carl Furillo. He was the first. Soon a host of enormously talented young men would arrive to bring Brooklyn baseball into its years of glory.

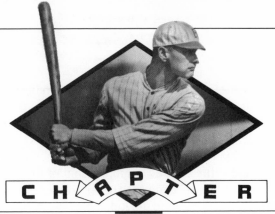

25

Black Baseball

L ess than twenty-four hours earlier, in a little red schoolhouse in Reims, France—the headquarters of General Dwight D. Eisenhower—the war in Europe had ended with the signing of the German surrender.

Now, at the Dodger offices on Montague Street in downtown Brooklyn, Branch Rickey was taking a step that would ultimately bring an end to baseball's color barrier.

On this Monday morning, May 7, 1945, the Dodger president announced formation of the United States Baseball League, a Negro circuit that would have a team at Ebbets Field called the Brown Dodgers.

Rickey made a point of saying the new league might some day be part of organized baseball, but he refused to commit himself to favoring integration of the big leagues. And so his press conference did not make especially big news.

Unknown to the public that day was Rickey's real intention in creating the Brown Dodgers. He would use them as a cover for finding the first black man to wear a major league uniform in the twentieth century. Scouts would be dispatched to games of the already existing Negro leagues on the pretext of seeking candidates for the Brown Dodgers, but they would really be on the trail that would lead to Jackie Robinson.

When the Brown Dodgers took the field in mid-May, they brought Negro league baseball to Ebbets Field for the first time in ten years. But black baseball had a long history in Brooklyn reaching back to the Civil War era.

In October 1862, the *Brooklyn Eagle* reported on a local game between black teams called the Unknowns and the Monitors. The North may have been fighting the forces of slavery, but the headline reflected the mores of the day. "Sambo as a Ballplayer," it read.

Games between black squads were quite a social occasion, at least so far as the *Brooklyn Daily Union* told it in reporting on plans by the Excelsiors of Philadelphia to visit Brooklyn for an October 1867 game against the Uniques to decide "the colored championship of the U.S."

"These organizations are composed of very respectable colored people, well-to-do in the world . . . and include many first-class players," the newspaper reported. "The visitors will receive all due attention from their colored brethren of Brooklyn; and, we trust, for the good of the fraternity, that none of the 'white trash' who disgrace white clubs, by following and bawling for them, will be allowed to mar the pleasure of these social colored gatherings."

Boasting a fine set of uniforms—white shirts with a large *E* in script, blue pants and blue caps—the Excelsiors made quite a show of things, marching during the morning accompanied by a fife and drum corps.

But the big game, held at a ballpark adjoining the Union Grounds, disappointed the white press. The afternoon was filled with arguments, and after the game was called because of darkness with seven innings played and the Excelsiors ahead, 42–37, the *Daily Union* decided that black baseball was just as disreputable as the white variety. It described the Philadelphia team's rooters as a "pretty rough crowd" and declared:

"The contest was in no way creditable to the organizations. In fact it put us in mind of the old style of nines which used to prevail among the white clubs."

In December 1867, organized baseball created the first formal color line when the National Association of Base Ball Players, the sport's governing body, barred from membership "any club which may be composed of one or more colored persons."

"Gentlemen's agreements" would suffice to keep blacks out in the decades to come.

A minor breach in the color barrier came in 1884 when a pair of brothers—Moses Fleetwood Walker, a catcher, along with Welday Walker, an outfielder—saw action for Toledo of the American Association, then considered a major league. The franchise finished eighth and then disbanded. And that was that. No one known to be black got into a major league game again until the arrival of Jackie Robinson.

By the 1880's, all-black teams, among them the Atlantic and Remsen clubs of Brooklyn, were common.

Professional black baseball came to Brooklyn in 1906 when John W. Connors, the black owner of the Royal Cafe and Palm Garden on Myrtle Avenue in what is now the Bedford-Stuyvesant section, formed the Brooklyn Royal Giants.

The stars of his first squad were Grant (Home Run) Johnson, a slugging shortstop, and Bruce Petway, the catcher, who gave up studies at Meharry Medical College in Nashville to play ball.

Johnson, the Royal Giants' manager and captain as well, came to the team after eleven years in black baseball, first in the Midwest and then in Philadelphia.

He may have been the first black player to provide published instructional material. In Sol White's *History of Colored Base Ball*, published in 1907, Johnson wrote an article on the "Art and Science of Hitting," citing "confidence" and "fearlessness" as the key elements at the plate.

His advice: "Stand firmly and face the pitcher, thinking you are going to hit, without the least atom of fear about you."

Johnson put his theories to good use for many a season. When he played his last game, with the Buffalo Giants, he was fifty-eight years old.

The Royal Giants were among the East's leading black teams in their first decade of play. In 1914, they appeared in the "colored World Series," but were swept in four games by the American Giants of Chicago.

One of the Negro leagues' greatest pitchers—Dick (Cannonball) Redding—fired away for the Royal Giants in the twilight of his playing career and managed the club in the 1920's and 30's.

Redding was at his most overpowering in the years before World War I, winning forty-three games and throwing several no-hitters in 1912. He was a showman as well, developing a hesitation pitch long before Satchel Paige became noted for it. Redding would show the batter his back for a couple of seconds while balancing on his right foot, then pour his fastball past the presumably over-anxious hitter.

In July 1920, pitching for the Bacharach club of Atlantic City, Redding faced another great pitcher, Smoky Joe Williams, then with the Lincolns, in the first game between black teams at Ebbets Field. Appearing before a crowd of 16,000, Redding was masterful in a 5–0 victory.

Williams later joined the Royal Giants and, at age thirty-eight, pitched a magnificent game in a losing effort. He struck out twenty-five batters on the white semipro Bushwicks in a twelve-inning game in which he was beaten, 4–3. In 1952, a poll of black baseball figures voted Williams the greatest Negro leagues pitcher ever, giving him one vote more than Satchel Paige.

Although his pitching days were essentially over by the mid-1920's, Redding would take to the mound for the Royal Giants in fall barnstorming games against the greats of baseball.

In October 1927, Babe Ruth, playing for a Trenton, New Jersey, semipro club, faced Redding.

George Glasco, who promoted the game, recalled a little chat he had with Redding before the teams took the field.

◆ *Two of the greatest pitchers in the Negro leagues' history, Dick (Cannonball) Redding (left) and Smoky Joe Williams, teaming up for the Brooklyn Royal Giants. Men between them are unidentified. (National Baseball Library, Cooperstown, N.Y.)*

Glasco: *"Now look, you know why all these people are here. You know what they came to see. They're out here to see Ruth hit home runs, right?"*
Redding: *"Right."*
Glasco: *"Now, when the Babe comes to bat, no funny business."*
Redding (winking): *"Got ya. Right down the pike."*

Ruth flied out, popped to second, and then hit three huge homers over the right-field wall.

The Royal Giants had a clown of sorts in Country Brown, a third baseman who sometimes came to bat on his knees. Brown also entertained from the coaching boxes by playing pantomime dice games and holding imaginary telephone conversations with a girlfriend.

In 1923, the Royal Giants joined the newly formed Eastern Colored League, a circuit with largely white ownership. By then, they were owned by Nat Strong, a white booking agent who would eventually control the scheduling of most semipro clubs in the New York area. Strong also was an owner of the Bushwicks. Both teams played at Dexter Park in Queens, just across the Brooklyn line, a field that held about 15,000 seats with room for perhaps 3,000 more sitting on a slope behind the outfield.

The Royal Giants were one of the weaker teams in the Eastern Colored League, finishing in sixth place twice, in seventh twice and in eighth place once. They left the league after the 1927 season, continuing play as an independent, and the circuit itself disbanded late in the spring of 1928.

In the 1930's, games at Dexter Park between black squads and the white semipro teams—particularly Sunday doubleheaders—were big draws.

"We outdrew the Dodgers every year on Sundays," recalled Overton Tremper, who played for the Bushwicks from 1931 to 1934 after his stint with the Dodgers. "Brooklyn would have 5,000 or 10,000—that's when Brooklyn was pretty bad, of course. Once the Giants came in, I think it was in '34, and we had an overflow crowd of about twenty or twenty-two thousand."

The Bushwicks' attendance was boosted in the early 1930's by an innovation the majors hadn't tried yet. Nat Strong installed lights at Dexter Park.

Just as the New York area semipros played night games a few years before Larry MacPhail brought night ball to the majors at Cincinnati, so they pioneered headgear safety six years before MacPhail unveiled his plastic protectors for the Dodgers.

"After the Bushwicks, I managed the Springfield Grays in Queens from 1935 to '41," Tremper recalled. "Back in '35 we had a fella named Dutch Werner who was a shortstop from Fordham. He got beaned playing against the Pennsylvania Redcaps and he was taken to a hospital. Our owner went out and bought those hard polo hats. I guess we were the first club in baseball to wear the protection over our heads."

The games provided a nice Depression-era payday for the white semipros—players on their way up to or down from the majors—and for the black players they faced.

"We'd get $10 for a night game and $25 to $40 for a Sunday doubleheader, but pitchers probably got $10 more than the outfielders or infielders," Tremper remembered.

To provide tip money of sorts, fans would chip in with a few bucks when a hat was passed around.

In 1935, Brooklyn got a new black ballclub, the Eagles, who were founded by Abe and Effa Manley of Jersey City and played in the Negro National League.

The Eagles rented Ebbets Field for their home games and debuted with all the trappings the white big leaguers were accustomed to. The mayor and police commissioner were on hand and almost 200 special guests were in the stands on opening day.

But it was a disaster.

George Giles, who had played for the Kansas City Monarchs and St. Louis Stars in a career going back to 1927, was the Eagles' first baseman. More than a half-century later, Giles recalled that dismal day.

"Mayor LaGuardia threw out the first pitch," he remembered. "We opened with the Homestead Grays and I think they ran us out of Brooklyn. It was a pretty good score."

21–7 to be exact.

"It was an awful game," Mrs. Manley would recall. "I never saw so many home runs before in my life. The mayor had to stay for the whole game. I went home in the third inning and had my first drink of whiskey."

But the embarrassment suffered by the team and its manager, Candy Jim Taylor, a long-time Negro leaguer, brought good fortune for Giles.

"After the Grays ran us out of Ebbets Field, Mrs. Manley wanted me to run the ballclub, so I took over."

Taylor's tactics had not made a particularly good impression on Giles.

"We had guys like Fats Jenkins who were fast," Giles noted. "As fast as our guys were, you should play a lot of hit and run. But Taylor was from the old school. He didn't know how to use the material he had."

Leon Day, at age nineteen the Eagles' best pitcher that season with a 9–3 record and a one-hitter, would remember Taylor from a more personal perspective:

"He'd spit on the feet of young kids. He waited until I got right in front of him—ptui, right on my foot."

The Eagles struggled through the eight-team league's split season, finishing with a 15–15 record for fourth place in the first half, then going 13–16 for sixth place in the second half.

The Manleys purchased a new bus for the team, but things weren't much easier off the field than on it.

"We'd be riding all night, then get off the bus and play a game," recalled Day. "We weren't eatin' right, and my corns would be killin' my feet. The only time I got rubbed down was by myself. You had to love it to go through it."

But Giles recalled that by Depression-era standards, the pay wasn't bad.

"I got $450 a month, playing and managing. It was beautiful. The salaries then averaged from $150 to $200 a month, but the ballplayers never did know what each other got. They never did publicize it."

And there was little publicity for the Negro league players in the white

◆ *The ex-Dodger Overton Tremper as manager of the '34 Bushwicks, the powerful white semipro team that often took on Negro league clubs at Dexter Park. (Brooklyn Public Library-Brooklyn Collection)*

press. Their games were largely ignored. Giles did, however, remember with pleasure how he impressed one prominent columnist: "Dan Parker had me pegged in the *Mirror* as the black Bill Terry."

By the time the color barrier was broken, Giles had been retired for nine years. But a family member did make it to New York as a major leaguer. His grandson Brian Giles played the infield for the Mets in the early 1980's.

Although the '35 Eagles didn't exactly tear up the league, there were some bright spots. Four Eagles played that summer in the Negro leagues' annual showcase event, the East-West All-Star Game at Comiskey Park in Chicago. Giles was at first base for the East, Fats Jenkins played left field, Leon Day pitched and Ed Stone pinch-hit.

After the season, there was a bonus for the Eagles. Mrs. Manley arranged for about half the squad, plus stars like Buck Leonard and Ray Dandridge, to make a playing tour of Puerto Rico to pick up extra cash.

The Eagles' Dick Seay would recall how the Puerto Rican fans showed their emotions. If they liked the players' performances, they would throw oranges at them; if not, they tossed lemons.

But at Ebbets Field, there had been little excitement. With money tight in those Depression days and with the Eagles a mediocre ballclub, attendance had been poor. So in 1936, after one season in Brooklyn, the Manleys moved the club to Newark. The franchise would remain there until the waning days of black baseball.

In 1947, the Eagles returned to Ebbets Field for some home-away-from-home games, but by then few blacks cared about the Negro leagues. Jackie Robinson was in his rookie year with the Dodgers.

Robinson's first step toward the majors—the signing of a contract with the Dodgers' Montreal farm club—came five months after Rickey's news conference announcing the birth of the United States Baseball League and its Brown Dodger franchise.

Rickey's statement that day in May '45 that the new league might become part of organized baseball—opening the prospect that its players could be drafted by big league clubs—stirred speculation on his motives. The remark, coming amid increasing pressures for an end to the color bar, "tossed a hand grenade into the gathering," according to the *Brooklyn Eagle.*

But Rickey would not pull the pin.

"It is not my purpose today to discuss Negro players becoming members of clubs in our present organized baseball league or of white players becoming members of the proposed Negro baseball league," he said.

"My sole idea in becoming identified with the United States League is to attempt to place Negro baseball on a sound basis," he insisted.

The established Negro leagues, according to Rickey, were merely fronts for monopolistic game-booking enterprises and were "in the zone of a racket."

The *Eagle* reflected skepticism over Rickey's motives.

"The recent agitation to let down the bars and admit Negro players into pro baseball has had baseball by the ears," the newspaper observed. "Cynics declare that the formation of the new league is primarily to quiet the de-

◆ *The Brooklyn Eagles at Jacksonville, Florida, for spring training in 1935. Manager Candy Jim Taylor is at far left in top row. George Giles, the first baseman (sixth from left in rear), would succeed Taylor soon after season began. Leon Day, who would become one of the Negro leagues' best pitchers, is in front row at far right. (National Baseball Library, Cooperstown, N.Y.)*

mands of various Negro groups."

Quiet there would not be.

Frank A. Young, writing in *The Defender,* a black publication, declared: "We want Negroes in the major leagues if they have to crawl out there, but we won't have any major league owners running any segregated leagues for us. We have enough 'black' this and 'brown' that in tagging ballclubs in various cities now and we don't need any more."

Ignoring the hostility, Rickey put the Brown Dodgers on the field. Oscar Charleston, one of the Negro leagues' greatest players, was named the manager. He commuted between Brooklyn and Philadelphia, where he was the manager and first baseman of the Philadelphia Stars.

The Brown Dodgers debuted at Ebbets Field the night of May 24, defeating the Hilldale club of Philadelphia, 3–2. They were greeted with a yawn: Only 2,000 fans turned out. As the season moved along, interest remained low.

The United States Baseball League never threatened the established Negro leagues, and it disbanded along with the Brown Dodgers in 1946. But as that final chapter of black baseball in Brooklyn was played out, a momentous step had been taken by the Brooklyn Dodger organization.

On an August '45 evening at Comiskey Park in Chicago, the Dodger scout Clyde Sukeforth approached a Negro leagues infielder and arranged for him to travel to Brooklyn. Branch Rickey's search had ended.

26

Rickey and Robinson

For three hours, they talked in the Dodger offices on Montague Street. It was as extraordinary a meeting of two men as there had ever been in the world of sports. For what happened that day would have an impact far beyond the narrow confines of baseball.

It was mostly a lecture, a calculated incitement, a monologue by Branch Rickey, a testing of the man before him as a prelude to the infinitely more severe trials that lay ahead.

On August 28, 1945, the shortstop of the Negro leagues' Kansas City Monarchs was escorted into the Dodgers' executive offices by Clyde Sukeforth, who had returned with the ballplayer from the Chicago stadium where they met.

Jackie Robinson was five months shy of his twenty-seventh birthday—a muscular man a drop under six feet tall—intelligent, well-spoken and fiercely proud. He had been a superb college athlete a few years before, had encountered a stormy time as an Army officer, now was enduring with great distaste the Jim Crow world of Negro league baseball.

Rickey told this black man before him—the columnist John Crosby would call Robinson "the blackest black man, as well as one of the handsomest I ever saw"—why he had been called to Brooklyn. And then the Dodger president provided a graphic description of what would await the first black ballplayer in modern organized baseball. Rickey launched into the epithets he knew would come—from the stands, from opposing players, perhaps even from teammates. And then he made it clear that for a long time to come, there could be no retaliation, by word or deed.

"His acting was so convincing that I found myself chain-gripping my fingers behind my back," Robinson would remember.

Finally, Robinson asked, "Mr. Rickey, do you want a ballplayer who's afraid to fight back?"

Rickey shouted, "I want a ballplayer with guts enough not to fight back."

To enlighten Robinson on the burden, he presented him with a copy of Papini's *Life of Christ* and asked him to read the portions on "Nonresistance."

Rickey also presented him with a contract providing a $3,500 bonus and $600 a month to play the following season with the Dodgers' top farm club, the International League's Montreal Royals.

"Mr. Rickey, I think I can play ball in Montreal," Robinson said. "I think I can play ball in Brooklyn. But you're a better judge of that than I am. If you want to take this gamble, I promise you there will be no incident."

Rickey was not ready to reveal what had transpired. He hoped to sign more black players soon—though Robinson was his prime candidate to break the racial barrier—and wanted to wait until the baseball and football seasons had ended, then announce the signings all at once to attract maximum attention. So Robinson agreed to tell only his fiancée and his mother what he had embarked upon.

Jack Roosevelt Robinson was born on January 31, 1919, in Cairo, Georgia, the youngest of Mallie and Jerry Robinson's five children. When he was six months old, the family was deserted by the father, a sharecropper. Eight months later, Mallie Robinson moved with her children to the largely white Los Angeles suburb of Pasadena. She worked as a domestic and saved up enough money to buy a home.

The threat of serious racial violence, always present in the deep South, was essentially absent in California. But white neighbors harassed the Robinson family, and the boys got into many a fight spurred by a slur.

An older brother, Mack, had won a silver medal as a sprinter in the 1936 Olympics at Berlin, and now Jackie Robinson turned to athletics as well. After attending junior college, he enrolled at U.C.L.A. in 1940 and went on to star in baseball, basketball, football and track.

In his senior year, Robinson dropped out of college to support his mother, and in 1942 he was drafted into the Army. Denied entry into Officer Candidate School at Fort Riley, Kansas, because of his race, he enlisted the aid of another black serviceman at the post—Joe Louis—and prevailed, emerging as a lieutenant. But the gold bar provided no immunity from discrimination in the Army of World War II. He was denied a spot on the post's baseball team—only whites could play.

Then came a transfer to Fort Hood, Texas, and trouble. In August '44, Robinson was court-martialed for defying a driver's order to go to the back of a military bus. The directive was, in fact, illegal as the Army had recently ended segregation on its military buses. Robinson was acquitted, and in November he received an honorable discharge.

The following year, Robinson joined the Negro leagues' Monarchs. It was not a pleasant summer. He disliked the haphazard scheduling and often boisterous life and bristled at the segregation he encountered in trips through the South.

But he would not be playing black baseball for long. Rickey's scouts were out during the spring and summer of '45 combing the Negro leagues for those phantom Brown Dodger candidates. As the reports came in, Robinson's name stood out. He wasn't a superstar, but his skills were evident. Just as important as talent on the diamond, to Rickey's thinking, was the character of the man who would be so severely tested. Robinson had all Rickey was looking for. He was bright and articulate, didn't drink or carouse.

And the time was right.

The war years had seen strides toward the ideal of racial equality. The Roosevelt Administration had banned discrimination in defense industries and the Supreme Court had struck down the all-white primary. Blacks were organizing in great numbers, swelling the ranks of the National Association for the Advancement of Colored People tenfold.

Baseball, however, had bent not at all. Paul Robeson, the distinguished black actor and singer, and a delegation of black publishers had met with Commissioner Landis in December '43 to seek an end to the color barrier. Landis told them: "Each club is entirely free to employ Negro players to any and all extent it desires."

Jackie Robinson discovered what that meant. In the spring of '42, just before he withdrew from U.C.L.A., he obtained a tryout at the White Sox's Pasadena spring camp. Jimmy Dykes, the Chicago manager, was impressed, but that was that. In April '45, bowing to local political pressure, the Boston Red Sox gave Robinson and two other black players a brief tryout at an otherwise deserted Fenway Park. It came to nothing.

But the tide was building elsewhere. When the Yankees opened their '45 season at the Stadium, pickets marched outside demanding an end to the racial bar. "If We Can Stop Bullets, Why Not Balls?" read one sign. The hypocrisy of an America fighting totalitarianism abroad while denying many of its citizens equality at home was clear.

Ten days before Robinson's workout with the Red Sox, Rickey himself came under pressure at the Dodgers' Bear Mountain camp. Joe Bostic, a sportswriter for a pro-Communist publication, arrived uninvited with two Negro league players, Terris McDuffie, a pitcher, and Dave (Showboat) Thomas, a first baseman, and demanded they be given a tryout. A furious Rickey allowed a forty-five-minute drill, then sent them on their way.

"I'm more for your cause than anybody else you know, but you are making a mistake using force," Rickey told the black journalist.

Rickey had already taken the first step. Back in 1943, he told the Dodgers' board of directors that he hoped to sign black players at some point. The board members gave their approval, then swore themselves to secrecy.

Rickey's motives have been debated. Was he inspired by the ideal of brotherhood or was he moved primarily by the prospect of building winning ballclubs and thereby enhancing profits?

He often cited a commitment to racial equality going back to his days as a coach at Ohio Wesleyan University in 1904. His first baseman, a black named Charlie Thomas, was refused a room when the team stayed at an inn in South Bend, Indiana. The player wept as he looked at his hands, anguishing—as Rickey told the story—"Black skin, black skin, black skin. If I could only make them white."

Rickey would tell how "the scene haunted me for many years."

But in October '45, in a letter to the sportswriter Arthur Mann confidentially relating Robinson's signing, Rickey wrote: "I don't mean to be a crusader. My only purpose is to be fair to all people and my selfish objective is to win baseball games."

Rickey was not about to stop at Jackie Robinson. With the signing of Robinson still secret, he looked to the next men on his list, Roy Campanella and Don Newcombe.

Campanella had grown up in an interracial family in Philadelphia. Though only twenty-four years old in the fall of 1945, he had been catching for nine years with the Negro leagues' Baltimore Elite Giants. At five feet nine inches and 215 pounds, he hardly had a typical ballplayer's build, but he possessed power at the plate, good speed and a strong arm.

Newcombe, raised in New Jersey, was only nineteen years old. A six-foot-four-inch, powerfully built right-hander, he had displayed a terrific fastball pitching for the Newark Eagles during the '45 season. He was hardly a polished pitcher and had control problems, but his potential seemed vast.

Campanella and Newcombe were invited to meet with Rickey in mid-October.

"I played in the Negro National League and I never had the idea that the Dodgers were scouting me until I played an exhibition game one night, and Charley Dressen was the coach and manager for the major league team I played against, and he asked me to come to the Dodgers' office that Saturday morning," Campanella would recall.

"Mr. Rickey had a book on his desk approximately three inches thick—had all my school transcripts and everything I ever did on the baseball field. And he knew that my father was Italian, he knew that my mother was an American black woman."

Newcombe signed, but Campanella would not come aboard just yet. Asked by Rickey if he would like to join the Brooklyn organization, he assumed he was being recruited for the fledgling Brown Dodgers, noted he was receiving a fine salary with his current Negro league team, and turned the offer down.

Now Rickey decided to wait no longer in going public.

On October 23, the Montreal Royals called a news conference at their Delormier Downs ballpark to introduce Jackie Robinson.

Robinson appeared confident in fielding the questions that day, but later he would write, "I was nervous as the devil."

There was little comment from the top executives of the major leagues or from individual club owners, though Rickey would later charge that his fellow owners condemned him in a secret document drafted in February '46, a charge he never proved.

Many minor league officials were outright hostile, and none expressed himself more scathingly than William G. Bramham, the president of the organization overseeing the minors.

"Father Divine will have to look to his laurels for we can expect Rickey Temple to be in the course of construction in Harlem soon," said Bramham.

Little reaction was sought immediately from Dodger players or members of other teams. One comment that did receive notice came from Dixie Walker. "As long as he isn't with the Dodgers, I'm not worried," said that most popular of Brooklyn ballplayers.

For another Dodger brought up in the South, the news carried particular impact. Kentuckian Pee Wee Reese, on his way home from the Navy, would remember vividly how he got the word.

———

I was coming back from overseas. I was aboard ship, coming back from Guam, I'd spent about nineteen or twenty months overseas. Someone on the ship knew who I was. He told me, "Pee Wee, the Dodgers signed a black"—or nigger, whatever he said at the time—and I kind of laughed about it. I said, "You gotta be kidding. They wouldn't sign a black." They always said the blacks couldn't play under pressure; things got hot, they would fold up.

Maybe an hour or two later, he came back and told me— this same kid—said he was not only a black, but he was a shortstop. Now, then, he caught my attention.

———

This was far beyond a sports story in the black press, which hailed Robinson's signing in front-page stories and editorials.

The hope it presented for young black athletes could hardly be overstated. The outcome of the experiment was far from certain, but there might never again be a scene like the one that occurred back in 1940 in the clubhouse of northern New Jersey's Plainfield High School. Long afterward, Plainfield's star player that year would recall the moment when his dream vanished.

———

My junior year I hit .357, my senior year I hit .380. And the scouts are signing guys, and nobody said a word to me. My foolish self, I went to a scout and said, "Hey, I'm the best hitter on the team. How come you don't sign me up?" And he said the dreaded word. He said, "Colored guys don't play in the big leagues."

I said, "You're crazy, man, you seen me playing baseball." He said, "I didn't say you can't play baseball, but they don't play in the big leagues."

And they got silent in that clubhouse. I looked at the coach and the kids and I ran all the way home, about two and a half miles to my house from the field house, and went up in the attic and got my scrapbook. Hank Greenberg, Charlie Gehringer, Rudy York, Carl Hubbell, Harry Danning, Joe DiMaggio, Lou Gehrig—and he was right—there wasn't a face of color there. And I tore them all up except Greenberg, and just laid in the bed and just cried.

———

The young man eventually went to the only place that would have him: the Negro leagues. He pitched for the Baltimore Elite Giants, his catcher Roy Campanella. But in 1952, Joe Black would pitch the Dodgers to the National League pennant.

After the announcement of his signing, Robinson played ball in Venezuela.

On February 10, 1946, he was married in Los Angeles to Rachel Isum, a woman from a middle-class Los Angeles family whom he had met at U.C.L.A.

Two weeks later, they set out together for Daytona Beach, Florida, the spring camp of both the Dodgers and Montreal Royals. It was a miserable journey, and for Rachel, her first encounter with the South. They were bumped twice at southern airports, slept over at a filthy blacks-only hotel in New Orleans, were ordered to the jammed rear section of a long-distance bus, were relegated to a colored bus-station waiting room in Jacksonville infested with flies, and went hungry rather than seek food at the back doors of restaurants.

At Daytona Beach, the couple lived in the home of Joe Harris, a local black politician. Soon, it developed that Robinson would have a black teammate. Rickey had earmarked Newcombe and Campanella for the Dodgers' farm system, but he did not want to inflame an already tense situation in segregated Florida so he kept them away from spring camp. He did bring in John Wright, a twenty-seven-year-old Negro leagues pitcher who was a questionable prospect, and assigned him to Montreal, essentially as a companion for Robinson.

Robinson's first manager in organized ball would be a southerner. The sensitive role was entrusted to Clay Hopper, a cotton broker from Greenwood, Mississippi, who had long managed for Rickey in the Cardinal and Dodger farm chains. Whatever his personal views, he would treat Robinson fairly.

Robinson's first appearance came at Daytona Beach on March 17 when the Royals played the Dodgers. One thousand blacks filled the segregated seating area in right field and hundreds more stood behind the foul pole. The applause drowned out a few boos as Robinson played five innings, stole a base and scored a run. But there was trouble ahead. Municipal officials in Jacksonville canceled a scheduled game between the Royals and their International League rival Jersey City Giants. Two days later, the Royals arrived for an afternoon game at Deland, only to find it had been called off on the curious grounds that the lighting system had malfunctioned. On April 7, the Royals did play at Deland, meeting the St. Paul Saints of the American Association. Robinson got a single in the first inning, stole second and later came home, sliding under the catcher's tag. After the second inning, the chief of police walked onto the field and demanded that Robinson and Wright leave. The Royals complied with the order.

Finally, the Royals left camp and headed for their season opener.

Jersey City's Roosevelt Stadium was customarily packed on opening day, and April 18, 1946, when the Jersey City Giants opened against the Montreal Royals, the house was jammed. The composition of the crowd was, however, markedly different from other years. Large numbers of black people had come from all over the East Coast and even from the Midwest. And the press box was crowded, the field lined with photographers. When Jackie Robinson came to the plate, he would be the first black man in organized baseball since the nineteenth century.

As they played the "Star-Spangled Banner," Robinson sang along "with a lump in my throat and my heart beating rapidly, my stomach feeling as if it were full of feverish fireflies with claws on their feet."

He came to the plate in the first inning, met by polite applause. For the first five pitches, he didn't swing. Then he hit a bouncer to shortstop and was thrown out. Mild applause again. In the third inning, with two men on base, Robinson connected on a fastball. The drive sailed high into the afternoon sunlight, coming down over the left-field fence, more than 330 feet away. By the time the day was over, Robinson had gotten four hits, had driven in three runs and had stolen two bases. He scored four times, once when he harassed a Jersey City pitcher into a balk by dancing off third base. He was the star of a 14–1 victory.

But disheartening times were to come as the Royals stayed on the road over the following two weeks. In Syracuse, Robinson was heavily booed and a black cat was shoved onto the field by an opposing player. In Baltimore, where violence had been feared, Rachel Robinson, sitting behind the Montreal dugout, heard a man shout: "Here comes that nigger son of a bitch. Let's give it to him now." A stream of abuse poured from the stands. That night, Rachel cried in their hotel room and thought that maybe Jackie should give it up.

The emotional toll on Robinson was enormous—he would be on the verge of a nervous breakdown by August—but in Montreal, he was received warmly. Rachel encountered no discrimination in finding an apartment. The fans, most of them French speaking in a city of few black persons, showered enormous affection on Robinson. He didn't force himself socially on his teammates and had minimum contact with them off the field. But they respected his skills and there were no incidents.

On the field, Robinson was a smashing success. He went on to take the batting title with a .349 average and was the league leader in runs scored with 113 and runner-up in stolen bases although missing almost thirty games due to injury. He had the highest fielding percentage among second basemen.

The Royals won the International League pennant in a runaway, then captured the Little World Series—the minor league championship—by defeating the Louisville Colonels of the American Association. A crowd of 19,000 filled Delormier Downs to watch the Royals capture the title, and after the game, Robinson was mobbed by ecstatic fans. They kissed him, hugged him and lifted him onto their shoulders. There were tears in his eyes.

John Wright, the Royals' other black, pitched infrequently in the early spring and was demoted in mid-May to the Three Rivers club of Quebec in the Canadian-American League. He was quickly replaced on the Royals by Roy Partlow, a left-handed pitcher who had been a standout in the Negro leagues since 1934. Partlow pitched erratically, and early in July he too was sent to Three Rivers. Robinson remained the only black player in the International League for the rest of the season.

The previous March, Roy Campanella had been called to Brooklyn from Venezuelan winter ball and had been signed to a Dodger organization contract. Rickey envisioned Campanella and Newcombe as his second tier—they would come up to the Dodgers after Robinson. A Rickey aide at first tried to place them with the Danville, Illinois, club of the Three-I League, but it was territory hostile to blacks, and management said no. Buzzy Bavasi, the young general manager of the Dodgers' Nashua, New Hamp-

◆ *Jackie Robinson, Dodger rookie, with (l. to r.) John (Spider) Jorgensen, Pee Wee Reese and Eddie Stanky. (National Baseball Library, Cooperstown, N.Y.)*

shire, club in the New England League, was next on Rickey's list. Bavasi accepted the ballplayers without hesitation.

The two men and their wives, the only blacks in town, were treated well, and they flourished. The only incident of note came early in the season. Campanella would recall how Sal Yvars, a catcher for Manchester, tossed a handful of dirt in his face while he was at the plate. Momentarily disregarding Rickey's admonition not to fight back, Campanella told Yvars, "Try that again and I'll beat you to a pulp." The dirt-throwing stopped.

One day in mid-June, Nashua's manager-first baseman, a thirty-four-year-old Ohioan named Walter Alston, was ejected from a game against the Lawrence Millionaires. He turned the managing over to Campanella. In his first major move, Campanella sent Newcombe up to pinch-hit, and he delivered a two-run homer to tie the game. Nashua went on to win, 7–5. And so Campanella emerged with a perfect record as the first black manager in organized baseball.

Receiving little national attention, Campanella and Newcombe went on to outstanding seasons in leading Nashua to the league championship. Campanella hit .290 with 14 homers and was named the all-league catcher. Newcombe had a 14–4 record with a 2.21 earned run average.

A month after Robinson's triumphant finale to the 1946 season, the couple's first child, Jackie Jr., arrived. The following March, Robinson set out for spring training still attached to the Montreal team.

Now there were four black players on the Royals. Campanella and Newcombe had been promoted, and Roy Partlow was back.

Seeking to avoid further problems with southern segregation, Rickey took both the Royals and the Dodgers to Havana for the '47 spring camp.

Rickey hadn't said whether Robinson would be promoted to Brooklyn, but he set out to find a spot for him. Reese was entrenched at shortstop and Eddie Stanky at second base, so Robinson was handed a first baseman's mitt and given a crash course by Hall of Famer George Sisler, then a Dodger scout.

He was also given separate and decidedly unequal accommodations by the Dodger organization. Fearing there might be incidents in the Royals' camp, Rickey assigned the four blacks to a small hotel while the Dodgers stayed at the plush Hotel Nacional and the Royals were housed in a classy military academy.

But trouble there would be— and not from the Montreal players. Soon the Dodgers and Royals traveled to Panama for a few games. One night, after drinking heavily, Kirby Higbe confided to Harold Parrott, the Dodgers' traveling secretary, that an anti-Robinson petition was being circulated.

Higbe was a South Carolinian and was personally opposed to playing with Robinson. But he felt loyalty to Rickey, who had brought him to Brooklyn back in '41, so he unburdened himself by revealing the budding revolt. " 'Ol Hig ain't going to join any petition to keep anybody off the club," the pitcher told Parrott.

The petition had been instigated by Dixie Walker, but it was unclear how many of his teammates would go along.

Parrott reported Higbe's remarks, and the protest was quickly dealt with.

Durocher, wearing pajamas and a robe, called the ballplayers together for a midnight lecture. They gathered in various stages of undress in the kitchen of the Army barracks the club was housed in and heard some choice language.

"You know what you boys can do with that petition—you can wipe your ass with it," Durocher snapped. "I'm the manager of this ballclub, and I'm interested in one thing. Winning. I'll play an elephant if he can do the job, and to make room for him I'll send my own brother home."

The next evening, Rickey summoned the players suspected of involvement in the petition, lectured them on democracy and offered to trade them if they couldn't face playing with a black. The petition got nowhere.

Soon afterward, Walker asked Rickey to trade him "for reasons I don't care to go into." Early into the season, Rickey did send Higbe to the Pirates, but he couldn't get what he wanted for Walker, and so Dixie would remain a Dodger for the time being.

Robinson had a strong training camp though slowed by stomach problems and a back injury suffered in a rundown. Finally, the Dodgers and Royals went to Brooklyn to play a couple of exhibition games at Ebbets Field. And then the speculation over whether Robinson would be promoted was overshadowed by a startling development. On April 9, Durocher was suspended for one year by Commissioner Happy Chandler on grounds of conduct "detrimental to baseball," a punishment supposedly prompted by Durocher's past association with gambling figures. Burt Shotton, an old associate of Rickey, would take over the ballclub.

The day after Durocher was banned, Robinson became a Dodger. He was at bat in the sixth inning of the Royals' game with the Dodgers when the announcement was made.

Robinson played in three exhibition games against the Yankees, and then, on April 15, he made his major league debut at first base when the Dodgers opened the season at Ebbets Field against the Braves. As Rickey had envisioned, Robinson was alone. Campanella had been sent to Montreal, Newcombe was returned to Nashua and Partlow was released.

The drama that surrounded Robinson's debut with Montreal was missing at Ebbets Field, though some 14,000 blacks turned out for the opener on a cold, gray day.

Robinson managed only a bunt single in his first two games. But he went on to have a pair of terrific afternoons at the Polo Grounds, hitting a home run in the series opener with the Giants and following that up with a three-hit performance on a Saturday afternoon before a crowd of 52,000.

Then came the reaction Rickey had feared. When the Dodgers returned to Ebbets Field to play the Phillies, the Philadelphia manager, Alabama native Ben Chapman, instigated brutal racial taunting.

Robinson would write years later of what he heard that day:

"Hey, nigger, why don't you go back to the cotton field where you belong?"

"They're waiting for you in the jungles, black boy."

"Hey, snowflake, which one of those white boys' wives are you dating tonight?"

Robinson remembered how "for one wild and rage-crazed minute I thought, 'To hell with Mr. Rickey's noble experiment.' "

He had wanted to "grab one of those white sons of bitches and smash his teeth in with my despised black fist," but he kept his emotions in check.

Chapman had gone too far, even by the standards of the day. Two of his fellow Alabamans on the Dodgers—Dixie Walker, who hadn't even wanted to play alongside Robinson, and Eddie Stanky—condemned the Phillie manager. Walter Winchell denounced him on his Sunday radio program. And then Happy Chandler threatened to punish the Phillies if the abuse continued.

When the Dodgers visited Philadelphia in early May, there were other distasteful developments. The Benjamin Franklin Hotel, where the team customarily stayed, denied Robinson admittance though his name had been included on the reservation list. He found lodging elsewhere, and on subsequent trips to Philly the Dodgers switched to the Warwick, where Robinson was welcome. On the field, there was another unsavory scene. Robinson was pressured by the Dodger and Phillie management into posing for a photograph with Chapman. The Philadelphia players, ordered by Chandler to drop racial taunts, switched to pointing bats at Robinson from the dugout and making machine gun-like noises, a gesture inspired by death threats Robinson had received.

While the Dodgers were in Philadelphia, a supposed plot against Robinson was reported by Stanley Woodward, the sports editor of the *New York Herald Tribune*. Woodward wrote that members of the St. Louis Cardinals had planned to strike rather than take the field against the Dodgers for a series a few days before but that warnings by Ford Frick, the National League president, and Sam Breadon, the Cards' owner, had averted trouble. Cardinal officials denied the report, and Woodward did not provide names of players involved. But the allegations created a furor dashing hopes diehards may have had that an organized protest would be tolerated.

Under intense pressure, Robinson struggled early in the season, going 0 for 20 at one point, but in May he began to show the talents he had displayed with Montreal. By late June, he was hitting over .300, leading the league in steals, bedeviling opponents with bunts and drawing big crowds wherever the Dodgers played.

As the season moved along, Robinson encountered few serious incidents on the field, though opposing pitchers were hardly bashful about throwing at him. The Dodger ballplayers—southerners included—accepted Robinson within a few weeks, and Dixie Walker even provided unsolicited batting tips. Pee Wee Reese, the Kentuckian, became Robinson's closest friend on the club.

Late in August, with the Dodgers battling the Cardinals for the pennant, Rickey looked for additional pitching help and decided to sign Dan Bankhead, a fastballing right-hander with the Negro leagues' Memphis Red Sox. But Bankhead, promoted ahead of Campanella and Newcombe, would appear in only four games during the '47 season and never live up to his notices.

By the time Bankhead came to the Dodgers, three black players had seen action in the American League. The Indians obtained Larry Doby, who would be a top outfielder for many seasons, while the Browns signed Hank Thompson and Willard Brown.

Robinson continued to play aggressive, exciting baseball through the summer. He finished with a .297 average, led the league in stolen bases with twenty-nine and no doubt fattened teammates' batting averages by disconcerting opposing pitchers with his daring on the basepaths. The *Sporting News* named him rookie of the year.

He was deluged with mail—most of it praise for his courage—and his presence spurred the overall attendance at Dodger games to nearly four million for the season.

Wherever the Dodgers played, thousands of blacks turned out to cheer him on, sometimes embarrassing him with their adulation.

"The colored fans applauded Jackie every time he wiggled his ears," commented one black sportswriter following a game at Cincinnati's Crosley Field.

Rickey had been mightily concerned about the reaction of black America, fearing that unrestrained celebrations and boisterous conduct in the stands could result in racial incidents.

The previous February, appearing tense and chewing on an unlit cigar, he unburdened himself before a middle-class black audience at a Brooklyn Y.M.C.A.

"If Jackie Robinson does come up to the Dodgers as a major leaguer," said Rickey, "the biggest threat to his success—the one most likely to ruin that success—is the Negro people themselves."

He warned: "Every one of you will go out and form parades and welcoming committees. You'll strut. You'll wear badges. You'll hold Jackie Robinson Days . . . and Jackie Robinson Nights. You'll get drunk. You'll fight. You'll be arrested."

When Rickey had begun to speak, the reaction was one of shock. But by the time he had finished, the gathering burst into applause in appreciation of the admonition, patronizing as it was. A committee was formed to spread the word in the black community. Its theme: "Don't Spoil Jackie's Chances."

Rickey's fears were unrealized, and at Ebbets Field white fans joined with blacks in cheering Robinson on. Crowds would wait outside for Robinson to appear after the games. "Many wanted autographs and others simply wanted to touch him," wrote Sam Lacy, a black sportswriter. It was as if "he had suddenly been transformed into some kind of matinee idol."

On September 23, the day after the Dodgers clinched the pennant, it was Jackie Robinson Day at Ebbets Field. Among the speakers was Bill (Bojangles) Robinson, the famed black dancer.

"I'm sixty-nine years old but never thought I'd live to see the day when I'd stand face-to-face with Ty Cobb in technicolor," he said.

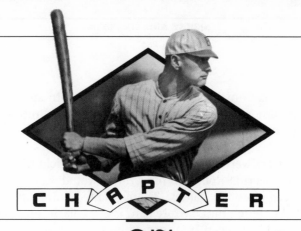

27

Building a Winner

On that March day in 1946 when Jackie Robinson debuted for the Montreal Royals against the Dodgers, he was the big story. But even had he not been making history, it was no ordinary spring for baseball.

The ballclubs were training in the South for the first time since 1942, and scores of old faces had returned from the war. The key men from the Dodgers' 1941 pennant-winners—Pee Wee Reese, Pete Reiser, Billy Herman, Cookie Lavagetto, Hugh Casey and Kirby Higbe—were in Dodger uniforms again as camp opened in Daytona Beach. Dixie Walker and Eddie Stanky, a couple of wartime stalwarts who could hold their own in any season, were back as well. And there were promising newcomers, foremost among them a powerful-throwing center fielder, Carl Furillo.

While a host of Dodgers had returned from overseas, a couple of them left the country. A Mexican businessman named Jorge Pasquel and his four brothers were offering fat contracts to big league ballplayers willing to join their newly formed Mexican League, a circuit outside of organized baseball. More than a dozen players were lured by the big money, among them the Dodgers' Mickey Owen and Luis Olmo, the Browns' Vern Stephens, the Giants' Sal Maglie and the Cardinals' Max Lanier. Most of those who jumped became disillusioned with conditions in Mexico and tried to return. But Happy Chandler, who had taken over as commissioner in April '45 after Landis's death, imposed a five-year ban on deserters who had not come back by opening day. Owen and Olmo would be out of big league ball until the ban was lifted in 1949.

Soon after the season began, Leo Durocher appeared in court over a wartime battle having nothing to do with the Germans or Japanese. Leo and Joseph Moore, the chief of the Ebbets Field special police, were tried on assault charges brought by John Christian, the fan who claimed they had broken his jaw the previous June in retribution for his heckling.

Testifying before a Kings County Court jury, Christian repeated his story that Durocher had attacked him though he admitted having called Leo "a crook" and "a bum." Durocher, taking the stand, said he had admonished Christian for his "ungentlemanly" behavior, but claimed "I never touched him" and denied seeing the park policeman hit the fan. Durocher acknowledged settling a civil suit by Christian for $6,750, but Durocher's lawyer maintained that Leo would not have been re-hired as manager unless he agreed to a cash settlement.

It took thirty-eight minutes for an all-male jury to acquit Durocher and the ballpark cop to the glee of 200 spectators jamming the courtroom.

"I am glad for the sake of the Brooklyn baseball team that their manager has been vindicated and that no discredit has been placed on the great American game of baseball," gushed Judge Louis Goldstein.

That summer Durocher came up with an off-the-cuff remark that would give him an unlikely place in the world of letters. He would be immortalized in *Bartlett's Familiar Quotations*.

One night at the Polo Grounds, chatting with reporters before a game, Durocher was praising Eddie Stanky's competitive fire. Leo looked at the Giant players going out for batting practice and dismissed them for lacking the Stanky killer instinct. "All nice guys," said Durocher of Mel Ott and his crew. "They'll finish last."

The *New York Journal-American*'s Frank Graham printed Durocher's remark the next day, and thus was born the philosophical observation— twisted a bit out of context—"Nice Guys Finish Last."

On Memorial Day, there was a bit of mayhem at Ebbets Field—a blow inflicted on the Bulova clock atop the right-field scoreboard. Bulova had promised a watch as a reward for anyone hitting its clock. In the second game of the holiday doubleheader, the Boston Braves' Carvel (Bama) Rowell did just that, sending a blast that showered glass down on Dixie Walker and brought the clock hands to a halt. Eventually, art would imitate life. Rowell's feat would be duplicated in Bernard Malamud's 1952 novel *The Natural*. This time, Roy Hobbs of the New York Knights would do the clock-smashing.

In the summer of 1987, the writer Bert Randolph Sugar came across the Rowell-Hobbs connection while working on a magazine article, and he located the seventy-one-year-old Rowell at his home in Citronelle, Alabama. Rowell remembered his prodigious shot, but complained, "I never got no watch." Sugar made a few phone calls to Bulova, and in a ceremony in his hometown, the old ballplayer was presented with his reward, forty-one years late.

As the 1946 season moved along, the Dodgers were beginning to make changes. With Stanky established at second base, Billy Herman, approaching his thirty-seventh birthday, became expendable and was sent to the Braves. Goody Rosen, an outfield regular in '45, went to the Giants. Late in August, Goody would remind the Dodgers he was still in the league when he spiked Stanky sliding into second base at the Polo Grounds, sparking a fistfight.

Joe Medwick, having been shipped to the Giants in '43, returned to the Dodgers, but he didn't have much left. There was, however, some young blood. Furillo took over in center field and fellow rookie Gene Hermanski also saw outfield action. Bruce Edwards was called up from Mobile to catch, replacing Mexican-bound Mickey Owen. Two other rookies, lefty Joe Hatten and the Brooklyn-born Hank Behrman, helped keep the pitching afloat.

The Dodgers and Cardinals went into the final week battling for first place. St. Louis had been favored to take the pennant, so any special help for the Brooklyn camp would be welcome. Enter the Rev. Benney S. Benson, minister of the Greenpoint Reformed Church. The clergyman appeared on the steps of Brooklyn Borough Hall one noontime, got down on his knees and pleaded for divine intervention before a couple of hundred bemused onlookers.

"Everybody is praying for the Bums to win," the Rev. Benson intoned. "Oh Lord, we pray, give to the Dodgers an even chance to win the pennant."

The Lord seemed undisposed to render the Dodgers an edge for the moment. The following day, Pete Reiser fractured an ankle on a pickoff play in a game against the Phillies. But the Dodgers managed to finish in a tie with the Cardinals, forcing the first playoff in major league history.

They opened the two-of-three-game series at Sportsman's Park with the Dodgers starting Ralph Branca against Howie Pollet. The Cards knocked Branca out in the third inning and went on to a 4–2 victory. Game 2, at Ebbets Field, pitted Joe Hatten against Murry Dickson. Hatten was routed in the third inning, and the Cards went to the ninth with an 8–1 lead and the pennant apparently wrapped up. But the Dodgers rallied for three runs and had the bases loaded against lefty Harry Brecheen with one out. Now Stanky came to the plate. He may have been Durocher's favorite for his fortitude, but this time he struck out. The right-handed-batting Howie Schultz, who had homered in Game 1, was sent in as a pinch-hitter for Dick Whitman, a lefty batter. Another home run would tie the game. But Schultz fanned on a screwball and the Cardinals were champions.

When the Dodgers opened in '47, they had baseball's first black player, but they were without a manager. Six days before Jackie Robinson's debut, Happy Chandler suspended Durocher for the season.

Durocher's banishment from the game may have had its roots in what was alleged to be a less-than-sporting game of another type three years before. During March '44, the actor George Raft had borrowed Durocher's Manhattan apartment while the Dodgers were training at Bear Mountain. Some weeks later, a complaint was filed with the Manhattan District Attorney's office by an airplane parts manufacturer named Martin Shurin, Jr., who charged he had been cheated out of $18,500 in a crooked crap game at the apartment. It was the stuff of tabloid headlines.

Soon after the '46 season ended, the Hearst columnist Westbrook Pegler—the man who dubbed the Dodgers "The Daffiness Boys" in the more carefree 1920's—dredged up the crap-game incident in a campaign against Durocher. Reminding readers of the Black Sox scandal, Pegler charged that "the moral 'climate' of Durocher's circle and Raft's is ominously similar to that in which the corruption of 1919 occurred."

The columnist then telephoned Rickey to demand that Durocher be fired, and informed him that, as they spoke, Leo was a guest at Raft's Hollywood home. The publicity was hardly the kind Rickey welcomed, so he prevailed on Chandler to talk with Durocher about breaking off ties with people baseball might regard as undesirable.

Chandler met with Durocher at a northern California golf course, gave him a list of people he was not to see, and ordered him out of Raft's home. Among the people on the list were Memphis Engelberg, a handicapper who occasionally had joined Durocher at racetracks, and Connie Immerman, the manager of the casino at Havana's Hotel Nacional, the Dodgers' headquarters for their upcoming spring training. Soon those two names would loom large.

Now, hard feelings between Rickey and Durocher on one side and Larry MacPhail on the other would enter the picture. After leaving the Army, MacPhail had become a co-owner of the Yankees, purchasing the franchise with Dan Topping and Del Webb. In November '46, MacPhail announced the hiring of Bucky Harris as manager, Joe McCarthy having quit during the previous season. MacPhail also plucked Charley Dressen from the Dodger coaching staff, naming him as one of Harris's coaches. The switch angered Rickey since Dressen had a verbal agreement to remain in Brooklyn for two more years unless offered a managing position. Then Rickey became even more furious when MacPhail claimed that Durocher had actively sought the Yankee managing job.

Late in November, when Durocher signed for another season as manager, he claimed that MacPhail had, in fact, come to him with an offer to manage the Yankees, but that he turned him down. Soon MacPhail created more bad blood by hiring another Dodger coach, Red Corriden.

In December, Pegler stepped up his attacks, charging that Durocher was continuing to live in Raft's home and that Chandler—a former Senator from Kentucky—was, in essence, a do-nothing commissioner from a politically corrupt background.

◆ *Burt Shotton doing his Connie Mack imitation in April '47, a few days after taking over the Dodgers upon Leo Durocher's suspension. While Mack stuck to a business suit, Shotton yielded to baseball custom a bit here by wearing a windbreaker. (National Baseball Library, Cooperstown, N.Y.)*

By now, Durocher was making more headlines with his courtship of actress Laraine Day. When they began dating, Day was in the process of seeking a divorce from Ray Hendricks, the manager of a small California airport. Hendricks replied to the divorce petition by charging that Durocher had stolen away his wife while posing as a family friend. That made for even juicier stories than the crap-game incident.

Day was granted a divorce in January 1947 by a California Superior Court judge named George Dockweiler, but under terms of the decree, she was not permitted to remarry in that state for one year. After twelve months, the divorce would become final there. Day and Durocher promptly flew to Juarez, Mexico, obtained a second "quickie" divorce, then were married in El Paso, Texas. An angry Judge Dockweiler summoned the newlyweds and berated Durocher for going outside his jurisdiction. Leo retorted by blasting the judge as an unethical publicity-seeker. Dockweiler in turn raised the threat of having Durocher held in contempt.

Now a minor chapter in the tempest was played out in Brooklyn. Soon after the Dodgers departed for spring training in Cuba, the Rev. Vincent J. Powell, director of the Catholic Youth Organization's Brooklyn diocese, withdrew his group's participation in the Dodger Knot Hole program under which free tickets were distributed to youngsters.

"The present manager of the Brooklyn baseball team is not the kind of leader we want to idealize and imitate," the priest declared.

On Saturday, March 8, the Rickey-MacPhail feud took a new turn following a Dodger-Yankee game in Havana. Rickey angrily pointed out to reporters that Memphis Engelberg and Connie Immerman—two of the men Chandler had expressly forbidden Durocher to associate with—had been seated next to MacPhail that very afternoon.

The next day, the two men were again in box seats adjoining Mac-Phail's box. Durocher, asked by reporters for his reaction, charged that Chandler had a double standard. MacPhail claimed he didn't know who the two men were and said he had nothing to do with their being at the ballpark.

Five days later, MacPhail filed a complaint with Chandler over Rickey's statements about him. MacPhail also demanded that the commissioner determine whether articles in the *Brooklyn Eagle* under Durocher's byline taking shots at MacPhail and Dressen were really Leo's words. (The column, "Durocher Says," was, in fact, ghostwritten by Harold Parrott, the Dodgers' traveling secretary, who was formerly an *Eagle* sportswriter.)

In response to MacPhail's plea, Chandler summoned Durocher and others in the feud to a closed hearing in Sarasota, Florida, on March 24. A notable absentee was Rickey. He requested a postponement because he had to attend his brother-in-law's funeral, but Chandler rejected any delay.

Parrott admitted at the hearing that he had written the "Durocher Says" column, but Durocher took full responsibility for it and apologized to MacPhail for any overly hostile remarks. MacPhail accepted the apology. Dressen, meanwhile, acknowledged that he had violated an agreement with Rickey when he went to the Yankees.

Then Chandler began to question Durocher about high-stakes card games in the Dodger clubhouse, and soon he turned to the matter of the two gambling figures who had been sitting next to MacPhail.

Durocher insisted his anger over seeing Immerman and Engelberg next to MacPhail had been justified. If he couldn't associate with the two men, was it proper for MacPhail to be an elbow's length away? Chandler then asked MacPhail if he had tried to hire Durocher as the Yankee manager, in effect tampering with Dodger property. MacPhail, according to Durocher's autobiography, "consistently avoided making any flat statement about offering me the job."

The hearing was adjourned, and five days later, Chandler met with Rickey in St. Petersburg. Rickey admitted to expressing outrage over the Immerman-Engelberg matter and refused to retract his statements. Chandler then questioned Red Patterson, the Yankees' public relations man, about how the two men had gotten their tickets. Patterson said he was unsure whether he had provided the seats.

The commissioner ordered all parties not to discuss what went on at the hearings. Then, on April 9, the silence was broken. Chandler stunned the baseball world with the announcement he was suspending Durocher for one year, declaring he "has not measured up to the standards expected or required of managers of our baseball teams."

Without giving any specifics, Chandler said he was punishing Durocher over "the accumulation of unpleasant incidents in which he has been involved which the commissioner construes as detrimental to baseball."

Chandler suspended Dressen for thirty days, finding he had broken a verbal agreement with the Dodgers by taking the Yankee coaching job. He fined Parrott $500 for ghostwriting "a deliberately derogatory column about others in baseball." (Parrott later claimed that Chandler returned the money secretly.) The Dodgers and Yankees were each fined $2,000 for engaging "in a public controversy damaging to baseball."

Chandler took no action against MacPhail. He absolved him of tampering, finding no evidence he offered the Yankee managing job to Durocher. But Chandler did find that MacPhail had acted unethically by delaying the appointment of Bucky Harris to give Durocher time to negotiate a more lucrative contract with Rickey. As for Immerman and Engelberg, the commissioner determined they had not been MacPhail's guests at those two spring training games.

The next day, Durocher met with his players, told them to "put your faith in Mr. Rickey," then left with Laraine Day for California.

Clyde Sukeforth filled in for the first two games, and then Rickey reached for an old friend who presented a stark contrast to Durocher. Named as manager was sixty-two-year-old Burt Shotton, then living in Florida in retirement. Durocher was famous for his brashness and he was a practiced umpire-baiter. The white-haired Shotton was mild-mannered and couldn't very well come on the field to fight with the umpires since he preferred to wear street clothes in the dugout.

Shotton, like Rickey, was raised in southern Ohio. He played the outfield for the Browns and Cardinals when Rickey was managing the clubs and so impressed his boss that he became an assistant manager, filling in on Sundays when Rickey absented himself. Later, Shotton managed in Rickey's Cardinal farm chain and was the Phillies' manager for six years in the late 1920's and early 30's, never finishing higher than fourth.

The only tinge of color about Shotton was his nickname, Barney, his base-stealing skills as a ballplayer having brought comparisons with Barney Oldfield, the auto racing champion. He had done some troubleshooting for Rickey in the Dodger system, but the fans knew little about him, and he evidently knew little about Brooklyn. The first time he set out for Ebbets Field, he got lost on the subway.

As the storm over Durocher's suspension ebbed, the spotlight once again focused on Jackie Robinson. Having weathered the intense pressure, the hate mail, the racial taunting of the Phillies and their manager, Robinson was proving himself as spring moved into summer.

Aside from the installation of Robinson at first base, the Dodger lineup was little changed from the '46 squad. Stanky was still at second base and Reese at shortstop. The rookie Johnny (Spider) Jorgensen took over at third base as Cookie Lavagetto went to the bench. The outfield was the same: Reiser in left, Furillo in center and Walker in right. Bruce Edwards returned as the No. 1 catcher.

In May, Rickey sent Kirby Higbe and four other players to the Pirates for $300,000 and a five-foot-six-inch outfielder named Al Gionfriddo. The joke was that Gionfriddo had been thrown into the deal so Rickey would have someone to carry all that cash to Brooklyn.

Once again, it was a Dodger-Cardinal pennant race. Brooklyn took a ten-game lead in August, weathered a late-season threat, then coasted to the pennant by five games over St. Louis. Robinson provided the spark, and Walker and Reiser hit over .300 with Pistol Pete stealing home seven times. Ralph Branca, who had been with the club since coming off the New York University campus in 1944, emerged as the ace of the pitching staff, turning in a 21–12 record. Joe Hatten was the No. 2 pitcher with a 17–8 mark.

The Yankees romped to the pennant by twelve games over the Tigers, setting up the first of six post-war World Series between Brooklyn and the

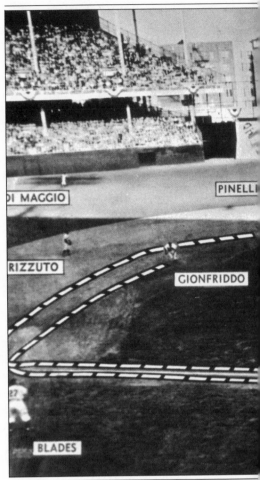

◆ *Cookie Lavagetto's game-winning double breaks up Bill Bevens's 1947 World Series no-hitter. (Los Angeles Dodgers)*

Yanks. As the teams took the field on September 30 at the Stadium, all of America would now be watching: This was the first World Series to be televised.

The Yanks took the first two games, Joe Page turning in a fine relief job in the opener and Allie Reynolds going all the way in Game 2. Then the Series moved to Ebbets Field, and the Dodgers came back with a 9–8 victory as Hugh Casey closed down the Yankees in relief of Hatten and Branca.

For Game 4, the Yanks started twenty-nine-year-old Bill Bevens, a husky fastballer from Oregon who had slumped to a 7–13 mark for the season after two fine years. The Dodgers went with Harry Taylor, a rookie curveballer who had won ten games.

Bevens went into the last of the ninth with a 2–1 lead having yielded eight walks. What he had not given up was a hit.

Three outs away from the first no-hitter in World Series history, he retired the leadoff man, Bruce Edwards, on a long fly ball to left. Then Carl Furillo got the ninth Dodger walk. Spider Jorgensen followed by fouling out to George McQuinn, the first baseman.

Now Shotton removed Furillo for a pinch-runner, Al Gionfriddo, the little outfielder. Pete Reiser, who had injured an ankle sliding the previous day, came to the plate, batting for the reliever Hugh Casey.

"I used to run the 100 in 10-flat in high school," Gionfriddo would recall. "I was probably the fastest guy on the team. Furillo that year I think missed seven bases. When he was going from first to third, he'd miss second. Carl was a good runner, a fast runner, but he was in the habit of missing bases."

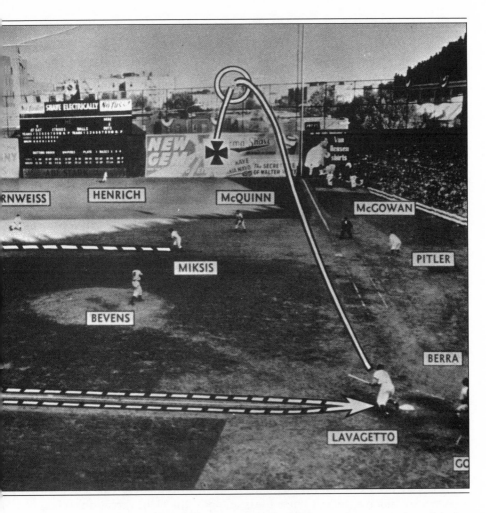

Gionfriddo looked into the dugout, and with the count 2-and-1, he got the steal sign. If he made it, the Dodgers could tie the game on a single. If he was thrown out, Bevens had his no-hitter.

"I sort of slipped a little bit when I took off for second," Gionfriddo remembered. "I slid in head-first under the throw. It was a little close."

Moments later, Reiser was given an intentional walk and limped to first. Going against accepted wisdom, Bucky Harris had put the winning run on first base, but Reiser was a dangerous lefty hitter, and now the Dodgers had no left-handed batters remaining to face the right-handed Bevens. Shotton made a move, too, sending Eddie Miksis in to run for Reiser.

Eddie Stanky was scheduled to bat next, but Shotton sent Cookie Lavagetto to the plate. Fast approaching his thirty-fifth birthday, Lavagetto had batted only 69 times during the season and had managed just one extra-base hit.

Cookie swung at the first pitch and missed. The second pitch was high and outside. Lavagetto connected and sent a drive to right field. Tommy Henrich went back, but he ran out of room. The ball hit the fence and then bounced off the heel of Henrich's glove. By the time the relay throw arrived home, Gionfriddo and Miksis were across the plate. Lavagetto had broken up Bevens's no-hitter and had given the Dodgers a 3–2 victory. It was arguably the most dramatic finish ever to a World Series game.

The next afternoon, the Yankees bounced back to take a lead of 3 games to 2 as Spec Shea pitched a four-hitter in a 2–1 victory.

They went back to Yankee Stadium with the Dodgers' Vic Lombardi, a little left-hander, opposing Allie Reynolds. The Yanks took a 5–4 lead, but then the Dodgers rallied for four runs in the top of the sixth.

Joe Hatten, the third Dodger pitcher, came on in the bottom of the inning. Shotton made a defensive switch as well. Gene Hermanski had been the starting left fielder, but Miksis batted for him in the top of the fifth inning and then replaced him in the outfield. In the bottom of the fifth, Miksis experienced trouble with the sun so Shotton sent Gionfriddo in to left as the Yanks came to bat in the sixth.

Trailing by 8–5, the Yankees got two men on with two out, and then Joe DiMaggio stepped to the plate.

Gionfriddo sought instructions from Shotton as DiMaggio waited for Hatten to deliver.

"I looked into the dugout to see how they wanted me to play," Gionfriddo would recall. "They moved me close to the line. I played Joe to pull."

DiMaggio sent a drive to deep left-center field. It was headed for the bullpen, seemingly a three-run homer to tie the game.

"I put my head down and ran," Gionfriddo remembered. "I looked over my shoulder once and knew I was going in the right direction. When I got close to the fence, I looked over my left shoulder and then jumped practically at the same time and caught the ball over my shoulder. I turned in the air coming down and hit the fence with my butt. I caught it in the webbing."

DiMaggio was nearing second base when Gionfriddo made one of the greatest catches in World Series history. Normally loath to show emotion on the field, DiMaggio kicked at the dirt in frustration.

The Yanks later got another run but the Dodgers won it, 8–6, forcing a seventh game.

The heroics by Lavagetto and Gionfriddo weren't enough. The Yankees won the Series the next day as Joe Page pitched one-hit ball over the last five innings to nail down a 5–2 victory.

Gionfriddo had grown up in Dysart, Pennsylvania, "just a small coal-

◆ *Al Gionfriddo robs Joe DiMaggio in the '47 World Series. (Los Angeles Dodgers)*

mining community of a couple of hundred people," and had played semipro baseball there as a teenager. Now he came home to a hero's welcome. Some 5,000 people from the little towns in the area greeted him, and then he took his place in center field for Dysart in a game against a club from nearby Coalport.

More than forty years later, Gionfriddo was living in retirement in the Santa Barbara, California, area after being in the restaurant business and then serving on the physical education staff of a local high school.

His moment in the October sun at Yankee Stadium had not been forgotten with the passing of the years. He had been back to Brooklyn several times for ceremonies honoring the old Dodgers, had appeared at several old-timers' games at Yankee Stadium and Shea Stadium, and, he noted, "I get quite a few autograph requests, and I go to card shows."

Yet there was a certain amount of bitterness as Gionfriddo looked back.

In the spring of '48, Rickey had sent him down to Montreal, telling him—according to Gionfriddo's account—that he would be back if he had a good season. He was just sixty days short of qualifying for the major league pension plan.

"I knew it at the time and Rickey knew it at the time," Gionfriddo said. "That's why he promised to bring me back if I had a good year at Montreal."

"I hit .320, hit about 20 home runs," Gionfriddo recalled. "Now he wants to send me to the West Coast. I refused to go. I said, 'You promised to bring me back up to the big leagues.' "

Gionfriddo stayed at Montreal, played there a few more seasons, but never made it back to the majors.

"Baseball is a dog-eat-dog business," he observed. "They make you promises. Unless it's on paper, they never live up to it.

"I will never forgive Branch Rickey, even though he's passed away, for not keeping me up there on the big league roster, which I think I well deserved, so I could receive my pension. I don't get anything."

The tumultuous '47 World Series also marked the final major league appearances of Cookie Lavagetto and Bill Bevens. Lavagetto was simply too old to play anymore. Bevens hurt his arm pitching that one-hitter, and it was never right again. One of baseball's great characters would be gone as well. As the Yankees were celebrating the Series victory in their clubhouse, Larry MacPhail announced he was quitting baseball. He sold out to Dan Topping and Del Webb and never returned to the game.

Although Shotton won a pennant, Rickey announced in December that Durocher, upon completing his suspension, would return as manager.

The '48 season would see the emergence of the men who would bring the Dodgers dominance in the National League for the next decade.

In December '47, Rickey finally traded Dixie Walker, sending him to the Pirates in what would be a wonderful deal for Brooklyn. Coming to Ebbets Field in a six-player swap were Preacher Roe and Billy Cox.

A wily left-hander from the Ozarks, Roe would have a string of fine seasons, courtesy of a spitball he would ultimately admit to creating from the juice of Beechnut gum. Cox, a skinny loner from central Pennsylvania with fantastically quick hands, would become the league's finest defensive third baseman.

Joining Roe on the pitching staff was Carl Erskine, a product of the Brooklyn farm chain with an outstanding overhand curveball. Erskine won only six games in '48, but the following season he would begin to blossom. Another young pitcher seemed to come of age during the summer of '48. Rex Barney, a right-hander from Nebraska with a terrific fastball, won fifteen games and pitched a no-hitter at the Polo Grounds in September. But wildness bedeviled him and ultimately ruined what might have been a spectacular career.

Carl Furillo would eventually move from center field to right, taking the spot vacated by Walker. Raised in the small community of Stony Creek Mills, Pennsylvania—not far from Reading—the son of a Sicilian immigrant farmer, Furillo displayed a dazzling arm bringing him renown as The Reading Rifle. (He was also known as Skoonj, for his fondness for scungilli, but that seemed neither here nor there so far as the Dodgers' pennant chances went.)

Furillo worked hard at learning the peculiarities of the right-field barrier, an easy target only 297 feet down the line. The top twenty feet consisted of a wire screen. The bottom twenty feet—plastered with advertising—was divided into a vertical concrete section, a moderately sloping concrete portion and a base partly padded with rubber and sloping away at a 30-degree angle.

In a 1954 photo spread for *Collier's* magazine titled "Craziest Wall in Brooklyn," Furillo would provide a guided tour of the scoreboard, screen and wall, showing how the ball could bounce back at fourteen different angles.

The "Esquire Boot Polish" sign (the one to the right of "Gem Razors and Blades: Avoid '5 o'clock Shadow!' ") presented four separate angles. A baseball striking the top, around the Esquire letters, would come back hard off the vertical concrete. A ball smacking just below that, against the concrete slope, would rebound high into the air. If a baseball hit the seam between the two concrete sectors, all bets were off: It could go zooming up or angling down sharply. A drive hitting the rubber padding at the bottom would have a deadened bounce.

Furillo had to decide in a split second where to position himself for a carom. He did it superbly.

◆ *"We're Number 1" says young lady at parade for the 1949 pennant-winners. (Brooklyn Public Library-Brooklyn Collection)*

Duke Snider, the southern Californian who first wore a Dodger uniform as a teenager at a Bear Mountain wartime camp, had a taste of big league ball in 1947, appearing in forty games. He was back in '48, showing good power but not yet a regular. Snider was temperamental and he had trouble figuring out the strike zone, but his powerful left-handed swing was made to order for that short right-field fence. And he came to be the picture of grace in center field. In the spring of 1949, he would crack the lineup for good.

During spring training of '48, Rickey sent Eddie Stanky to the Braves in order to open the second-base spot for Robinson. Gil Hodges, a quiet man from Indiana with enormous physical strength, was converted from a third-string catcher to the first baseman, taking Robinson's rookie position. It was a master move. Hodges would have no peer for finesse around the bag, and his powerful right-handed stroke would send the ball flying out of Ebbets Field.

Durocher had seen enough of Roy Campanella during spring camp to make him the No. 1 catcher. But Rickey had other plans. He wanted Campanella to integrate the American Association by playing at St. Paul. Campanella stayed with the Dodgers when the season began but saw little action at Rickey's insistence as Bruce Edwards did the catching. If Campy played well, there would be pressure to keep him. On May 15, the cutdown date, Campanella was sent to St. Paul. He hit 13 homers there in 35 games, then, having completed the integration mission, was called back to Brooklyn in early July, this time to stay.

The men who would star in the years to come were on the field, but this was a young team, still a year or two away. The ballclub got off to an

awful start, even spent a day in last place toward the end of May, and as July arrived, it was still floundering.

There was little excitement that summer at the Polo Grounds either, and Horace Stoneham, the Giants' owner, had tired of Mel Ott. Stoneham asked Rickey if he could talk to Burt Shotton about taking over his club. By now, Rickey had soured on Durocher. He told Stoneham he could have the Dodgers' current manager if he wanted. Stoneham leaped at the chance. Rickey called Durocher in and told him the Giants were interested and that he was free to leave. Leo took a not very subtle hint, and on Thursday, July 15, the stunning announcement was made. After leading the Dodgers' battles against the Giants for a decade, Durocher would be wearing their uniform.

Rickey brought Shotton back to the dugout, this time without the specter of Durocher over him. The Dodgers came to life in late summer, but it was not to be their year. They finished in third place, a game back of the Cardinals and seven and a half games behind Boston, which rode the pitching of Warren Spahn and Johnny Sain to the franchise's first pennant since the Miracle Braves of 1914. The Giants of Leo Durocher came home fifth.

By the spring of '49, Rickey's techniques for developing ballplayers could be played out on a grand scale. He had converted a former naval air base at Vero Beach on Florida's Atlantic Coast into a baseball college. A myriad of instructional facilities and ballfields filled the complex, designed not only for the Brooklyn ballclub but the extensive farm system Rickey had built. Everyone in the organization would be learning the same system—the Rickey system—at Dodgertown, eating planned meals, listening to chalk talks, running against stopwatches, sliding into sawdust pits and fathoming a strike zone put together by interconnected strings.

One old favorite would be gone. Pete Reiser, ruined by encounters with outfield walls and a collection of other injuries, was sent to the Braves. He would knock around the majors for a few more years, but never again would show the flashes that had him marked as a future Hall of Famer.

As the '49 season went into September, the Dodgers and Cardinals were once again locked in a pennant race. They went into the last day with the Dodgers a game in front. The Cards ended a four-game losing streak by routing the Cubs, 13–5. The Dodgers went into extra innings in Philadelphia tied with the Phillies, 7–7. In the top of the tenth, Reese singled, Miksis bunted him to second and Snider singled to center, bringing in the go-ahead run. After Robinson was walked, Luis Olmo—back from exile after his Mexican League sojourn—singled to drive in Snider. With a skinny right-handed rookie from Kansas named Jack Banta pitching four and one-third innings of scoreless ball, the Dodgers won it, 9–7, and they had the pennant.

Back in May, with the arrival of Don Newcombe after three seasons in the minors, the final piece had been put in place for the great Dodger teams to come. Newk quickly made his mark with a record of 17–8, becoming the majors' first outstanding black pitcher and joining with Campanella, who hit twenty-two homers, to form the first black battery. Robinson was spectacular. He won the batting title with a .342 average, drove in 124 runs, stole a league-leading 37 bases and was named the National League's most valuable player.

On July 12, in the first All-Star Game ever played at Ebbets Field, black players were in the lineup for the first time. Robinson, Newcombe and Campanella made the National League squad while Larry Doby was on the American League team.

The Yankees were again in a tight pennant race, this time under a new manager who was, however, a most familiar face. Casey Stengel, saddled with a reputation as a clown and a string of second-division finishes as manager of the Dodgers and Braves, took over in the Bronx. He brought the Yanks home first by one game over the Red Sox.

And so the Dodgers and Yankees met in the World Series for the third time in the 1940's.

Newcombe faced Reynolds in the opener at Yankee Stadium. They were locked in a scoreless game for eight innings, and then Tommy Henrich led off the last of the ninth by hitting a low curveball into the right-field seats. The next day there was another terrific pitching duel, but this time the Dodgers emerged on top, Preacher Roe besting Vic Raschi, 1–0, with Gil Hodges's second-inning single driving in the run.

Then they shifted to Ebbets Field. Game 3 went to the ninth inning tied at 1–1, Ralph Branca pitching against Joe Page, in relief of Tommy Byrne. Rain began to fall as the Yankees loaded the bases with two out. Up came brawny Johnny Mize to pinch-hit, and there went the game. Mize slammed a single off the screen sending home two runs. Another run scored later on Jerry Coleman's single off Jack Banta. The Dodgers struck back with homers by Olmo and Campanella, but then Page struck out Bruce Edwards and the Dodgers were beaten, 4–3.

Starting with only two days' rest, Newcombe was routed in the fourth inning the next afternoon and the Yanks went on to a 6–4 victory. Rex Barney delivered 37 pitches in the first inning of Game 5. He escaped with only two runs coming across, but the Yanks were just warming up. They took the game, 10–6, for their third World Series victory against the Dodgers in three tries.

With their flock of young, powerful ballplayers starting to mature, the Dodgers seemed a good bet to take another pennant in 1950. But they weren't the only good young ballclub. The Philadelphia Phillies, a franchise that had ranged from mediocre to moribund since the days of Grover Cleveland Alexander, had come alive. Dubbed "the Whiz Kids," the Phils had a pair of excellent starting pitchers in Robin Roberts and Curt Simmons, a superb reliever in Jim Konstanty and a talented lineup led by Del Ennis, Richie Ashburn, Granny Hamner and Dick Sisler.

The Dodgers had little pitching depth, and on September 19 they were in third place, nine games back of the league-leading Phils. Then Brooklyn got hot and Philadelphia faded. Going into the final weekend at Ebbets Field, the Dodgers had pulled to two games back of the Phils. They would face them Saturday and Sunday with a chance to force a playoff.

The Dodgers won the first game, 7–3, behind Erv Palica, their ninth straight victory, and it seemed as if the Phillies were going to crumble.

On Sunday, it was Newcombe against Roberts. They matched fastballs for five scoreless innings, and then the Phils got a run in the top of the sixth. In the bottom of the inning, Pee Wee Reese hit the most bizarre homer in Ebbets Field history. His fly to right struck the screen about five feet from the foul pole, then dropped to the top of the wall above the Esquire Boot Polish sign. And there the baseball stayed as Reese scampered around the bags with an inside-the-park homer. The ball was finally grabbed by a fan who emerged from the stands to scale the wall.

They went to the ninth tied at 1–1. Cal Abrams, a journeyman out-fielder, led off the bottom of the inning with a walk and took second when Reese singled. Snider followed with a single to center field. Richie Ashburn, the Phillie center fielder, had been playing shallow and grabbed the ball on one bounce. But Ashburn had a weak arm. Milton Stock, the third-base coach, decided to send Abrams home. Ashburn delivered a perfect throw to the catcher, Stan Lopata, and nailed Abrams by a good ten feet. Now, instead of bases loaded with no one out, there were runners on second and third with one down. Robinson was given an intentional walk, and then Roberts escaped, getting Furillo on a foul pop-up and Hodges on a fly ball to deep right.

The Phils made the most of their reprieve. Dick Sisler, the Philadelphia left fielder and son of the Dodger scout and Hall of Famer George Sisler, nailed an outside fastball by Newcombe and drove an opposite-field homer into the left-field stands with two aboard in the tenth. The Phillies won the game, 4–1, capturing their first pennant since 1915.

On the afternoon of October 26, reporters were called to a news conference at the Hotel Bossert in downtown Brooklyn. An era was about to end.

First, Branch Rickey rose to speak.

Rickey smiled, and in a characteristic biblical allusion, began by asking the reporters, "Comest thou here to see the reed driven in the wind?"

The man who built the emerging Dodger powerhouse said he had resigned the club presidency on the eve of his contract's expiration. He announced it was his "duty and pleasure" to introduce the new president, "a man of youth, courage, enterprise and desire, a man you all know, Walter F. O'Malley."

Now O'Malley came forward and the proceedings became even more syrupy. "I have developed the warmest possible feelings of affection for Mr. Rickey as a man," said the new Dodger boss. "I do not know of anyone who can approach Mr. Rickey in the realm of executive ability in baseball."

O'Malley added he was "terribly sorry and hurt personally that we now have to face this resignation."

But beneath the flowery language there was bitterness brought by a struggle for power and a financial deal Rickey had worked out when he finally decided he had to depart.

Harold Parrott, who held a variety of executive positions with the Dodgers, would later write of O'Malley's gatherings with his cronies in Room 40 of the Hotel Bossert, their private eating and drinking place.

"Making jokes about Rickey was the main sport at Room 40," Parrott recalled. "O'Malley began to nitpick and deplore almost everything that went on in Rickey's office.

"For his own part, Rickey would have soon as cultivated a cobra as O'Malley, although he masked his feelings like the actor he was."

Rickey had borrowed heavily to come up with the $350,000 he needed to purchase a 25 percent interest in the team during the war. Over the next few years, he became increasingly uncomfortable with his financial burdens. Then, as the final year of his five-year contract as club president approached, the rift with O'Malley cast uncertainty over his future in Brooklyn. Rickey decided it was time to get out. At least a year before that farewell gathering at the Bossert, Rickey had informed his partners—O'Malley and the drug company executive John L. Smith—that he was looking to sell his stock.

Under an agreement among the three men, who together controlled 75 percent of the club, each partner had the option of meeting any bona fide offer that an outsider might make to the others.

With the assistance of John Galbreath, the Pirates' owner, Rickey was able to get a $1.05 million offer for his $350,000 investment from the New York real estate developer William Zeckendorf.

O'Malley and Smith's widow—Smith had died the previous July—were now faced with the prospect that an outsider, having purchased Rickey's 25 percent of the franchise, could team up with Steve McKeever's daughter and son-in-law, Dearie and Jim Mulvey, the owners of the remaining 25 percent, to frustrate them.

So O'Malley and the Smith widow had to come up with a $1 million payment to Rickey, and on top of that had to pay Zeckendorf $50,000 for his trouble.

"That may have been the only time O'Malley was outmaneuvered in a deal, for his financial acumen was legend," Red Smith would write. "It was this talent that ultimately made him the most powerful figure in baseball, where no other quality is held in such high reverence as the ability to make one and one equal three."

Walter Francis O'Malley was 47 years old when he took control of the Dodgers. Born in the Bronx, the son of a New York City commissioner of public markets, he attended Jamaica High School in Queens, then went on to Culver Military Academy in Indiana, where he played baseball until a broken nose ended his diamond career.

He attended the University of Pennsylvania, graduating in 1926 as president of his class, and then he obtained a degree from Fordham Law School.

While practicing law, O'Malley got a taste of big league baseball by bringing clients to Ebbets Field. He became a director of the Dodgers in

1932, and during the war years he replaced Wendell Willkie as the team's lawyer and bought into the club as part of a syndicate with Rickey and Smith.

An extroverted man adept at charming sportswriters, he was given to expensive cigars and convivial afternoons over a friendly drink and poker game with his associates at their Hotel Bossert hangout.

Now he had taken control of the premier franchise in the National League.

The man who put together that powerful ballclub pondered the future as he met with reporters that afternoon.

"If I listen to Mrs. Rickey, I will have no connection with baseball," said the sixty-eight-year-old Branch Rickey in bidding Brooklyn farewell. "The word she uses is 'retire,' but I don't know what that means. I don't see how a man can get any fun out of doing nothing."

He surely would not retire. There had been rumors Rickey would be going to the Pirates, and that he did, running the team through some awful years while building a youth movement.

Rickey was now a rich man, but he did not leave Brooklyn a happy man, according to Harold Parrott, who talked with Rickey on the street outside the Bossert after his farewell.

"He was in tears, despite the million bucks in his pocket," Parrott would write. "He did not want to leave this baseball juggernaut he had built, with all its fine, upcoming young stars."

A week after O'Malley took over, Rickey's old friend, Burt Shotton, was gone as well.

The managing job went to fifty-two-year-old Charley Dressen, who most definitely was not a Rickey protégé, having been fired by the old man during the war years for his gambling and then, after coming back, having walked out on him to join MacPhail's Yankees.

Dressen was a small man—five feet six inches—with a large ego who would be best remembered for telling his ballplayers, "Just you fellows hold them and I'll think of something."

Born in Decatur, Illinois, he was a pro football pioneer of sorts despite his lack of size. In 1920, he played quarterback for George Halas's Decatur Staleys, the forerunner of the Chicago Bears.

Dressen was a third baseman for the Reds in the 1920's, later played with the Giants, then managed in the minors and eventually got the Cincinnati managing job when Larry MacPhail took over the ballclub.

While MacPhail tried to rebuild a dreary franchise, Dressen's teams finished in the second division four times—twice in last place—and when MacPhail moved on to the Dodgers in 1938, Dressen was dropped.

A year later, Dressen was reunited with MacPhail as a Dodger coach and stayed on in Brooklyn through the '46 season, except for that brief exile during the war. After coaching with the Yankees for a few seasons, he went to the Pacific Coast League and managed Oakland to the 1950 pennant.

Dressen kept Jake Pitler as his first-base coach and Clyde Sukeforth for the bullpen, but Milton Stock was fired, presumably for sending Cal Abrams home in the finale against the Phillies. Dressen would be his own third-base coach.

O'Malley promoted two men from the organization—Buzzy Bavasi and Fresco Thompson—to run the operation. Both had initially been hired not by Rickey, but by MacPhail. Bavasi, in effect the general manager, would make the personnel decisions for the Dodgers. Thompson would run the farm system.

As 1950 came to an end, the future looked bright for the Brooklyn ballclub even without the shrewd hand of Branch Rickey to guide it. An experienced corps of baseball men would be running the daily operation with a sophisticated businessman overseeing the show. And all those terrific ballplayers who had arrived soon after the war were coming into their prime. Surely 1951 would be the Dodgers' year.

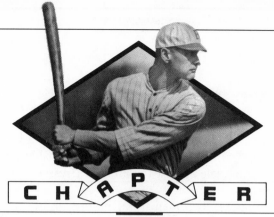

28

And In Came Branca

O n the evening of July 18, 1989, Donnie Moore, a former pitcher
for the California Angels, shot his wife three times with a pistol
at their Anaheim, California home, then committed suicide by
turning the gun on himself.

Moore's agent said afterward that the ballplayer had never recovered
emotionally from giving up a home run to the Red Sox's Dave Henderson
with the Angels one strike away from the 1986 American League pennant.
Boston went on to capture the title a few days later.

Soon after Moore wounded his wife and killed himself, an old-timers'
game was staged in Pittsburgh. It seemed inevitable that one of the former
players at Three Rivers Stadium that afternoon—a man whose career was
far removed from the 1980's—would be asked his thoughts about the night
Donnie Moore had snapped.

A reporter for the *Pittsburgh Press* did, in fact, seek out a comment,
and he got one.

"I cannot visualize being that depressed that you would take your
own life. I threw a home run pitch. So what? We lost the game. So what?
Life goes on," said Ralph Branca.

Thirty-eight years later, they were still reminding him about the
afternoon of October 3, 1951, when Bobby Thomson rocketed a line drive
into the lower left-field seats at the Polo Grounds to produce what is
arguably the most dramatic moment in baseball history.

The Dodger ballclub that went into the '51 season was little changed
from the '50 team that just missed winning the pennant.

Having finished strongly in 1950, the Giants seemed likely to give
Brooklyn plenty of competition. But they began the season as if they were

◆ *Ladies Day, the buck-and-a-quarter general admission seat, and Ebbets Field are long gone. But a happy afternoon seemed in store back in August '51 for 14-year-old twins Arlene (l.) and Rochelle Citron of Brooklyn, first in line for the Ladies Day admission. (Brooklyn Public Library-Brooklyn Collection)*

destined to wind up last, losing twelve of their first fourteen games. They gradually battled back, however, and then in May, the player of a lifetime arrived. A twenty-year-old Alabaman named Willie Mays was summoned to the Polo Grounds from Minneapolis of the American Association where he had been hitting a mere .477.

Installed in center field in place of Bobby Thomson, who went to the bench, the youngster got off to a horrible start, going 1 for 27, but Leo Durocher stuck with him. Mays would not be the only new face in the outfield. Durocher later switched Whitey Lockman, his left fielder, with Monte Irvin, who had been playing first base, a move that proved to be a huge success. Late in July, Durocher made another change, sending Thomson to third base after Hank Thompson went to the minors. Thomson would bat .357 for the remainder of the season.

The Dodgers moved into first place in mid-May, and in June they seemed to eliminate their one weak spot by getting Andy Pafko for left field in an eight-player deal with the Chicago Cubs.

Early in July, the Dodgers swept three games from the Giants, and Charley Dressen blustered, "We knocked them out; they'll never bother us again."

On the afternoon of Saturday, August 11, the Dodgers held a thirteen and a half game lead over the Giants after winning the second game of a doubleheader against the Braves.

On Sunday, it was Wes Westrum Day at the Polo Grounds. The catcher got a new Mercury, and the Giants got started on a roll to the top. Sal Maglie and Al Corwin stopped the Phillies in a doubleheader sweep that launched a sixteen-game winning streak.

The Giants gradually crept closer to the Dodgers, and on Friday night, September 28, as the season went into its final weekend, they moved into a tie for first place. While the Giants were idle, Brooklyn blew a three-run lead and lost to the Phillies at Shibe Park, 4–3, on a ninth-inning homer by catcher Andy Seminick.

Maglie shut out the Braves in Boston Saturday afternoon, but that night, Newcombe pitched a shutout against the Phillies.

So they went into the final day of the season still tied.

The Giants beat the Braves, 3–2, on Sunday behind Larry Jansen, finishing their game while the Dodgers and Phillies were in the seventh inning. The Phils had knocked out Preacher Roe and had taken a 6–1 lead in the third. But with the Giants nervously sitting around radios in their clubhouse at Braves Field, the Dodgers started coming back, and they tied it with three runs in the eighth. The Giants finally left for the Boston railroad station, and as the Dodger game went into extra innings, their train departed for Grand Central Terminal.

There would be no popping of champagne corks aboard the Giants' railroad car. Jackie Robinson saw to that.

The Phillies loaded the bases with two out in the bottom of the twelfth against Newcombe, the sixth Dodger pitcher of the afternoon. The count went to 3 balls and 2 strikes on Eddie Waitkus, the first baseman whose off-the-field misadventure two years before would make him a footnote figure in literature: He had been the real victim in the shooting of Roy Hobbs described in Bernard Malamud's *The Natural*. Waitkus hit a line drive that seemed certain to go into center field and bring a pennant for the Giants. But Robinson made a spectacular diving catch and held on to the ball as he hit the dirt hard and jammed his elbow into his chest.

In the fourteenth, Robinson completed his heroics, hitting a drive deep into the left-field seats off Robin Roberts to give the Dodgers a 9–8 victory and force a three-game playoff.

They opened at Ebbets Field on Monday afternoon, October 1, a beautiful day with temperatures in the 70's.

The drama would capture the city. At the New York Stock Exchange, the ticker intermingled play-by-play accounts with the Dow Jones averages. Bars with television sets—not quite a household staple yet—were jammed. An advertisement for the General Electric Black Daylite seventeen-inch TV offered a markdown from $379.95 to $299.95 as a playoff special.

The Dodgers started Ralph Branca, 13–12 for the season, against Jim Hearn, a Cardinal castoff who had come through with a 17–9 record.

Andy Pafko homered in the second inning for a 1–0 Dodger lead, but then Bobby Thomson delivered a preview of sorts, slamming a two-run homer in the third. Monte Irvin hit a home run later and the Giants won it, 3–1.

On Tuesday, the scene shifted to the Polo Grounds with the Dodgers starting the curveballing rookie Clem Labine, who had been called up late in the season. Labine was without the benefit of Roy Campanella's wisdom that afternoon. Campy had injured a hamstring muscle on Sunday and couldn't run anymore, so Rube Walker went behind the plate.

The Giants' pitcher was Sheldon Jones, only 6–11 for the year. Maglie could have started, but Durocher was saving his ace for a possible Game 3. The playoff would indeed go to a third game. Labine pitched a six-hitter as the Dodgers romped, 10–0.

For the showdown, it was a weary Maglie—winner of twenty-three games and master of the curveball—against an equally tired Newcombe, whose fastball had brought him twenty victories.

There was a threat of rain in the air at the Polo Grounds as they got under way, and a crowd of only 34,320 turned out. The day was dark enough to bring the lights on at 2:04 P.M. with the game in the third inning.

The Dodgers opened the scoring with a run in the first inning on walks to Reese and Snider and a line single to left by Robinson. In the Giants' second, Lockman singled and then Thomson sent a drive to the left-field wall. He was sure he had a double and tore to second base with head down. But Pafko played the carom perfectly, and as Thomson arrived at second, Lockman was standing there. Thomson was tagged after a brief rundown, and a rally was killed. If the Giants were to lose, he might become the "goat."

The Dodgers maintained a 1–0 lead until the seventh when the Giants tied it on Irvin's double, Lockman's sacrifice and Thomson's fly to deep center.

On returning to the dugout, Newcombe pleaded exhaustion and wanted relief help. He got little sympathy from Robinson. "Don't give me that shit—go out there and pitch," Jackie told Newk.

Soon the Dodgers gave Newcombe a cushion, getting to Maglie for three runs in the eighth. A walk, a wild pitch and four singles—two of them balls hit by Pafko and Cox that got past Thomson at third base—did the damage.

As he took the mound in the bottom of the ninth with a 4–1 lead, Newcombe had allowed only four singles and he had breezed through the eighth inning despite his weariness.

The Giants got a scrap of hope when Alvin Dark, the first batter, singled off the glove of Gil Hodges as he lunged to his right. Next came Don Mueller, known as Mandrake the Magician for his place-hitting skills. Hodges was holding Dark on though his run meant nothing. Mueller sent a bouncing ball to the hole on the right side, and it went just past Hodges's reach into right field as Dark sped to third.

Now the power-hitting Irvin came to the plate. In the Dodger bullpen, Carl Erskine and Ralph Branca were warming up. Irvin swung at the first pitch and lifted a pop foul near the first-base line. Hodges snatched it. The Giants were down to their final two outs.

The left-handed batting Lockman was next. As Newcombe prepared to pitch, there was an announcement over the press-box loudspeaker.

"All accredited writers should pick up their press passes for tomorrow's World Series game at Ebbets Field immediately after this game. Passes will be distributed in the Dodger clubhouse until 5 P.M."

Lockman fouled a pitch back to the screen, then went to the opposite field, sending a line drive down the left-field line. By the time Pafko chased it down, Dark had scored, Mueller was at third and Lockman was on second. Now it was 4–2.

As the crowd went wild, Mueller lay in pain, having snapped an ankle tendon sliding into third. He was carried off on a stretcher, and

◆ *It's the morning of October 3, 1951. Ralph Branca's fiancée, Ann Mulvey (far left), is determined to bring good luck to her man. Joining her in ill-fated effort are (second from left to right) the wives of Bud Podbelian, Carl Furillo, Rube Walker and Gil Hodges. (Brooklyn Public Library-Brooklyn Collection)*

Clint Hartung, once branded a star of the future but now a benchwarmer, ran for him.

Charley Dressen went to the mound. He had been told by Clyde Sukeforth, the bullpen coach, that Erskine had bounced some curves warming up. So he summoned Ralph Branca.

Moments later, Branca arrived at the mound still wearing his warmup jacket. Newcombe reached out with his left arm to give the reliever some pats of encouragement. Branca responded with a pat of his own and then Newcombe ambled off to the center-field clubhouse.

Bobby Thomson arrived at the plate. He had hit 29 homers during the season, 7 of them against Brooklyn. Two of the drives had come against Branca, including a key homer in Game 1 of the playoffs. That afternoon, Thomson already had two hits, but he had pulled a baserunning gaffe and had let two balls get by him in that big Dodger eighth inning.

Branca went into a full windup as the runners led off second and third.

The Giant announcer Russ Hodges was doing the radio play-by-play.

"Brooklyn leads it, 4 to 2, one out in the last of the ninth. Branca pitches. Thomson takes a strike call on the inside corner."

The delivery had been a little above the belt. Thomson had moved his bat just slightly.

♦ *Ralph Branca begins the long walk to the Polo Grounds' center-field clubhouse as Jackie Robinson watches the Giants mob Bobby Thomson. (National Baseball Library, Cooperstown, N.Y.)*

"That first pitch was a blur, not because it was so fast but because I was so nervous my eyeballs were vibrating," Thomson would recall.

Branca wound up and delivered again. Another fastball, this one a little higher and a bit more inside than the first one.

Thomson swung and the baseball headed on a rising line drive to the sixteen-foot-high green wall in left field, about forty feet to the fair side of the foul line.

Russs Hodges again:

There's a long drive . . . it's gonna be . . . I believe—the Giants win the pennant, the Giants win the pennant, the Giants win the pennant, the Giants win the pennant.

Bobby Thomson hits into the lower deck of the left-field stands. The Giants win the pennant and they're going crazy, they're going crazy.

I don't believe it, I don't believe it, I do not believe it.

In left field, Andy Pafko slumped against the wall as the ball cleared the top by a few inches. In center field, Duke Snider dropped to his knee in frustration and slammed his glove against the grass.

Branca had never moved to back up home plate in the event of an extra-base hit. As the baseball took off, he turned and watched its flight. "Sink, sink, sink," he would remember telling himself. He was frozen on the mound as Thomson approached the first-base bag and Hartung leaped onto home plate with his hands over his head in exultation.

Just after rounding first, as the realization of what he had done gripped him, Thomson took a couple of big, bounding strides and then broke into a trot. Eddie Stanky, the Giant second baseman, came tearing out of the dugout, still wearing his warmup jacket, and raced out to Durocher's third-base coaching box.

Stanky and Durocher hugged each other in a madcap dance and they grabbed at Thomson as he reached third. Thomson had the presence of mind to get away from them and head to the plate. He arrived there with a leap as his teammates surrounded him and then carried him aloft.

It was, as the *Daily News* would call it, "The Shot Heard 'Round the World."

Erskine and Labine, who had been throwing in the bullpen after Branca came in, turned for the Dodger clubhouse a few steps away.

Those final moments would remain vivid for Carl Erskine through the years.

———

I was warmed up, felt okay. Sukeforth has been held responsible for helping make that decision to bring Branca in, but my recollection was that he answered the phone call that we were both ready but that I had bounced my curve some, which was an overhead straight-down curveball. Sukeforth also was aware that I'd had intermittent arm trouble. He didn't tell Dressen, as I recall, "Take Branca." I think Dressen made that decision. Branca was a seasoned pitcher.

Labine had gotten up and was throwing alongside me now after Branca went in the game. So Clem and I would throw a pitch or two, then we'd watch the game. When the ball was hit, Labine and I just looked at each other and immediately started for the clubhouse, which was around the bend in the outfield. We were the first to go in.

What I saw was that the TV cameras that were being set up on our side were all being hustled across into the Giants' side. The cases of champagne were all being carried over. They were all stacked on our side, ready for the celebration. When

◆ *The Giants are in the 1951 World Series and the Dodgers decidedly are not. Ralph Branca shows Bobby Thomson there are no hard feelings. (National Baseball Library, Cooperstown, N.Y.)*

that finished, when they got out of there and went to the other side, our clubhouse was like a tomb, it was so deathly silent it was unbelievable. Most of the team hadn't gotten there yet. So I sat on my stool and watched one by one our players come in, and this bedlam was going on outside, this deafening roar and this madness was taking place outside.

I watched Robinson come in. Jackie threw his glove into his locker with great force. Dressen came in. He took his shirt and ripped the buttons off the front and threw his shirt in the locker. Hodges very quietly came in, head down, and placed his great big first-baseman's glove very carefully in his locker. It was silence in there, it was just death.

Then the classic picture of Ralph. He came in. There was a trainer's room at a level about five or eight or ten steps up. These steps were maybe eight feet wide. They were wooden steps, they were chewed up from all the spike marks going up into the trainer's area. Branca was seated about the fifth step up or so and he was pitched forward, and his hands and arms reached the floor between his feet. The big number 13 was visible on his back.

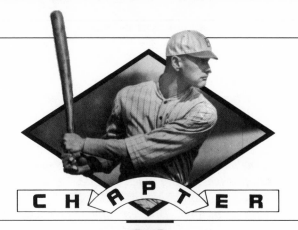

29

Damn Yankees

When Ralph Branca finally left the Dodger clubhouse that unbelievable October afternoon, he was joined by his fiancée.
Seventeen days later, he was to marry Ann Mulvey, a woman
whose family had seen many a dark day in Dodger history, though none
comparable with this one. Ann happened to be the granddaughter of Steve
McKeever.

When they got to their car, Ann began to cry. Her cousin, Father Pat
Rowley, had joined the couple for the ride home. Branca's mood seemed
to match his fiancée's. He asked the priest, "Why me?"

The father told him, "God chose you because he knew your faith
would be strong enough to bear this cross."

When the Dodgers assembled for spring training at Vero Beach in
March '52, the bad luck continued for Branca. He was about to sit in a
folding chair when it slid out from under him on a newly waxed floor. He
landed on top of a Coke bottle and suffered a tilted pelvis. The injury,
which wasn't properly treated until the following season, affected Branca's
throwing motion, and he saw little action in 1952, going 4 and 2. There
would be speculation the Thomson homer ruined him, but he would maintain it was the injury, not any emotional damage, that did him in. By the
following summer, Branca would be pitching for Detroit. His pelvic injury
was repaired by then, but he would never regain his form.

Another figure in the Branca-Thomson episode was already gone from
the Dodgers when the '52 spring camp opened. Dressen was ultimately
responsible for the decision to bring Branca in. But Clyde Sukeforth paid
the price for telling Charley that Branca's bullpen partner, Erskine, had
bounced his curves. Like Milton Stock before him, Sukeforth was fired over

◆ *The Dodgers are about to open their 1952 home season against the Giants. Barbara Anne Greene and Anita Tinkoff, 18-year-old Brooklynites, seek revenge for Bobby Thomson's homer as Joseph Santangelo offers encouragement to Ralph Branca. (Brooklyn Public Library-Brooklyn Collection)*

a final-day disaster.

The Dodgers opened the '52 season without Newcombe, who went into the Army as the Korean War entered its third year. But the Giants had suffered a loss as well—Willie Mays was also in the Army.

Brooklyn's top starter was gone, but a brilliant fastballing rookie arrived. Joe Black would become the Dodgers' first relief ace since Hugh Casey. The Giants had an outstanding rookie reliever as well in knuckeballing Hoyt Wilhelm.

The Dodgers and Giants had been viewed as the chief pennant contenders, and so they were.

All of Brooklyn's heavy hitters were back, and when everything went right, the results could be awesome.

On Wednesday night, May 21, the Dodgers faced the Reds' Ewell Blackwell at Ebbets Field. Known as "the Whip" for his sidearm deliveries, Blackwell was fearsome against right-handed batters. But he hardly proved intimidating this time. Before the Dodgers' half of the first inning was over, Blackwell had made it back to the Reds' Manhattan hotel, and Bud Byerly, Herman Wehmeier and Frank Smith had followed him to the mound. The Dodgers came up with 15 runs in the inning on 10 hits, 7 walks and 2 hit batters.

The Dodgers took a comfortable but hardly insurmountable lead over the Giants as the season went into the stretch.

On Monday, September 8, the clubs played a twilight-night doubleheader at the Polo Grounds. Before the first game was over, the evening had produced enough rough stuff for an entire season series.

The mayhem began in the fifth inning with the Dodgers leading by 5–0. Wilhelm hit Hodges with a pitch. When Furillo followed with a double-play grounder, Hodges came into second with spikes high and opened a three-inch gash on Bill Rigney's leg. In the seventh, the Giants' Monte Kennedy threw two consecutive pitches at Joe Black's head. The umpires called time and summoned Dressen and Durocher for a warning.

◆ *The main men: (l. to r.) Duke Snider, Jackie Robinson, Roy Campanella, Pee Wee Reese and Gil Hodges. (Los Angeles Dodgers)*

Things were quiet for a while, but with two out in the ninth, Larry Jansen hit Billy Cox on the backside with a fastball. Umpire Lee Ballanfant was fed up by now and ejected the Giant pitcher.

It ended with a 10–2 Dodger victory as Black pitched seven and two-thirds scoreless innings in relief of Kenny Lehman. The Giants won the nightcap, 3–2, but the Dodgers had survived the series in good shape and they went on to take the pennant by four and a half games over New York.

Hodges, Robinson, Snider and Campanella had outstanding seasons. Black, starting only 2 games in 56 appearances, led the club in victories with a 15–4 record while earning 15 saves. Erskine went 14–6 while Billy Loes, a product of Astoria, Queens, in his first full season, was 13–8.

Joe DiMaggio retired after the '51 season, but the Yankees rolled along as usual with Mickey Mantle, back from knee surgery, touted as the next generation's superstar. The Yanks took their fourth straight American League pennant, edging the Indians by two games. So for the third time since World War II, it was the Dodgers and the Yankees in the World Series.

Dressen took Black out of the bullpen for Game 1 at Ebbets Field, starting him against Allie Reynolds. Black came through with a 4–2 victory, helped by homers from Robinson, Snider and Reese. But the Yanks won the next game, 7–1.

The Dodgers regained the edge with a 5–3 victory at Yankee Stadium and then, in Game 4, it was the same pitching matchup as in the opener. This time Reynolds bested Black in a 2–0 Yankee victory. The Dodgers won the next one, 6–5, in eleven innings on Snider's double off the Yankee bullpen railing in right, bringing home Cox. Erskine pitched all the way, retiring the last nineteen batters.

So the clubs went back to Ebbets Field with the Dodgers a game away from their first Series victory after five failures.

Loes, starting against Vic Raschi, sailed along for six innings, but then he came undone on a pair of bizarre plays. Pitching with a 1–0 lead, he gave up a home run by Yogi Berra and a single by Gene Woodling. Then Loes let the baseball slip out of his hand while he was on the rubber. It was a balk, and Woodling was awarded second base. After the next two men were retired, Raschi hit a ball off Loes's leg, and it caromed into right field, scoring Woodling to make it 2–1. Babe Herman might have had perilous duels with fly balls, but Loes had managed something not even the Babe could claim: He later maintained he had lost Raschi's grounder in the sun. In the eighth, Mantle homered and the Yanks won, 3–2.

It was Black against Lopat—a fastballer versus a master of slow stuff—in Game 7. The Yanks took a 3–2 lead in the sixth on Mantle's home run. In the seventh, with the right-handed Raschi pitching, the Dodgers loaded the bases with one out. Stengel brought in an unheralded lefty named Bob Kuzava to face the left-handed batting Snider.

"Kuzava went to 3 and 2, and I fouled off about five pitches," Snider would recall. "And then he threw me a fastball, low and away, and I tried to hit it to left center, and I popped it up. One of those perfect pitches."

Now Robinson was at the plate, yet Kuzava, without the lefty pitcher versus lefty batter edge, was allowed to stay in there. He delivered a pitch on the fists, and Robinson hit a pop-up to the right side near the mound. Billy Martin came charging in and grabbed the ball off his shoetops. The rally was over. Kuzava breezed through the next two innings and the Yankees went on to a 4–2 victory for their fourth straight World Series title.

The next year brought the first change in the major league map since the fledgling American League's Baltimore club became the New York Highlanders in 1903.

On March 18, 1953, the Boston Braves' owner, Lou Perini, was given permission to move his franchise to Milwaukee. A seventh-place team in '52, the Braves would hardly be missed. They had drawn only 281,278 at home the previous season and were decidedly second to the Red Sox in the hearts of Boston fans.

At first glance, the shift seemed to mean little so far as the Dodgers' fortunes went. But what would happen at Milwaukee's County Stadium that season would surely be noticed by Walter O'Malley.

The Dodgers seemed excellent bets to be atop the National League again. But one of their stars was struggling in the early weeks, carrying over a wretched slump from the year before.

It had been a frustrating 1952 World Series for Gil Hodges, who went 0 for 21 after having gone hitless in his last 10 at-bats during the regular season. Hodges beat out an infield single against the Pirates' Paul LaPalme on opening day of '53, but he continued to struggle. On May 17, carrying a .187 average, representing 13 singles and a homer in 75 at-bats, he was finally benched.

If Hodges couldn't get untracked, it wasn't for lack of support from the fans. He was getting thirty letters of advice a day. A Philadelphia man suggested he try pure carrot juice to improve his eyesight and supplied the name of the only store in Philly that sold it. Another fan asked for custody of Hodges for ten days and promised to return him as "a boy who could hit most anything." Scores of rosary beads, mezuzot, rabbits' feet, four-leaf clovers and miniature horseshoes came in the mail.

After a few days on the bench, Hodges returned to the lineup and he gradually got his batting eye back, perhaps with the help of divine intervention. Father Herbert Redmond was celebrating a 10 o'clock mass at Brooklyn's St. Francis Xavier school one Sunday in early June. It was a humid day and worshipers were mopping their brows.

"It's too warm this morning for a sermon," the priest told the congregation. "Go home, keep the Commandments—and say a prayer for Gil Hodges."

Perhaps no Dodger provided a sharper contrast with Hodges than Russ Meyer, a right-handed pitcher obtained from the Phillies after the '52 season. Hodges may have been the strongest Dodger, but he was famous for his even temper. Meyer was a firebrand, nicknamed the Mad Monk. On the afternoon of May 25, he was at his tempestuous best.

The Dodgers pounded the Phillies' Curt Simmons and four relievers for twelve runs with none out in the eighth inning at Connie Mack Stadium that Monday afternoon, setting a record for most runs scored at the start of an inning. Meyer was the Dodger starter but he wasn't around at the end to savor the 16–2 drubbing.

Back in the fourth inning, Meyer had been storming around over the ball-and-strike calls of Umpire Augie Donatelli. With outfielder Mel Clark at bat, Meyer finally rushed toward the plate to confront Donatelli. Campanella shooed him back. Then Meyer took out his anger on the resin bag, flipping it thirty feet into the air. It eventually came down—right on top of his head. To make matters worse, Donatelli then threw him out of the game. Meyer trudged from the mound, flinging his glove into the dugout as a parting salute.

◆ *A classic Jackie Robinson image: Stealing home against the Chicago Cubs in 1952. (Los Angeles Dodgers)*

◆ *Gil Hodges is the center of attention on camera day. (Los Angeles Dodgers)*

That wasn't the end of the Mad Monk's misadventures. A few minutes later, the cameras of the local television station, WPTZ, caught him making an obscene gesture at Donatelli from the dugout.

A few days afterward, the Philadelphia police commissioner, Thomas J. Gibbons, reported receiving dozens of angry phone calls and letters from viewers. If a similar scene occurred, Gibbons warned, the police would take "appropriate action."

The commissioner let it be known that laws against "indecent and disorderly conduct apply to baseball players just as they do to everyone else."

Meyer confined his TV performances to the pitching mound after that while the Dodgers went about pounding the rest of the league.

In August, Charley Dressen declared, "The Giants is dead," and they were. But not without a fight.

The obligatory annual uproar between the teams came on September 6 at the Polo Grounds. Ruben Gomez, a rookie pitcher, hit Carl Furillo on the right wrist in the second inning. Furillo tossed his bat aside and headed for the mound. Before anything more serious happened, the benches emptied and Furillo was persuaded to go to first base. Soon after arriving there, he heard Durocher heckling from the Giants' dugout.

Furillo made the tactical mistake of rushing into the Giants' lair. He got into a wrestling match with Durocher, and in the pile of bodies, someone stepped on his left hand, fracturing the palm and breaking the little finger.

The league-leader in batting at the time, Furillo would be out for the rest of the regular season. But his .344 average stood up to give him the title. When he made it back for the World Series, he played with a bandage on his hand and used a sponge to tape the hand to his bat.

The Dodgers wrapped up the pennant with a victory in Milwaukee on September 13, the earliest clinching in National League history.

If the season was a great one for the Dodgers, it proved a spectacular success for the Braves as well. Rejuvenated by their move, they wound up in second place, although thirteen games behind. Televising none of their home games, they played before 1,826,397 at County Stadium—the largest home attendance in National League history.

The Dodgers, continuing to televise all their home games and offering only 700 parking spots at Ebbets Field in an era of suburban flight, drew 650,000 less than the Braves. Walter O'Malley was not happy.

But for the Dodger fans, all was joy for the moment. Brooklyn had won two consecutive pennants for the first time since 1899 and 1900.

The '53 Dodgers were the most awesome team Brooklyn would produce. Furillo's batting crown was only one gem in the lineup. Campanella had his best summer, winning the most valuable player award for the second time in three seasons. He slugged 41 homers and had 142 runs batted in, becoming the first catcher to lead the league in both categories in a single year. Both totals were single-season records for a catcher. Snider hit .336 with 42 homers and led the league in runs with 132. After his awful start, Hodges went on to hit .302 with 31 home runs. Robinson yielded second base to a promising rookie, Jim (Junior) Gilliam, but had a .329 season playing at third.

Erskine enjoyed his finest year, going 20–6. Loes tailed off after a strong start but finished at 14–8 while Meyer was 15–5 despite an earned run average of 4.57. Labine became the mainstay of the bullpen as Black, frustrated by Dressen's demands he develop a good breaking ball, lost his confidence and contributed little.

The Yankees having swept to their fifth consecutive pennant, the World Series opened at the Stadium with Erskine opposing Reynolds. Hodges snapped an 0-for-25 slump in Series play going back to 1949 by hitting a home run into the left-field seats in the sixth, and George Shuba had a pinch-hit, two-run homer, but the Yankees won it, 9–5.

Game 2 was a duel of junk pitchers—thirty-eight-year-old Preacher Roe against Eddie Lopat. The Yanks won again, this time by 4–2, getting homers from Mickey Mantle and Billy Martin.

They went to Ebbets Field, and now Erskine came back, facing Vic Raschi. Campanella had been struck on the hand by a pitch in the opening

game, but he overcame the pain to smack a bases-empty homer in the bottom of the eighth to break a 2–2 tie. In the top of the ninth, Erskine struck out the first two batters—pinch-hitters Don Bollweg and Johnny Mize—to give him 14 strikeouts. It broke the Series record of 13 set by the Athletics' Howard Ehmke against the Cubs in 1929. After walking Irv Noren, Erskine got Joe Collins on a bouncer to end the game.

Next came a matchup of pitchers who had grown up within a few blocks of each other in Queens: Billy Loes against Whitey Ford. The Dodgers won it, 7–3, and the Series was even.

The Yankees were 11–7 winners in Game 5, the big blow a grand slam by Mantle in the third inning off Meyer, who was pitching in relief of rookie Johnny Podres. Batting left-handed, Mantle hit a screwball into the upper left-field seats.

The clubs went back to Yankee Stadium, and Erskine started against Ford in Game 6. It went to the bottom of the ninth deadlocked at 3–3 with Labine pitching. The Yanks got two men on with one out. Martin came to the plate. The second pitch was a good sinker, but he stroked it up the middle and the winning run came home. Martin had batted only .257 during the regular season, but the hit was his twelfth of the Series, tying a record.

◆ *The Dodgers extend a welcome to former Korean War P.O.W.'s at the Ebbets Field clubhouse in August '53. On the pitching end are (l. to r.) Clem Labine, Carl Erskine, Jackie Robinson and Preacher Roe. Enjoying the hospitality are (l. to r.) Sergeant Wesley Murra of Manhattan with Sergeant Pedro Pereira and Corporal Leonard Chiarelli, both of Brooklyn. (National Baseball Library, Cooperstown, N.Y.)*

The Dodgers were losers for the seventh time in seven World Series.

A week later, Walter O'Malley called a news conference. Charley Dressen was at his side, but he wasn't accepting congratulations for winning two straight pennants.

Dressen's wife, Ruth, had written to O'Malley demanding a three-year contract for her husband. Observing that "the Brooklyn club has paid more managers not to manage than any other club"—Max Carey and Casey Stengel certainly fit in that category—O'Malley said he would offer only a one-year deal. If Dressen wouldn't agree to that, he was out.

"The door is still open for Charley," said O'Malley. "All he has to do is say the word and I'll pull a contract out of the drawer here and sign him to it. It'll have to be a one-year contract, however."

The door was, in fact, closed. A few days later, Dressen did try to reopen negotiations, but O'Malley rebuffed him.

Another familiar name in Brooklyn would be departing as well. Red Barber, after fifteen seasons at Ebbets Field, decided he didn't want to work for O'Malley anymore. The following spring—strange as it seemed—the 'Ol Redhead would be the new man in the broadcasting booth for the New York Yankees.

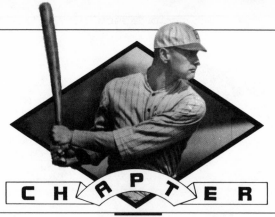

30

Beyond the Baselines: From Happy to Hilda

When Bill Stewart and his two fellow umpires took their positions at Ebbets Field one day in May 1942, they were greeted with an unwanted serenade. From an organ in the stands came the strains of "Three Blind Mice."

The mischievous touch was courtesy of a woman who had just been hired by Larry MacPhail after six years of entertaining hockey, basketball and boxing crowds at Madison Square Garden. Gladys Goodding had debuted with a flourish.

From the summer of '42 until the final season at Ebbets Field, Goodding was a fixture at the ballpark, one of the personalities who added spice to a day in Flatbush.

The rendition of "Three Blind Mice," a little joke inspired by Goodding's acquaintance with Stewart from his years refereeing hockey at the Garden, was not well received.

"You should have seen them," she remarked years later, the image of the umpires still vivid. "The three of them turned on me as if they were on a stick, with their eyes bugging out.

"That was the one and only time I played it. After the game I apologized, and Bill forgave me."

Like many in the Brooklyn baseball family, Goodding—a small woman with fluffy brown hair—came from somewhere else. She was born in Macon, Missouri, and as a young girl was taught the piano by her mother. Later she learned the basics of playing the organ in two weeks, filling in when the regular organist went on vacation at her church in Independence.

Arriving in New York City in the early 1920's, Goodding hoped for a career in musical comedy. But she was divorced with two small children and needed to earn a regular wage. So she settled for a job playing the organ at silent movies in the Loew's chain. In 1936, Goodding was hired by the Garden to play at hockey games, and she eventually got the Ebbets Field job after writing a letter to MacPhail offering her services.

In all her years playing for the Dodgers, she never lived in Brooklyn. Home was an apartment at the Hotel Belvedere across from the Garden. She would ride the subway to Ebbets Field, sometimes accompanied by her fox terrier, who would sit beside her at the organ.

Goodding played the "Star-Spangled Banner" to her lyric soprano rendition and, during seventh-inning stretches, provided a touch of Mexico with "Chiapenecas" as the fans clapped and stamped their feet. She saluted the players with their favorite numbers, ranging from Goody Rosen's "Warsaw Concerto" to Dixie Walker's "Wish You Were Jealous of Me." And she composed a theme song for the team, "Follow the Dodgers."

One purported Dodger fan who didn't find Goodding's organ-playing an inspiration was a seventy-year-old retired music teacher named J. Reid Spencer, who lived in an apartment near Ebbets Field. Claiming that the music disturbed his afternoon rest, he took the Dodgers to court several times in 1942, trying to get the organ banned as a public nuisance.

In an effort to placate the man, Goodding decided to play an organ composition titled "Canzonetta" that he had composed in 1914. She publicized the impending performance, hoping he would show up at the ballpark and that all would be forgiven. But Spencer was preoccupied with wartime rationing that day. He was far from Ebbets Field, getting gasoline for his automobile with temporary coupons that were about to expire.

Even a legal genius would be unlikely to win a suit against the Dodgers in a Brooklyn court. The complaint finally was thrown out on a technicality.

Spencer would have found

◆ Gladys Goodding adorns sheet-music cover for the Dodger theme song she composed. (New-York Historical Society)

Goodding's organ music positively soothing compared with the racket emanating from Ebbets Field late one summer night in 1951.

Anyone carrying a musical instrument or a reasonable imitation of one was admitted free to the left-field grandstand for the August 13 game with the Braves. It was Music Appreciation Night, a bit of zaniness in support of a group of Italian-Americans from the Greenpoint section calling themselves the Dodger Sym-Phony.

Formed in 1938, this little troupe would show up at all the ballgames to inspire the Dodgers and torment their foes.

The efforts weren't appreciated at first—Larry MacPhail wouldn't give the group free seats. But the Sym-Phony outwitted management.

"Some sneaked in with the hot-dog guy, some with the ice man, and some with the roll guy," Louis Soriano, the conductor and snare drum player, recalled years later. "We had a rope over the back of the stand. We'd haul the instruments up and hide them under our seats till we were ready to play. It was tough in those days."

◆ *Dodger Sym-Phony helps Spider Jorgensen (left) and Bobby Bragan warm up for first game of 1947 World Series. Doing the serenading are Pat Palma on cymbals, Jerry Martin on snare drum, Lou Soriano on trombone, Matty Pecora on trumpet and Jo Jo Delio on bass drum. (Brooklyn Public Library-Brooklyn Collection)*

◆ *Manager Charley Dressen, on trumpet, and Walter O'Malley, baseball mogul and miniature-saxophone player, lend their support to Music Appreciation Night at Ebbets Field in August '51. Politicians knowing a captive audience when they see one are (l. to r.) Joseph T. Sharkey, president of the New York City Council; John Cashmore, Brooklyn Borough President; Mayor Vincent Impellitteri and Bronx Borough President James J. Lyons. (Brooklyn Public Library-Brooklyn Collection)*

The Sym-Phony members eventually had seats reserved for them behind first base. In a takeoff on the military's provision for a mental-case discharge, the Dodgers put them in the first row of Section 8.

Long after the Sym-Phony overcame the Dodgers' objection to freeloading, it ran into problems with the musicians' union. Organized labor wanted the Sym-Phony members who held union cards to play for union-scale wages.

To provide backing for the Sym-Phony, the Dodgers threw open the gates to fellow musicians, and 2,248 fans—one-tenth of the total crowd—showed up on Music Appreciation Night with instruments ranging from a glockenspiel to a nine-inch trombone. Mayor Vincent Impellitteri came over from Manhattan and was led to the outfield grass by Sym-Phony members, who were attired in top hats and tails. The mayor serenaded the grandstand music makers with "Take Me Out to the Ballgame."

Long after the Dodgers departed, Sym-Phony members Lou Dallojacono and Jo Jo Delio remained celebrities of sorts, appearing at baseball card shows with former Brooklyn ballplayers.

Dallojacono, who played the cymbals and bass drum when he wasn't working at the Williamsburgh Savings Bank building in downtown, would recall the Sym-Phony's tour de force: serenading visiting players when they returned to the bench.

"When a batter made out and he'd walk to the dugout, we'd play 'da-da da-da, da-da da-da.' The song was 'Go wash your feet, go wash your feet.' And we used to keep in tune with his stepping. As soon as he was ready to sit down, we used to bang the bass drum."

It could become a minor battle of wits.

"Lots of times, Walker Cooper, the catcher with the Cardinals, would kid with us. He'd make believe he was gonna sit down. We'd bang the drum but he'd go for a drink."

The Sym-Phony had specialty numbers for some players.

◆ *Hilda Chester and cowbell. (Los Angeles Dodgers)*

"Ed Stanky was noted for his bases on balls," Dallojacono remembered. "When he got up, we used to play, 'Would You Like to Take a Walk?' "

There was a particular affinity, Dallojacono noted, between the band members and fellow Italians on the field.

"I'd kibitz with Augie Donatelli, the umpire, in Italian. He'd turn around and laugh. We'd kid Carl Furillo a lot. Jo Jo used to give him salamis."

The Dodgers' most famous fan improvised some music of sorts to complement her vocal exertions. Bearing a white banner proclaiming "Hilda Is Here," a deafening truck horn and a cowbell, Hilda Chester was as much a celebrity as some of the players in the 1940's and 50's.

"I used to come to the park every Ladies Day," she once told an interviewer. "I was like any other fan. Then I started to get bored. I went out and bought a cowbell for a dime and things began to happen."

Hilda, who sold hot dogs at the racetracks when she wasn't sounding off in support of the Dodgers, received national recognition one evening. She was flown to Los Angeles for a television appearance on "This Is Your Life" when it featured the umpire Beans Reardon.

One day in the early 1940's, Hilda's zealousness could have cost the Dodgers a game. As Pete Reiser trotted out to center field at the beginning of an inning, Hilda dropped a note from the bleachers and asked him to give it to Leo Durocher.

Moments later, when Reiser returned to the dugout, Larry MacPhail, who was sitting in a nearby box, waved a greeting, and Reiser responded with a brief hello. He then handed the note to the manager. Right away, Durocher got Hugh Casey warmed up in the bullpen. Though Whitlow Wyatt was pitching a good game, Durocher brought Casey in as soon as a few balls were hit hard.

"Casey got rocked a few times, and we just did win the game," Reiser would remember.

In the clubhouse afterward, Durocher was steaming and pointed his finger at Reiser.

———

Durocher: "Don't you ever give me another note from MacPhail as long as you play for me."
    Reiser: "I didn't give you any note from MacPhail."
    Durocher: "Don't tell me. You handed me a note in the seventh inning."
    Reiser: "That was from Hilda."
    Durocher (screaming): "From Hilda?"

———

"I thought he was going to turn purple," Reiser recalled. "I'd never even looked at the note, just handed it to him. Leo had heard me say something to MacPhail when I came in and figured the note was from Larry. It seems what the note said was, 'Get Casey hot, Wyatt's losing it.' So what you had was somebody named Hilda Chester sitting in the center-field bleachers changing pitchers for you."

Rivaling Hilda for zealotry was Jack Pierce, a Cookie Lavagetto fanatic who camped behind the Dodger dugout.

Pierce, a restaurant owner and contractor, would buy ten seats for each game and fill an entire box-seat sector with his equipment: a host of balloons reading "Cookie" and a hydrogen tank to inflate them.

He would warm up with a few belts of scotch mixed with mineral water ice tips, place a blue and gray banner emblazoned "Cookie" on the roof of the Dodger dugout, inflate the balloons, scream "Cookie" and then puncture them to climax the tribute.

Even after Lavagetto joined the Navy at the beginning of World War II, Pierce's devotion was undimmed. He kept up the ritual though Cookie was thousands of miles away.

Long before Hilda and Jack, an infamous "fan" known variously in later accounts as Abie the Iceman or Abie the Truckdriver plagued the Dodgers. Abie was a rotund little man who would sit in the upper tier behind third base and heckle the team, win or lose. One day—so the story went—Uncle Robbie called for Abie and offered him a season's pass on condition he end the harangues. Abie accepted and all was quiet from his sector for a few days. But soon he walked into the Dodger offices and gave up his pass. He couldn't bear to be muzzled.

Then there was another Abe, a man whose advertising sign at Ebbets Field brought his name before all of Brooklyn and helped launch a political career.

At the base of the right-field scoreboard was the "Hit Sign, Win Suit" ad for Abe Stark's clothing store on Pitkin Avenue.

Born in 1894 on the Lower East Side to poor immigrant parents from Russia—his father was a tailor—Abe went to work at age six as a newsboy. The family later moved to Brooklyn, and at age twenty-two he opened his own clothing shop in the Brownsville section.

It's questionable whether the outfield sign cost Stark many suits. A popular caricature showed him standing in front of the right-field wall with glove in hand, trying to shield his advertisement from line drives. In the late 1940's and 50's he had an accomplice who really did protect the sign from being dented. With the sharp-fielding Carl Furillo patrolling right field, Stark could rest relatively easy when opposing batters were at the plate.

As the Dodgers' days in Brooklyn neared an end, Stark's political career was on the rise. He became the president of the City Council in 1954 and would later serve as Brooklyn Borough President.

In the 1950's, the Abe Stark sign was a backdrop for televised pregame shows featuring a six-foot-one-inch, 275-pound show business personality who emceed workouts involving a Dodger player and sandlot youngsters.

The right-field corner was the site of Happy Felton's Knot Hole Gang show.

Born in Bellevue, Pennsylvania as Francis J. Felton, Jr., Happy had been performing since age seven when he was a violin soloist with the Pittsburgh Symphony. He got his nickname at Allegheny College where he played a Dr. Happy in an undergraduate show.

Happy later had his own nightclub orchestra, was a host on radio's "Guess Who?" and "Finders Keepers," and acted in the films "Swing Shift Mazie" with Ann Sothern, "Whistling in Brooklyn" with Red Skelton and assorted Dodger players, and "A Guy Named Joe" with Spencer Tracy and Irene Dunne. He also appeared on Broadway, doing a fourteen-month stint in "Hellzapoppin" and playing a venal southern political boss in the short-lived "Flamingo Road."

One afternoon, Happy met Walter O'Malley on a tuna-fishing trip and suggested a program involving young ballplayers. In 1950, the Knot Hole Gang show got under way.

The program featured three youngsters who would be put through their paces by a Dodger player. All three received baseball equipment as

◆ *Abe Stark advertisement inviting batters to "Hit Sign, Win Suit" tucked away at base of right-field scoreboard in 1941. (NYT Pictures)*

◆ *Happy Felton, at 275 pounds the biggest Dodger of them all. (Brooklyn Public Library-Brooklyn Collection)*

♦ *A sandlot youngster exchanges catching tips with Roy Campanella as Happy Felton plays impresario on Knot Hole Gang program. (National Baseball Library, Cooperstown, N.Y.)*

prizes, and the one judged best by the ballplayer would come back the next day to talk with his favorite Dodger.

Cal Abrams, a reserve outfielder, seldom got to test the youngsters—and earn the $50 appearance fee, which meant something then—since the likes of Duke Snider and Carl Furillo provided greater appeal for the TV audience. On one rare occasion when he was selected for the show, Abrams hit upon a scheme to earn another $50 the next day.

Long after Ebbets Field was gone, he reminisced about his plan:

I got hold of this one kid, and I said, "Look, I'm going to pick you as the best fielder, and in turn I want you to say that you want to talk to me in the dugout." That way I would get an extra $50. So he said, "All right." And so I was throwing the ball to the three kids, and Happy Felton says, "Cal, who do you think is going to make it?" I said, "Number 3." And the kid who I had made the deal with comes over, and Happy says, "Congratulations, here's an autographed ball, a Baby Ruth candy bar. Now who do you want to talk to in the dugout?" I'm waiting out there, and the kid says "Carl Furillo." I almost died.

In 1951, Happy started his post-game program, "Talk to the Stars," featuring the top two players in the day's game fielding questions from viewers.

For this show, too, the players made 50 bucks per appearance. The financial bonanza might bring a strange shift of loyalties as Carl Erskine found out after pitching a no-hitter against the Cubs on June 19, 1952.

I started against the Cubs and it was drizzling rain and threatening real bad. We got some runs early. The main thing was now to get the game in. I think Warren Hacker started for the Cubs. We got him out, and Willard Ramsdell came in to pitch. The worst hitter who ever picked up a bat.

But in the haste of trying to get the game in, I walked him on four straight pitches. Well, anyway the rains did come. We all rushed to the clubhouse, and Clyde King had introduced bridge to our team and it caught on like wildfire. Somebody would yell "deal 'em" and we'd sit around the trunks, two or three games of bridge would start. That's what I did during the forty-minute delay.

They came in and said, "Hey, we're taking the canvas off, they're gonna restart this thing." I changed my suit, which was real damp from perspiration. I went back and re-warmed up, and the game went on. Finally, Ramsdell was taken out for a pinch-hitter.

But Larry McDonald, who was Happy Felton's leg-man, about the eighth inning or seventh inning, went around to the Cubs' dugout, and he said to Ramsdell, "Don't get dressed and please stay available because if nobody else gets on base, you're the star of the game for the Cubs today."

So McDonald took him into the clubhouse. As I finished pitching the ninth inning, Ramsdell is watching on the monitor. He gets fifty bucks if he's the star of the game. That was real money in those days. So Happy tells me that Willie now is yelling at the last batter—it was Eddie Miksis. He says, "Why, you popcorn, how many times you popped up when I needed you, if you get a hit now, I'll kill you." He's pulling for his teammate to make an out so he can win his 50 bucks.

The 3-and-2 pitch was a curveball, he hit a ground ball to Reese, and that was the end of the game. So Willie was star of the game and the only baserunner.

I also got 50 bucks plus Mr. O'Malley came down. We had these one-year contracts, they weren't very big. It was typical of a no-hitter, the owner would come down to the clubhouse and be in the picture and say, "Well, we're tearing up Carl's contract and we're gonna give him a 500-dollar bonus." I got 500 bucks.

◆ Carl Erskine and wife, Betty, proudly display bonus for June 19, 1952, no-hitter against Cubs to go with the fifty bucks Erskine got for appearing that day on Happy Felton's "Talk to the Stars." (Los Angeles Dodgers)

31

"This Is Next Year!"

"**W**HO HE?" asked the headline in the *Daily News*.

Who, indeed. The Brooklyn Dodgers—a collection of big-name players at the top of their form—would be managed in 1954 by a virtual unknown.

Pee Wee Reese and then Fresco Thompson, the Dodgers' vice president for minor league operations, reportedly turned down offers to succeed Charley Dressen.

So Walter O'Malley chose 42-year-old Walter (Smokey) Alston, a career manager in the Dodger farm chain who had most recently been at Montreal. Alston had managed Campanella and Newcombe in their first season of organized ball, at Nashua, New Hampshire, and was known to the men who had come up through the Dodger system. But he had not proven himself as a ballplayer. He had a brief fling in the majors, but it lent itself more to quips than prideful memories.

On a Friday night at Ebbets Field in July '53, a catcher named Dick Teed was contemplating life as an almost-major leaguer. Teed had spent six years in the Dodger farm system without ever playing for the big club. But now he had been called up as the No. 2 catcher because of an injury to Rube Walker, the backup for Campanella.

"I was down in the bullpen and we were losing 11–3 or something, and they called me in to pinch-hit," Teed would recall. "I came running in. I didn't have any of my own bats so Carl Furillo threw me one of his."

Batting for reliever Jim Hughes, Teed faced the Braves' Max Surkont. He struck out. Soon after that, he was back in the minors for good.

Later, while a Dodger scout, Teed couldn't resist comparing experiences with the man who had become the boss of the Brooklyn superstars.

◆ *Walter Alston is about to make his debut as Dodger manager. His opening-day 1954 lineup is (l. to r.) Jim Gilliam, Pee Wee Reese, Duke Snider, Jackie Robinson, Roy Campanella, Gil Hodges, Carl Furillo, Billy Cox and Carl Erskine. (National Baseball Library, Cooperstown, N.Y.)*

"At one time I mentioned to Walter Alston that we had something in common," Teed remembered. "He asked me what, and I said, 'You and I both got to the plate one time and K'd.' "

Alston's major league career had come and gone in a matter of minutes back in 1936 with the St. Louis Cardinals.

"It was the last game of the season, and I'd come up like a lot of kids," he recalled long afterward. "I went up as a first baseman. They had Johnny Mize and Rip Collins. I'd been up there about six weeks and I hadn't played a game. I think the only reason I got into that game was they'd used Collins as a pinch-hitter, and Mize got thrown out of the game."

Alston played the last two innings in a game against the Cubs. He fielded .500, making one putout and being charged with one error. His batting average was .000.

"Lon Warnecke was pitching," he remembered. "I struck out. But he struck out a lot of fellas."

Although he didn't possess the playing credentials, Alston would call upon his vast experience running ballclubs and an imposing, yet quiet personal manner, to exert his authority in Brooklyn. At six feet two inches and 210 pounds, he was the strong, somewhat silent type.

"He should have been born in another time period," the Dodger announcer Vin Scully would later remark. "He would have been comfortable back in the days of the Old West, riding shotgun on a stagecoach."

The year Alston took over, Scully would begin to blossom in his own profession. With Red Barber gone, Connie Desmond, his partner for a decade, was now the senior man in the broadcast booth. But Scully, hired by Barber in 1950, would quickly make a name for himself.

Don Newcombe returned from the Army in 1954, but so did Willie Mays, who played a sensational center field that summer with his basket catches, hit .345 to lead the league, slugged 41 homers and was voted most valuable player. It was the year for the beginning of the great debate: Who was the No. 1 center fielder, Mantle, Mays or Snider?

The Giants took a lead of six and a half games in July, but Brooklyn began to narrow the gap. After the Dodgers won three straight from the Giants in mid-August at Ebbets Field, they trailed by only a half game.

In September, a rookie named Karl Spooner arrived at Ebbets Field. He looked like a left-handed Bob Feller. In his debut on September 28, against the Giants, Spooner struck out the first six batters to face him and finished with fifteen strikeouts and a shutout. Four days later, he struck out twelve Pirates and pitched another shutout.

But it was too late for the Dodgers. The day before Spooner pitched his first game, the Giants clinched the pennant. Brooklyn settled for second place, five games out.

The lineup was little changed from the two pennant-winning teams, but the Dodgers hadn't caught the breaks while everything went perfectly for the Giants. Robinson, now out in left field, got off to a fine start, but was hurt late in the season. Campanella suffered a hand injury in a spring exhibition against the Yankees and underwent surgery in May for removal of a bone chip from his left wrist. He would get into only 111 games and bat .207. Erskine was erratic, Podres was sidelined for an appendectomy, and Newcombe suffered from a stiff right shoulder, winding up 9–8 with a 4.55 earned run average.

It wasn't the Yankees' year either, although they won 103 games. The Indians happened to win 111. Yet Cleveland met its match in the World Series as Dusty Rhodes's home-run heroics led the Giants to a sweep.

In December '54, the Dodgers signed a left-handed pitcher who was coming back home after a brief stay at the University of Cincinnati. He was a Brooklyn boy out of Lafayette High School, not quite nineteen years old. Because he was a so-called bonus baby—signed for $20,000—he would have to remain on the Dodger roster for two seasons, ready or not. He had a terrific fastball but most certainly was not ready for the big time. The Dodgers would be in Los Angeles before Sandy Koufax would get started on the road to the Hall of Fame.

The new year began on a sad note for Brooklynites. On January 28, 1955, in the midst of a reporters' strike, the *Brooklyn Eagle* printed its last edition following 114 years of publication.

"We had some cold bitter days on that picket line," recalled Dave Anderson, the last man to cover the Dodgers for the *Eagle*. "They had an oil drum with wood and a fire in it to keep warm. When we were on strike, nobody thought it would close."

Anderson had become the paper's Dodger writer in May '53 after Harold Burr, its long-time beat man, broke a hip in a fall. He took over what was a year-round assignment.

"Our office was at 24 Johnson Street," remembered Anderson. "The Dodger office was on Montague Street. You could walk over there in three minutes. In the winter, you had to have at least one story on the Dodgers every day, whether it was on a farmhand or a rookie or a contract thing. If you had a day off, you were expected to do another story to cover you on that day. If you were off on Friday, you'd better do two stories on Thursday."

Anderson, who would eventually become a Pulitzer Prize-winning columnist for the *New York Times*, recalled how the Dodger players of the 1950's made things a lot easier for the sportswriters than the stars of the 1980's would.

Besides the *Eagle*, Anderson noted, "there were nine newspapers then that covered the Dodgers on a day-to-day basis—the *Times, Herald Tribune, News, Mirror, Journal-American, World-Telegram*, the *Post* and the *Long Island Press* and *Long Island Star-Journal*."

But in the 1950's, there were few television or radio reporters at the ballpark creating a crush around the star or goat of the game.

Now, Anderson observed, "the ballplayers see this horde of media coming at them" and sometimes disappear.

In the days of the Brooklyn Dodgers, it was simply a print reporter chatting with a ballplayer.

"They use the word interview today," Anderson reflected. "In those years it wasn't an interview, it was just a conversation you had with guys."

———

You'd walk into that old Dodger clubhouse. It was down in the right-field corner. There was a big metal door. The players' clubhouse was to the left and there was an anteroom in the middle where the big black equipment trunks would be, and then to the right was the manager's office and next to the street was the trainer's room.

You'd go to the left and the first locker you would see was Snider's, and then Reese's. He had a little rocking chair and there was also a trunk there. Hodges's and Robinson's locker was right there, and Campanella's, I think, was behind Snider's. That was the corner of the room where everything happened.

You'd just sit there and talk to these guys. They were always available. Nobody said, "Gee, I have to go to the trainer's room," or "I have to call my agent." There were no agents. It was a lot calmer, a much more comfortable atmosphere.

―――――

With no microphones being shoved in ballplayers' faces, the reporters may have found it relatively easy to get them to open up. But the sportswriters at Ebbets Field worked in a no-frills environment—a cramped press box offering only basic ballpark fare.

"They had hot dogs but they didn't have the meals like they have today," Anderson noted. "There was a guy named Benny Weinrig who was the press box steward. Bill Roeder of the *Telegram* didn't like the ice cream in the ballpark. But there was an ice cream stand across the street, and about the sixth inning every game, Bill Roeder would send Benny Weinrig down for some ice cream."

The *Eagle*'s death would bring an often-repeated quip, inspired by the Dodgers' long quest to find a third outfielder approaching the caliber of Snider and Furillo.

"The joke in those years after the *Eagle* folded," remembered Anderson, "was Brooklyn was the only city in America without a newspaper, a railroad station and a left fielder."

Brooklyn's image as a community perpetually overshadowed by the great city across the East River was underlined in a more serious vein by the *Eagle*'s publisher, Frank D. Schroth. In a front-page column on the newspaper's final day of publication, he offered an epitaph:

―――――

Again Brooklyn falls victim to the Manhattan pattern. It has been that way since Brooklyn became a part of New York City. The borough has been a stepchild in government services, charity, social activities, and indeed in every phase of community life. The Manhattan pattern now closes . . . the last voice that is purely Brooklyn. All the other Brooklyn newspapers fell by the wayside years ago. The borough seems to be doomed to be cast in Manhattan's shadow.

―――――

But the '55 Dodgers would not be in the Giants' and Yankees' shadow, nor in anyone else's.

The Dodgers set a modern record by winning their first ten games.

When they finally lost, it wasn't without raising an uproar. The normally self-controlled Alston got thrown out of a big league game for the first time while the Giants were scoring a 5–4 victory at Ebbets Field the night of April 22. Alston wound up on the losing end of an argument with the home-plate umpire, Babe Pinelli, who had called Don Zimmer out on a squeeze bunt by Robinson in the eighth inning.

After the clubs split their next two games, the Dodgers captured another eleven in a row. By the time the Cubs ended their second streak on May 11, the Dodgers were eight and a half games in front.

On Friday night, July 22, the Dodgers threw a huge party. They weren't celebrating another pennant yet, though no one was getting very close to them. It was the eve of Pee Wee Reese's thirty-seventh birthday.

In the biggest extravaganza ever put on for a Dodger player, 33,003 fans turned out to honor the captain in pregame ceremonies that lasted fifty minutes. President Eisenhower conveyed best wishes in absentia while Vice President Nixon sent a letter exhorting, "Long may you wave—that bat." Among the gifts was a deep freeze with 200 pounds of food ranging from frankfurters to shrimp. Seven different automobile models were driven onto the field, and Pee Wee's eleven-year-old daughter, Barbara, reached into a fishbowl and pulled out one of seven ignition keys. It fit the Chevy. In the middle of the fifth inning, two huge birthday cakes were wheeled onto the field. The lights were dimmed, and the fans, striking matches or flicking cigarette lighters, stood and sang "Happy Birthday to You."

As August moved along, the Dodger fans looked forward to another shot at that elusive World Series championship. But then Walter O'Malley sent a chill through Brooklyn.

On August 16, O'Malley announced that the Dodgers would play seven night games the following season in New Jersey. They would face each of the other clubs once at Jersey City's Roosevelt Stadium, once the home of the Giants' International League team.

The Dodger boss coupled the startling announcement with a polite—though firm—warning that the ballclub had to find a new home.

"We plan to play almost all of our home games at Ebbets Field in 1956 and 1957," O'Malley said. "But we'll have to have a new stadium shortly thereafter."

He hoped it would be in Brooklyn.

Maintaining he had been seeking a new site in the borough since 1948, O'Malley raised the possibility that the team might go elsewhere.

"We will consider other locations only if we are finally unsuccessful in our ambition to build in Brooklyn," he said.

O'Malley noted that attendance had been declining, and he placed the blame on Ebbets Field, dismissing it as an antiquated structure unequal to the age of the automobile.

As one storm brewed in Brooklyn, Hurricane Diane, with winds of 115 miles an hour, was heading toward the South Carolina coast.

"If you wish you may call it Hurricane Dodger," O'Malley playfully characterized his stunning announcement. "And the core of the hurricane is now passing over Brooklyn."

The Dodger home attendance had peaked in 1947—Jackie Robinson's rookie season—with a turnout of 1,807,526, the National League record until the Braves' first year in Milwaukee. But by 1954, with the games free on television and many Brooklynites having moved to the Long Island suburbs, the second-place Dodgers played before only 1,020,531. Mighty as the '55 ballclub was, as of mid-August it seemed unlikely to draw more than one million.

Roosevelt Stadium, the old home of the defunct Jersey City Giants, had only 24,170 seats to Ebbets Field's 32,111. But its parking lot could hold 7,000 autos, 10 times the capacity in Flatbush. More important, playing a few games in Jersey would send a powerful message to the people who could bring O'Malley a new ballpark.

Brooklynites were startled and angry. The Jersey City Dodgers? Even for seven games, it seemed ludicrous. And the chagrin was fueled by concern that the team might wind up a lot farther west of the Hudson.

"If O'Malley can't resettle in Brooklyn, he'll move to Queens, or Long Island or—who knows?—California," warned the *New York Times* columnist Arthur Daley.

Three days after setting Brooklyn astir, O'Malley went to Mayor Robert Wagner's Gracie Mansion residence, accompanied by John Cashmore, the Brooklyn Borough President. They met with Wagner and Robert Moses, whose control of several key government agencies made him a man with tremendous power. O'Malley asked that the city condemn a decaying section of downtown Brooklyn so the Dodgers could build a ballpark as part of a large-scale urban renewal project.

The site he wanted was the intersection of Flatbush and Atlantic avenues. Nearby was the worn-out Long Island Rail Road commuter terminal, which would be renovated under O'Malley's plan as part of the overall reconstruction program.

Moses rejected O'Malley's proposal, citing legal limitations on the purpose for which land in that area could be used following condemnation.

"Then, if you don't get this particular site, you'll pick up your marbles and leave town?" Moses asked.

"I didn't say that," O'Malley replied. "I don't even want to consider leaving Brooklyn."

The day of O'Malley's meeting with Wagner and Moses, a couple of telegrams arrived at City Hall—the first pleas from Dodger fans for a way to save their ballclub.

HONORABLE ROBERT WAGNER
CITY HALL NYK

I HAVE AVAILABLE A DESIRABLE CENTRAL LOCATION IN THE HEART OF DOWNTOWN BROOKLYN FOR THE BROOKLYN BASEBALL CLUB. IF INTERESTED CALL ME AT OXFORD 52200.

LOUIS LEISER

MAYOR ROBERT WAGNER
CITY HALL NYK

TO KEEP OUR DODGERS IN BROOKLYN PLEASE BE ADVISED THAT THE HEBREW NATIONAL KOSHER SAUSAGE COMPANY LOCATED IN THE SUGGESTED STADIUM SITE AT 178 SOUTH ELLIOT PLACE WOULD BE WILLING TO RELOCATE OUR ENTIRE PLANT ELSEWHERE IN BROOKLYN. FOR FURTHER INFORMATION CALL

LEONARD PINES PRESIDENT STERLING 93000

One week later, the *New York Times* ran a small item out of Los Angeles noting that the L.A. City Council had approved "official reconnaissance into the matter of bringing big league baseball here."

Amid the distractions, the Dodgers kept rolling. When they beat the second-place Braves, 10–2, on September 8, with Karl Spooner pitching five and two-thirds hitless innings, they bettered by five days their own record—set in '53—for the swiftest pennant-clinching in league history.

On September 24, Leo Durocher, rumored to be on his way out, announced his retirement after seven and a half years at the Polo Grounds. Bill Rigney, managing the Giants' Minneapolis farm club, would succeed him.

Brooklyn finished thirteen and a half games ahead of Milwaukee, with the Giants in third place.

The Dodgers were beginning to age, but their power was undiminished. On the night of June 1, they belted six homers against the Braves, three by Snider, who finished with 42 home runs, 136 r.b.i.'s and a .309 average. Coming back from an injury-ruined season, Campanella hit 32 homers, drove in 107 runs, batted .318 and was featured in a *Time* magazine cover article. Hodges had 27 homers and 102 r.b.i.'s, and Furillo hit 26 home runs and batted .314.

Newcombe won his first ten starts and finished at 20–5. He was a terror with the bat as well, slugging 7 homers and batting .359. Labine went 13–5 with 11 saves. Podres, Erskine, Loes and Spooner along with three rookies—Roger Craig, Don Bessent and Eddie Roebuck—did the rest. Preacher Roe, having pitched on three Dodger pennant-winning teams, was gone. He took his spitball back to Missouri, retiring after the '54 season without a World Series ring.

The Yankees, returning for their customary October appointment after a one-year lapse, took the American League pennant by three games over the Indians.

So it was the Dodgers and the Yankees again. An old story, but for the first time televised in color.

They opened at Yankee Stadium with Newcombe, weakened by a virus and hampered by a sore back and shoulder, opposing Whitey Ford. Furillo and Snider homered and Robinson stole home, but the Yanks won, 6–5.

♦ *Jackie Robinson steals home against Whitey Ford in Game 1 of the 1955 World Series. Yogi Berra is about to rant and rave at Umpire Bill Summers. The batter is Frank Kellert. (Los Angeles Dodgers)*

The Dodgers went with Billy Loes in Game 2. The Yanks started Tommy Byrne, once a wild fastballer but now, at age thirty-five, enjoying a second life in the majors. Having discovered a slider and breaking ball, Byrne had gone 16–5 for the season. The Yanks won again—this time by 4–2—as Byrne pitched a five-hitter and drove in a pair of runs with a single. He became the first lefty to pitch a complete-game victory over the Dodgers all season.

As the scene shifted to Ebbets Field, the Dodgers seemed destined for another October defeat. No team had ever won a four-of-seven-game World Series after losing the first two games.

Tex Rickards, the Dodgers' public-address announcer, unintentionally provided some laughter amid the tears just before Game 3 began.

After the singing of the "Star-Spangled Banner," Rickards intoned: "Now, if you will direct your attention to the box near the Dodger dugout, Borough President John Cashmore will throw out the first ball."

A one-bouncer was promptly uncorked to Campanella—not by Cashmore, but by New York's Governor, Averell Harriman. The arrangements had been changed at the last moment, but nobody had told Rickards.

Johnny Podres started Game 3 on his twenty-third birthday, going against Bob Turley, a hard-throwing right-hander. It had not been a happy summer for the Dodger lefty, who had gone 9–10 and had not even expected to be on the Series roster. He had begun strongly, but hurt his shoulder pitching against the Cardinals in mid-June and went on the disabled list for a month. In early September, he was standing in the infield before a game at Ebbets Field, about to hit fungoes, when the ground crew, wheeling the batting cage across the diamond, whacked him with it. His ribs were banged up, and for a few weeks he had difficulty breathing. Podres's last complete game had come on June 14 and he had failed to complete his next thirteen starts. But he had a good outing in late September against the Pirates, so he was kept aboard when the Series began.

Though hobbled by a hamstring injury, Mickey Mantle hit a 400-foot homer to center in the top of the second. But Podres, showing a fine changeup, pitched an 8–3 complete-game victory, yielding seven hits. As his teammates congratulated him, Gladys Goodding played "Happy Birthday to You."

Erskine started Game 4 on a gray afternoon, opposing Don Larsen, who had come to the Yanks along with Turley in a huge trade with the Baltimore Orioles. By the fifth inning, both starting pitchers were gone. The Dodgers went on to win it, 8–5, with homers from Campanella, Hodges and Snider.

Newcombe was still ailing, so Alston went next with Roger Craig, a six-foot-four-inch rookie right-hander who was 5–3 for the season. He was opposed by Bob Grim, the American League's rookie of the year in '54 when he had 20 victories, but only 7–5 in his second season. A crowd of 36,796—the largest ever for a Series game in Brooklyn—was on hand. Craig left in the seventh with a 4–2 lead and then Labine, appearing for the fourth time in the Series, held the Yankees off. Snider smacked his third and fourth homers of the Series as the Dodgers won, 5–3, to complete a sweep of the three games at Ebbets Field.

Now, as they went back to Yankee Stadium, Brooklyn was a game away from that long-sought World Series victory.

The Dodgers went with Karl Spooner in Game 6. After his spectacular debut in September '54, he had hardly been a world-beater, going just 8–6 for the '55 season. Casey Stengel, having started right-handers at Ebbets Field, gave the ball to the left-handed Ford, counting on the left-center field expanse at the Stadium to frustrate the Dodgers' right-handed power hitters. Spooner lasted one-third of an inning in what would be his final major league appearance, and Ford went to the mound with a 5–0 lead. He had little trouble as the Yanks won it by 5–1.

For Game 7, it was Podres against Byrne, a duel of lefties who were hardly star material. Podres had to convince autograph hunters outside the Stadium that morning that he wasn't the journeyman outfielder George Shuba. Byrne boarded the Independent subway line at Fifty-ninth Street in mid-Manhattan and rode all the way to the Stadium unrecognized.

The Dodgers would have to do it without Jackie Robinson, who had strained an Achilles' tendon and was replaced at third base by Don Hoak. But Mantle, having aggravated his hamstring injury, was sidelined as well.

The Yanks got a rally going in the third inning with two men out. Phil Rizzuto walked and Billy Martin singled to right, sending Rizzuto to second. Then the Dodgers were handed a bit of luck. Gil McDougald hit a chopper down the third-base line. Hoak was playing back. Before the ball could reach him, it struck Rizzuto as he slid into third. He was automatically out. Instead of a possible bases-loaded situation, the inning was over.

Carl Erskine would recall how he was buoyed by that moment.

"It was pent-up frustration. We had a great team. Every year that team would post some great numbers, virtually dominate the National League for ten or eleven years.

"This batted ball hit Rizzuto and he was out. And I thought to myself, that's the first time in five World Series I ever saw what I considered to be a break in a crucial time that went our way. I know that's not entirely true and I'm not saying the Yankees were lucky. They were great. But that play gave me a sense of 'Hey, this may be a different finish.' Nothing like that ever happened to the Yankees before."

The Dodgers broke through in the fourth when Campanella doubled to left, moved to third on Furillo's infield out and came home on Hodges's single over Rizzuto's head.

In the top of the sixth, the Dodgers loaded the bases with one out, and Stengel called for Grim to replace Byrne. Hodges made it 2–0 on a long fly to center field scoring Reese. After Grim walked Hoak intentionally, Alston set in motion a couple of moves that would loom large a few moments later. He sent Shuba up to hit for Don Zimmer, the second baseman. Shuba grounded out, and the inning was over. With Zimmer gone, Jim Gilliam was shifted from left field to second base. Sandy Amoros, the little Cuban who had been around for a few years without causing any particular sensation, was put in left.

Martin walked to lead off the bottom of the sixth and then McDougald beat out a bunt. Up came Yogi Berra. Alston shifted the outfield toward right, figuring the left-handed batting Berra would pull the ball. Podres delivered a high fastball, and Berra instead went to the opposite field, poking a fly ball down the left-field line.

Amoros raced for the ball as the runners went flying. As he neared the foul line and the low barrier, he reached out with his right— or gloved—hand and picked the ball off. As in the third inning, when Rizzuto was hit by the batted ball, good fortune smiled on Brooklyn. Had Amoros been right-handed, as was Gilliam, who had just vacated left field, he would have had to make a much more difficult back-handed catch.

Now Amoros had more work to do. He made a perfect relay throw

◆ *Sandy Amoros saves the day in Game 7 of the '55 World Series. (Los Angeles Dodgers)*

◆ *The Dodgers have finally won a World Series as Brooklyn goes wild. (National Baseball Library, Cooperstown, N.Y.)*

to Reese, who fired to Hodges, doubling up McDougald. Hank Bauer then grounded out.

Podres had escaped another jam, but the Yanks had three innings left to them. Early in the game, Podres had gone to his changeup, the pitch that proved so effective in his Game 3 victory. As the autumn shadows began to fall on the infield, making it harder for the batters to follow the ball, he began to rely on his fastball and a hard curve.

The Yanks threatened again in the eighth, getting two men on base with one down. But Podres survived once more, retiring Berra and then Hank Bauer.

They went to the bottom of the ninth with Brooklyn holding a 2–0 lead.

Bill Skowron, the muscular Yankee first baseman, sent a hard one-hopper back to Podres. He grabbed it but the force of the ball tore the webbing of his glove. Podres ran toward first, struggling to free the baseball and wondering whether he should keep going until he reached the bag. Finally, he tossed the ball to Hodges. One out. Bob Cerv flied to Amoros. Two out. Now Elston Howard came to the plate. He fouled off several fastballs and then Podres shook off Campanella's sign for another fastball and threw a changeup. Howard hit a slow grounder to shortstop. Reese picked it up and threw to first—low and wide. Hodges stretched and grasped the baseball. At 3:43 P.M. on October 4, 1955, the Brooklyn Dodgers were finally World Series champions.

Carl Erskine, one of the Brooklyn players who had been waiting so long for that moment, would recall the scene in the clubhouse:

> *It was such an emotional finish—and to have it happen in Yankee Stadium—when we went into the clubhouse there was a lot of celebration naturally. But there were a few guys—and I looked around—the key guys on that ballclub were very quiet because this was like a spiritual experience more than a celebration. It was just a deep feeling to have finally won a Series in the Stadium and to be world champions.*

If a few of the older players were contemplative, the long-frustrated Dodger fans proved anything but.

The flood of phone calls in the city was the greatest since V-J Day.

◆ *The 1955 World Series champions:* Top row (l. to r.): *Russ Meyer, Jim Gilliam, Billy Loes, Clem Labine, Gil Hodges, Ed Roebuck, Don Bessent, Duke Snider, Johnny Podres, Rube Walker and Jackie Robinson.* Middle row (l. to r.): *John (Senator) Griffin, clubhouse man; Carl Erskine, Sandy Koufax, Lee Scott, traveling secretary; Roger Craig, Don Newcombe, Karl Spooner, Don Hoak, Carl Furillo, Frank Kellert and Harold (Doc) Wendler, trainer.* Bottom row (l. to r.): *George Shuba, Don Zimmer, Coach Joe Becker, Coach Jake Pitler, Manager Walter Alston, Coach Billy Herman, Pee Wee Reese, Dixie Howell, Sandy Amoros and Roy Campanella. (Los Angeles Dodgers)*

Firecrackers exploded and Brooklynites stood on doorsteps banging silver-ware against pots and pans. Stuffed pillows, inscribed "Yankees" and molded into effigies, were strung from lampposts. A blizzard of ticker tape and torn telephone books rained down from the Court Street office buildings in downtown. On Utica Avenue, Joseph Faden, the owner of Joe's Delicatessen, set up a sidewalk stand and gave out free hot dogs. With horns blaring, motorcades raced up and down Flatbush Avenue, Ocean Parkway and Eighty-sixth Street.

Johnny Podres appeared that night on Steve Allen's television show and then went over to the Hotel Bossert for the Dodgers' victory celebration.

"There was a helluva party," he would remember. "The champagne was really flowing. There was one old guy who told me over and over that he had been waiting for this since 1916."

The following morning, the *Daily News* said it best: "THIS IS NEXT YEAR!"

◆ *The '55 Dodgers at a 30th anniversary reunion in Vero Beach, Florida. (Some of those in photo, including, in bottom row, a certain Dodger manager, did not make the official '55 photo because they weren't with the club when the picture was taken.)* Top row (l. to r.): *Russ Meyer, Billy Loes, Clem Labine, Ed Roebuck, Don Bessent, Johnny Podres, Rube Walker and Joe Black.* Middle row (l. to r.): *Jim Hughes, Carl Erskine, Sandy Koufax, Roger Craig, Don Newcombe, Carl Furillo, Bob Borkowski and Walt Moryn.* Bottom row (l. to r.): *Tommy Lasorda (four innings pitched, 13.50* ERA*), Charlie Templeton, George Shuba, Joe Becker, Pee Wee Reese, Dixie Howell, Sandy Amoros and Roy Campanella. (Los Angeles Dodgers)*

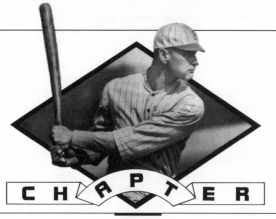

32

One More October

Now that the Dodgers had brought a World Series championship to Brooklyn after sixty-six seasons in the National League, what could they do for an encore?

Go west to Jersey.

On April 19, 1956, a cold, windy day, Act I in Walter O'Malley's war of nerves unfolded. The Dodgers played their first game at Jersey City's Roosevelt Stadium.

Opened in 1937 as a Works Progress Administration project of the New Deal and named for Franklin D. Roosevelt, the ballpark had last been the scene of a pro baseball game in 1950, the final year of the Giants' Jersey City farm team.

In its heyday, Roosevelt Stadium was famous for huge opening-day turnouts engineered by the Jersey City mayor and political boss Frank Hague. On an April afternoon in 1946, Jackie Robinson had made his organized-baseball debut there for the Montreal Royals.

But the park had faded. In recent years, a banked asphalt track had been installed for stock-car racing.

The Dodgers edged the Phillies, 5–4, in their Jersey opener, but the greeting was tepid at best. Only 12,214 fans turned out, and many of them—evidently unreconstructed followers of the old Giant farm club—rooted for Philadelphia.

Two days later, there seemed to be movement on O'Malley's quest for a new stadium. Governor Harriman went to Brooklyn to sign legislation giving Mayor Wagner the power to create a Brooklyn Sports Center Authority. To be composed of three private citizens, the authority would be empowered to issue $30 million in bonds to redevelop 500 acres surrounding the Long Island Rail Road terminal for use as a stadium complex. O'Malley had supported the plan and had announced the Dodgers were prepared to invest $4 million in the bonds.

But the authority didn't exactly get off to a flying start. Wagner waited until July 24 before appointing its members.

By the '56 season, the Dodgers were growing old—the average age of the starting lineup was almost 32—yet they played good baseball as the summer moved along.

Podres had gone into the military, but Newcombe won five of his first six starts and Labine emerged as a top relief pitcher.

On May 12, Erskine became the first Dodger to throw two no-hitters when he held the Giants hitless at Ebbets Field, yielding two walks. Soon he would be joined by an old nemesis. Late in the '55 season, the Giants sent Sal Maglie to the Indians. Now, at age thirty-nine, the old Dodger-killer was purchased from Cleveland. Strange as it seemed, Maglie would be coming out to the Ebbets Field mound wearing a blue cap with a white *B,* glowering not at Jackie Robinson but Willie Mays.

Dodger fans were stirred by another curious development that month. Duke Snider collaborated with Roger Kahn on an article for *Collier's* magazine titled "I Play Baseball for Money—Not Fun."

◆ *The road to Los Angeles begins on April 19, 1956, as the Dodgers play their first game in Jersey City's Roosevelt Stadium. (Los Angeles Dodgers)*

Complaining about travel demands, second-guessing from sports-writers and rough treatment by fans, Duke told his devotees, "The truth is that life in the major leagues is far from a picnic."

"I'm explaining, not complaining," he went on, "but believe me, even though deep down I know it isn't true, I feel that I'd be just as happy if I never played another baseball game again."

Reaction was swift.

"For all its bluster, the story was genial, no more mature than either author, harmless," Kahn would write years later in his book that would bring the Dodger stars of the 1950's the enduring image as "The Boys of Summer."

"But the sporting press hurried to flagellate us for unorthodoxy. At least fifty newspaper articles described Snider as an ingrate."

On September 18, a long-time Dodger who had once managed Snider in the minors was honored with a "night" at Ebbets Field. Rumor had it the Dodgers employed Jake Pitler as their first-base coach so they could announce to their Jewish fans that someone on the team was taking off for Yom Kippur. But Pitler, on the coaching lines since 1948, had an extensive baseball background. He played second base for the Pirates and later managed in the Dodger chain at Olean, New York, and Newport News, Virginia. It was Pitler who spotted Gil Hodges at a tryout camp in Olean during the war years. Now, at age sixty-two, Pitler was presented with a Cadillac sedan before a game with the Cardinals.

After coasting to the pennant in '55, the Dodgers were in a tight race with the Braves and Reds. Going into their final five games, they trailed Milwaukee by a half-game but were at Ebbets Field for the windup.

Maglie opened the last homestand by pitching the first no-hitter of his career in a 5–0 victory over the Phillies. He allowed just two walks and a hit-batsman. But the next day, the Dodgers lost to Philadelphia, 7–5, and fell a game behind the Braves.

On the final Friday night of the season, the Dodgers were rained out of their game with the Pirates, but the Braves lost to the Cardinals in St. Louis.

On Saturday, Maglie and Labine pitched the Dodgers to a double-header sweep of Pittsburgh that eliminated the Reds. That evening, the Braves were edged by the Cards, 2–1, in twelve innings. So the Dodgers moved a game in front.

Newcombe started against Vernon Law on Sunday. Snider and Amoros each hit a pair of homers, Robinson added a home run, and Don Bessent, a bespectacled right-hander in his second season, pitched well in relief as the Dodgers won, 8–6, to wrap up another pennant.

The ballclub still packed punch, but as the team got older, the lineup grew less fearsome. The only .300 hitter in '56 was Jim Gilliam, who batted

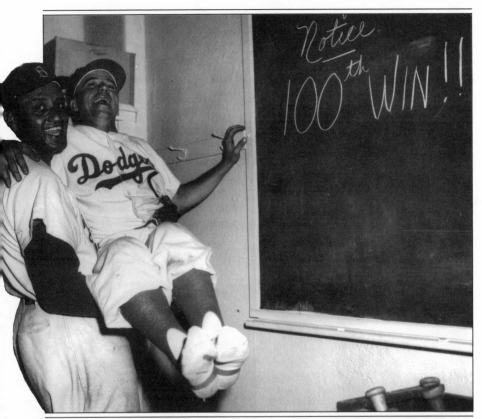

♦ *Don Newcombe celebrates his pitching milestone in 1956 with the help of Pee Wee Reese. (Los Angeles Dodgers)*

exactly that. Snider had another outstanding year, however, with a league-leading 43 homers while Hodges hit 32. Newcombe, coming back from a poor season, went 27–7 and was voted both the National League's most valuable player and the winner of the Cy Young Award as the majors' best pitcher.

The Yankees were atop the American League as usual, and so the Dodgers and Yanks met in the World Series for the fourth time in five years.

With President Eisenhower in the box seats, taking his re-election campaign against Adlai Stevenson to Ebbets Field, the Dodgers captured the opener, 6–3. Maglie, who had gone 13–5 after arriving from the Indians, struck out ten, besting Whitey Ford.

Newcombe and Don Larsen were both knocked out early in Game 2 as the Dodgers outlasted the Yanks, 13–8, in a three-hour-twenty-six-minute encounter, the longest nine-inning game in Series history.

Brooklyn was well on its way to a second successive championship. But then the Yanks evened things at the Stadium with Ford and Tom Sturdivant turning in complete games.

They played Game 5 on October 8, a bright Monday afternoon, before a Yankee Stadium crowd of 64,519.

The Dodgers seemed in good shape as Maglie, impressive in the Series opener, got the ball again.

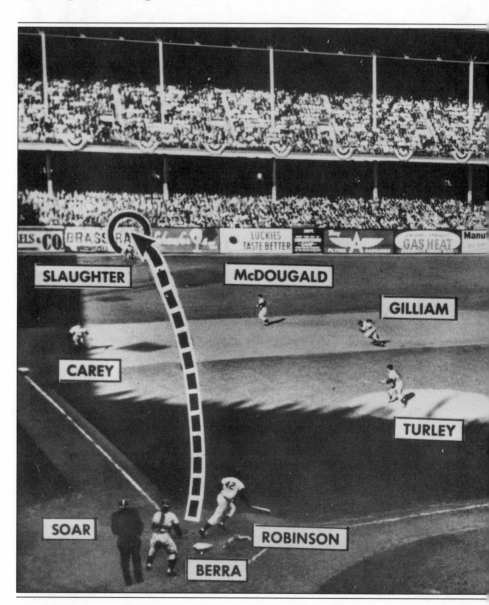

Stengel settled for Larsen, who lasted only one and two-thirds innings in Game 2 and had pitched just six complete games all season.

The twenty-seven-year-old right-hander had broken in with the lowly St. Louis Browns in 1953. The following season, when the franchise moved to Baltimore, he turned in one of the more unenviable records in major league history: 3 victories and 21 defeats. But he cut an imposing figure on the mound at six feet four inches and 215 pounds, and the Yankees

Jackie Robinson hits a tenth-inning drive over a leaping Enos Slaughter to drive home Jim Gilliam with the winning run in Game 6 of the 1956 World Series. It is the last Series game a Brooklyn team will win. (Los Angeles Dodgers)

figured he had potential. They got him in 1955 along with Bob Turley in a wholesale swap of players. He had gone 9–2 his first year with New York and then 11–5 for the '56 season.

Both Maglie and Larsen were in command as the afternoon moved along. Twenty-three batters came to the plate before the game's first hit, a bases-empty homer by Mantle in the fourth inning just inside the right-field foul pole. The Yanks added a run in the sixth on Hank Bauer's single, driving in Andy Carey.

The Dodgers got in a few good cuts during the early going. In the second inning, Robinson hit a liner to third. Carey knocked the ball down and then Gil McDougald, the shortstop, picked up the baseball and fired to first to nip Jackie by half a step. In the fifth, Hodges sent a drive to deep left-center, but Mantle made a one-handed catch.

Having survived those scares, Larsen kept breezing along with his no-windup delivery. Behind him, the zeroes stood out—ever more distinctive—on the auxiliary scoreboard.

When Robinson led off the eighth with an easy grounder to the mound, the crowd roared as if a great play had been made. The tension was rising. The next two Dodgers went down as well, and Larsen walked back to the dugout having faced twenty-four batters and retired them all.

Moments later, Carl Furillo led off the top of the ninth. After fouling off four pitches, he flied to right. Campanella was next. He hit a drive that curved foul, then grounded to Billy Martin at second base.

Up to the plate came Dale Mitchell, batting for Maglie. Thirty-six years before, a Dodger pitcher named Clarence Mitchell had become a footnote to World Series history when his liner was turned into an unassisted triple play by the Indians' Bill Wambsganss. Now Dale Mitchell—a former Cleveland outfielder in his eleventh and final big league season—was Larsen's final obstacle.

"My legs were rubbery and my fingers didn't feel like they belonged to me," Larsen would remember in recounting the moment Mitchell approached the plate. "I said to myself, 'Please, help me out, somebody.' "

The first pitch was ball one. Larsen went to the resin bag, looked at his outfielders, then threw a slider for a called strike. Next came a fastball. The left-handed batting Mitchell swung and missed. Now another fastball, and Mitchell fouled it off. Finally, a third fastball. Mitchell watched it go by over the outside part of the plate. Umpire Babe Pinelli shot his right arm into the air—strike three. Yogi Berra raced to the mound and leaped onto Don Larsen's back. He had pitched the only perfect game in World Series history.

The next afternoon, Labine outpitched Turley in a 1–0 game at Ebbets Field with Robinson winning it on a tenth-inning drive to left over Enos Slaughter's head.

For the seventh game, it was Newcombe—having been battered in Game 2—against Johnny Kucks, a young right-hander from Jersey who had won eighteen games during the season. There was little drama. Bill Skowron blasted a grand slam, Yogi Berra slugged two homers and Elston Howard hit another in a 9–0 Yankee rout.

Afterward, Newcombe said he had hurt his arm on the final Sunday of the season. Alston, however, claimed to know nothing about that.

In November, the Dodgers toured Japan. One day, a message arrived there for Newk. It was from the White House.

"I was pulling for you in the World Series, but hard luck is something that no one in the world can explain," wrote Ike.

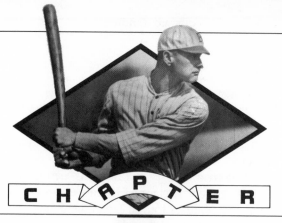

CHAPTER

33

Final Innings

T he Dodgers had gone to the East after the World Series, but there was no question they would be back. It seemed increasingly likely, however, that they would journey to the West before long and never return.

The hot '56 pennant race—a sharp contrast with Brooklyn's runaway the year before—brought the fans out. The Dodgers drew 1,199,775 to Ebbets Field, a gain of 166,000 over their championship season. Yet O'Malley pressed ahead in a quest for a new Brooklyn ballpark.

Late in October, Ebbets Field was sold for $3 million to Marvin Kratter, a real estate developer who envisioned middle-income housing for the site. The Dodgers took a three-year lease with an option to renew for two more years. In theory, they could remain through 1961. No one thought they would.

As 1956 neared its end, the New York City Board of Estimate granted the Sports Center Authority—the unit overseeing that dimly glimpsed vision of a new stadium in downtown Brooklyn—a miserly $25,000 for an engineering and economic survey. O'Malley quickly responded by warning there was only "a short time" left before he might start to take steps to "commit the Dodgers elsewhere."

The Dodgers were still in Brooklyn, but as of December 13, Jackie Robinson wasn't. In a move almost as shocking as the thought they would desert their fans, the Dodgers sold Robinson to the Giants for Dick Littlefield, a well-traveled pitcher, and $30,000. The heart of the ballclub—the man whose pioneering had set Brooklyn apart from all the rest of baseball—was almost thirty-eight years old by now, the waistline expanding, the sparkling moments less frequent. Yet it boggled the mind to see Robinson in a Giant jersey. A bizarre image emerged: Jackie bouncing up and down on the baselines harassing a Dodger pitcher—maybe Sal Maglie?—and then stealing home to beat Brooklyn at Ebbets Field.

It wouldn't happen. Robinson announced his retirement on a Sunday afternoon in January at a news conference in *Look* magazine's offices off Madison Avenue. "From now on I'll be just another fan—a Brooklyn fan," he wrote in an exclusive piece for *Look* distributed that day to the reporters. The magazine had paid him $50,000 for his article "Why I'm Quitting Baseball." Robinson would take a personnel job with the Chock Full O'Nuts lunch-counter chain, staffed almost entirely by blacks.

The week Robinson retired, O'Malley was in Los Angeles exploring 300 acres of downtown real estate known as Chavez Ravine. If big league baseball came to L.A., there might be a ballpark there some day.

O'Malley briefly turned his sights toward Brooklyn in January, hiring Ringling Brothers' Emmett Kelly to entertain at home games. The sad-eyed clown—seemingly the embodiment of Willard Mullin's cartoon character "Bum"—might ease the tension at Ebbets Field, O'Malley suggested.

But events kept moving, and not in Brooklyn's direction. In late February, O'Malley bought the Los Angeles Angels, the Cubs' Pacific Coast League team, in exchange for the Fort Worth franchise of the Texas League. The Dodgers now had territorial rights to the Los Angeles area.

In March, Norris Poulson, the Los Angeles mayor, met with O'Malley at the Dodgers' Vero Beach training camp.

"We got to know each other, but the Dodgers are still in Brooklyn," said O'Malley.

Poulson, who would see O'Malley four times that spring, assured him Chavez Ravine would eventually be the site of a new stadium. If the Dodgers were to go to Los Angeles the following season, they could play awhile at Wrigley Field, the ballpark of the minor league Angels, or at the Los Angeles Coliseum.

Later that month, City Council President Abe Stark proposed that the Dodgers move his "Hit Sign, Win Suit" ad to Prospect Park, envisioning a ballpark at the Parade Grounds, a thirty-nine-acre site on the park's southern end. O'Malley rejected the idea.

In mid-April, Robert Moses, having rebuffed O'Malley on a downtown Brooklyn site, proposed construction by his Parks Department of a 50,000-seat stadium for the Dodgers at the site of the 1939 World's Fair in Flushing Meadows, Queens.

The Queens Dodgers? O'Malley did not reject the proposal outright, saying instead he would look at it in detail if it ever "achieves political maturity."

On Friday, May 3, Poulson and O'Malley met in Beverly Hills at the Beverly Hilton Hotel. This time, another mayor was there as well: George

◆ *It's early 1957. Walter O'Malley has purchased this 44-seat Convair to transport the Dodgers in comfort just in case some long journeys loom. (General Dynamics)*

Christopher of San Francisco. O'Malley had not been alone in his restlessness. The Giants' owner, Horace Stoneham—his club floundering and the Polo Grounds aging—had been clamoring for a new ballpark as well. Back in March '56, the Manhattan Borough President, Hulan Jack, had concocted a grandiose plan for a 110,000-seat stadium to be built on stilts over railroad tracks on Manhattan's West Side. But Stoneham, like O'Malley, was making no real progress. Now San Francisco was hunting for the Giants.

The following Monday, O'Malley telephoned Christopher from Brooklyn and told him Stoneham was anxious to listen. By Friday, Christopher had arrived at the Giants' offices with his plans for a municipal ballpark.

In mid-May, having gotten nowhere with his Parade Grounds idea, Abe Stark proposed an expansion of Ebbets Field through acquisition of surrounding run-down property. O'Malley rejected that plan too.

As the impossible moved toward becoming inevitable, Brooklynites turned to City Hall for a way to save their Dodgers. Alternately pleading and threatening, they unloosened their emotions in postcards and letters to Mayor Wagner.

Decades later, the mail from Brooklyn—often filled with misspellings and mangled English—lies in gray boxes at the New York City Municipal

Archives. From youngsters, from old-timers, from men and women who could hardly imagine a summer without the symbol of their hometown, are long-forgotten voices of desperation in a cause that would soon be lost.

=====

Dear Mayor Wagner,

We Brooklynites are a proud people and the Dodgers are a part of our lives. If we ever lose them, it will be the same as taking the heart out of a person.

Sincerely
Paul W. Hagman

=====

Dear Sir:

We think it only fair that the Dodgers should stay in Brooklyn, for it was born here. Here in Brooklyn, no-place else has the Brooklyn Dodgers created a legend. Could you pictured a Dodger-Less Brooklyn?

So please Mr. Wagner, let our Dodgers stay here. Don't break our hearts.

We fans of all different faiths are offering up our prayers, Masses, and Communions, that our beloved team will stay, so please Mr. Mayor help us.

Very truly yours,
Theresa Harting Sponser

=====

Mayor Wagner
Dear Sir,

What is the matter with you people. The only good thing we have in Brooklyn is the Dodgers. Keep them here.

Anna Motiaytis

=====

To Whom it May Concern,

I have always been a Dodger fan ever since I can remember. I've only gone to school for 4 yrs. but when it comes to baseball I know which team is best. Pleas help them.

Thank you
Jane Turner

=====

Sir:

I cannot impress upon you too much how important it is to keep the Dodgers in Brooklyn. It keeps the children off the streets during the day, it gives them someone to look up to, someone to try to imitate. Instead of acting like "tough guys," they try to imitate Duke Snider, Pee Wee Reese, Roy Campanella, etc. It also gives them a feeling for "fair play." And the Dodgers, being composed of Negroes, Spanish, and Whites, are a good example of how good you can get if everyone works together regardless of race or color.

Respectfully yours,
Mr. T. Ciappina

Dear Mayor Wagner

Please. Please do all you can about saving the Dodgers, and keeping them in Brooklyn. Its something to be saved for the future generations of New Yorkers, some of the greatest times of my boyhood were spent with my father watching the Dodgers, and god willing I hope I can do the same for my kids if I have some.

Bernhard Steil

Dear Mr. Mayor,

Like my daddy I am too a Dodger fan I am 9 years old and I have been a dogers fan all that time like many kids like myself I would be lost without the dodgers, Please make sure the Dodgers stay in Brooklyn, Thank you very much.

Joseph Batteria

Dear Sir,

I am 11 and I am speaking for my family, my cousin, and all of my uncles and aunts.
If Brooklyn moves not only us, but all of the Brooklyn fans will be heartbroken.
As for myself Ive rooted for Brooklyn all my life and I sure would not want to see them go.

Sincerely,
William Eisenhardt

Honorable Mayor Wagner:

My family, friends & relatives have been registered Dem-
ocrats for 20 years. If the Dodgers move out of town the Re-
publican Party has gained our votes for the rest of our lives.

Citizen M. Franco

Dear Mayor Wagner:

Please get busy on the stadium for our Dodgers. I have
been a Dodger rooter since the days of old Washington Park,
when as a kid I could see them play for 10 cents from the (so
called) Dago flats. It would be a terrible thing to me and millions
of other fans if the Dodgers had to leave Bklyn.

We've lost the Bklyn Eagle, department stores downtown
& now the Dodgers? Say it ain't so Mr. Mayor. Please think it
over very carefully Mayor Wagner. Your political future could
hinge on your decision.

Yours sincerely,
Henry Holmes

As the summer of '57 moved along, Brooklynites began to organize
in a bid to pressure City Hall. A "Keep the Dodgers in Brooklyn Committee"
was formed. Some 10,000 buttons were distributed and 25,000 signatures
were collected demanding a solution.

Many of the committee's members were youngsters. One of them was
a sixteen-year-old Erasmus Hall High School student named Ron Gabriel.

On October 4, 1975—twenty years to the minute after the Brooklyn
Dodgers won their only World Series title—Ron Gabriel would declare
formation of a Brooklyn Dodger Fan Club. He would become a collector
extraordinaire of Dodger memorabilia, creating a shrine of sorts at his
home in the Washington, D.C., suburbs. But in 1957, he was simply a
young fan scrambling for a way to save his team.

"During those last several weeks there were rallies and petitions,"
Gabriel recalled. "We had pins—one or two of which I still have—blue and
white with the Dodger logo, reading 'Keep the Dodgers in Brooklyn.' There
were long sheets, they were maybe 14 by 18, that people signed.

"I stood out every night by the subway, usually downtown around
Flatbush Avenue, Fulton Street, Borough Hall. My father said, 'If you don't
come home for dinner—you go out collecting signatures—you'll lose your
allowance.' I said, 'Fine, that's a fair deal. I may never eat again.' Because
I felt this was a real crusade."

◆*Empty seats on opening day set the mood for the Dodgers' final season in Brooklyn. (Los Angeles Dodgers)*

Then came the day when Brooklynites massed outside their Borough Hall to voice what would be a final collective cry. The scene remains sharply etched in Ron Gabriel's memory.

"John Cashmore was the Borough President—it seemed like forever—he was presiding. There were a number of speakers, mostly older men. They seemed to have a prepared text. They went all the way back. They cited Charlie Ebbets and Dazzy Vance and Zach Wheat and Babe Herman, Jackie Robinson and Dixie Walker. They always ended with the same phrase: 'That's baseball, that's the Dodgers, that's Brooklyn.' They went on for hours. There were people as far as you could see. The excitement was phenomenal."

But the National League wasn't listening. The Braves' move to Milwaukee in 1953 had proved a spectacular success. Since then, the American League had granted two transfers. The St. Louis Browns had become the Baltimore Orioles and the Philadelphia Athletics had moved to Kansas City. Of course, the Braves, Browns and A's had been flops on the field and at the gate while the Dodgers were powerful and prosperous, the Giants not without hope.

The contrast made no difference to the league's clubowners. On May 28, meeting in Chicago, they granted the Dodgers and Giants permission to go to Los Angeles and San Francisco respectively, providing they made application before October 1.

It would be a dreary season at Ebbets Field. Snider, Hodges and Furillo could still whack the ball, but the lineup was graying. Opposing pitchers need be terrified no longer. Robinson was gone, Campanella had a mediocre year, and Reese, at age thirty-nine, had become a part-timer, seeing action mostly at third base as Charlie Neal took over the shortstop job. The pitching staff did have its moments, and there was some young blood. Don Drysdale, a big, sidearming right-hander in his second season, emerged as a power pitcher. Yet Newcombe was fading, Erskine was plagued by continuing arm problems, and Maglie, completing his tour of New York, was sent to the Yankees during the summer.

On the night of July 11, the torpor was broken by a brawl in the best tradition of Ebbets Field's rowdy history. Raul Sanchez, a Cincinnati Reds right-hander, had been knocked sprawling in the fifth inning when he tagged Jim Gilliam, who had dragged a bunt. In the seventh, Sanchez retaliated by knocking Gilliam down with a head-high pitch. On the next delivery, Gilliam bunted again, and when Sanchez approached the first-base line in pursuit of the ball, Gilliam bowled him over. They began flailing away, and the benches emptied. Charlie Neal and the Reds' Don Hoak, a Dodger only two years before, got into a splendid fight of their own.

One week later, a crowd of 28,274 turned out at Ebbets Field for Gil Hodges Night. In ceremonies between games of a twilight-night double-header with the Cubs, Hodges received gifts ranging from a Dodge convertible to a year's supply of dill pickles. It would be the last festive evening at the old ballpark.

On August 19, the Giants made it official. Horace Stoneham, who had owned the team for two decades and whose father, Charles, had run the franchise before him, announced he was bound for San Francisco. A 45,000-seat municipally owned stadium with ample parking—and more than ample winds, he would learn—was to arise at a spot called Candlestick Point. While it was being built, the Giants would trade in the Polo Grounds for Seals Stadium, San Francisco's minor league ballpark.

Still, O'Malley would not commit himself.

Dodger fans glimpsed a ray of hope during September when Nelson Rockefeller put forward a plan to keep the team in Brooklyn. A Rockefeller corporation would purchase land condemned by the city in downtown Brooklyn and then lease it to the Dodgers, who would build a ballpark there. But like all the other proposals, the plan came to nothing.

By the final week of September, it was all but official. The Brooklyn Dodgers were history.

On Tuesday evening, September 24, the Dodgers met the Pittsburgh Pirates in the season's final game at Ebbets Field. It was a cool night, and only 6,702 fans were in the stands.

Gladys Goodding captured the moment at her organ. After the first inning, she played "Am I Blue" and "After You're Gone." In the third, she chose "Don't Ask Me Why I'm Leaving." Later came "Que Sera Sera," "Thanks for the Memories" and "How Can You Say We're Through."

The game ended with the Pirates' Dee Fondy grounding out to Gil Hodges. The Dodgers had won it, 2–0. As the players headed for the clubhouse, Tex Rickards, the public-address announcer, repeated a message he had conveyed hundreds of times before, as if this were just another night.

"Please do not go on the playing field. Use any exit that leads to the street."

Gladys Goodding began to play "May the Lord Bless and Keep You." Then someone turned on the amplified recording of "Follow the Dodgers," the ballclub theme Goodding had composed. Soon that was silenced, and as the last few fans filed through the exit gates, Goodding played "Auld Lang Syne."

Moments later, the ground crew raked the infield smooth and protected the pitching mound with canvas.

The Dodger pitcher that evening was a twenty-four-year-old rookie left-hander named Danny McDevitt.

As he threw the final pitches, Gladys Goodding's sentimental outpouring went unheard.

"When I was pitching a ballgame—and I had a pretty good ballgame going—I had tuned out everything else," McDevitt would recall. "You sort of put yourself in that trance. I don't hear people talking in the stands and I'm hardly aware of the ballplayers sitting on the bench with me."

McDevitt's outing—a five-hitter with nine strikeouts—had a very personal significance for him far removed from sentimentality.

He thought: "That's a good way to end the season because maybe they won't cut my salary."

There were three more ballgames to play. The Dodgers went down to Philadelphia, and on Sunday, September 29, they wound up the season with a 2–1 loss to the Phillies and a third-place finish, eleven games behind the Milwaukee Braves.

O'Malley still had made no announcement. When the October 1 deadline for notifying the league of his intentions arrived, he was given a two-week extension. The next day, the baseball spotlight turned to Yankee Stadium, where the Yanks and Braves opened the World Series.

On Monday, October 7, the Los Angeles City Council took the action O'Malley had been waiting for. It approved an ordinance turning over a huge chunk of real estate to the Dodgers for a ballpark at Chavez Ravine.

◆ *Paul Katz, 12, of Brooklyn's Sheepshead Bay section, puts his personal stamp on a Willard Mullin cartoon showing the Bum being dragged out of Brooklyn. (National Baseball Library, Cooperstown, N.Y.)*

At four P.M. the next day, publicity representatives for the Dodgers and the National League called reporters to the press room at the Waldorf-Astoria, the New York headquarters for the World Series.

The Dodgers handed out a bloodless statement announcing that "the stockholders and directors of the Brooklyn Baseball Club have today met and unanimously agreed that necessary steps be taken to draft the Los Angeles territory."

Walter O'Malley was nowhere in sight.

Baseball may have been a gentleman's pursuit when Brooklyn's Putnam players toasted their vanquished foes, the Excelsiors, at that lavish

◆ *Poodle power didn't quite do the trick. (National Baseball Library, Cooperstown, N.Y.)*

banquet in Trenor's Dancing Academy in Williamsburgh back in the autumn of 1856. But what had been a game developed quickly into a hard business. By 1857, delegates from Brooklyn and Manhattan had drawn up a formal set of rules at baseball's first convention. When asked once whether he planned to build a new field to replace Washington Park, Charlie Ebbets had retorted, "The question is purely one of business; I am not in baseball for my health."

The Brooklyn fans were not especially naive, yet they felt an overwhelming sense of betrayal when their Dodgers departed. The bond between the people of Brooklyn and the players had been strong in a time when professional athletes were not only celebrities but considered members of the community.

Carl Erskine, Rube Walker, Pee Wee Reese, Duke Snider and Preacher Roe rented homes during the summers in Bay Ridge, a pleasant neighborhood near the Narrows separating Brooklyn from Staten Island. The Erskine family lived on Lafayette Walk. The owner of the home they occupied would spend her summers visiting a sister upstate in Saratoga Springs.

Reminiscing on those years, Erskine would recall long afterward the time when he was truly a Brooklynite.

We'd go back to the same neighborhood every year. We got very well acquainted with the neighbors. We became citizens in a way rather than just ballplayers who moved in for a season and left. There were so many ties for some of the Brooklyn players of that era. Gil Hodges lived in a different section but he married a girl in Brooklyn, Joanie, and moved there permanently.

That team was unique in that we had a second home. In my case a second home from Anderson, Indiana, was Brooklyn, New York. Our kids went to the same doctor most of the time, Dr. Morris Steiner, who lived out on East Nineteenth Street. He took care of our kids from the time they were tiny babies. I often jokingly say, but it's almost true, when my son Danny, who's now forty, gets a bad cold or something, my wife is tempted to call Morris Steiner. He was really closer to our families than our own doctors back in our hometowns because we spent more time in Brooklyn than we did in the off-season in Anderson.

Abe Meyerson owned a deli and he also owned about six red-headed kids. Abe was a big Dodger fan. He would come around to my house on Lafayette Walk from over on Ninety-

second Street. On the day after I'd pitched, he'd be over at my house the next morning—win, lose or draw. Abe Meyerson would bring me two big bags of deli groceries. This guy had his own kids to feed—I wonder if they all got fed. I said, "Abe, you can't give me that stuff." Beautiful ham slices. He said, "Oh, you guys shouldn't have to buy anything in Brooklyn. You shouldn't have to pay rent, buy gasoline, you guys are wonderful, here, take this."

That was typical of the people who took us into their lives—the babysitters, the families, they all celebrated our victories and died with us in some of our tough losses. We were very much integrated into the community of Brooklyn.

Carl Erskine thought back to one particular fan, and that man's sense of loss when the Dodgers departed.

There was a gentleman that lived at 404 Caton Avenue, Captain Joe Dowd. He was a tugboat employee of Moran Towing Company, a dispatcher. He'd been with the company for many years. He had lived through the eras of Brooklyn baseball probably back to the early 1900's. He knew a lot of history. He lived and died with the Dodgers. Gil Hodges and I got to be close friends with Captain Dowd, and he'd take us and our families around the harbors in tugboats. It was beautiful. We'd go fishing with him in Sheepshead Bay and we got to be very close friends.

Captain Dowd was nearly ready to retire and he geared his whole life around the retirement years when he could go to Ebbets Field every day, not just on his off day. The year he retired was the year we moved to Los Angeles, and it sort of typified the heartbreak of the Dodger fan for me to talk to Captain Dowd.

He was broken-hearted and he never forgave the team for causing him to devote his life interest to them, and then without even asking him, they just left.

34

The $1,420 Seat

The rain is pouring down as Tom Knight sloshes his way up the hillside at Greenwood Cemetery. He stops at a modest gray monument inscribed simply "Ebbets."

It is a Saturday afternoon in April, and Knight thinks back to another afternoon that same month sixty-five years before.

"Charlie was buried on a day like today," he observes. "I hope we don't get pneumonia like Ed McKeever."

A semiretired insurance executive, Tom Knight had been designated some years back by then-Brooklyn Borough President Sebastian Leone as the borough's historian for baseball. He is among a small band of Brooklynites dedicated to keeping the memories aglow. This day, thirty-three years after the Dodgers last saw a springtime in Flatbush, he is taking a guest on his little tour through the sites of Brooklyn baseball past.

Now Knight is recalling the time Charlie Ebbets was buried on a stormy April day and then how Ed McKeever, his successor, catching a cold from standing in the rain as the gravediggers struggled with the oversized coffin, would be gone as well a week later.

That tale is the stuff of Brooklyn baseball legend. But Knight has an anecdote or two to share beyond that. He glances at the small headstones: "Charles Ebbets, 1859–1925" and "Grace S. Ebbets, 1884–1959."

Grace was actually Charlie's second wife; before her there was Minnie, Knight notes.

"Rumor had it that Grace washed the Dodger uniforms, but she was once asked about it and said that was ridiculous, so maybe it was Minnie.

"Minnie was at Ebbets Field, she was eighty years old, the night of Vander Meer's no-hitter."

That bit of arcane Ebbets genealogy having been revealed, it is time to move on.

"Good-bye, Charlie," chuckles Knight.

"I'm the only one who comes to see him," he suspects as he leaves the gravesite.

The next stop is the monument to baseball's first sportswriter, only a few hundred yards away.

The stone column is inscribed "In Memorium—Henry Chadwick—Father of Baseball." Crossed bats and a glove are engraved on one side of the marker and crossed bats and a catcher's mask are carved on another side. Atop sits a sculptured baseball.

"You can see the stitching on the ball," Knight notes. But there is one detail that has even this aficionado puzzled. Observing that four stone bases are cemented into the soil around the monument, he wonders, "Why didn't they put in a home plate?"

Next comes a visit to the places where the Dodgers played their games before Charlie Ebbets built his ballpark in Flatbush.

A few minutes' drive from the cemetery, Knight stops in Park Slope, the neighborhood he grew up in during the Depression years. He is at the site of the original Washington Park. It's a cement playground now, a spot for youngsters to play softball. Knight points to a brick building used by the city Parks Department for an office. It was put up in 1935, he notes, a replica of the structure used by George Washington as a headquarters during the Battle of Long Island, then taken over by the ballclubs of the 1880's.

"Thousands of people go by here every day and they never know this was the ballpark the Dodgers used," Knight laments.

He moves on, and a few blocks away comes to a spot where blue is everywhere. But it is not Dodger blue, simply the color of Consolidated Edison trucks. This is the site of the Dodgers' second Washington Park, built in 1898, last used by the Federal League's Tip-Tops in 1915, now an electric utility plant.

A remnant of the old days still stands. Knight notes that the red brick walls surrounding the plant were part of this latter day Washington Park. He points out indentations signifying where the clubhouse windows had been placed.

Nearby, there is one more stop, an attractive two-story brownstone at 328 First Street, the Ebbets family home in the 1890's.

"He couldn't have been too unpopular or he'd have been killed walking back and forth to the ballpark," Knight laughs. "Could you imagine Steinbrenner walking back and forth to Yankee Stadium?"

The mirth is gone when Knight turns his thoughts to another baseball mogul, the man who took the Dodgers out of Brooklyn.

"It was incredible," he says. "It's still unbelievable. It's just a tragedy. It took a certain type of individual to pull a stunt like that, and Walter was it."

Knight recalls a conversation a while back.

"A guy said to me, 'How could a man from Brooklyn do a thing like that?'

"I said, 'Well, he wasn't from Brooklyn. He came from Amityville [the Long Island village O'Malley lived in].' "

Knight pauses, and then comes his punch line, delivered with gusto.

"He was the original Amityville Horror."

The deep feeling of betrayal is shared by Ron Gabriel three decades after he stood outside Borough Hall with those petitions to keep the Dodgers in Brooklyn.

Now a management consultant, Gabriel carries a torch for the old days at his Maryland home through the Brooklyn Dodger Fan Club he founded and a hoard of memorabilia—World Series programs, trading cards, miniature bats, pins, and a replica of the right-field scoreboard complete with Abe Stark sign.

"I just went into a state of shock," he says, remembering the day the Brooklyn Dodgers were no more. "I was very disillusioned. I didn't think it could happen. I thought that for sure O'Malley would have gotten assassinated before he could pull something like that. The emotion was running sky high.

"I knew I could never root for any team again because there'd never be anything like Ebbets Field again. There'd never be an atmosphere like that again—and there hasn't been."

The intensity of the fans and the improvised entertainment from the likes of the Dodger Sym-Phony made Brooklyn baseball unique for Gabriel.

"It was spontaneous, it was sincere," he says. "Brooklyn's an amalgamation of ethnic groups that came over from other countries, usually with pretty strict and repressed environments, and I think going out to Ebbets Field served as a perfect outlet. They could let themselves go. There was this tremendous unity. It was something in common that brought them all together."

As Gabriel warms to his theme, visions of the 1950's return.

"The identity with everything that Brooklyn did was phenomenal. Who was better—Snider, Mantle or Mays—we used to debate over that, and we'd debate Reese versus Rizzuto and Campanella versus Berra. We'd have wild fights with Yankee fans that Red Barber was better than Mel Allen or that Schaefer beer tastes better than Ballantine beer. Anything that was identified with the Brooklyn Dodgers was part of you personally."

What did the loss of the Dodgers mean for Brooklyn?

"What it did for Brooklyn as a society, as a culture, it destroyed it,"

Gabriel maintains. "That was a rallying point, it was a tax base, it was clearly what Brooklyn was best known for."

Gabriel sends out a newsletter these days to a fan club with some 150 members. "If I ever advertised, I'd probably have thousands, but that's a full-time job," he observes.

Occasionally, he shows visitors his collection of memorabilia, including such personal items as "a few blades of grass inside one of my autographed ball holders that has some red paint on the edge. I was near the box seats. They had sprayed the railing red. One game I went to, I just leaned over and scooped up some grass."

The Dodgers come alive again as well in Brooklyn's Greenpoint section. Dressed in their baggy flannels, they look down at customers in Bamonte's Restaurant on Withers Street, a block from the elevated Brooklyn-Queens Expressway.

There's a black-and-white photo of the 1949 pennant-winners, a color shot of the 1955 champions and, on a contemporary note, an autographed photo of a recent guest named Tommy Lasorda ("To Anthony: The food was really great. God bless you.").

The object of Lasorda's effusiveness is the restaurant owner, Anthony Bamonte. He's fifty years old now, the hairline receding, but on the wall of his restaurant, in another of the photographs, he's just a kid. And standing at his right in the picture, bocci ball in hand, is none other than Carl Furillo.

Back in 1900, Bamonte's grandfather, an Italian immigrant from the Salerno region, opened a social club at 32 Withers Street called Liberty Hall. Eventually it became a restaurant specializing in Neapolitan food, and among its patrons were those neighborhood celebrities from the Dodger Sym-Phony and the ballplayers they presumably inspired.

Bamonte remembers how he got into Ebbets Field for free as a Sym-Phony imposter.

"They'd give you one cymbal. You'd hold it and another guy would hold the other one."

Sometimes the Dodger players would eat at the restaurant as guests of the Greenpoint crowd.

"We had steak parties," Bamonte recalls. "Carl Furillo would come in with a few other players. We had bocci courts in the yard and he'd play with the fellas.

"The players were all working people. They didn't have a lot of money like the players today who are millionaires. You had more closeness. It was a different lifestyle."

But there was an evening, Bamonte remembers, when one popular Italian ballplayer received something less than a warm reception.

"My grandmother, Rose, had a chow named Skippy. The dog would

◆ *Just a memory. (Los Angeles Dodgers)*

stay in the hallway underneath the vanity. Sometimes if you moved your hand too fast, he'd bite. He nipped Cookie Lavagetto on the hand."

The photos at Bamonte's spring from a sense of community with the Dodger players. At the other end of Brooklyn, the old ballplayers are recaptured in a more commercial vein.

On Third Avenue in Bay Ridge, a blue and white awning proclaims "The Brooklyn Dodger." It's a sports bar, the walls lined with photos of the Brooklyn ballclubs but also with pictures of the Mets, the Yankees and the Knicks.

In the spring of 1990, the bar's owners, Kevin and Brian Boyle, reaped a publicity bonanza after becoming embroiled in a dispute with the Los Angeles Dodgers over ownership of the name Brooklyn Dodger.

In a column in the *New York Times* headlined "Guarding The Family D-Word," George Vecsey imagined Peter O'Malley, his father's successor as Dodger owner, saying:

"When those nice people in Los Angeles gave us Chavez Ravine, they also gave us the rights to the word 'dodger.' . . .

"We worked very hard for the rights to that word . . . Look at the dictionary: 'Dodger. (doj'er.) n. 1. One who dodges; a tricky fellow.' That's our name. Ours alone. We earned it."

A column by Mike McAlary in the *Daily News* carried the headline, "O'Malley Stix It to B'klyn Again."

It was already the decade of the 1990's, but O'Malley was still a fighting word in Brooklyn.

Thirty-three years after the cheering stopped, a visitor to Bedford Avenue can find a few strained reminders that there once was a ballpark across the street.

The stroll begins at Bedford and Sullivan, behind what used to be the right-field corner where Happy Felton played host for the Knot Hole Gang show.

The Dodgers Service Station once stood here. Preacher Roe used to park his powder blue Cadillac by the gas pumps, and youngsters would hang out looking for autographs. Now there's a nearly empty Kentucky Fried Chicken fast-food spot at the corner.

Next comes a dry cleaners, a small supermarket, and then the Ebbets and Raymond Deli Grocery. (So who is Raymond?) Finally, as Bedford reaches the corner of Montgomery, there is the tiny Ebbets Field Donut and Coffee Shop, then a closed window grating with a red, white and black sign reading "Coming Soon Bedford Check Cashing."

Young Motors, a Plymouth-DeSoto salesroom, used to dominate this stretch of Bedford Avenue, its windows an inviting target for Duke Snider's smashes. About a dozen times each summer, the Duke would knock letters off the Young Motors sign above the glass.

Across the way, on the once-green plot of land bounded by Bedford, Sullivan, McKeever and Montgomery, stands a twenty-story, brown brick housing development: Ebbets Field Apartments.

The neighborhood has long since slipped into inner-city poverty. One does not have to be an old Dodger fan to consider this an altogether depressing scene. Yet there are signs of hope. A block to the north, on Bedford between Montgomery and Crown, stands the modern, low red-brick campus of Medgar Evers College, a branch of the City University of New York.

At 46 McKeever Place, behind what used to be the third-base stands, is another school. This one honors the sports figure who, like Medgar Evers, was a civil rights pioneer. The sign reads "Jackie Robinson Intermediate School 320."

The school's assistant principal, Marty Adler, is one more guardian of the Brooklyn Dodger tradition. A wiry, fast-talking, fast-moving man, exuding the sort of hustle one might expect from a native Brooklynite, he uses the custodian's office on the second floor as a headquarters for the Brooklyn Dodger Hall of Fame.

The school opened in 1967 and was named for Robinson five years later, soon after his death. Toward the end of the 1970's, the idea was born for, as Adler puts it, "a memorial to the history of the Dodgers." He sent out letters to former players, and as the word got out, memorabilia began to arrive.

"I got a brick from a lady in Queens," Adler recalls. "She had been in the hospital getting her appendix out. In the next room was a Dodger having his foot taped up. He gave her a brick from Ebbets Field. He signed his name—Spider Jorgensen."

That piece of Dodger history came from the 1940's. More exciting for Adler was a remnant of the '30's, courtesy of a man who learned about the father he never knew thanks to the Dodger Hall of Fame.

Adler tells the story:

───────

A guy calls my house two years ago. My wife answers the phone. He says, "My name is T. Wilson, I'm a doctor." And he starts crying and hangs up. A month later, he calls again, starts crying, hangs up.

Summer comes, he calls, I get the phone call. His name is Ted Wilson. He's a doctor at the University of Pennsylvania. His father was Ed Wilson, who played for the Dodgers in 1936, a reserve outfielder. He broke something, was never the same again. He quit baseball. He got married. T. Wilson was born. He divorced his wife. T. Wilson never saw his father.

He contacted us. Could we get the names, addresses and phone numbers of those guys with whom his father played so he could get something about his father, which we were glad to do.

Ten months later, he calls back. "Thank you, I contacted Lonny Frey, I contacted Hassett, Van Lingle Mungo, Camilli."

And he says, "Can I help you guys in any way? I got a uniform."

I said, "Would you donate it to us?"

He said, "Yeah, sure. I wanna get it cleaned."

I said: "Don't clean it. We want the dirt. Whose uniform was it, your father's?"

"No. Casey Stengel's when he was the manager."

So we got Casey Stengel's uniform.

───────

Much of the Dodger esoterica is housed at the Brooklyn Historical Society in downtown. But a few items are at the custodian's office in the Jackie Robinson school, among them a bizarre combination: a photo of Pee Wee Reese autographed by Peter O'Malley. Walter's son was in New York on business when he decided to visit the site where pop ran a ballclub.

In 1984, the Hall began annual inductions, bringing Brooklyn Dodger players back for ceremonies each June outside the Brooklyn Museum on Eastern Parkway.

"I'm reliving my childhood," Adler exults.

He launches into a joyful remembrance of the final years at Ebbets Field—he was a teenager then—and begins with the Dodger Sym-Phony.

"They were a bunch of ragtime guys who went around the ballpark with *mishugene* instruments. They can't play music, they'd never be hired for this, but it was fun. They'd tease the opponents. The fans saw 'we're part of the action.'

"The Dodgers lived in the neighborhood. Their kids went to the schools. Their wives shopped in the shopping places. They were an integral fabric of the pattern of this whole community and we loved the guys.

"You could walk down the street and put a radio on—a black person or a white person, 'How're the Bums doing?' It was one common denominator that tied everybody up together."

Adler's tribute concludes with an attack on the haughty followers of the hated pinstripers from the Bronx.

"We as Brooklyn Dodger fans felt we were more knowledgeable about the sport and about our heroes. Here's a Yankee fan, he could have a 180 I.Q., come from Harvard. Here I am, a schleppy Bum, I knew more about baseball than he did by virtue of the fact that I'm a Brooklyn Dodger fan.

"We knew how to fake a throw, we knew how to bunt, we knew that Carl Furillo was the greatest right fielder who ever lived and Billy Cox was the best third baseman that ever put a glove on."

How did Marty Adler feel when the Dodgers left?

"I didn't watch baseball for a good ten years. I could say that honestly. I'd walk in the living room and my father's sitting there with my brother. I'll ask, 'Who's playing? Who's winning? That's nice.' It was never, ever the same.

"I feel sorry for the kids growing up now in Brooklyn who don't have a team to identify with."

Adler says that each year he makes an announcement over the school's public address system telling about Jackie Robinson: "This is what took place here, this is American history. Everybody deserves a chance, regardless of race or creed."

But he wonders what impact Robinson's life has on his students, virtually all of whom are from minority groups.

"The city game in New York is basketball, especially among the black children," he notes.

And efforts to pay tribute to Robinson sometimes yield frustration. There is an oil painting of Jackie in the school lobby. But an ash tree planted outside the building in Robinson's memory is long gone.

"The kids just broke it up—for toothpicks, I don't know," says Adler. "You plant a tree, it grows, it's life. Not here. Nothing lives here."

Adler points to a spot outside his office.

"See this ground here? At the very end there's a piece of concrete. There was a plaque there."

A marker in tribute to Jackie Robinson is now a stub, vandalized like the ash tree.

But enough for lamentations about the tree that didn't grow in Brooklyn. It's time to do some business this particular afternoon. Adler finances the trips for old Dodgers to his Hall of Fame ceremonies by selling memorabilia, and now he has a customer.

A forty-year-old New York City fireman named Tom Kelly has arrived at the school custodian's office. He sports a reddish mustache giving him the look of one of those 1890's Brooklyn ballplayers and is wearing a blue and white shirt with a picture of a certain ballpark and the words "Ebbets Field—Home of the Brooklyn Dodgers."

Kelly has come to buy a chair that survived the demolition of Ebbets Field. Adler asks for $1,450. Kelly offers $1,300. After a bit of haggling, they tilt mostly in Adler's favor: The price will be $1,420, but Adler throws in a jar of honest-to-goodness Ebbets Field soil, taken from Holy Cross Cemetery, where it was used as landfill.

Tom Kelly removes his wallet and peels off fourteen one-hundred-dollar bills and a twenty-dollar bill. The seat—newly repainted Dodger blue—is his.

Kelly lives on Staten Island and he works in Manhattan, a member of Ladder Company 15. But his roots are in Brooklyn.

"We lived at Nostrand Avenue and Lincoln Road, about ten, fifteen blocks from Ebbets Field," he remembers. "We'd wait for the trucks from the *News* and *Mirror* around nine o'clock, and you could hear the cheering."

Only once, at age seven, had he been to the ballpark.

"It was the summer of 1957," he recalls. "I was with my father and three brothers. We sat on the third-base side. I remember Roy Campanella and Duke Snider. They were playing the Giants.

"When we left, there was a vendor's stand outside. My father said, 'You can pick out anything you want.'

"I was a Mickey Mantle fan. There was a New York Giant cap hanging. I pointed to it because I thought it was a Yankee cap.

"My father said, 'Take a Brooklyn hat or nothing.'

"I said, 'Gimme the Dodger hat.' "

At a considerable cost, that uncomfortable old Ebbets Field chair now brought a return to innocence for Tom Kelly.

"This is the ultimate," he says. "It reminds me of when I was a kid. It brings back memories of a happier time and of family. Ebbets Field was like the cathedral of Brooklyn. It was our representation to the rest of the world. We were proud of it. Now it's gone. They took the heart out of Brooklyn."

There will be no baseball game across the street this April day nor on any other day. But as Tom Kelly carries his little piece of Ebbets Field out of Jackie Robinson Intermediate School toward where the wonderful old rotunda once stood, he is a happy man—and a boy once again.

Sources

I'm grateful to the men who supplied firsthand accounts of Brooklyn baseball. Most were interviewed during 1989 and early '90. In some cases, I have drawn on conversations going back a number of years.

Recollections were provided by Marty Adler, Walter Alston, Dave Anderson, Anthony Bamonte, Red Barber, Ray Berres, Dolph Camilli, Lou Dallojacono, George Daubert, Harry Eisenstat, Carl Erskine, Ron Gabriel, George Giles, Al Gionfriddo, Buddy Hassett, Babe Herman, Billy Herman, Jack Kavanagh, Tom Kelly, Tom Knight, Hank LeBost, Al Lopez, Danny McDevitt, Cal McLish, Les Munns, Tom Seats, Joe Stripp, Dick Teed, Overton Tremper, Lloyd Waner and Phil Weintraub.

The Sporting News and the many New York City and Brooklyn newspapers—particularly the *New York Times* and *Brooklyn Eagle*—provided on-the-spot coverage.

BOOKS

Adelman, Melvin L. *A Sporting Time: New York City and the Rise of Modern Athletics, 1820–70.* Urbana: University of Illinois Press, 1986.

Allen, Lee. *The Giants & the Dodgers: The Fabulous Story of Baseball's Fiercest Feud.* New York: G.P. Putnam's Sons, 1964.

—————. *100 Years of Baseball.* New York: Bartholomew House, 1950.

Barber, Red, and Creamer, Robert. *Rhubarb in the Catbird Seat.* Garden City, N.Y.: Doubleday, 1968.

Campanella, Roy. *It's Good to Be Alive.* Boston: Little, Brown, 1959.

Church, Seymour R. *Baseball: The History, Statistics and Romance of the American National Game,* 1902. Princeton: Pyne Press, facsimile edition, 1974.

Conner, Anthony J. *Baseball for the Love of It.* New York: Macmillan, 1982.

Creamer, Robert W. *Stengel: His Life and Times.* New York: Simon and Schuster, 1984.

Durocher, Leo, with Linn, Ed. *Nice Guys Finish Last.* New York: Simon and Schuster, 1975.

Fleming, G.H. *The Dizziest Season: The Gashouse Gang Chases the Pennant.* New York: William Morrow, 1984.

Frommer, Harvey. *New York City Baseball: The Last Golden Age, 1947–1957.* New York: Macmillan, 1980.

Goldstein, Richard. *Spartan Seasons: How Baseball Survived the Second World War.* New York: Macmillan, 1980.

Golenbock, Peter. *Bums: An Oral History of the Brooklyn Dodgers.* New York: G.P. Putnam's Sons, 1984.

Graham, Frank. *The Brooklyn Dodgers: An Informal History.* New York: G.P. Putnam's Sons, 1945.

Holmes, Tommy. *The Dodgers.* New York: Macmillan, 1975.

Holway, John. *Blackball Stars: Negro League Pioneers.* Westport, Conn.: Meckler Books, 1988.

—————. *Voices from the Great Black Baseball Leagues.* New York: Dodd, Mead, 1975.

Honig, Donald. *Baseball Between the Lines.* New York: Coward, McCann & Geoghegan, 1976.

—————. *Baseball When the Grass Was Real.* New York: Coward, McCann & Geoghegan, 1975.

Hynd, Noel. *The Giants of the Polo Grounds: The Glorious Times of Baseball's New York Giants.* New York: Doubleday, 1988.

Kahn, Roger. *The Boys of Summer.* New York: Harper & Row, 1971.

Kazin, Alfred. *A Walker in the City.* New York: Harcourt, Brace & World, 1951.

Kiernan, Thomas. *The Miracle at Coogan's Bluff.* New York: Thomas Y. Crowell, 1975.

Kirsch, George B. *The Creation of American Team Sports: Baseball and Cricket, 1838–72.* Urbana and Chicago: University of Illinois Press, 1989.

Latimer, Margaret. *Two Cities: New York and Brooklyn the Year the Great Bridge Opened.* Brooklyn: The Brooklyn Educational & Cultural Alliance, 1983.

Leitner, Irving A. *Baseball: Diamond in the Rough.* New York: Criterion Books, 1972.

Lieb, Fred. *The Baseball Story.* New York: G.P. Putnam's Sons, 1950.

Lowry, Philip J. *Green Cathedrals.* Cooperstown, N.Y.: Society for American Baseball Research, 1986.

McCullough, David. *The Great Bridge.* New York: Simon and Schuster, 1972.

McCullough, David W. *Brooklyn . . . And How It Got That Way.* New York: The Dial Press, 1983.

Ment, David. *The Shaping of a City: A Brief History of Brooklyn.* Brooklyn: The Brooklyn Educational & Cultural Alliance, 1979.

Okkonen, Marc. *The Federal League of 1914–1915: Baseball's Third*

Major League. Garrett Park, Md.: Society for American Baseball Research, 1989.

Orem, Preston. *Baseball from the Newspaper Accounts, 1845–1881,* 1961.

Parrott, Harold. *The Lords of Baseball.* New York: Praeger Publishers, 1976.

Peterson, Harold. *The Man Who Invented Baseball.* New York: Charles Scribner's Sons, 1969.

Peterson, Robert. *Only the Ball Was White.* Englewood Cliffs, N.J.: Prentice-Hall, 1970.

Quigley, Martin. *The Crooked Pitch: The Curveball in American Baseball History.* Chapel Hill, N.C.: Algonquin Books, 1984.

Rice, Damon. *Seasons Past.* New York: Praeger Publishers, 1976.

Ritter, Lawrence S. *The Glory of Their Times.* New York: Macmillan, 1966.

Robinson, Jackie. *I Never Had It Made.* New York: Fawcett, Crest, 1974.

Rogosin, Donn. *Invisible Men: Life in Baseball's Negro Leagues.* New York: Atheneum, 1983.

Roth, Philip. *Reading Myself and Others.* New York: Farrar, Straus and Giroux, 1975.

Seymour, Harold. *Baseball: The Early Years.* New York: Oxford University Press, 1960.

——————. *Baseball: The Golden Age.* New York: Oxford University Press, 1971.

Shannon, Bill, and Kalinsky, George. *The Ballparks.* New York: Hawthorn Books, 1975.

Smith, Robert. *Baseball.* New York: Simon and Schuster, 1970.

Spalding, Albert G. *America's National Game.* New York: American Sports Publishing, 1911.

Sullivan, Neil J. *The Dodgers Move West.* New York: Oxford University Press, 1987.

Syrett, Harold Coffin. *The City of Brooklyn, 1865–1898.* New York: Columbia University Press, 1944.

Thorn, John, and Palmer, Pete, eds. *Total Baseball.* New York: Warner Books, 1989.

Tiemann, Robert L. *Dodger Classics.* St. Louis: Baseball Histories, 1983.

Tiemann, Robert L. and Rucker, Mark, eds. *Nineteenth Century Stars.* Kansas City, Mo.: The Society for American Baseball Research, 1989.

Tygiel, Jules. *Baseball's Great Experiment: Jackie Robinson and His Legacy.* New York: Random House, 1983.

Voigt, David Quentin. *American Baseball: From Gentleman's Sport to the Commissioner System.* Norman: University of Oklahoma Press, 1966.

——————. *American Baseball: From the Commissioners to Continental Expansion.* Norman: University of Oklahoma Press, 1970.

Weld, Ralph Foster. *Brooklyn Is America.* New York: Columbia University Press, 1950.

White, Sol. *History of Colored Base Ball.* Philadelphia: H. Walter Schlichter, 1902.

Willensky, Elliot. *When Brooklyn Was the World.* New York: Harmony Books, 1986.

Wolfe, Thomas. *The Portable Thomas Wolfe,* edited by Maxwell Geismar. New York: The Viking Press, 1946.

MAGAZINE ARTICLES

Bulkley, George. "The Day the Reds Lost," *The National Pastime, Society for American Baseball Research,* Fall 1982.

Crichton, Kyle S. "The Great Hoiman," *Collier's,* August 19, 1933.

Frank, Stanley. "Fan—As In Fanatic," *Collier's,* April 24, 1943.

——————. "Yes, You Can Buy a Pennant," *Saturday Evening Post,* September 20, 1941.

Kavanagh, Jack. "Bill 'Brickyard' Kennedy, the First of the Daffy Dodgers, Helped Create Brooklyn History," *Sports History,* May 1989.

Lane, F.C. "The Man Who Was Run Out of Baseball" [Ed Reulbach], *Baseball Magazine,* May 1915.

——————. "R.B. Ward, the Master Baker, Vice-President of the Feds," *Baseball Magazine,* July 1915.

——————. "Why Brooklyn Doesn't Appreciate Ivan Olson," *Baseball Magazine,* December 1920.

Meany, Tom. "Craziest Wall in Brooklyn," *Collier's,* August 6, 1954.

——————. "When Gil Hodges Slumped," *Collier's,* August 21, 1953.

Rice, Robert. "Profiles: Thoughts on Baseball" [Branch Rickey], *The New Yorker,* May 27 and June 3, 1950.

Snider, Duke with Kahn, Roger. "I Play Baseball for Money—Not Fun," *Collier's,* May 25, 1956.

Taylor, Robert Lewis. "Profiles: Borough Defender" [Larry MacPhail], *The New Yorker,* July 12 and July 19, 1941.

"What Makes the Robins Soar?" *Literary Digest,* July 12, 1930.

VIDEO

"The Boys of Summer," VidAmerica, 1984.

PUBLIC PAPERS

Mail received by City Hall on the issue of a new ballpark for the Dodgers is filed in the Robert F. Wagner papers, New York City Municipal Archives.

Index